PRISONER 1167

THE MADMAN WHO WAS

JACK THE
RIPPER

PRISONER 1167

THE MADMAN WHO WAS
JACK THE
RIPPER

James Tully

Carroll & Graf Publishers, Inc.
NEW YORK

For Anne Hounslow – without whom nothing would have been possible

Carroll & Graf Publishers, Inc.
260 Fifth Avenue
New York
NY 10001

First published in the UK by Robinson Publishing Ltd 1997

First Carroll & Graf edition 1997

Copyright © James Tully 1997

Picture Credits: Public Records Office,
author's collection, Mary Evans Picture
Library and Popperfoto.

ISBN 0–7867–0404–7

Printed and bound in the United Kingdom

10 9 8 7 6 5 4 3 2 1

Contents

Acknowledgements

When I began my research for this book I found myself in a situation rather akin to being confronted by a 100-piece jigsaw puzzle with only three of the pieces present.

It took nine long years to find all the missing pieces, and many people were kind enough to help me look for them. I now have pleasure in acknowledging that assistance.

My deepest debts of gratitude are to:

John Morrison, who was the first to identify James Kelly as a possible suspect. Ever generous, he provided me with much material about Kelly's life prior to Broadmoor and has given me his constant and unstinting support over the years.

Alison Carpenter and David Webb – of the Bishopsgate Institute Reference Library – who went far beyond the normal call of duty in replying to my stream of enquiries. Ever friendly and efficient, they ferreted out answers to even the vaguest of my questions.

Jonathan Ogan, who was always willing to make time for me, despite his many other commitments. It was only with his aid that I was able to ensure the accuracy of many points, and our discussions about criminal psychology increased my knowledge of the subject immeasureably.

The late Dr F.D.M. Hocking, who died so tragically just over a year ago. It was I who first kindled his interest in 'the Ripper', but from that moment on he delved into the mystery with great enthusiasm. He was of immeasurable help with the medical aspects of the murders, and provided me with numerous suggestions about others. His common sense and infectious sense of humour saw me through many a dark patch – I miss him very much.

I am also deeply grateful to:

Matthew Taylor, MP, for espousing my cause so willingly and with such perseverance.

Mrs Virginia Bottomley, MP, and Tim Renton, MP, for cutting so decisively through the bureaucracy and red tape which threatened at one point to engulf me.

Mr C. Kaye – of the Special Hospitals Service Authority – for overcoming some of the same obstacles which I had encountered and for preparing my way to Broadmoor Hospital.

Mrs Mary Lane – formerly of Broadmoor Hospital – who, ever efficient and courteous, made the actual arrangements for my visits. She and other members of the staff showed great friendliness in completing my knowledge of the history of the Hospital.

Many others aided me in my quest. I have named them below in alphabetical order, and therefore their position in the list should in no way be taken as indicative of the value of their assistance. There were those whom I pestered constantly; their patience with me was remarkable, as was the amount of information which they found time to search out and forward, sometimes with ideas that had not occurred to me. Conversely, some provided mere snippets of knowledge, but often they were of vital importance. Even negative replies had their value.

Unfortunately, because of a lack, directly or indirectly, of government funding, some institutions have been forced to close or to curtail their facilities drastically. That is a great shame and a major handicap to researchers. It can only be hoped that the shortsightedness of such policies will be realized sooner rather than later. Sometimes as a result of such 'economies', several of those who were so kind to me are no longer in the posts which they occupied when I was making my enquiries. Their going is a sad loss to future authors on many subjects, and I wish them well wherever they may be.

My great thanks, then, to:

Patricia Allderidge – The Bethlem Royal Hospital and the Maudsley Hospital.

Tim Ashworth – Salford Local History Library.

Maggie Bird – Archives Branch of the Metropolitan Police Service.

D.J. Blackwood – Home Office.

Philip Davies – Archive Section of the Bank of England.

Naomi Evetts – Liverpool Record Office.

Dr William J. Eckert – Milton Helpern International Center, Wichita State University.

Eileen Ephithite – Society of Licensed Victuallers.

Mrs J.P. Farrell – District Central Library, Preston.

Robert Gilby – Metropolitan Police Museum.

Malcolm Holmes – Camden Local Studies Library and Archives.

Jeremy Johnson – Guildhall Library.

Roger C. Kershaw – Reader Services Department, Public Records Office, Kew.

Richard Knight – Camden Local Studies Library and Archives.

D. Mander – Hackney Archives Department.

Phyllida Melling – Guildhall Library.

Peter A. Moll – Greater London Record Office.

Robert C. Morris – National Archives, New York.

Mrs H. Murray – Licensed Victuallers' Association.

D.J. Richards – Holborn Library.

Janet Smith – Liverpool Record Office.

C. Stewart – Home Office.

Mrs Pauline Wale – Office of Population, Censuses and Surveys.

H. Watton – Bancroft Library.

D. Withey – The Finsbury Library.

Almost last, but certainly not least in the value of their contributions, I would like to express my sincere appreciation to:

David Blomfield, my editor, for his patience and courtesy. He showed me great understanding and worked extremely hard in reducing my original manuscript to a practical but effective length.

Stewart Evans, for his correspondence, the material which he sent me and his encouragement, despite the fact that at one point he thought we were hot on the heels of the same suspect.

Toni Fernandez – of Multy Copy, Benidorm – for his efficient and practical expertise and his help in so many other ways.

Jack Herman, for his graphic photograph of the ripping chisel.

Andrew Holloway, for his correspondence, his many suggestions and his friendship and encouragement over the years.

Nick Robinson – my publisher – and his excellent team, who demonstrated great patience in educating me in the mysteries of publishing and who worked extremely hard on every aspect of this book.

Phillip Schofield, for his information about the tools, past and present, employed in the upholstery trade.

Peter Underwood, who first introduced me to professional writing and who predicted that my contribution to his book 'could lead to other things'.

Paul Wilson, for his generous practical assistance and friendship.

In conclusion, I feel that it would be very remiss of me were I not to express my heartfelt apologies to all those, but especially to my wife and sons, whom I have bored to death over the years with my talk of 'the Ripper'. They, and my wife in particular, have been most forebearing, and it seems poor reward merely to say that I am thankful for their toleration – but I am.

Introduction

I am sure that there will be some who will sigh wearily at the appearance of yet another book about 'Jack the Ripper'. They will imagine that surely everything worthwhile on the subject has already been written – but they will be wrong. The identity of the elusive killer is an abiding mystery which has engaged the minds and imaginations of every generation, and will continue to do so until incontrovertible evidence is produced. Until that time (should it *ever* arrive) research and the debate will continue, and even more suspects will be submitted for consideration because – and make no mistake about it – the field is still wide open.

It was in the 1950s that I read my first book about 'Jack the Ripper' – and I was hooked immediately!

In those early days I merely read everything on the subject upon which I could lay my hands, and found that authors who came up with a suspect usually managed to convince me that they had finally solved the 'Ripper' riddle.

Later, however, as my knowledge grew, I became more sceptical. Rarely did I sense that an author was really *involved* with what he had written, or that he had researched his subject in any depth. The same old errors were trotted out as facts, fresh mistakes made and, sometimes, downright lies were told in order to bolster a theory. Padding and superficiality abounded, and there seemed to be a complete absence of basic commonsense and simple curiosity. That manifested itself in an apparent willingness to accept without question most of what had been written by others.

It was both frustrating and infuriating. No author appeared able to produce a candidate who was even half convincing, and my fingers itched with a longing to put the record straight about undisputed facts, and to provoke debate about the others.

I settled down to studying the mystery properly, and have now been doing so for over thirty years. I am sure that my wife and sons will consider it the understatement of all time when I say that the whole business became something of an obsession.

Inevitably, I began to speculate if there might not be some suspects who would seem more convincing if only they were researched more carefully. I therefore found myself spending much of my spare time checking and expanding on the dossiers of various candidates – only to abandon them one by one. What intrigued me, however, was the fact that, despite the memoranda, notes, auto-biographies and nods and winks of senior policemen of the day, none of them ever came out openly and named a specific suspect. That leads to but two conclusions. Either they did not know who the 'Ripper' was when the murders were committed, or else they became aware of his identity then, or later, but were unable – for some reason – to reveal it.

It was not until 1987 that my good friend John Morrison brought James Kelly to my attention. He had come across him, and his escape from Broadmoor, in the *Guinness Book of Records*, and from that moment he was utterly convinced that Kelly was 'Jack'. However, his notion was based solely upon the facts that Kelly had cut his wife's throat, that he had got away from Broadmoor in 1888, and that two of the victims were also named Kelly.

John put together a good story, which he set out in a booklet called *Jimmy Kelly's Year of Ripper Murders 1888*. Unfortunately, most of what he stated as being factual was nothing of the sort, and he was quite unable to produce any documentary evidence to substantiate his assertions. However, in response to his enthusiasm, I decided to turn my attention to James Kelly. I did so half-heartedly and, in truth, only so that I might dismiss him with a clear conscience.

John Morrison, ever generous, supplied me with Kelly's birth, marriage and death certificates, newspaper cuttings about his trial, and a plethora of other material. However, I decided to begin my research from scratch.

Unused then to the bureaucratic delays to which all researchers seem to be subjected, I was surprised by the time my initial investigations took. However, it was not until I moved on to Kelly's career from 1883 that my real frustrations began.

I was amazed at the reactions of Broadmoor Hospital and the Home Office, especially the former, and I found myself accumulating a file of correspondence with them that would have provided many scripts for the television comedy *Yes, Minister*.

It was only when – with the patient help of my MP, Matthew Taylor – the Home Office at last allowed me to see what it held that I began to understand why so many obstacles had been, and were being, placed in my way.

I received a telephone call to say that, if I would nominate a date when I could be at the Public Records Office at Kew, the Home Office file would be delivered there, by special messenger, for my inspection. That I did, and duly presented myself on the appointed day.

Right from the outset, I discovered that special arrangements had been made. My 'Document Request' form was significantly unlike those of every other reader I met that day. A rubber stamp had been applied which read: 'TO BE SEEN UNDER PERMIT. NOT TO BE PHOTOCOPIED.'

Somewhat daunted by that, but undismayed, I then proceeded to the appropriate counter where, after what seemed an eternity of waiting, I was told that the file I had 'requested' was not held at the P.R.O.! It was only after I had explained the situation, and waited even longer, that it was found that the file had been delivered the previous day and had been locked away until my arrival.

Finally came the magical moment when file number H.O. 144/ 10064 was placed in my eager hands.

It was contained in a simple brown cover, bound with once-white tape. On the top left-hand corner was the reference number – H.O. 144/10064 – whilst on the bottom corner on that side was a red sticker bearing the reference 'E 503'. Towards the top of the right-hand side was a green sticker with the words 'CLOSED

UNTIL 2030', and beneath that was written: 'This file should never be destroyed. 5/11/52. T.J.H. Hetherington.' However, when I opened the cover I found that Mr Hetherington's injunction had come too late. Pinned to the inside was a piece of paper bearing the following:

<u>A 30356</u>

3
5–9
11–14
16–18
25
28
31–32
<hr>
Destroyed

(Date Stamp) 25.OCT.1952.

So seventeen documents had been removed from James Kelly's Home Office file and destroyed. Why? And upon whose instructions? To what did they refer, and why had they been done away with after lying intact for anything up to seventy years? It all seemed very odd, and my interest in Kelly began to grow.

It grew even faster when, at last, I managed to get to Broadmoor, though that took far longer to achieve – nearly six years in all.

My first contact with the Hospital was when I wrote, in 1988, asking for the answers to two questions. Ralph Partridge, in his book *Broadmoor*, had paid tribute to the help he had received from the Hospital in 1953, but *I* was told that my queries could not be answered 'for reasons of confidentiality'. I replied by pointing out that both questions were of a non-medical nature, but received a letter which stated that: 'The issue of confidentiality has become a BIG thing.' I was told: 'Legislation and guidelines have become more prescriptive . . . Our protection of the confidentiality of named patients, past or present, whether alive or dead, is subject only to the likelihood that a patient presents a risk of serious harm to others.' That last sentence did not make sense to me, then or now, as I fail to see how a dead person can present a serious risk to anyone, but my comments to that effect did no good.

Year after year dragged by as Broadmoor officials came and went, with my having to start from scratch with each new arrival. Most of the replies I received were evasive, but some contained what I later discovered to be deliberate lies. Eventually I lost patience with the Hospital's version of 'musical chairs' and wrote to the then Secretary of State for Health, Mrs Virginia Bottomley.

My request, which by then was for direct access to Kelly's file, was passed to Mr C. Kaye, the Chief Executive of the Special Hospitals Service Authority, with commendable speed. He then wrote to say that he had asked Broadmoor whether the information which I required could be made available to me, and that he would let me know when he had their response.

It all seemed very hopeful, but then Mr Kaye ran into the same procrastinations that had bedevilled me and three months elapsed before he was able to tell me that I *could* visit Broadmoor and examine Kelly's file, and that I should contact the Hospital for an appointment.

So, at last, it came about that, on the morning of Tuesday, February 1st, 1994, I found myself driving up the hill to Broadmoor. When I presented myself to the reception centre, everything had been arranged perfectly. I was expected and, after only a very few minutes, a young lady arrived to escort me, unlocking and locking door after door as we went to the administrative wing.

There, on a table in an office, James Kelly's file awaited me. It was contained in a rather dilapidated blue box file covered in blue paper. On the title edge, machine-printed on to blue adhesive tape, I read: '3510 – KELLY J'.

The contents of the file were in a sorry state, especially the older documents, with the impressive 1883 warrant for Kelly's detention in pieces. Many of the papers had come away from the metal rings of the file, and I was told that many more had disappeared completely over the years – 'until we became more strict'. (Unlike the Home Office file, it contained no indication of what might have been destroyed, removed, purloined or simply lost, but what remained was a positive treasure trove – well worth waiting for, and well worth fighting for.)

We cannot know for certain what was removed from those two files, nor why it was removed. Yet, from what they still contain, it is easy to see that Kelly was a source of acute embarrassment to the police and the government of his day. I hope that this book will convince others – as I am myself convinced – that their embarrassment was not due simply to their failure to recapture a homicidal maniac, but to the fact that many of them believed, with good reason, that this particular homicidal maniac was responsible for the 'Ripper' murders.

I have chosen deliberately to begin this book by telling the story – or as much as is known – of Kelly's life. It is a fascinating story in itself. I then give accounts of the murders, and conclude by exploring the links between them and Kelly.

Also deliberately, I have elected to recount the 'Ripper' story largely in the words of the actual testimony given by the main witnesses at the inquests – not the snippets gleaned from inaccurate newspaper reports, upon which some very tenuous theories have been built. I have also done my best to explain the precise locations and features – and some of the history concerned.

There are many minor mysteries surrounding these killings, my comments on which I have included at the end of the book as 'Points to Ponder'. Some have little or no relevance to the identification of 'Jack', and the solving of them will not, therefore, necessarily be of major significance. Nevertheless they exist, and need to be discussed more fully than hitherto. The more enquiring minds that can be brought to bear upon them the sooner they can be, as the police have it, eliminated from our inquiries.

In this way readers have the main facts laid out before them. I know what I believe, but readers should have the chance to reach their own conclusions.

It is also right that everyone should have the opportunity of understanding just how terrible life was in the East End at that time. For this reason and also because I had personal experience of life in the pre-war London slums, and my grandfather lived in the nineteenth-century East End – I have paid especial attention to the lives of the poor women who were slaughtered so brutally – to give them the dignity which they deserve. They were not merely victims; they were *people* like you and me.

Jim Tully,
ALTEA,
Spain.
March 1997.

1

Murder in the Parlour

THE 'JACK THE RIPPER' murders began in 1888, and were perpetrated in the parishes of Spitalfields and Whitechapel in the East End of London. However, our story begins about 200 miles away, and some twenty-nine years earlier.

It was in the second half of 1859 when, to her horror, an illiterate fifteen-year-old Liverpudlian working-class girl, Sarah Kelly, discovered that she was pregnant by a clerk named John Miller. Those were the days when a child born out of wedlock was a bastard, pure and simple. Often the mother was abandoned by her lover, disowned by her family, and ostracized by the local community. No decent man would look at her, and her innocent child could expect to be taunted at school, sneered at in later life, and, if he was a boy, barred from certain professions.

John Miller deserted Sarah, but she was fortunate in that her family stood by her. However, not even they were prepared to face the shame of the situation, and her mother, Teresa Kelly, resorted to a stratagem often employed in such situations. Some pretext for her absence was devised, and arrangements were made for Sarah to have her baby in Preston, some thirty miles from the family home. It seems likely that she was sent to her aunt, Mary Motler – her mother's sister – who later moved to Eccles near Manchester.

The baby, a boy, was born on April 20th, 1860, in No. 43, St Mary's Street. A small terraced house, it stood in the shadow of the forbidding Preston Prison – formerly the House of Correction – and perhaps that was an omen. Sarah named her son 'James', and registered his birth on May 26th, 1860, making her mark with an 'X'. She did not name the father.

Upon her return to Liverpool, Sarah left her son to be brought up by his grandmother and went her own way. Little James therefore grew up believing Teresa to be his mother. He received little affection, and was never to meet his true parents.

No one knows how Sarah supported herself over the next ten years, but in 1870 she found herself a husband. His name was John Allan, and he lived at No. 76, Aubrey Street, Everton, Liverpool. He was a Master Mariner with a share in his ship – a very attractive catch. Apparently, Sarah did not reveal the existence of her illegitimate son, and after the wedding the couple moved out of the area. They went to live at No. 95, Manchester Road, Southport, Lancashire – a pleasant and rather select seaside resort, which was equidistant from Preston and Liverpool.

It was a far better marriage than Sarah could ever have expected, but it was childless and did not last long. John Allan died on May 16th, 1874, at Pisagua, in the Republic of Peru. In his will, dated April 23rd, 1870, he left everything to his widow, and appointed her his sole executrix.

The news of her husband's death shattered Sarah. For four years she had been in constant pain because of a liver disease, and her friends in Liverpool became very concerned. They urged her to end her isolation in Southport, and she did not take much persuading. Before long she was being looked after at the home of one of her husband's friends, a victualler named John Munro, who lived at No. 10, Walker Street, Low Hill, Liverpool – quite near John Allan's former home in Aubrey Street.

Despite the care she received, Sarah's health deteriorated rapidly, and it was then that, after all those years, she decided to try to make some form of recompense to her son. Both before and after her marriage, Sarah had met her mother from time to time to ensure that she was not short of money, and may even have been introduced to her son without her true identity being revealed. On July 22nd, 1874, she made her will. She must have received some form of education since James's birth because she was able to sign her name, and in a good hand at that. Her signature was witnessed by Thomas Edward Sampson, a partner in the firm of solicitors Messrs. Woodburn J. Pemberton and Sampson, and E. Killewell, of No. 20, Winter Street, Low Hill, Liverpool.

At last Sarah made public acknowledgement of her 'natural son', as she called him – although she was not quite sure of his age! She left him her watch and chain, and made provision for his future. Teresa was to receive her jewellery, personal effects and clothes, but everything else – her 'real and personal estate and effects of every kind' – was placed in the hands of two executors and trustees who had been friends of her dead husband. These friends, John Hind, a licensed victualler of Lime Street, Liverpool, and John James Wren, a clothier of St George's Cresent [*sic*], Liverpool, were required to call in all debts and sell everything saleable. The proceeds were to be placed in a trust, the income from which was to be paid to Teresa for James's maintenance and education. Once he had attained the age of twenty-five everything was to be his.

If his grandmother died before James was twenty-five, the trustees were empowered to advance up to a quarter of the capital 'for or towards the advancement or settlement in life of the said James Kelly'. In the event of Teresa and James both being dead before he reached the age of twenty-five, and his leaving no children, the estate was to go to Sarah's aunt (mentioned above) a Mary Motler of Eccles, near Manchester, and her heirs.

Sarah died on July 29th. Probate was granted to John Hind on August 8th, 1874. John Wren had renounced his nomination as executor and trustee when he realized that there were legal complications which would cause far more work than he had anticipated.

Problems arose because John Allan had died so far from home, and because the greater part of his estate was tied up in his share of the ship and her cargo. His will could not be proved until the necessary documents had arrived from Peru, and then there would be further and longer delays before the ship returned to England where precise values could be placed upon the assets.

The situation was eased somewhat by Sarah and John having the same solicitors but, even so, the solicitors and John Hind were forced to tackle the situation in three stages. First, Sarah's will was proved, and the value of her estate was declared at 'Under £200'. Then, on November 25th, 1874, Letters of Administration were granted in respect of her husband's assets, on the sureties of William Roskell, a jeweller, of No. 21, Church Street, Liverpool, and James Crellin, 'Gentleman', of No. 181, Islington, Liverpool. At that time, John Allan's effects were valued at 'Under £100. No leaseholds'. Much later, however, in June 1876, when his share of the ship and her cargo had been sold, the value of his estate was resworn at 'Under £600'.

In 1876 £1 would have been worth a little less than £38 today, so if we take Sarah's 'Under £200' to have been £150, and John's 'Under £600' to have been £550, we arrive at an approximate present-day figure of £26,600.

James Kelly was fourteen years of age when his mother died but, because of the legal delays, he was not told of her death and the contents of her will until early in 1875. Only then did he learn of the circumstances surrounding his birth. One can but attempt to imagine what a shock the revelations must have been to the boy. He had been reared in a religious household, and was already deeply religious himself. Now his whole world was turned upside down. His 'mother' was actually his grandmother, whilst his true mother, who had abandoned him at birth, was regarded as having been of loose morals. He also discovered that, on his mother's side, he had a cousin who was insane.

Such was his confusion that in Liverpool he was always to be known as 'Jim Kelly' or 'Jim Allan', but when away he preferred to adopt the name of 'John Miller'.

It would appear that Kelly had left school when he was about thirteen, and then he was apprenticed to a firm of upholsterers, Messrs. Ray and Miles, of London Road, Liverpool. He liked the work, and had been getting on well. Now, however, all that was changed. In accordance with the terms of his mother's will, money was available for his education. The next thing that the confused boy knew was that his apprenticeship was terminated and he was packed off back to school.

All concerned had decided that he should be prepared for a life in 'trade', and therefore young James was sent across the River Mersey to Dr Robert Hurworth's Commercial Academy at No. 1, Albert Terrace, Egerton Street, New Brighton. There he would complete his education, and learn the intricacies of double-entry book-keeping and other office duties.

Kelly was at the Academy for over two years, and appears to have been a good pupil. Nevertheless, it must have been a lonely and bewildering time for him. He had been uprooted from everything which he knew, and thrust into an entirely different environment with lads from much wealthier backgrounds. Gradually he became divorced from his former acquaintances, and found himself living in a limbo between two worlds, to neither of which he felt he belonged.

Lonely and friendless, he left the Academy when he was seventeen and discovered, once again, that his future had been decided without consultation. A position had been found for him with a pawnbroker, Isaac H. Jones, at No. 102, West Derby Road, Liverpool, and he was placed in lodgings at No. 49, Fielding Street – which was only a stone's throw from Walker Street where his mother had died. One of the reasons why lodgings were found for him may have been that his grandmother was now dead, because from that time on he appears to have had direct access to his trustee and his mother's solicitors.

The new situation lasted only for about eighteen months, during which he made the occasional trip to Eccles to see his great-aunt Mary Motler and her family, by whom he was liked and always well received. Apart from them, he appears to have had no friends, male or female, and his daily life seems to have consisted only of going to a job with which he was not enthralled, and then returning to lonely, brooding evenings in his room.

Gradually, symptoms of mental instability began to appear. His work was unreliable, and any comparatively minor incident was enough to send him into a rage. He was filled with an ever-increasing desire to leave Liverpool, and everyone who knew of his background. Eventually this became an obsession. Various people, including his priest, tried to talk to him, but they could not change his mind and finally he decided to leave.

The solicitor acting for the trustee of his mother's estate was Mr T. E. Sampson, who was by now the senior partner in the firm of Sampson, Williamson, Inglis and Edgecombe – whose offices were in the Guardian Assurance Building at No. 35, Dale Street, Liverpool. James Kelly went to see him, and made it quite clear that he was no longer prepared to stay in Liverpool. London attracted him, and he wanted to go there and resume his trade as an upholsterer. He asked for enough money from his trust fund to sustain him until he was working and settled.

His proposal was soon agreed. Mr Sampson and the trustee, John Hind, who were probably only too pleased to see the back of such an erratic and troublesome young man, provided him with what was thought to be a suitable amount of cash, and gave him what advice they could. One suggestion was that he should contact the East London Upholsterers Trade Society, in Shoreditch.

Before heading south, young James made the twenty-five-mile trip to say farewell to the Motlers whom, to a large degree, he had come to consider as his family. Mary was then fifty-seven years old, and lived with her husband Philip, who was a shoemaker and one year younger. They had several sons, one of whom may well have been Kelly's insane cousin, but at that time only one, John, still lived at home. He was twenty-two and worked in a local grocer's shop. He and James, with only four years' difference in their ages, had become quite friendly, with Kelly tending to regard his cousin as the older brother he never had.

The good-byes were said, and James departed for the city of his dreams. The eighteen-year-old Liverpudlian arrived at Euston Station with sovereigns clinking in his pocket and carrying a piece of paper which bore the name and address of his trade society.

Somehow Kelly found his way the two miles across London to the Horse and Groom pub at No. 89, Curtain Road, Shoreditch, EC2, where the East London Upholsterers Trade Society had its lodge. The Horse and Groom is still there. It has been altered slightly inside, but it is still possible to identify the original layout, and it retains its Victorian atmosphere.

For many years Shoreditch had been the centre of the furniture trade, which extended to Bethnal Green in the east and Finsbury in the west. Over 15,000 upholsterers were employed in mainly small workshops in which from four to twenty-five men eked out a precarious seasonal living.

Young Kelly was received well enough at the Horse and Groom, but he was told that steady jobs were in short supply, especially for an 'improver', as he was now termed. The few vacancies that did occur were usually snapped up by men with more experience – and friends in the right places. In the short term, his only hope for work lay in the sweatshops, and even there, he was warned, he would face competition from redundant shipwrights from Poplar. The Society would do its best to help him, but any assistance would be limited and, in effect, he would need to seek out any work himself.

It was probably at this time that James met John Merritt, a thirty-five-year-old cab-driver who lived with his wife and four children (and ten other people!) at No. 31, Clarendon Square, almost next to Euston Station. Kelly took lodgings at No. 15A, Woburn Buildings, Tavistock Square – which was only about half a mile from where Merritt lived and which he may have recommended.

From then on it was a matter of going over to Curtain Road every morning to see what, if any, casual labour was required. Sometimes he found work in his trade but then, as he came to know his way around, he took anything that was going.

Only a few hundred yards from Curtain Road was the beginning of what was regarded as the 'real' East End of London, which ran east from a line roughly north and south of the Aldgate Pump. The 1871 stone pump is now at the junction of Fenchurch Street and Leadenhall Street, and no longer gives water. Originally, however, it was built over St Michael's Well, which adjoined the City wall close to where the Aldgate gibbet was to be erected.

In the 1880s, the East End contained the worst slums and the most deprived people in London. For years the poor of London had been moved farther and farther east as the City proper expanded and spilled over its original boundaries. Their number was to be increased by successive waves of the many thousands of immigrants who were allowed to flood into the country resulting in a steady annual increase of paupers.

At the end of the seventeenth century, many thousands of Huguenots arrived in Spitalfields, having been forced to leave their native France to avoid religious persecution. They were mainly silkweavers, and were so diligent in building houses and establishments in which to continue their craft that what had once been pleasant rural countryside soon began to take on the appearance of a small town.

Then, in the first half of the nineteenth century, came the Industrial Revolution, and hordes of agricultural labourers were lured to the cities in search of higher wages – with London being the greatest magnet. In due course, however, as mechanization increased, thousands of those workers found themselves unemployed and were forced, with their families, into the cheaper, but more over-crowded, accommodation of the East End.

1881 saw the beginning of a vast immigration of Jews from Russia and Poland. It was a seemingly never-ending tide of humanity fleeing from the bloody pogroms, and much of it washed up upon the East End bringing its own particular problems. Until then, long-established, but much smaller, Jewish communities had lived in relative harmony with their neighbours. In the main, they were industrious and respectable people who kept themselves to themselves and looked after their own. Now, however, the overwhelming increase in their numbers provoked adverse reactions from all sides. There was fear and resentment from the native population, which already envied the Jews' ability to prosper, and hostility from the resident Jews who felt that such large numbers of their poorer and illiterate brethren would disturb the status quo.

Many who had begun their business lives by selling second-hand clothes from stalls in the street markets now saw their chance and became clothing manufacturers running sweatshops in the former Huguenot premises. The poor and homeless immigrants were paid next to nothing, but allowed to sleep on the floor under their machines.

As the years went by, the Jews came to comprise a close-knit and thriving community in Whitechapel and Spitalfields, with the more philanthropic ensuring the establishment of its own social services, schools and places of worship. However, the Victorians made no comparable provisions for the indigenous population, which suffered even more overcrowding and, with such a free availability of cheap unskilled labour, a lowering of wages which were already desperately poor. It is hardly surprising, therefore, that there was a steady increase in anti-Semitism which, from time to time, exploded into open hostility and violence.

Somehow the very poorest of all nationalities always seemed to drift to the East End. By the time James Kelly went to live there it was estimated that some 900,000 of them were packed into overcrowded slums, causing conditions that almost beggar description, and by 1888 the total number of paupers, excluding vagrants and lunatics in asylums, was to be well over 90,000.

In Spitalfields and Whitechapel, in particular – both names record happier times, when there was a twelfth-century hospital in the fields outside the City, and when a fourteenth-century whitewashed chapel became a landmark in the Essex Road – the labyrinths of unlit alleys and courts were populated by wretches who, often through no fault of their own, had sunk to the very lowest levels of degradation. Here thousands eked out a bare existence in rented accommodation, where sometimes as many as ten members of a family were crammed into one small room and incest was commonplace. Sanitation was virtually non-existent. Usually there was only one filthy outside privy for a whole household of sometimes scores of tenants.

There was little or no furniture in the rooms: broken windows remained broken, and were stuffed with rags or paper; the walls were alive with almost every species of creeping and crawling creatures, and rats and mice ran freely from cellars to attic. The yards and courts were choked with stinking rubbish and worse, which was not moved from one year to the next. Inevitably, such appalling conditions resulted in all manner of diseases, most of which went untreated and contributed to the high mortality rate, especially amongst infants.

Common lodging-houses catered for the more transient adult population. In Whitechapel alone, there were about 200 such establishments sheltering some 8,000 souls on any given night. A double bed in the many mixed-sex dormitories could be rented for 8d (3½p) a night, and a single cost 4d. Those whose pockets did not permit of such luxuries sometimes resorted to trying to sleep on a 'line' – a webbing of rope – stretched across a room, for which the price was only 2d.

The nearest of those notorious parishes to Curtain Road were Spitalfields and Whitechapel in the east and south-east respectively, and south of them were the dock areas of St George's-in-the-East and Stepney. Casual work was to be had there, and a strong young man could earn up to a pound a week if he was willing to take whatever was offered.

In James Kelly's early days in London, his work, and the search for work, took him all over the East End, especially Shoreditch, Bethnal Green, Spitalfields and Whitechapel. Sometimes it would have taken him ages to discover the whereabouts of a place to which he had been sent, and he would finally arrive at his destination, via narrow alleys, to find a dilapidated workshop at the end of a filthy court. Still, he would have felt very much at home with many of the place and street names. Whitechapel, Islington, Wapping, Kensington, Mount Pleasant, Commercial Road, the Strand, Cable Street and Oxford Street, were but a few of the many names with which he had grown up in Liverpool.

Nowhere was busier than the road which began as Aldgate High Street and then continued eastwards from the City of London boundary to become in turn Whitechapel High Street, Whitechapel Road and the Mile End Road. As well as the many and varied pubs, shops and rows of stalls, there was the added attraction of what was known as 'The Mile End Waste' – a stretch of undeveloped land between the southern side of the roadway and the pavement. It was at its narrowest where it began – at the Church of St Mary Matfelon (the original 'White Chapel'), almost opposite the entrance to Osborne Street – and it widened gradually as it progressed. It reached its maximum width at the Cambridge (now Cambridge Heath) Road junction, and then continued to Stepney. Over a mile and a half long, The Waste was used for a variety of purposes. During the week, shopkeepers adapted it as extensions to their premises, but there were also stalls, side-shows, shooting-ranges, quack doctors and all manner of diversions to capture the interest of a young man.

On Sundays, The Waste was ideal for public meetings and open-air preaching; in fact it was opposite the Blind Beggar pub that William Booth – founder of the Salvation Army – held his first meeting. It was on Sunday evenings, however, that The Waste really came into its own in the form of the Sunday Fair. Although it usually started quietly enough, as the hours passed it became, according to the *East London Observer*, 'a scene of bacchanalian revelry – an indescribable mixture of stalls, oil lamps, betting tips, and the foulest of language'.

There was little that Kelly had not already seen and heard in Liverpool, but not on such a large scale and never had he witnessed so much activity in so small an area. Everything was a-bustle, almost all around the clock.

The scores of pubs, of which there were forty-eight in the White-chapel Road alone, opened at 5 a.m. A multitude of small traders was not too long behind them, and soon the streets were filled with noise and traffic. Then began the babel of many nationalities; the hoarse, and mainly incomprehensible, shouts of the stall-holders in the street markets; the squeals of pain and terror from the herds of animals being driven to slaughter; and the neighing of horses, mingled with the clatter and scraping of their hooves on the cobbles.

It was not until dusk that this frenzy finally calmed down, and then an entirely different atmosphere began to creep over the neighbour-hood. At first the change was almost imperceptible but, as the darkness deepened, more and more of another population began to emerge from the nether world which lay behind and between the main thoroughfares.

From the maze of alleys and courts, through the Stygian blackness of narrow covered passages and dingy lanes came prostitutes, beggars, bully-boys and criminals of every description, lured by the prospects of easy money and a night of drunken forgetfulness. Then the pubs filled, the music played, and the streets were crowded with those in search of a 'good time', and others only too willing to relieve them of their cash.

Although things tended to calm down in the small hours there was still virtually continuous movement. The pubs did not close until midnight or half an hour later – if at all – and some of the local inhabitants had to rouse themselves as early as 2.30 a.m. in order to arrive at their places of work for a four or five o'clock start. Swelling their ranks would be the prostitutes who had had no customers and were without the price of a bed, and paupers and vagrants constantly moved on by the police to wander the streets aimlessly until dawn brought them another dreary day to survive.

At first, James Kelly knew very little of that mysterious world, and tended to make any evening excursions in the vicinity of his lodgings and, increasingly, in the company of John Merritt, who no doubt would have learned of the amount of money held in trust for Kelly. Soon he was drinking regularly, and becoming known in the pubs in Euston Road, Somers Town and St Pancras. Sometimes, he went farther afield to Camden Town, the Caledonian Road and Islington.

However, the time came when Kelly was forced to face reality. Not only was he spending more than he was earning, he was living in the wrong place. He now knew that he was paying more than enough for his lodgings, and every morning he was wasting time and money in travelling to the East End. To precisely where in the East End he moved is not known for certain; however he was to say later that he always stayed with friends and his only known friend in the district was a fellow upholsterer named Walter Lamb, who lived with his family in a private house at No. 37, Collingwood Street, Bethnal Green.

Here, and in the area of Whitechapel and Spitalfields, the streets were packed every evening. Sailors of all nationalities, and soldiers from the Tower of London, brushed shoulders with pickpockets and prostitutes. Food vendors, selling everything from hot potatoes to jellied eels, did a roaring trade. Street entertainers, with the occasional hurdy-gurdy man prominent, vied with the attractions of drunken brawls and fights – often between women. The theatres and music-halls were full, and drink – especially gin – was cheap.

Free of all ties, and with money in his pocket, James Kelly would wander around absorbing everything eagerly. The drinking which had begun with John Merritt continued and increased, and it was not long before he was a regular visitor to the bright lights and drunken cheeriness of the pubs. There, obviously not short of a shilling, he soon attracted the attentions of the many ladies of the night. They fluttered around him like the moths drawn to the stall-holders' lamps.

The prostitutes in the East End came in all ages, shapes and sizes – from the prettiest of young girls to the most broken-down hags – and they catered for all classes and requirements. In 1888, the Metropolitan Police were to estimate that there were over 60 brothels and 1,200 prostitutes, 'of the lowest order', in Whitechapel alone, and there is no reason to suppose that the figures were very different a decade earlier.

However, those statistics by no means tell the whole story because there were also hundreds of 'casuals'. Driven by the desperate needs to pay the rent and feed the children, these were prepared to succumb to the vilest of sexual practices for just a few pennies. Then there were the 'enthusiastic amateurs', girls quite happy to sell the use of their bodies in return for a night out and an extra shilling or two in their purses. Saddest of all, however, were the very young girls – children – who were pushed on to the streets in order to supplement the family income, or to provide drinking money for dissolute parents.

Such a supply fulfilled more than a local demand. 'Toffs' came by carriage from the West End to places like Aldgate, where the better class of girl was to be found; soldiers flooded in from the Tower and other garrisons; but above all there were the seamen. Sailors from every quarter of the globe swelled the crowds that packed the pubs and thronged the streets. A free and easy bunch, with no local ties and usually with months of back-pay burning holes in their pockets, they were generous and not too fussy about whom they picked up. The only unwelcome exceptions were the Lascars, who were held responsible, possibly unfairly, for the high incidence of venereal disease. Only the most desperate of whores would have anything to do with them. VD was rife, and was one of the reasons why such high prices were paid for disease-free young virgins in the white slave traffic to France.

Forbidden by his faith to have sexual intercourse outside of marriage, and distrusting and disliking most females, James Kelly had had no girlfriends or sexual experience in Liverpool. However all that changed shortly after he arrived in London. It was probably whilst he was lodging in Tavistock Square that Kelly lost his virginity to a prostitute as a result of, one suspects, a combination of unaccustomed drinking and encouragement from John Merritt. For a man in his situation, the impersonal services on offer were part of the answer to his problems with women. It was possible to obtain instant sexual gratification without emotional involvement. Afterwards he could discard them with contempt.

It may well have been a realization that he could not continue upon this path of self-destruction that eventually, at the age of nineteen, drove him away from London.

We know almost nothing of what happened to James Kelly over the next two years. All that we have to go on are the briefest of details supplied some years later by Dr R. F. M. Treadwell, the Assistant Surgeon-in-Charge at Clerkenwell Prison, who recorded that after leaving London Kelly was: 'for some time in lodgings in Brighton – does not know street. Then in an American man-of-war.' The paucity of this information is frustrating in the extreme. We are not told why, or for how long, he went to Brighton, nor what on earth he was doing in an American warship or where he went in it. It is a fascinating episode in Kelly's life, and one that apparently influenced him strongly in later life.

Two years later he was drawn back to London, physically stronger and more mature but still mentally unstable. He had kept in touch with John Merritt, and once again he became a regular visitor to Clarendon Square. A trip to Liverpool resulted in his returning with some money from his trust fund, but he resumed contact with his trade society in Curtain Road.

His work took him all over the East End and other parts of London, and there is reason to suppose that he stayed in several lodging-houses. Between upholstery jobs he, as before, turned his hand to whatever was available, and appears to have worked in and around the docks on occasion. In the light of subsequent events, it is also probable that sometimes he secured casual employment on some of the many boats which made regular trips to and from the Continent. Certainly he came to know the docks area very well, and made some good friends there who were to stand by him in years to come.

During those months, Kelly seems to have spent most of his evenings drifting around the pubs of the East End. He was drinking much more heavily now, and the indications are that he was patronizing prostitutes on a fairly regular basis. Sometimes he was accompanied by Walter Lamb, but it is not known whether he ever stayed at Collingwood Street during this brief period. There were also occasional evenings when he went out with John Merritt, especially if he happened to have work in the area, and then he may have stayed overnight in Clarendon Square. It was a careless way of life which might have continued indefinitely had not Fate taken a hand and introduced him to Sarah Brider – a meeting which was to change his life for ever.

Sarah lived with her parents at No. 21, Cottage Lane – a short thoroughfare just off City Road. She was employed as an 'Indian envelope folder' by Thomas De La Rue, the security printers, wholesale stationers and publishers, of Nos. 107/115, Bunhill Row. (The block was destroyed by bombing in World War II.) It was only about 750 yards from where Kelly attended meetings at the Horse and Groom.

Sarah was later described by her mother as a 'pious girl, a thoroughly good-living girl; she was very reserved, she never spoke to a person in the street – she had never misconducted herself in any way . . . she was always modest and proper'.

Perhaps she was all of those things at the time she met Kelly – although there is some evidence to the contrary – and perhaps it was those very qualities which, in addition to her undoubted physical charms, drove Kelly wild with desire.

It is doubtful whether, at that stage, Sarah realized the intense emotions which she had aroused. She saw a quiet, religious twenty-one-year-old: orphaned and apparently alone in the world; a young man with not only a good trade in his hands but with 'expectations'.

Sarah was in her twenty-first year when they met, quite old in those days for a girl to be without a steady boyfriend, and she was not enamoured of her boring repetitive job nor her overcrowded home. She responded to his tentative advances, and soon they were 'walking out' together.

An essential part of the 'courting' process was being taken home to meet the parents, usually over a traditional Sunday high tea. It was therefore only a matter of weeks after their meeting that, around Christmas 1881, James Kelly found himself being ushered into the small double-fronted house in Cottage Lane.

Her beau must have been rather taken aback by what awaited him. Double-fronted or not, No. 21 could not have been termed large by any stretch of the imagination, yet at least eight people were crammed into its tiny rooms. In addition to Sarah (according to the 1881 Census) they were: John Charles Brider (Father), aged forty-two, a bricklayer. Sarah Brider (Mother), aged forty. Mary Ellen Brider (Sister), aged 17 – also an envelope folder. Harry Charles Brider (Brother), aged 14, a die sinker. Frank Brider (Brother), aged 12, a schoolboy. William Brider (Brother), aged nine, a schoolboy, and an unnamed lodger.

Kelly continued to see Sarah who, he discovered, was known within the family as 'Titty'. He had been well received by the Briders, and became a regular visitor to Cottage Lane. There he felt part of the family, a role for which he had yearned, and the homeliness was in marked contrast to the bare and impersonal lodging-houses. He must have told Sarah how he felt, but we do not know who eventually took the initiative: suffice it to say that by the beginning of March 1882, he had moved into No. 21, Cottage Lane as the second lodger whom the Briders had been seeking.

The Briders had previously had two lodgers in one room. They had moved on. One male replacement had been found, but there was a potential problem.

The previous lodgers had been a married couple, and very happy to be together, but would a man wish to share a room with a stranger? There was no alternative to the problem because sleeping accommodation was at such a premium that the two girls were already sharing one of the two downstairs parlours.

From what we shall learn of Kelly, in normal circumstances nothing in this world would have induced him to share a room, especially with a stranger, but he was so strongly attracted to Sarah that he seems to have been prepared to suffer many inconveniences to be near her.

We are not told how the existing lodger viewed the situation. It may well have been a condition of his tenancy, or it could be that he had already become used to a lack of privacy because some of the arrangements in that house were rather peculiar. For instance, there was a wash-stand in the lodgers' room, with wash-basin, jug and soap-dish – but the lodgers were not permitted to wash there! That privilege was reserved for Mrs Brider and, most probably, her daughters. The males had to make do with the outside tap and the Public Baths!

Time passed, Kelly settled in and he must have been well pleased. Although he continued to work on a casual basis, and sometimes travelled quite long distances for employment, at least he now had a permanent base. What few belongings he possessed were safe whilst he was out, and at the end of the day he returned to a meal in warm and friendly surroundings.

When the idea of his going to lodge at No. 21 had first been mooted, living under the same roof as Sarah must have conjured up some alluring possibilities. Kelly lusted after her, but any intimacies had been very restricted.

That may have been due to Sarah's reputed virtue, but the lack of opportunities to take matters further would also have played a part. Whatever mild familiarities in which they had indulged had, of necessity, taken place out of doors but now, he thought, surely things would be different.

However, there was scarcely a nook or cranny in that house that was ever free from prying eyes. Had both partners been of the same mind no doubt something could have been contrived – but Sarah needed to be wooed.

No question here of a quick coupling in the outside wash-house; in addition to privacy Kelly needed time and warmth to bring her round to his way of thinking, and all three were never available at the same time. It was all very frustrating for a lusty young man, especially one who had become accustomed to having sex whenever and wherever he wished.

Now that he was living that much closer to Clarendon Square, Kelly saw more of John Merritt but, for the first couple of months at least, any drinking jaunts were restricted. When he had been faced with the prospect of spending his evenings in a lodging-house, going out on the town had been a far more attractive, and almost necessary, alternative. Now that situation no longer arose, and also Sarah did not take kindly to the idea of his spending evenings out of her sight. Kelly was quite content, therefore, to spend only the occasional evening out, especially as he constantly entertained hopes of getting the virtuous Miss Brider into his bed.

After a while though, when he had come to realize that there was little chance of his hopes being fulfilled, things changed.

During that brief spell of domesticity Kelly, and whoever he happened to be going around with at the time, had not strayed very far from the pubs of the City Road and Islington areas for their pleasures. They were relatively innocuous evenings which came to a sudden end when Jim Kelly's sexual frustration finally became unbearable.

He could, of course, have found what he wanted close to home, but the snag was that the whores of Islington and King's Cross were *too* local. Then, as now to some extent, the many districts of London were little more than interlocking villages in which everyone knew everybody else. Had he gone astray so near to Cottage Lane it would have been but a matter of time before word got back to the Briders. He realized that he would have to go out of the area, and he already knew the ideal place – the East End!

The summer and autumn of 1882 came and went and, to all outward appearances, things were very much the same at No. 21. Kelly was still lodging there, and appeared still to be the same quiet, religious young man whom the Briders had taken to their hearts. As Mrs Brider was to say later, at that time, 'he was much beloved by the whole family'. However he might have been just a little less beloved had they known what he was getting up to in his spare time.

He had now been back in London for over a year and his knowledge of the capital, and of the East End in particular, had increased immeasurably. No longer did he cling resolutely to the main roads; gradually he had explored what lay behind and between them, and he was horrified by what he had seen.

Kelly had by no means lived a sheltered life in Liverpool. Although he had little knowledge of the more violent and vice-ridden districts of that city, he had seen slums and human degradation. Nothing, however, had prepared him for the sights, smells and sounds which awaited him in these squalid tenements and lodging-houses, in and out of which passed young men and women aged prematurely by poverty and long hours of arduous work.

At one point, he had seriously considered leaving London and returning to Liverpool. However just one visit had served to change his mind about the idea. During the summer he had gone back for more money – even in the East End, the more desirable prostitutes were not cheap – and he had realized that nothing there had changed. For better or worse, it seemed that his future lay in London.

Something of his unrest had transmitted itself to Sarah, who was already bothered about what she thought to be a cooling in their relationship. She had worried when he began to spend more evenings out of her company, and had become even more concerned when his advances became less ardent. Although she had permitted increasing intimacies as their friendship deepened, she had always drawn the line at the full sexual intercourse for which Kelly pressed. That previous persistence had annoyed, and possibly frightened, her and at times she had reacted angrily.

Now, with female contrariness, she was puzzled, and not a little piqued, because he was not so demanding. Thoughts that she might be losing his affection had begun to plague her. Little did she realize to what lengths her refusals had driven him, or how much he still wanted her.

There were moments when Kelly's frustration at being denied what was so freely available elsewhere neared explosion point. At such times he wondered despairingly when, if ever, she would succumb. Christmas 1882 was to provide the answer.

*

Christmas with the Briders was an entirely new experience for Jim Kelly. Kelly drew a present-day equivalent of £1,000 from his solicitors in anticipation of the event. As Sarah's 'steady', he had found himself included in the family's plans, and had shared the growing excitement. When the festivities finally began he joined in wholeheartedly, and was very generous with presents. It was a time of almost frenetic activity. Once the women had completed the really hard work, they joined the rest of the household in the almost constant comings and goings. Visits were made, and visitors received.

Drink flowed freely. Kelly was introduced to members of the Brider clan of whom he had never even heard, and visited their homes and those of family friends. He was taken to backstreet pubs previously unknown to him, took part in the boisterous banter, the horseplay and the drunken singsongs, paid more than his share of the rounds and at some time during the jollifications managed at last to seduce Titty.

Various allegations were to be made later, but all we know for sure is that what should have been a moving and pleasurable experience for both parties was a total disaster.

The few facts available indicate a combination of sexual ignorance and physical disabilities. He was accustomed to women who, both physically and mentally, were no strangers to sexual intercourse, but there is no hard evidence to suggest that she was not a virgin. Both were unlikely to have had much knowledge of some of the functions of the human body, and the seduction was almost certainly a furtive and hurried affair.

Kelly later claimed 'a malformation' existed in Sarah 'which he thought unfitted her, to a serious extent, for fulfilling the functions of a wife . . . and when he spoke to her [about it] she cried and threw the blame on her Uncle who had taken her upon his knee . . .'

It is quite possible that Sarah was suffering from vaginismus, or that there was a constriction of a temporary nature caused by the unhelpful circumstances surrounding the intercourse. With either of those situations, penetration would have been difficult, if not impossible.

It is also likely that he had never even heard of a hymen, let alone the implications of a broken one. Those were the days when sex education for children was not even considered. Any 'knowledge' that was acquired was usually picked up from those only marginally better informed – and was usually wrong anyway. As for Sarah, her mind would have cast around in desperation for a possible explanation, and she had obviously responded by mentioning the only incident of which she could think.

There must have been a reason why whatever had happened with her uncle had remained so firmly embedded in her mind, but unfortunately, we are not told her age at the time of the occurrence, and can therefore only speculate upon whether it was innocent horseplay with a young child or part of a sinister design upon an older girl. Be that as it may, Kelly was not convinced by her stammered explanation, and said that she should see a doctor. As far as he was concerned, the whole business had been a disaster. Only his fondness for her prevented him from leaving the household.

From that time on, he was a changed man – and the change was very much for the worse.

He fell into a deep slough of depression. No steady job; no home of his own; only one true friend in the world; and now the added complication of his damaged relationship with Titty. Every way his mind twisted the outlook was of gloom and doom, and soon he began to suffer stabbing pains in his head.

Sarah, also, was troubled. Not only does the act of intercourse with Kelly appear to have been a shocking and unnerving experience, but his accusations had left her bewildered and hurt. As far as she was concerned she had done nothing wrong, but nevertheless she felt guilty.

It is hardly surprising that relations were strained for a few weeks – something which did not go unnoticed by the rest of the household. Kelly resumed his trips to the East End, whilst Sarah sat at home and wondered about their future together.

Fortunately, their domestic arrangements did not permit such a sorry state of affairs to continue. Living as they did in the same small house, they were constantly thrown together. Under the surface, their feelings for each other were unchanged and so, gradually, things got back to normal, encouraged in no small measure by a decision made by Kelly. He had reached the conclusion that only marriage, and the setting-up of home together, could halt what, in his darkest moments, he regarded as his otherwise certain spiral to poverty and the workhouse.

However his subsequent proposal of marriage was not received with the degree of warmth which he had anticipated. Only a few months before it was something Sarah would have welcomed, literally, with open arms. Now she was not so sure. Jim Kelly was no longer the happy-go-lucky young man to whom she had been attracted, and with whom she had fallen in love. She resented his constant exhortations to see a doctor. Sarah took time to think, and consulted her mother, but all the time, in her heart of hearts, she knew that she would accept his proposal, and finally she did.

Her decision would, almost certainly, have been very different had she known of the discovery which Kelly had made whilst she was shilly-shallying. To his horror, he found that he had contracted a venereal disease. His whole world collapsed about him, and he was never to be the same again.

It is difficult to judge just how worldly-wise James Kelly was. It is possible that he had not been aware of the dangers he was running in consorting with whores, and did not even *know* about venereal diseases, but of one thing we may be sure; whatever Kelly did or did not know about the dangers of catching such a disease, he certainly knew nothing about curing them. It is possible that someone unqualified – a workmate, or Jack Merritt, for instance – told him what *might* be wrong with him. In that case embarrassment, and fear of the news getting back to the Briders, may well have deterred him from seeking expert help. The truth of the matter is just not known but, as will be seen later, there is very strong evidence that Kelly resorted to trying to treat himself. What, however, there can be *no* doubt about is that his contracting of the disease intensified the changes which were taking place in his personality. He became even more introspective, and began to act in a most peculiar manner.

Now he wished that he had not proposed, although his reasons for those regrets varied with his moods. There were times when he vowed not to become involved with Sarah. At others – and they were in the majority – his love for her made him fearful of passing on the disease after marriage, and he resolved to delay the wedding until he was cured.

As it happened, however, he was to be carried along upon a tide of events over which he had little control.

It all began when he secured a more or less permanent job with an upholsterer named John Hiron whose premises were at No. 4 Orchard Buildings, off Acton – now Arbutus – Street, Haggerston. He started there on April 1st.

Needless to say, Sarah and her parents were delighted. At the time of his proposal he had said that the wedding would take place as soon as he had a steady job. Now, to their way of thinking, there was no reason why a date should not be set.

Kelly tried desperately to slow matters down, but his success was limited and his clumsy tactics so puzzled the family that, at one point, Sarah seemed to be having doubts about his intentions. The most he was able to achieve was the acceptance of his suggestion that it would be rather pleasant were the wedding to be held as near as possible to Titty's twenty-second birthday – Monday, June 18th – but he was somewhat thwarted even in that. As is often the way, his potential mother-in-law took over all the arrangements and, for some reason, decided on June 4th. Kelly had little option but to agree, and became quite fatalistic about the whole business. To be sure, the venereal disease was a problem, but he had stopped going out at nights and the treatment appeared to be working.

However, to his dismay, the pains in his head became more frequent and were accompanied by some very nasty discharges from both ears. At times he was in such agony that he could hardly think straight. Although he became convinced that he had an abscess in his head, he refused to see a doctor; instead, he relied upon dropping 'sweet oil' – perhaps olive or camphorated oil – in his ears. His work began to suffer, and all his former moodiness reappeared.

That was enough of a set-back, but the consequences were to be much worse. This time disaster struck only a few days before the wedding, and it was a blow which placed all the plans in jeopardy. He was sacked from his job.

As may be imagined, Sarah and her family were not exactly, overjoyed at the news, and they would have been even less ecstatic had Kelly told them the reason for his dismissal. John Hiron, his employer for only two months, had dismissed him because 'he was obviously not right in the head'.

For a time it seemed that the wedding would be cancelled, but Kelly still had most of the present-day equivalent of £400 which had been advanced to him from his mother's estate during the previous month and, after many discussions, it was decided to proceed with the arrangements.

On June 4th, 1883, James Kelly, aged twenty-three, bachelor, and upholsterer by trade, was married to Sarah Ann Brider, aged twenty-one, spinster and Indian envelope worker, at St Luke's parish church, Old Street, EC1, in the county of Middlesex, not a hundred yards from Bunhill Row, where Sarah worked. The ceremony was conducted by the curate, Frank H. Dalby. Kelly named his father as 'John Miller, clerk'.

There was no wedding breakfast, and no honeymoon. The couple returned to Cottage Lane, changed their clothes, and then Sarah went off to De La Rue's whilst Kelly set about trying to find a job.

One way and the other, it was his lucky day, because his trade society told him of a vacancy, just off the Regent's Park end of Euston Road, and he was engaged on the spot.

His new employer was Cornelius Vincent Smith, who ran an upholstery business in what was known as 'Marshall's Yard', at No. 4, Henry Street. Henry Street was the better part of two miles from Cottage Lane, but it was a job – and Kelly could travel by tram.

Kelly and Sarah may have been married, but there was nothing different in the domestic arrangements at No. 21. Shortage of space precluded any notion of the couple having a room of their own, and they did not sleep together – not even on their wedding night! The sleeping arrangements were unchanged. Sarah continued to share with her sister, and Kelly with the lodger. The lack of privacy made any intimacies virtually impossible, and even a private conversation was rare. The only time when they were able to snatch a regular moment to themselves was in the early evening, and even then it was out of doors. Sarah usually got home from work at around 8 p.m., but Kelly did not arrive until some time during the next hour. It therefore became her custom to walk along City Road and down Pentonville Hill until she met him. Then they would chat as they strolled back to Cottage Lane.

It was an unnatural situation, and nowhere near satisfactory as far as Kelly was concerned. Now that he was a married man he felt that he should be sleeping with his wife, and free from intrusion. His conscience told him that he could pass on his disease to Sarah, but his powerful sexual urges overcame all scruples and on several occasions he tried to persuade Sarah into intercourse. However the same practical difficulties existed as when they were single, and she baulked at the quick and furtive coition which he suggested. Kelly could not understand her objections, and furious rows broke out during which he constantly asked why she would not see a doctor about her 'condition' if she had nothing to fear.

As we have seen, his mental condition had been deteriorating for months, and had been aggravated by the discovery of his disease, the almost constant pains in his head, and the loss of his job. Now the sexual frustrations which he was experiencing finally tipped him over the brink into active insanity. He began to brood; his hatred of women grew even stronger, and his mind filled with all manner of suspicions. Although there were periods when he appeared to be quite normal, it became increasingly obvious to all around him that something was very wrong.

There were times when, somehow, he convinced himself that every disaster that had befallen him was Sarah's fault. It was then that he saw quite clearly that she had deceived him from the moment of their first meeting and that, even now, she was laughing at him behind his back. No wonder she was always putting him off; she'd never really cared for him; she just wanted a wedding ring on her finger in order to get at his money. She was no better than all the others, and had probably been seeing other men all the time he had known her. For all he knew, she might actually be 'on the game' herself. That would explain her malformation and, come to that, what about the VD? He'd never had any trouble like that until he'd bedded *her* – *that's* where he'd got it from! Well she needn't think she was going to get away with it; he'd soon settle *her* little game.

So his thoughts went, on and on, round and round, day and night, during that first week of marriage. Sometimes he would come to his senses and laugh at his suspicions, but it was never too long before he was once more plunged back into the welter of sinister fancies.

Matters began to come to a head on Saturday, June 9th, with his final demand that Sarah be examined by a doctor. He was now determined to find out just what *was* wrong with her and *why*, and was no longer prepared to be put off. When she began to make excuses for not going he would have none of it. He told her that she should see a doctor on the following Monday without fail, and that she should speak to her mother and get her to go with her.

Sarah did consult her mother, but Mrs Brider was not at all pleased to learn of Kelly's insinuations. Her indignation was such that she went straight to her husband and demanded that he remonstrate with his son-in-law.

Little is known about John Brider. His is a shadowy figure, who makes only fleeting appearances in our tragedy. Either he was dominated completely by his wife or he preferred to lead a quiet life leaving most things to her; certainly Mrs Brider was the partner usually to the fore. It was, therefore, with a great deal of reluctance that her spouse allowed himself to be drawn into what he regarded as interference between husband and wife, but he did as he was asked and took Kelly off for what he thought would be a quiet chat. It did *start* quietly enough, with John Brider asking what all the trouble was about, but he cannot have been prepared for the tirade his gentle enquiry provoked.

Inside, Kelly was seething. When he gave his wife instructions he expected them to be followed to the letter, and without further ado. Yet here he was, the injured party, being interrogated like a criminal because of his meddling mother-in-law. What right had she to interfere in *his* affairs – hadn't she done enough damage?

Out it all poured. According to him, Mrs Brider had known full well that something was wrong with Titty, but she had not said a word to him. Never mind that her daughter would be unhappy when the truth was discovered after their wedding; all that *she* wanted was to cover up what the uncle had done in order to get Sarah married off. Allegation piled upon allegation.

Mr Brider was quite taken aback. He did not really understand what his son-in-law was going on and on about. Certainly all this business about the uncle and an internal disability was news to him, but it was only when the torrent of words had slowed to a trickle that he was able to ask a few questions.

By then Kelly was much calmer, and was able to answer in a rational manner. However, the ranting had upset Mr Brider, who now realized that the family's concern about Kelly's state of mind was more than justified. Obviously there was little for it but to humour the man, and hope that acquiescing with his wishes would alleviate the situation. He said that the best thing *would* be for Sarah to be examined. The two men shook hands, and off he went to tell a disbelieving wife and daughter what had transpired, and to what he had agreed.

As for Kelly, he may have got his way but the episode had taken its toll. He was quite spent, and utterly depressed. Less than a week married, he had not only alienated his wife but had also damaged his relationship with her parents irredeemably. What *was* to be done? He wrestled with the problem all over the weekend, and by Monday morning he had come to the conclusion that the only solution was for him and Sarah to leave Cottage Lane and set up in a place of their own. Then they could have a normal married life, and settle any differences without the constant interference of others. A new beginning would, however, cost money, and that meant that he would have to make another trip to Liverpool and try to obtain more money from his mother's estate.

No sooner the thought than the deed. Any thought of work that day was abandoned and, before 9 a.m., he was at Euston Station waiting for a train to his home city. He used that quiet interval to write the following letter to Sarah:

Euston Station.
My dear Wife,

Through the trouble between your father and mother and I, I feel I can never live with them more. You and I must leave them soon, and to do so we want money. When you read what I am going to do, do not fret, as it will only make things worse. I am going down to Liverpool to see the solicitors, but shall come back late to-night. Dear Sarah, don't fret, but be quiet and let them all at home see how you can trust me. God knows that they have distrusted me, which is one of the things which has upset us. Dear Sarah, it is hard to go away from you, but it is for the best; rather let me be away from you one day than for ever. Dear Sarah, if you have not been examined today do not be so. I say again, it will make no difference between you and I. I am afraid the friendship between your mother and I is ended. Dear Sarah, it is strange, but before I married you I thought it would turn out like this; I shall always believe your mother knew you; but never mind, we shall both be happy when living alone. The fault is not yours. Dear Sarah, believe me, I love you with all my heart, although I have acted funny at times. Remember, allow no one to come between us. Dear Sarah, I cannot say any more at present. I go at 9.30. Please not to go near Smith's, I shall telegraph to you when I arrive. Dear Sarah, believe me to be your ever loving husband,

James K.

His visit to the solicitors was successful, and Kelly was able to tell Sarah that they had agreed to advance him the present-day equivalent of £800; but he looked, and felt, terrible whilst he was doing so. It may have been the aftermath of all the rowing, the travelling, the putting of his case to the solicitors, the apprehension of returning with nothing solved, or a little of everything, but his head pains had intensified to a completely unbearable level. Whatever the Briders had had in mind to say to him was swept aside in their concern about how ill he appeared. He had not told the family of the pains previously, but now, in reply to their anxious enquiries, he blurted out that his head was 'very bad'.

For the whole of that week he was in agony, and all his mental turbulence was resurrected. He watched every move his wife made, and questioned her continually about what she did, and whom she met, whilst they were apart. The Briders were also affected by his behaviour: he was rude and surly, and would swear upon the slightest provocation. Every day that passed witnessed an increase in the episodes of insanity.

What probably caused his final breakdown was the discovery Mrs Brider made in the room that Kelly shared. Whether she merely went in unexpectedly, or whether it was her habit to poke around whilst her tenants were out, we shall never know but, as she later said, she saw 'things in his bedroom that were used for an immoral purpose; a syringe, a small phial, and ointment, with directions'. She tackled Kelly about her find and 'he said he hoped I did not think they were his. I said I had not seen them there before.' Clearly she had not believed Kelly's denials. She cornered her daughter, told her of what she had found, and asked whether she knew of Kelly's disease. Sarah did not answer her immediately, but there was no need; the look of disbelief and horror which she had displayed told their own tale. With her mother present, she confronted Kelly when he came in.

Kelly flew into a terrible rage. He shouted at her that *she* had passed the disease to him, and made many of the other accusations which, until then, he had bottled up in his tormented mind. Then he vented his anger on her mother, saying that she had known all along of everything that was wrong with her daughter, and accusing her of tricking him into marriage. It was a violent and unpleasant scene which resolved nothing, and ended with Kelly slamming out of the room leaving his wife in tears.

Mrs Brider was furious. Yet again she and her daughter had been maligned, and in the coarsest possible terms. She was all for telling her husband what she had found, and of how Kelly had behaved, but her daughter persuaded her otherwise. Sarah had loved James Kelly, and probably still did. She had tried to understand his moods, and had felt for him when he was racked with pain. Hurt though she was by his outbursts, she saw that nothing would be gained by dragging her father into it again. Far better to leave things until she could speak to Jim quietly, and possibly prevail upon him to seek medical help. In any case, the next day, June 18th, was her birthday. It was something to which she had been looking forward for weeks, and she did not want it spoiled by more rows.

Kelly hardly slept that night. Once he had recovered himself he was, as usual, full of remorse. He also knew that he would have to face his wife and the Briders in the morning, and the prospect filled him with dread.

To his great relief and surprise, however, nothing untoward was said before he went off to work. His mother-in-law was a little distant, but Sarah seemed much as usual when he gave her his present. There was, in fact, little opportunity for serious conversation amidst all the birthday excitement, and he was able to slip away from the house virtually unnoticed.

All that day he tormented himself with regrets about his behaviour of the previous evening. He was ashamed of himself, and became determined to put matters right between Titty and himself. Somehow he'd have to get her on her own. He'd take her out for a birthday drink when she met him that evening. Everything would be all right – he'd *make* it all right. Full of resolve for a new beginning, he could hardly wait for the day to end.

That evening, during the long toil up Pentonville Hill his eyes were peeled for the first sight of his wife. There was, however, no sign of her; not there, not in City Road, not even in Cottage Lane. By the time he reached No. 21 all his eagerness had subsided, and he entered the house with a sense of foreboding.

To his amazement she was not there either, and nobody seemed to know where she might be. He did not know what to think or do, and fidgeted around the kitchen exclaiming that he could not think where she had got to. Someone suggested that they might have passed each other unwittingly, and that perhaps he should retrace his steps, but the idea fell on deaf ears. By that time Kelly was sitting quite still and staring into space. A creeping black shadow was taking possession of his mind, and slowly blotting out his sanity. All his good intentions were being ousted by a mad conviction that all his suspicions about his wife were true.

It was not until about 9 p.m. – and over an hour late – that they heard Sarah come in by the back door. She walked straight past the kitchen and into the parlour. Kelly did not stir, but Mrs Brider hurried after her and found her sitting in an armchair. Sarah did not say where she had been; all that could be got out of her was that she felt 'very ill'.

Still Kelly had not moved, and Mrs Brider had just returned to the kitchen to have a word with him when they heard Sarah sobbing. At that, Kelly stood up and listened for a few minutes, his face expressionless and his whole demeanour that of a man in a trance. Then, without warning, he leaped into the parlour, grabbed hold of his weeping wife, and began to drag her back to the kitchen, all the time hurling threats. She started to scream, and her mother intervened, shouting at him to stop. Stop he did, but then he pushed past Mrs Brider and began fumbling in the table drawer where the cutlery was kept. Abandoning her daughter, Mrs Brider made for the door but was overtaken by Sarah who was protecting her neck with her arms and shrieking that Kelly was going to kill someone. By now he was close on her heels, a large carving knife in his hand. When they reached the parlour, Mrs Brider caught him by the shoulders and screamed at him to drop the knife; but faintness overcame her and she slumped into a chair. She could merely watch as Kelly held the knife to her daughter's breast and threatened to 'run it through' her if she did not tell him where she had been.

According to Mrs Brider, Sarah had been to the Hackney Road on an errand for her father, but Sarah gasped out that she had been to Fox's in the Bethnal Green Road to fetch Kelly 'some bark [quinine] to gargle his throat', at which all the violence stopped as Kelly sat down and cried bitterly.

Yet again a complete transformation had taken place in a split second, and he was now dismayed by what he had done. Holding his head in his hands, he muttered that he thought he was mad; to which Mrs Brider had no hesitation in retorting that she was sure he was! Whilst that exchange was taking place, Sarah seized the opportunity to slip out of the room with the knife and return it to the kitchen. When she came back she once again begged her mother not to say anything to her father and, albeit reluctantly, Mrs Brider agreed.

Thus another episode of insanity passed, but they were now occurring more frequently and it was quite plain that Kelly was desperately in need of treatment.

Three days passed – days, and nights, during which he relived the events of the Monday evening over and over again until he felt that his head would burst. However, the more he thought about it the more convinced he became that he had done nothing wrong. Little by little, the remorse which he had felt was whittled away and replaced by all his usual suspicions. At times, in his twisted mind, he felt as if he was living through a recurring nightmare. His mother, Sarah Kelly, had been a woman of loose morals, and now his wife of the same name was also a whore. He was certain that Titty and her mother were in league against him, and he felt a quiet anger as he pictured them laughing together behind his back. Events were building to a climax.

On Thursday, June 21st, Sarah came home from work at her usual time of 8 p.m. She was carrying a small parcel which she laid upon the table before going to meet her husband. An hour passed, and then Kelly appeared. Mrs Brider was surprised that he was alone, and asked if he had not met Sarah on his way up. He replied that he *had* seen her, on the other side of Pentonville Road, but 'she was walking in such an upright style I did not cross directly to her'. His manner was peculiar and aggressive and, on his way out again, he snarled that no woman would master *him*.

About twenty minutes elapsed, and then he returned with his wife. Nothing appeared to be wrong, and they walked into the kitchen quietly enough. Suddenly, however, Sarah broke away from him and ran into her bedroom. That threw Kelly into a fury. He rushed after her and, finding the door locked, burst it open. A fierce argument then broke out: an argument of such violence that Mrs Brider felt bound to see what was happening.

As she entered the room she saw her daughter in tears, and Kelly standing over her. His hands were on her shoulders, and he was mouthing threats and accusations that she was 'a whore'. Sarah made a desperate appeal to her mother to refute what he was saying, and struggled free shouting that she would not live with him any more, and never wanted to see him again.

The result was dramatic, but nothing new. In a trice Kelly was out of his madness and full of contrition. He begged his wife to forgive him, and swore that it would never happen again. Sarah, however, had heard it all before, and this time she was not prepared to relent. She told him that she could *never* forgive him. Another abject appeal brought the same response, and Kelly sat down beside her looking quite dejected – but suddenly something snapped and, in a flash, he pounced. His arm went around her neck, he dragged her head down to the floor, stabbed her in the throat with a pocket-knife, and began digging away with the knife as if bent upon further damage.

Sarah screamed for help as best she could, and her mother tried to pull him away by his hair. It was all to no avail. Kelly was a strong young man, and even stronger when in one of his frenzies. He hurled Mrs Brider right over the bed, knocking her unconscious, and then, in a blind panic, he ran off to his room.

When Mrs Brider came to her senses she saw that her daughter was bleeding profusely. She dashed off for a towel and some water, but soon realized just how serious the wound was and ran into the street screaming for help. People came running from all directions, and in a very few minutes a doctor was attending to Sarah whilst her mother gave a gabbled account to a policeman.

The doctor asked for a cab to be summoned, and just then another constable appeared on the scene. Shortly after, his colleague accompanied Sarah, Mrs Brider and the doctor to St Bartholomew's Hospital, whilst he took Kelly to Old Street police station.

Before he did so, the policeman asked Kelly if he had anything to say for himself.

He replied: 'I don't know what I am about, I must be mad.'

2

Escape from Broadmoor

ON THE MORNING OF Friday, June 22nd, 1883, James Kelly was in the dock at Clerkenwell Police Court, charged with attempted murder.

Inspector Thomas Maynard, of 'G' Division of the Metropolitan Police, told the sitting magistrate, Mr Barstow, that the 'prosecutrix' was in St Bartholomew's Hospital, and was too ill to attend.

Mrs Brider was called to give evidence, and said that for a day or two there had been 'a slight quarrel' between Kelly and her daughter. On the previous night, the Thursday, the prisoner had accused his wife of keeping the company of girls of loose character in Islington. His wife had replied: 'I won't live with you any longer; you are unkind and cruel.' Kelly had then told her: 'You *won't* leave me – I'll stop you from doing so. I'll knock you down.'

After the witness had related the subsequent happenings, her place was taken by Dr Raynor of St Bartholomew's Hospital. He said that Mrs Kelly was unconscious when she was admitted. She had a 'punctured' wound below the left ear that was nearly three inches deep, and her life was very much in danger.

The court then heard further police evidence describing how Kelly had been taken into custody upon returning to the room where the stabbing had occurred, and how, on the floor of that room, a pocket-knife had been found 'with the blade broken sharp off from the handle.'

At the end of the hearing the prisoner was remanded to HM Prison Clerkenwell for a week.

There were dramatic developments on the following afternoon. Inspector Poule, also of 'G' Division, sought out Mr Barstow and told him that Mrs Kelly was 'in a dying state', and there was almost no hope of her recovering. It was vital that her deposition be taken as soon as possible. The magistrate wasted no time. He gave instructions for Kelly to be taken to the hospital and then, without further ado, he drove there himself, accompanied by the inspector and the Chief Clerk of the Court.

Shortly after their arrival, Inspector Maynard came in with Kelly. Sarah's evidence was taken, and the accused was allowed to question her.

That was on the Saturday. The next day Kelly wrote to Sarah c/o St Bartholomew's:

My dear Wife,

I scarcely know how to write a few lines to you, I feel so wretched, and have such pains in my head that I have no power to think, so if I omit anything you must forgive me. Dear Sarah, before I say more, I must ask you to write and let me know how you are; tell me if you are getting better. Dear Sarah, I am so sorry and repent to the utmost for what I have done, and I want you to write and say that you forgive me and love me still. I love you, dear girl, and I never meant to stab you as I sat by you asking you to forgive me and you answered no. I took out my penknife and meant to frighten you, but something seemed to come over me and I went mad and stabbed you. Dear Sarah, we have both been mistaken; I thought you did not love me, and you seemed to be sure that I did not love you. Dear Sarah, if it had been so, would not I have taken the opportunity to leave you when you told me to go? but, no, I could not leave you, Sarah. I loved you too much, and you drove me mad. Dear Sarah, I shall be tried next Wednesday. I shall not mention your faults, not even to save myself; you are too good for the world to know you. My dear Sarah, if you had trusted me and given way to me for a few days I feel sure this awful affair would not have happened. Dear Sarah, I am obliged to finish my letter now as I am wanted at Court. So good-bye for the present. Believe me to be, my dear wife, your loving and affectionate, but unfortunate, husband, James Kelly.

On the morning of Monday, June 25th, Kelly was taken, in handcuffs, to Clerkenwell police station. He was lodged in a cell whilst Inspector Maynard awaited the appearance of the magistrate for that day, a Mr Hosack. As soon as he arrived, the Inspector told him privately that Sarah Kelly had died at half-past ten on the previous evening. The post-mortem examination was to be held later that morning, but there was little doubt about what the result would be, and that would necessitate a fresh charge being brought against the prisoner.

This sequence of events throws some doubt on the sentiments expressed in Kelly's letter to his wife. They may well have been genuine, but Kelly wrote that he had to finish the letter as he was 'wanted at Court'. It is therefore obvious that although he *began* the letter on the Sunday he did not finish it until the next day, because it was not until the Monday morning that he was taken to Clerkenwell Police Court. This raises the question of whether he learned of his wife's death when he was only part way through his letter. Were that the case, and realizing the mortal peril in which he then stood, he would have had every reason to write what was, on the surface, a note of remorse and affection but was in reality a document of exculpation.

The cause of death was indeed held to have resulted from the injuries to the dead woman's neck. Kelly was then brought up from the cells and charged with his wife's murder, without any evidence being heard. He was remanded until the Thursday by when, it was thought, it would be possible to assemble the witnesses for a proper hearing.

On Thursday, June 28th, Kelly was once again facing Mr Barstow from the dock at Clerkenwell Police Court. The charge was that he had murdered his wife 'by stabbing her in the neck with a pocket-knife'.

When asked if he had anything to say, Kelly told the magistrate: 'I can say that I did it in my madness; I did not know what I was doing. I was led to do it by certain things that was said and done. I loved my wife and I love her still. She had many faults which I was not going to mention for my wife's sake, and as I had caused great trouble in the family I did not wish to cause more. I shall tell all now, as I can see a great many lies have been told, and a false witness brought up. That is all I have to say.'

As it happened, however, no witnesses were to be called that day. The inquest had been arranged for that very morning, and they were all required there. Kelly was therefore remanded for a week – again without any evidence having been heard.

Because Sarah had died in the sub-district of St Sepulchre, in the City of London, the inquest was conducted by Mr Samuel Frederick Langham, the Deputy Coroner for the City. He ruled that the cause of death was a 'Wound in throat by being stabbed with a knife', and recorded a charge of 'Wilful Murder' against James Kelly.

Eleven days later, on July 9th, Kelly wrote to his mother-in-law:

Dear Mrs Brider,

I feel I must write to yourself to say that I forgive you from my heart for any words you have said or anything you have done to satisfy yourself, and as you thought my poor wife Sarah, but which to me did and has made me unhappy. I know I have been very gay and reckless, but for what I have done to my dear wife I can say truthfully I never have or wished to ruin any girl's life. My dear Sarah and I had many troubles, and although I was a stranger and at liberty to do and go as I pleased, my love for your daughter was such that I could not leave her. Dear Mrs Brider, concerning my darling's illness, I did often ask Sarah to go to a doctor for her own sake, but she would not. I got wild and asked her to speak to you, which she did: then after Mr Brider spoke to me, and I said more than I wished about Sarah because I thought you had deceived me at the risk of making Sarah unhappy. I always felt more for her than myself on that point, and I never did or would allow myself to think that it was her own fault (I shall say no more), but I can see now I had not the sense to inquire in a quiet and proper manner, because I was out of my mind. I had no one to comfort or advise me, not even my only love Sarah. My dear wife seemed to me like a dead person, she could or would not speak. I cannot say more, as I wish you to get this tonight, Tuesday. [July 9th was in fact a Monday.] I should much like to know how you are all getting on. I have seen my solicitor this afternoon, but I would give no statement, as I wish to hear from you first. Please write soon. I hope that you and Mr Brider and all at home will accept my best wishes for your happiness, because I sincerely wish it. I remain, Mrs Brider, your forgiving but unfortunate son-in-law, James Kelly.

P.S. You have been much mistaken in me concerning a certain thing.

As mentioned in that letter, Kelly now had a London solicitor. After being charged with murder, he had written to Mr Sampson, the Liverpool lawyer handling his mother's estate. Mr Sampson had then engaged the services of a most reputable law firm, Messrs Cunliffe, Beaumont and Davenport, of No. 43, Chancery Lane, WC2, but they did not find Kelly an easy client. Time was short – the trial had been set for August 1st – but they were still no nearer in preparing an answer to the charge because Kelly refused to give *his* version of the events leading up to the killing. Despite having told Mr Barstow that he would 'tell all now', it was apparent that he was concealing something, something that he would not divulge until he had spoken to Mrs Brider. Time after time, his solicitors warned him of the seriousness of his predicament, and urged him to abandon any mistaken loyalties he felt towards his dead wife and her mother. They pointed out to him that Mrs Brider, as a Prosecution witness, would probably be allowed no contact with him even if that was her wish, but it was all to no avail.

On July 13th, he wrote to her again:

Dear Mrs Brider,

If it would not be asking you too much, I should much like to speak to you privately here; (if you will) please say when you can come. If you are going to the Clerkenwell Court tomorrow [where a further remand hearing was to be held], I should thank you much if you would bring with you those slippers dear Sarah worked for me. Please send them to me in my cell. Hoping that you and all at home are bearing up, I remain yours sincerely, James Kelly.

P.S. Dear Mrs Brider, – I am terribly afraid I shall have to tell all I know, but if you come and tell me any words my dear wife said which will comfort me, I will, with God's help, do what I think is right. I feel I would rather die than say a word against poor Sarah and cause you more trouble. I cry often and say to myself 'What shall I do? is there nothing to save me, and shall I have to tell all? I have seen the solicitor again this afternoon, but I will not write out my defence till I have seen you. As you know, I gave poor Titty 10L [ten pounds] which she put in the bank, and as I shall want all the monies as I can get I am asking my solicitor to get it. I should be very thankful for a letter from you, so good-bye from your sincere but unfortunate son-in-law, James Kelly.

On Wednesday, August 1st, 1883, James Kelly found himself in the dock at the Central Criminal Court, or 'Old Bailey' as it was and is better known. As he looked about him in that gloomy, gas-lit courtroom, unchanged since 1774 and where so many infamous murderers had preceded him, he, like many of them, must have been surprised by how small it was. Nevertheless, the majesty of the place was overwhelming, especially for any accused. The impressive royal coat of arms behind the judge (the Honourable Mr Justice Watkin Williams) the jury-box packed with those who were to decide his fate, the bewigged and robed counsel, the uniformed police and prison officers, the public seats crammed with those in search of a vicarious thrill – all combined to form the awesome panoply of English law. Even the most hardened of criminals, despite any outward appearance of unconcern, have felt a cold tremor of apprehension at the spectacle that awaited them as they climbed into the dock from the cells below.

Kelly was bound to have felt nervous, but he was still surprisingly optimistic. We know that during his time in prison he had experienced religious episodes during which he was convinced that he would come to no harm.

Leading for the Prosecution was Harry (later to be Sir Harry) Bodkin Poland. By 1883 he had been one of the counsel for the Treasury, and adviser to the Home Office on criminal matters, for eighteen years. His junior was Mr Eyre Lloyd. They constituted a formidable team for such a routine murder case, especially against a Defence so ill-prepared.

That is not to imply that any expense had been spared by Messrs Sampson and Hind in engaging counsel to represent Kelly. Mr Montagu Williams, whose fame was to be curtailed by his early death only nine years later, was to lead Mr Cavendish-Bentinck, a scion of the Dukes of Portland. The problem that faced the defence team was the reticence of their client who, despite all warnings and pleas, still refused to give his side of the story in full. They were faced with the prospect of trying very hard to make the best of a bad job.

The trial began. Kelly's plea of 'Not Guilty' was recorded, and Mr Poland lost no time in making his opening statement, producing Kelly's letters to his wife, and calling his first witness – Mrs Brider.

She was obviously nervous when she entered the witness box but, after some gentle leading by Mr Poland, she regained her composure somewhat and launched into a jumbled narrative. The sequences of events were muddled, and sometimes completely wrong. Nevertheless she painted a graphic word picture of the events leading up to the killing:

Mr Poland eventually finished with his witness, and she made to leave the box. She was halted, however, by Mr Williams who told her gently that he too would like her to answer a few questions.

He began his cross-examination softly enough by asking the ages of her daughter and Kelly, and upon what date they had been married, but the next question was more pointed:

'Was your daughter of good character?'

There was the briefest of intervals, and then Mrs Brider unleashed an absolute torrent of words at the hapless Mr Williams:

'She has always been an *excellent* daughter to me: a truthful, pious girl, a thoroughly good living girl. She was very reserved, she never spoke to a person in the street, she had never misconducted herself in any way. She had not given him the slightest provocation on this day, nor on any occasion. She was always modest and proper, and was very fond of him. When she begged me not to tell her father, the prisoner cried bitterly, and begged me to forgive him. He was perfectly sober on the Thursday – he was a strictly sober man – there is not the smallest suggestion for saying that she kept bad company with girls, or anything of the kind. Her church was her God.'

Counsel was wilting slightly under this spirited defence. Obviously a change of subject was indicated, and he managed to slip in another question when the witness paused for breath:

Q: 'I understand that the defendant is a Liverpool man?'

A: 'Yes, he *is* a Liverpool man. He went to Liverpool to get some money from some solicitors: he was entitled to a share in a ship.'

Q: 'Did he ever complain about pains in his head?'

A: 'Yes, he complained very much at one time of an abscess in the head, and running at the ears very badly.'

Q: 'Did that in any way affect his behaviour?'

A: 'I had known him about thirteen or fourteen months before the marriage, but he has been very different since Christmas last. He was very much beloved by the whole family until that time. He had conducted himself very properly till after his return from Liverpool: after he came back he said his head was very bad and he continued to complain of that up to this day.'

Police Inspector Thomas Maynard gave evidence: 'On the 23rd of June I took him [Kelly] to the hospital, and the Magistrate was there, and took the deceased's deposition. She was sworn, and her evidence was taken in the usual way. The prisoner had an opportunity of cross-examining her, and he *did* ask her some questions. The deposition was read over to her, and she put her cross to it.'

For the Defence, Mr Williams then produced a document, and asked the witness if it was the deposition to which he had just referred. When the inspector replied that it was, he was asked to read it to the Court. It went as follows: 'The man now present, the prisoner, is my husband. The night before last he stabbed me. I was sitting over in the back room. I am so insensible I cannot remember much. We had a few words about some boots, and he told me he would pay me when he got me home. I did not have time to make him an answer in the kitchen. He got the knife out of his pocket, and he stuck it into me two or three times. We had the words about the boots in the street, and we came home together. The kitchen and the back room are the same room. We were not ten minutes in the house before it happened. I cannot remember the words he used at the time. The knife stuck in my throat two or three times. This is the third time he has threatened my life, and this time he stabbed me. I told him in the street I would not live with him, and he said: "When we get home we'll see." I did not see the knife at all.'

Cross-examined by the prisoner: 'You *did* stab me two or three times. My mother was there too. You asked me to forgive you, and you told me you would let me see when you got me home.'

Re-examined: 'He did not say he would stab me when he got me home.'

The whole Court had fallen very quiet whilst the deposition was read, and it was obvious that it had had a profound effect upon the jury. Several of the jurors exchanged words as Inspector Maynard was dismissed and the next witness summoned.

He was Frederick Alfred Hammond, who stated what *he* had seen on that fateful night:

'I am a coachman, and live at 17, Old Ford Road. At about nine o'clock on the evening of the 21st of June I was in the City Road walking towards Cottage Lane, and saw the prisoner just by Duncan Terrace: he was alone, but he came across and met a young woman. He said to her: 'You bloody cow, I will give you something for walking Upper Street when I get you home.' She said: 'No you won't,' and ran across the road. He ran after her and caught her at the corner of Old Street. I followed them; I was going the same way. I saw them go into 21, Cottage Lane and then I went on home.'

The defendant's statement before the magistrate was read out, and then Oliver Treadwell entered the witness-box:

'I am assistant surgeon to Her Majesty's Prison, Clerkenwell. The prisoner was in that prison from the 22nd of June up to the present time. I have seen him from time to time – about three or four times a week. During the whole of the time I have seen him he has always conducted himself as a rational and sane man. I have not noticed any symptoms of insanity about him.'

With the exception of Mrs Brider, Mr Williams had been content to allow all the witnesses to pass without cross-examination, but what Dr Treadwell had said placed the whole of the Defence in jeopardy, and could not go unchallenged:

Q: 'You say that you have seen the defendant three or four times a week since he has been in prison. What form did these meetings take, and for how long did they last?'

A: 'I have had conversation with him for five or ten minutes at a time.'

Q: 'What did you make of the defendant's complaints about the pains in his head – did you prescribe any treatment?'

A: 'I never heard till today of his suffering from an abscess in the head.'

Q: 'But you would agree, would you not, that an abscess in the head, before bursting, might probably cause pain?'

A: 'I suppose in the interior is meant? A running abscess might discharge through the ear if in that region.'

It was an answer to a question which had not been asked, but counsel did not labour the point.

Q: 'In your opinion, might it temporarily affect the brain at times?'

A: 'It depends upon the position of the abscess, and whether it is acute or chronic.'

Very wisely, Mr Williams decided to stop whilst he was winning. He had taken a chance with that last question, insomuch as a flat 'No' would have made a bad impression on the jury, but his gamble had been worthwhile. There had been no medical evidence that Kelly had ever had an abscess, and yet Dr Treadwell had not only appeared to accept the existence of what could have been a purely fictional affliction, he had testified that it could have affected Kelly's brain! The doctor was the last of the witnesses, and his answer was the one that would linger in the jurors' memories.

Mr Poland then made his final address, and most of it was taken up with trying to anticipate any arguments for insanity which might be raised by the Defence and controverting them. However, Mr Williams had the last word, and he made the most of it.

He told the jury that the prisoner's acts and suspicions with reference to his wife's conduct, which were absolutely without foundation, proved conclusively that he had been labouring under 'a distempered imagination'. The deceased's conduct was shown to have been of exemplary propriety, and with the evidence of the mother and the letters could the jury believe that the prisoner was sufficiently master of himself to know the nature and quality of the act he committed? Did the jury believe that he intended to take her life?

Mr Williams then made the most of Dr Treadwell's last answer. He urged that it was evident that the prisoner, having suffered from pains in the head arising from an abscess, had acted 'under an uncontrollable impulse arising from a temporary aberration of intellect'.

If the prisoner was morally irresponsible for the act, he was entitled to be acquitted on the ground of insanity, and the result of that verdict would be that he would be detained during the Queen's pleasure for the remainder of his days. On the other hand, if it was not a malicious act, but one committed in a paroxysm of passion, it was open to jurors to find a verdict of manslaughter.

It was a performance typical of the time: great oratorical flourishes, unashamed appeals to sentiment, and a covering of all eventualities, which smacked vaguely of having one's cake and eating it. It is doubtful whether such an address would carry much weight with a modern jury, but it was the kind of thing Victorians expected to hear, and they had not been disappointed.

Mr Justice Williams then made a lengthy summing-up. He placed great emphasis upon what was then, and to a large degree still is, the test of criminal insanity. Known as the McNaghten Rule, it asks: 'Was the prisoner, at the time of the crime, suffering from such a defect of reason from disease of the mind as not to know the nature and quality of the act he was doing or not to know that it was wrong?'

The legal points raised by both sides were commented upon, and the jury was told of the verdicts open to it. All in all, it was a very fair assessment.

Obviously it had given the jurors food for thought, because they deliberated for an hour over what many considered to be a foregone conclusion. It may well be that the defendant and his lawyers were encouraged by the length of time which was taken but, were that so, they were doomed to disappointment.

The usual ritual was followed:

Clerk: 'Members of the jury, are you agreed upon your verdict?'

Foreman: 'We are.'

Clerk: 'Do you find the prisoner, James Kelly, guilty or not guilty?'

Foreman: 'Guilty, but we wish to recommend him to the mercy of the Court.'

Clerk: 'You find the prisoner guilty, and that is the verdict of you all?'

Foreman: 'It is.'

Clerk: 'James Kelly, you stand convicted of murder, have you anything to say why sentence should not be passed according to law?'

In most murder cases the prisoners have nothing to say. They are usually so overcome by a 'Guilty' verdict that it is as much as they can do to mutter a 'No' to the question posed by the Clerk. Kelly, however, was one of the exceptions.

He said that he would like Mrs Brider to be recalled to the witness-box, as he had some questions which he wished to put to her. Such a thing was, of course, unheard of. The chance to speak was given to a prisoner that he might express remorse, or say anything he wished to be considered in mitigation which might lighten his sentence. It was certainly not intended to be an opportunity to re-open a trial, and Mr Justice Williams made that quite clear. It was all academic anyway, because there was only one sentence for murder.

Kelly, however, was not to be silenced; he had the chance to speak, and speak he would. He said that, as a matter of justice, he wished to warn others against being deceived. In a lengthy, and somewhat incoherent tirade, he spoke of the deception which he had suffered at the hands of his wife, his mother-in-law and others, but said that he was out of his mind when he stabbed his wife, and was sorry for what he had done. He prayed God to forgive him, and felt sure that He had already done so. For that reason, he felt that he would like to live in order that he might serve God; but, as the jury had decided that he must die, he hoped the Lord would give him strength to show them that even a sinner like himself knew *how* to die.

He was allowed to have his say in full and then, when he declared himself finished, the judge glanced at his papers and prepared to deliver his own address.

Staring at the jurors, he told them: 'I cannot see a single circumstance in this case to reduce the criminality of the act in the slightest degree from an act of wilful murder of which the prisoner has been found guilty. *You*, however, have recommended him to mercy, and I shall take care that the recommendation is forwarded to the proper quarter, but if anything is likely to affect its being attended to it is the statements which the prisoner has just made with reference to the deceased and other persons. I shall not aggravate the agony of feeling which the prisoner must be undergoing by moralizing on the crime, or preaching to him, but shall confine myself to passing upon him the sentence of the law.'

The black cap was placed upon his head, and then he switched his attention to Kelly, who stood in the dock with his eyes downcast: 'James Kelly, it is my duty to pass upon you the only sentence which the law allows for the crime of murder. The sentence of the Court upon you is that you be taken from this place to a lawful prison, and thence to a place of execution, and there you suffer death by hanging, and that your body be buried within the precincts of the prison in which you shall have been confined before your execution, and may the Lord have mercy upon your soul.'

The two prison warders flanking Kelly then made as if to take him back down to the cells, but he would have none of it. He pulled himself back, glared at the judge, and then shouted that he was innocent. Mr Justice Williams ignored him, and Kelly, still ranting, was taken straight from the Court to the adjoining Newgate Gaol and lodged in the condemned cell.

On the day after the trial Judge Williams wrote to the Honourable Sir A. F. O. Liddell, KCB, Permanent Under-Secretary at the Home Office. He sent the Notes of Evidence which he had completed, accompanied by a letter which stated that: 'My own belief is that the key to the whole misery was that he had communicated a disease to her and, being frightened, begged her to seek medical advice, and afterwards, when the girl's mother reproached him with it, he tried to throw the blame upon her and insinuated that she was a girl of loose habits. The correspondence has many allusions of an obscure character which I believe to be thus explained.'

In the meantime, Kelly's London solicitors had lost no time in organizing a Petition for Clemency, which was also sent to the Home Office. It laid particular stress on the following arguments:

That the said James Kelly was born in 1860 and is now of the age of 23 years. That the mother of the said James Kelly died in 1875 [*sic*] when he was only 15[*sic*] years of age and as he was an illegitimate child he, after his mother died, having no friends or relations, was left without any relation [*sic*] or friend to guide or advise him.

That at the trial of the said James Kelly evidence was given by Mrs Brider, the mother of the wife of the said James Kelly, that up to Christmas 1882 the said James Kelly had been much beloved by all the family, but from that date his manner had been very strange and he was altogether an altered man. She also proved that the said James Kelly had been suffering for some months from an abscess in the head, and that by her advice he had dropped sweet oil into his ear to alleviate the pain, and at the time he committed the deed he was still suffering from this abscess, and had for some time previously complained of the great pains in his head.

That the said James Kelly had no medical advice in respect to the abscess, (though he had been advised to see a doctor), as he was strongly averse to both doctors and physic.

That at the trial of the said James Kelly it was proved that he had no reason at all for committing the act and that there had been great attachment between himself and his wife.

That the jury who tried the said James Kelly were nearly an hour considering their verdict, and though they found him guilty they very strongly recommended him to mercy.

That James Kelly was in the employ of Mr John Hiron of 4 Orchard Buildings, Haggerston, in the months of April and May last, and Mr Hiron has made an affidavit to the effect that the conduct of James Kelly was very strange and that he discharged him because he was of the opinion that he was not accountable for his actions.

Attached to the Petition was a sheet of paper which stated: 'We, the undersigned, earnestly join in the prayer of the above petition.' Then follows a list of seventy-one names of people from all over London, mostly fellow workmen but with a few notable exceptions.

The first signature is that of Cornelius V. Smith, Kelly's last employer; John Merritt is also there, and George Hogg (Clerk in Holy Orders), of St Alban's Clergy House, Holborn. However the great surprise is that, tacked on the end, are the names of Mr and Mrs Brider!

Had they but known it, those who had drawn up and signed the Petition were wasting their time, because the Home Secretary had already made up his mind.

It was obvious from the letter and Notes which the judge had sent to the Home Office that, as he had also made quite clear in court, he did not agree that Kelly should be shown any mercy. A trial judge's views carry great weight, and therefore it is hardly surprising that, on August 3rd, the Home Secretary, Sir William George Granville Venables Vernon Harcourt, wrote across the judge's papers: 'I don't see my way to commutation here.'

Kelly's solicitors were informed, and the date of the execution was arranged for Monday, August 20th, thus allowing for the three statutory Sundays to pass after sentence.

Now at this time, August 1883, a draft Bill was going through the Committee Stage in the Houses of Parliament. Eventually to become the Criminal Lunatics Act of 1884, it would oblige the Home

Secretary to appoint two or more doctors to make a special inquiry into the sanity of any prisoner under sentence of death whenever there was 'reason to believe such prisoner to be insane'. The inquiries were to be carried out by specialists in criminal insanity, and if they found that the prisoner was indeed insane he was to be transferred to a mental institution.

Probably because of the then prominence of the subject in the minds of politicians, and the certainty that the Bill would become law, just such an inquiry was now ordered in Kelly's case. He was examined by a team of doctors, the most notable of them being Dr W. Orange, Superintendent of the Broadmoor Criminal Lunatic Asylum.

On August 7th, 1883, he made this report to the Home Office:

To: The Hon. Sir A. F. O. Liddell, K.C.B.

Our examination has afforded us sufficient evidence to show that the prisoner is a man of defective mental capacity: and although tranquil at the present time yet that he has always been of unstable mind and a person whom one would expect to become actively insane from a comparatively minor cause.

That report saved Kelly. Only three days before he was due to be hanged, he was certified insane and removed from Newgate back to Clerkenwell Prison. On August 24th he was admitted to Broadmoor, firmly convinced that he had been saved by Divine Intervention.

Broadmoor Asylum stands on the summit of a ridge within a mile of the village of Crowthorne, in Berkshire. It was designed in 1856 by a military engineer, Sir Joshua Jebb, who, twenty years before, had drawn up the plans for Pentonville Prison in London. He made provision for two walled enclosures, to divide the sexes, with the Medical Superintendent's house between them. Within the enclosures, the Asylum was laid out on a system of very forbidding looking Blocks – seven for the men and two for the women – with heavily barred windows predominating. Originally the men's Blocks were numbered and each had a specific purpose. Now the Blocks have names (shown here in brackets), and their roles have changed.

Block 1. (Norfolk) Strong Block for disturbed inmates.

Block 2. (Essex) Privilege Block.

Block 3. (Kent) Infirmary Block.

Block 4. (Dorset) Admission Block, used also for the 'quite mad, but quietly so, and the suicidal'.

Block 5. (Gloucester) For the 'fairly sane and moderately trustworthy'.

Block 6. (Somerset) Strong Block for disturbed inmates.

Block 7. (Cornwall) Semi-Refractory Block, for 'the obstreperous'.

There was also a Block 8, but it will not be found on any plans: it was the inmates' term for the cemetery!

The Asylum opened on May 27th, 1863, and ninety-five lunatic women were the first inhabitants. In February, 1864, over two hundred men began to arrive in batches from the Fisherton House and Bedlam Asylums. Eventually the population stood at about five hundred, of which one hundred and fifty were convicts who had gone insane whilst serving sentences in normal prisons for every crime imaginable. It was not until 1875 that this convict element was removed to the specially prepared prison at Woking, Surrey – some fifteen miles away.

When James Kelly arrived he was taken to Block 4 to begin the usual admission routine. Kelly was given his number, 1167, and issued with a complete set of clothes. That included a uniform of black serge, with a cloak of the same material, a peaked cap, a distinctive red kerchief and a pair of working trousers which were of a brilliant 'canary yellow' corduroy.

Thus equipped, he was then marched off to his new quarters, but he did not have far to go because it had been decided that he should remain in Block 4. That in itself tells us how he had been classified – 'quite mad, but quietly so', and possibly suicidal. He was paranoid, deeply depressed and exhibited signs of religious mania.

The Blocks system provided an excellent incentive for those able to appreciate their situation. Those who responded to treatment could progress gradually from the Back Blocks, if that is where they had been placed, to the Privilege Block. Kelly did *not* respond. He was always to be regarded as something of a dormant volcano 'whom one would expect to become actively insane from a comparatively minor cause'.

It was only after three years of severe mental torment that he appeared to adapt to his surroundings – three years during which he became more and more convinced that he had done nothing wrong in killing his wife, and that it was *he* who had been wronged. For most of that time he was quiescent. He followed orders obediently, and did his work after a fashion. However, he was incapable of holding a rational conversation, and for that reason he was left more to his own devices than might otherwise have been the case. As a result, he withdrew even further into his world of anguish and fantasy and, on occasion, erupted into bouts of active insanity.

The doctors knew that Kelly was a virtual time-bomb who could explode at any moment, but they were given no obvious cause for alarm. There were lengthy intervals between examinations, and his case was not reviewed or, one suspects, even considered unless some symptoms which required attention were brought forcibly to their notice. In the main, he was merely regarded as a quiet enough young chap with delusions of persecution and signs of religious mania who, apart from his many complaints, kept himself to himself. (The Doctors may have overlooked one crucial element: in Broadmoor, Kelly had no contact with women – the spark most likely to set off an explosion.)

Unfortunately, few examples of those complaints survive, which is a pity because they might have given us a deeper insight into how his mind worked. However, the few instances of which we know go a long way in demonstrating his powers of persuasive cunning and false humility when there was something he really wanted. He may have been incapable of holding a rational conversation but, as we shall now see, he could write a good letter, and he soon learned that that was the best way of achieving his ends.

Each Block was divided into wards, some of which were dormitories sleeping a dozen or more, whilst others had small rooms of their own. Kelly had been placed in a dormitory and, after an initial settling-in period, had been urged to start thinking about a job. There were workshops where inmates could learn, or continue in, various trades which included those of tinsmith, shoemaker, tailor, carpenter and upholsterer. They also had the options of working in the kitchen or the bakehouse or, if their inclinations were for outside work, in the kitchen garden or on the farm. Newcomers were not expected to work for a full day but, to those rational enough to understand, it was made clear that labour was part of the recognized route to recovery.

It was to be expected that Kelly would choose the upholstery shop, and he appeared to be quite content there until one day – November 16th, 1884, to be precise – when he wrote a letter to a Broadmoor official, which is reproduced here exactly as written:

Mr Royston.

Sir,

I am sorry to have to inform you that I am going to leave the uphostering shop. As I can tell you my reasons for so doing in writing better than I can verbally I now write you this letter. But I must first tell you that since I have been here I have tried my best with the little mental & bodily power that I have to improve myself & thereby hoping if I succeed to be able to show my respect to those above me in other ways than touching my cap when I came in yours or their presence but I am sorry to say through circumstances I cannot continue as I have done lately.

By circumstances I mean the trying ordeals that one has to go through to gain anything for his comfort or benefit, & then worse still is the state of intimadation that he is brought to if he happens to be lucky enough to get something beneficial to the mind or body. No doubt you have a license to do all this, but I think if you have any feeling for us poor creatures you might find out whether a patient can stand it or better still whether it is beneficial to him or not. I know that your system of treatment of late has not been beneficial to me. I have always found a feeling of great anxiety both before & after asking you for anything so from my experience I can say that your treatment is not beneficial to me but the reverse. I am very sorry that it has come to this, viz – that I should write this letter to *you* because you have been kind to me but you take all the goodness out of your kindness by your style of lifting up a man one day & then putting him down another, which thing I cannot stand, – nor can I repeatly beg & pray for anything that is in your power to give me. I am unable to do this not through pride for I have none or through want of humility but simply through the feelings which I have before mentioned. I have not much more to say except this which you know, that I asked you for a violin & you did not refuse me but (*to me* weak mentally & bodily, & who wants something to keep him up) did worst than that by putting me in a state of anxiety & suspense. I also asked you in a few words to put me in a better block & you told me that it was not in your province to do so. If you wished to help me you would have recommended me. Then worst than all last Friday (I suppose through my stopping away from the shop) you came to me when I was painting *& spoke & looked in such a manner which has upset me.* All this I have come to the conclusion is a foretaste of how I am going to be served for any trifling offence I commit. I think all this is done on the fact of my showing a little willingness to work, (not a mania to work) as my actions after this day will prove for I intend not to strive anymore with any kind of labour whilst I am in the state that I am in now but would rather lie down first & die. My only hope (of course it is nothing from such as me) is that you with the power you have now will not when before God someday be accused of not raising & keeping up those that have fallen but who would wish to be something better than they have been in the past.

   I remain Yours Truly

James Kelly

It seems that Dr Hurworth's Academy had done a good job with the young James. It is true that there are a few spelling mistakes, but in the main it is an excellent letter in good handwriting, and with margins so exact that they might almost have been ruled.

   I do not know what position 'Mr Royston' held at Broadmoor, but Kelly's mention of 'treatment' would suggest that he was a doctor. One can therefore only guess at what emotions such a manipulative letter would have aroused in him. It had come from 'a decent enough young fellow', and Kelly had certainly tried his best to make Royston feel both pity and guilt – apart from the threat of his having incurred God's wrath! Royston would no doubt have received similar letters from other patients in the past, but all the indications are that Kelly touched a chord which they had not. Instead of consigning the letter to the nearest wastepaper basket, Royston took it to the Medical Superintendent, Dr Orange, who, it will be remembered, had been instrumental in saving Kelly from the gallows and may have had a special regard for him.

The Superintendent interviewed Kelly and, as it appeared that he was undergoing one of his episodes of active insanity, had him packed off to the infirmary ward of Block 4. He did, however, see to it that Kelly was given a room of his own and, eventually, the violin that he wanted so badly – kindnesses that his successor would rue.

Kelly was not unappreciative of what had been done for him. A month later he wrote directly to Dr Orange:

> Block 4
> 14th Dec 84
>
> 1167
> Dr Orange.
>   Dear Sir,
>   Although I am comfortable & have plenty of things to occupy my time I think – that after the kind manner in which you spoke to me & ordering me to take rest in the infirmary & also giving me a warm room to sleep in – that I ought to do a little work to show that your kindness is appreciated. I am glad to say I am in much better health so with your permission I would be pleased to commence work again soon.
>   Hoping that you will enable me to show in my poor and humble way that I have not forgotten the kindnesses that I have received both direct & indirectly from you.
>   I remain
>
> Yours Obedient.
> James Kelly

We are not told whether it was considered that a change of work might be beneficial to Kelly or whether, for whatever reason, he refused to go back there, but he was moved from the upholstery to the carpentry workshop. If, however, the transfer *was* made on medical grounds, it made absolutely no difference to his mental state.

The year of 1885 came and went. Kelly had received his violin and had joined the Asylum band, but there was no noticeable change in his condition.

Only one record remains of any episodes during 1886, and that is in the form of an internal memorandum addressed to Dr Orange and signed 'C.E.P.'. It reads:

1167   12.4.86.
I have seen Kelly and sent him to work and he is brooding over
the carpenter shop grievance mainly – but has some ill-defined
feeling of suspicion and of everyone being against him.

Unfortunately, that is all we are told of the incident, but it shows that there was no improvement in his state of mind. He was still paranoid and brooding over grievances both real and imagined.

Somewhere around the time that note was written, Kelly was transferred from the carpentry shop to the kitchen-garden working party, but it is not recorded whether his grievance lay in the transfer, or whether the transfer was as a result of something that had happened in the workshop. Be that as it may, to the kitchen garden he went, and from that moment the doctors noticed subtle changes taking place in his condition which they were unable to explain. Ralph Partridge put their dilemma well in his book *Broadmoor*: 'One of the elusive characteristics of insanity is that it obeys no rules; every case of madness is unique. A madman's symptoms constitute his individual protest against a world that is too hard for him. The medical profession may classify them for its convenience; but the patients do not tamely submit to classification.'

All in all, 1886 was an eventful year for Broadmoor.

As we have seen, the convict element had been removed to Woking in 1875. However, there were so few of them by 1886 that it was thought safe to bring them back, and fifty-eight were returned over a period of two years. It was a decision which was not greeted with unqualified delight at Broadmoor. Unlike the 'Her Majesty's Plea-sure' inmates, the lunatic convicts were those who had gone mad whilst serving sentences in ordinary prisons. Their insanity therefore merely overlaid their criminal instincts to conspire together, and to combine in attacking the attendants. They were also teachers and pupils in a virtual university of crime where, as in all prisons, they passed on their unlawful skills and acquired others. There was, therefore, a very real risk that, by allowing them access to the other inmates, they would spread their criminal propensities.

The year of 1886 also saw the departure of Kelly's friend and mentor, Dr Orange. He resigned on the grounds of ill-health, although the return of the convicts may have played a part in his decision. He was succeeded by his deputy, Dr David Nicholson who, no doubt with the arrival of the convicts very much in mind, wrote: 'It is not surprising that the idea of escape is much in the minds of a population situated as the inmates of Broadmoor are.'

Dr Nicholson was never to write a truer word. Escape *was* much in the minds of the population, and nobody was destined to think about it more than James Kelly!

In the beginning, working in the kitchen garden was, for him, just another job with its own boring routine. Each morning the working party was collected from the Blocks to be taken across the Airing Court – the exercise area – behind Block 4 and down some steps to a large barred gate. That gave access to a continuation of the steps down to another locked gate situated in the six-foot-high wall which bounded the kitchen garden.

Once in the garden there was a sense of freedom which was in no way diminished by the distant perimeter wall. Despite any initial misgivings which he may have had, it was an amazing experience for Kelly, whose life had alternated between his Block and a workshop for three long years. Now, for the first time during that dark and dreary period, there came a realization that there was an outside world, and one that had continued to function perfectly well without him.

The following year the changes in his condition became quite noticeable. A Broadmoor report states that he was 'more contented and cheerful', although continuing to be subject to 'periods of depression'. However, the doctors and attendants had not the slightest idea of what he was feeling or thinking, and the only clues to his secret thoughts lie in his subsequent statements.

He was still firmly convinced that there was a Divine Plan for him, and he just could not understand why it was taking so long for his destiny to be fulfilled. Almost daily he expected a sign, and his bouts of depression arose when it did not come.

In the event there were two events that could be interpreted as signs, but with a lengthy interval between, and it was only with hindsight that Kelly would have recognized the first.

It came in the unprepossessing form of George Stratton, about whom the little we know is all bad. He was one of the returned convicts, and an informer – a 'nark'. We do not know for what crime he had been convicted but, probably in return for services rendered, he had managed to have himself transferred from Block 6 to Block 4.

Apparently his first job after his move had been in the tinsmith's shop where, amongst other things, the inmates were taught to be locksmiths and to make keys! That was not *quite* so ridiculous as it may appear because the keys they cut were simple and unimportant – all the passkeys being supplied from 'outside'. Nevertheless they were curious skills to teach to men whose lives were governed by locks.

For whatever reason, Stratton was taken out of the tinsmith's shop and sent to the kitchen-garden working party, and a most unlikely alliance was formed.

We can be sure that it was he and not Kelly who made the first overtures, and he probably did so because he had heard that Kelly had money. Certainly Kelly would not have approached him. Kelly was essentially a 'loner', and his paranoia, coupled with the irrational way in which he spoke, had ensured that he had stayed that way.

Nevertheless, and in some way, the two became what may be described loosely as friends, and many conversations ensued. What happened next is the 'authorised version' of events, based upon Kelly's and Stratton's accounts.

It would seem that the second sign came in 1887 when, whilst digging in the kitchen garden, Kelly unearthed a piece of metal, said to have been from an old corset: 'Immediately George Stratton and myself got the thought that we could make a key and that I could escape from Broadmoor Asylum.'

Now that was not as easy as it may sound. For one thing, each door had *two* different locks with two different keys, one of which was of a far more complicated design than the other. Neither would have been simple to copy even with unlimited access to them, and that was far from the case as each attendant kept his keys looped firmly around his belt. The actual making of the keys also presented apparently insoluble problems. As one would expect, the issuing of tools was carried out under close supervision, and each had to be accounted for at the end of a working session. Nevertheless, where there's a will there's a way, and Kelly, especially, had the will.

Kelly's story of how the keys came to be made reads:

I got the mettle [*sic*] from the ground whilst digging in the kitchen garden and I worked it to this form

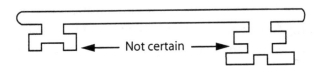

The tools which I used were a bent shoemakers awl & part of a broken small file. The impressions of keys were got from someone that was washing himself in the lavatory.

That is a good example of Kelly's secrecy. He knew very well who had been lax enough to allow his keys to be copied. Stratton, by contrast, was far more explicit, and at a time when his revelations could have spelled trouble for the member of staff concerned: 'The way the pattern was got was by looking at Mr Stephen's keys as they hung by his side. He is in the habit of putting the keys in his trousers that is sticking one in the top of his trousers and the others hang down below his waistcoat.'

The painstaking and nerve-racking task of cutting a key was a slow and laborious business. Stratton described how they would: 'put black-lead on it and then try it and where the black-lead rubs off to file that part away until it is complete.' It was not only the actual job which took up the time, but also the need to be ever on guard against intrusion. They had to work with the minimum of noise, and then ensure that that they had cleared up all traces of filing and hidden everything safely at the end of each session. Kelly's private room was, of course, a great advantage. It afforded them the secrecy in which to work and a hiding place for their tools, but not even Stratton was allowed to know where the embryo keys were concealed because Kelly trusted nobody more than he had to. What he had done, in fact, was to make 'a secret cavity in a violin case which belonged to me'.

The two men took turns with the work, but between times they went more deeply into the other aspects of the proposed escape, with Kelly by now the far more dominant partner. He needed Stratton, but had come to have no illusions about him and their discussions were strictly on a 'need to know' basis. There is some evidence that Kelly even went so far as to plant misinformation in Stratton's mind.

Right from the outset he had made it quite clear that the actual escape would be a solo effort. He did not trust Stratton completely, and certainly he had no intention of being handicapped by him. They came to an agreement that Kelly would leave the keys behind for Stratton to make his own escape later, but it is just possible that the latter was not particularly bothered. He was a lunatic convict – as opposed to being an 'HMP' – and, as such, would be allowed to walk free when his prison sentence expired. What may have interested him more was the cash which the keys would bring from other escape-minded inmates!

As their plans progressed, Kelly realized how justified he had been in supposing that he had been the subject of, to use his own words, 'Devine [sic] Help'. He had not appreciated it at the time, but being given his own room and a violin, and becoming a member of the band, were now crucial elements in the proposed escape.

By the beginning of 1888 the keys had been made and found to work properly, and it was decided that the escape attempt would take place on the evening of January 23rd.

The fateful day arrived, and somehow the conspirators managed to survive the long hours of waiting until darkness fell and the Asylum began to quieten. At 5 p.m. Block 4 was under the overall supervision of the careless Principal Attendant Stephens, but Number 1 Ward was in the immediate care of Charge Attendant Tyman and Attendants G. Davis and J. Green. Davis had the particular responsibility of the Day Room, whilst Green had something of a roving commission between the Gallery, the back door and any premises near the Day or Dining Rooms. His duties also included relieving any of the other attendants as required, seeing to the patients' suppers, and ensuring that they were in bed by the usual time.

At 5.20 p.m., Stephens 'put on' all the top – the so-called 'holding' – locks and, shortly after, he gave the the top key to Tyman, 'as Attendant Green was not quite ready to take charge of it'. He then went off to visit the other wards, spending some time in the Block's infirmary ward before going down to Number 2 Ward where he remained until 6.30 p.m.

The *News of the World* now takes up the story:

'At Broadmoor he [Kelly] was allowed to play in the band and commenced to learn the violin. Men in the band were allowed to wear ordinary clothes, and Kelly, having put on such a suit on the night of Jan. 23, 1888, it was assumed that he was going to attend band practice. He was playing his violin in the dining-room at 6.30 that evening, and then went downstairs.'

That report was inaccurate in one respect. Most of the staff may have *assumed* that Kelly and Stratton were going to band practice, but Charge Attendant Tyman *knew* that they were not because *he* had asked the specific question. In his own words, including the spelling mistakes, he deposed that: 'At 6 p.m. I ask Kelly and Straton if they were going to band practice, the answer was No.' We are not told whether he asked them why, in that case, they were wearing ordinary clothes.

Tyman spoke to them again at about 6.30 p.m., after they had gone to the dining room. Kelly was playing his violin there by then, and it would seem that Tyman cleared both men off 'downstairs', and out of the way, before P. A. Stephens returned and started asking questions.

He was only just in time, because Stephens returned from Number 2 Ward at about 6.30 p.m. and, as everything appeared to be in order, he remained in the Gallery, 'smoking', until Dr Baker, the Duty Medical Officer, arrived to make his rounds. Stephens accompanied the doctor, and then retired to his room to complete his Daily Report.

Aided, as he was to claim, 'by the power of goodness', James Kelly made his escape between 6.30 and 7.30 p.m.

There was nobody about as he and Stratton made their way along the corridor to the door that opened on to the Airing Court. Even so, Stratton kept a careful watch whilst Kelly unlocked the door quickly and slipped outside. Then, as arranged, he relocked the door and slipped the keys to Stratton through the bars of the nearest window.

Avoiding paths and steps, Kelly was across the terrace in a trice and encountered no real obstacles until he reached the wall to the kitchen garden. He was five feet seven inches tall and the wall was six feet high with no hand or footholds. Getting over it, he said, caused him 'much trouble and danger', and all his life he was to claim that he did so only with God's help. In contrast, the perimeter wall presented him with no problems and, in only a very short time, he was a free man and running for his life.

3

On the Run

AS SOON AS KELLY had disappeared, Stratton replaced the violin and case in his partner's room, hid the keys in a place of his own, and then rejoined the other inmates in the Day Room. Nobody had noticed anything amiss.

The patients were 'called for bed' at 7.30 p.m., and only then was Kelly missed. By that time he had at least a half-hour start on any pursuers, and that valuable time was to be increased because his absence did not, initially, cause any alarm. When it was realized that he was not about, the attendants looked in the places where he might have been and only when they could not find him anywhere did they start to panic.

Principal Attendant Stephens went to see the Chief Attendant and the whole Block was then 'thoroughly looked through'. Kelly was not discovered and, in Stephens's words, 'It was then certain that he had made his escape and scouts were sent out.'

The procedure to be adopted in the event of an inmate going over the wall was rusty in the extreme, and the hasty improvisations which were necessary resulted in quite basic errors. Nevertheless, the Broadmoor authorities did their best under such unexpected circumstances. All available staff was despatched to search 'the surrounding neighbourhood', and a description of Kelly was quickly cobbled together and transmitted to the police forces in Berkshire, Hampshire and Surrey and to various port authorities. A special messenger was despatched to Great Scotland Yard. His subsequent report is an interesting document.

Statement relating to search made for James Kelly who escaped on Monday evening, January 23rd, 1888.
Started from Broadmoor at 9.15 p.m. with instructions from the Superintendent to proceed to London and given information at Scotland Yard and other places respecting the above escape.

Left Wokingham Station at 10.9, South-Western Railways, rode in guard's van, wrote copies of description and left one at each station as far as Staines.

Reached London Waterloo at 11.50, waited until the last S.W. train for the night came in, walked to Scotland Yard, delivered papers to executive inspector on duty, returned Waterloo and caught the Southampton Mail at 3.40.

Then Attendants Franklin and Pulham got out of the train and proceeded to Hyde Park Corner to walk back to Broadmoor and tried to intercept him on the way.

Went to bed two hours, returned to station, met the 7.6 train from Kingston, saw all other trains as they came in up to 3.40 p.m.

Gave information and description to railway police inspectors, platform inspectors, guards and others.

Went again to Scotland Yard and ascertained whether the mother-in-law's house was being watched.

What is revealing here is that the Broadmoor authorities obviously suspected that Kelly had enough money for a train fare, and probably more. What the luckless Franklin and Pulham thought of walking the thirty or so miles back to Crowthorne in the middle of the night is left to our imaginations!

It goes without saying that a searching inquiry into the circumstances of the escape had begun at Broadmoor as soon as it was certain that Kelly had escaped. It was perhaps even more rigorous than might otherwise have been the case, because Dr Nicholson was already a worried man. Every year two of the Commissioners in Lunacy inspected Broadmoor and then reported back to the Home Secretary. Their findings for the first year of Dr Nicholson's regime had not been entirely favourable, but he had been given the benefit of the doubt because of the shortness of his tenure. Now, with another inspection due, the last thing he could have wanted was the escape of a murderer, and he was determined to shoulder as little of the blame as possible.

Attendant Tyman became the subject of much criticism and suspicion because there was a precedent for an attendant having been bribed to allow an inmate to escape. George Hage had made his getaway in 1864, and the attendant had received twelve months' hard labour. Tyman was therefore interrogated about his movements on the evening of the 23rd in order to establish just why he had not noticed Kelly's absence before he did. The two other attendants who had been on duty were also questioned at great length and, despite their precautions against being seen together too often, Kelly's friendship with Stratton was remarked upon.

Stratton was sent for immediately, but stoutly denied all knowledge of the escape. However, his manner was such that Dr Nicholson was not deceived. He now knew that Kelly and Stratton had been as thick as the thieves with whom they associated, and he was determined that Stratton should tell all he knew. Stratton had all his privileges withdrawn, and he was questioned repeatedly.

On the day after Kelly's disappearance, the Superintendent informed the Home Office of what had happened. In an obvious attempt to play down the seriousness of the matter, he wrote of Kelly that: 'For a long time previously to his escape the active indications of insanity had subsided and he conversed rationally. He showed no signs of being violent, or in any way dangerous.'

The final paragraph of Nicholson's report was revealing: 'Kelly is not unlikely to get in communication, personally or in writing,

with his mother-in-law Mrs Sarah Brider, 21, Cottage Lane
and who has always taken an interest in him since he came to
Broadmoor.'

Also on the 24th, it was decided that Tyman, as the Charge
Attendant at the time of the escape, should be the scapegoat and
the following report was sent to the Home Office:

BROADMOOR COUNCIL OF SUPERVISION
24th January, 1888

The Council, after careful consideration of the evidence in
this matter, felt it to be their duty to suspend Attendant Tyman
and they have informed him that he will be relieved from further
duty, his services being dispensed with.

Attendant Tyman is fifty-eight years of age and has a service
of close upon twenty years in which he has done good work.
Had it not been for these two considerations, the Council feel
that the gravity of his offence might have been dealt with by a
reduction in grade or by a forfeiture in seniority. But as it is, and
in view of all the circumstances, they have informed him that,
whilst they mark their sense of his want of vigilance by
removing him from active service, they will forward his super-
annuation papers in the usual way.

A week passed and then the Metropolitan Police finally got round
to asking for a photograph of Kelly.

There is a footnote to their letter, obviously written in Broadmoor:

31.1.88.
Two photographs of Kelly were forwarded to the Commissioner of Police yesterday.

On the same day that Scotland Yard wrote to Dr Nicholson he
received his first piece of information from Stratton. We shall never
know whether he had waited a week by arrangement with Kelly, or
that it was just that he could no longer stand the strain, but he finally

broke his silence and produced the duplicate keys. He admitted that he 'and others' had helped Kelly to make them, but refused to name names or say any more.

However, saying anything at all was a mistake: from that moment on he was given no rest. The authorities were determined in their efforts to learn the full details of the escape and Kelly's intentions. Stratton therefore found himself on the horns of a dilemma. His life was being made unbearable by persistent interrogation but he had a shrewd idea of what the consequences could be if he talked. Eventually he came to the conclusion that he would have to tell everything but, in an effort to safeguard his interests, he did so by way of two letters to Dr Nicholson.

The first letter contained his description of how the keys were made, but one paragraph of the second letter hinted – perhaps inadvertently – at what could have been a very different explanation for the escape:

Regarding Kelly having money he had no money that I know of only what he brought here. We had a threepenny piece found in the garden beside two shillings making two shillings and threepence and it was arranged by Finch [or fellow inmate] that when his sister came he would ask her for £5 which he said he knew he could get and something to escape which he was going to borrow for the occasion.

I wrote that the tale of Kelly's escape as set out in the last chapter was the 'authorized version'. There are, however, alternative explanations which somehow seem more plausible.

There were strong suspicions that he had been aided and abetted in his escape by either a member of staff or an outside agency – or both. Kelly never admitted having had any such help but – and it cannot be stated too often – he was intensely secretive and loyal to friends, acquaintances and accomplices. He only ever named one – Stratton – and even then it was only because he knew Stratton had already implicated himself.

Let us, therefore, examine the other escape possibilities.

We know that Kelly had a sizeable sum of money in trust, and that he had access to it. (The total amount at his disposal when he entered Broadmoor was over £11,000 in present values.) After he had been sentenced to death and was awaiting execution, his solicitors, on his instructions, paid John Merritt £5 – a 1995 equivalent of approximately £200 – but we are not told *why*. What we *do* know, however, is that Kelly was quite convinced that he would not hang and, in the light of what was to come, it would seem that it was arranged that Merritt, whom he regarded as his best friend, should have the cash to hold for any emergency.

Kelly escaped nearly four and a half years after Merritt was given that £5, but we know the latter had made regular visits to his friend in Broadmoor and, as George Stratton suggested, he probably still had the money in 1888, available to smuggle in to Broadmoor – perhaps via Finch's sister. (Presumably it was thought that a woman would be less carefully scrutinized than Merritt himself.)

On a similar theme, there is, in the 'Kelly File' at Broadmoor, a small, undated and anonymous pencilled note, probably from one of the patients:

James Kelly an inmate of this asylum escaped on the 23rd January and I have the time of Kelly's escape saw and conversed with Merritt (Kelly's friend).

It would be interesting to know whether this man has taken his departure from the neighbourhood if so why. The warder found that Merritt recently gone from number 31 to number 40 Clarendon Square.

Surely it is more than mere coincidence that Kelly asked Finch to persuade his sister to collect £5 for him 'which he said he knew he could get', and that at least one other inmate pointed the finger at Merritt. Certainly Broadmoor's attention became focused on Merritt after the escape, but the police were not much help. Part of a letter dated February 13th, 1888, from James Monro, the Assistant Commissioner of Police, CID, reads:

Inquiry has also been made at No. 31, Clarendon Square, St Pancras, and in the immediate neighbourhood, but no person named Merritt is known there.

There is no record of Broadmoor having informed Scotland Yard that Merritt had 'recently gone from number 31 to number 40 Clarendon Square', and perhaps they did not. Even so, had proper enquiries been made, there should have been no difficulty in finding him in such a small area. Broadmoor obviously felt the same way, because the authorities there wrote back asking for further enquiries to be made. Unfortunately there is no copy of that letter, but if No. 40 had not been mentioned before it seems that it was then.

Once more the reply came from James Monro. It reads:

GREAT SCOTLAND YARD

Ref: 49545-A30356

To Superintendent,
Broadmoor   23rd February, 1888

Sir,
    With further reference to the correspondence regarding James Kelly, whose arrest is sought for escaping from your establishment, I have to acquaint you that inquiry has been made and it is found that the man John Merritt is still at Number 4 [*sic*] Clarendon Square and has resided there for the past three years.
    He has been seen, and states he has not seen Kelly since he visited him at Broadmoor Asylum. He does not know of his present address.

I am, Sir,
Yours obediently,

There is no indication in that letter that Merritt was questioned very closely, and the fact that his address is stated carelessly as being No. 4, Clarendon Square, betokens a rather casual approach to the whole matter.

On October 6th, 1891, an inmate named Charles Harbour Junior
wrote to Dr Nicholson as follows:

Sir,
    About three or four weeks ago, as near as I can say, I was out
in Number 4 Airing Court and Patient Finch walking by my side
he brought up by some means or other I cannot say how James
Kelly made his escape from this asylum. He said that an
Attendant that used to be here that had to leave helped to
get him away and by what description he gave me of the
Attendant gave me an idea at once that he was Davis but he
would not say his name and that he sent away and got the key
made for him and received £5 for it and then he went on to say
that it was all planned beforehand that he was to go on a certain
night. He made his escape and that there was someone to receive
him as soon as he got out with clothes and other articles for
disguise and that about the time when they were searching the
woods for him he was on his way to Dover to take a boat for
abroad.
    This is a true and correct statement that as near as I can put it
together as Patient Finch told it to me in the Court.

So there it is. Once again the sum of £5 comes into the story and
Finch now makes it clear just *why* he was to ask his sister to smuggle
the money in.
    If the escape did *not* happen according to the 'authorized version',
there would, to say the least, appear to be a strong possibility that
Merritt managed to get the £5 in to allow Kelly to engineer the actual
escape. It is also odds-on that cabman Merritt was the 'someone' who
was there to help him at the perimeter wall and provide transport.
    Kelly's 'authorized version', however, paints a different picture.
Once he had overcome the problem of the perimeter wall Kelly,
without help from Merritt or anyone else, made for the woods and
then 'followed the moon, which he knew would take him in a
southerly direction'. By the time the alarm was raised completely
he was three or four miles away, and heading in a direction which he

hoped would not be amongst the first considered by the authorities.

Kelly had planted the idea in several inmates' minds that he intended to make straight for London, and then go across to France. Kelly had never had any illusions about his fellows, and may even have banked upon their relaying the misinformation. All in all, he had every reason to suppose that *somebody* would tell the Superintendent of his supposed plans, and that the search would be concentrated upon the wrong routes. As far as we know, in reality nobody said anything immediately, but Kelly was not aware of that and, whilst his pursuers directed their main attentions towards London, he was fleeing in almost the opposite direction.

He 'went as straight as he could, over hedges, dykes and private gardens, for some distance until he reached a road'. By daylight he had reached Alton, in Hampshire – some twenty miles south-west of Broadmoor as the crow flies. He was exhausted, and lost no time in finding a hiding place.

Only when it was completely dark again did he resume his journey. By then he had checked his bearings and initially he marched almost due south, towards Portsmouth. Then, after a couple of miles, and in an abrupt change of direction, he turned due east before veering to the north-east and setting his face firmly towards London. He tramped all night and by dawn he was on the outskirts of Godalming, in Surrey. Once again he concealed himself and prepared to wait out the long hours.

That night he was off again. He was wet, cold, tired and hungry, but he slogged on – passing through Guildford on the way – until it was time for his third day in hiding. By now he was almost at the end of his tether, but he was buoyed up by the knowledge that his destination was almost in sight.

He moved off at the earliest possible moment. Within a couple of hours he was on the outskirts of London, and from then on it was an even more nerve-racking experience. He imagined policemen where none existed, and was constantly avoiding those who did. When he finally reached his goal he was in a state of nervous and physical collapse.

According to Kelly, it was a particular lodging-house in the docks area of the East End that he had striven so hard to reach. There, he said, he had friends, and the material comforts of which he had been deprived for so long. Of course, we have only his word that he stayed at a lodging-house, and he never named the friends. Be that as it may whoever he went to certainly looked after him because he was so 'knocked out' by his privations that he was forced to lie up for a whole week.

It was only during that period – on February 3rd to be precise – that the police finally got round to taking some positive action. The following notice appeared in the 'Apprehensions Sought' section of the *Police Gazette*. It contains some factual inaccuracies which bear witness to the haste with which it had been compiled:

BERKSHIRE
£5 REWARD

6. – Wokingham (County). – Escaped from Broadmoor Criminal Lunatic Asylum, 23rd ult., – JAMES KELLY, an upholsterer, age twenty-seven, height five ft. seven in., spare build, complexion dark olive, thin pale face, hair black, moustache and eyes dark; clothing marked 'Broadmoor.' Is intelligent and converses rationally. Mother-in-law resides at 21, Cottage Lane, City-road. London, and an intimate friend at 31, Clarendon-square, St Pancras. Is well known at Liverpool. A native of London.

The above reward will be paid by Dr Nicholson, Broadmoor Asylum, for his apprehension.

Information to Supt. Atkin, Wokingham.

Kelly recuperated and regained his strength. Then, when he was ready to leave he 'got a little money from friends that knew nothing of my past'.

Of course he had never had any intention of going to Dover. His immediate need was for far more money than that with which his, as usual unnamed, friends had provided him, and the only place where he was likely to lay his hands on it was Liverpool. He knew that getting there would not be easy; however, his shortage of cash and the need to avoid public transport left him with no alternative but to walk the 200 miles.

He never said how long it took him, nor which route he took. His only statement on the subject was that 'I tramped to the North & touched Liverpool', but that comes as no surprise because Kelly was never precise whenever there was a possibility of incriminating himself or others. However, logic dictates that he did not reach his destination quickly. He would have known that there was a hue and cry for him, thus necessitating long detours around the larger towns on his route. There is also reason to believe that he took casual upholstery work in the Midlands. As to whom he saw when he finally reached Lancashire, what was brought out later, albeit indirectly, was that he almost certainly called upon the Motlers and was harboured by them. It was a sound move if he did visit them, because the authorities knew nothing of their existence, especially after the statements at his trial and in the Petition for Clemency that he had no relations. We know that he called upon various people in the Liverpool area but, true to form, he never named any of them.

Kelly's journey to the north took an unspecified time, and we do not know how long he stayed there. The only information which we have comes from Kelly himself who said that 'after a little time', in his usual vague words, 'I got some more money off friends that did not know what had happened to me', and that he then set off in what he hoped was a totally unexpected direction. He knew that the false trails which he had laid at Broadmoor would ensure that the Channel ports would be watched, and that there was always the possibility that someone would tell the police that he was in Liverpool. It seems, therefore, that the place from which he decided to depart for the Continent was the busy port of Harwich, in Essex. Ships made regular trips from there to destinations that included Sweden, Germany and Holland, and he had little doubt that he would be able to work his passage in one of them.

As the crow flies, it is about 210 miles from Liverpool to Harwich, but the circuitous route which he was forced to adopt made it much longer for Kelly. Nevertheless, he finally arrived there and managed to secure a berth. He must have thought that all his immediate problems were solved, but for once his guardian angel was looking the other way.

His ship was tied up alongside, and one day, whilst he was working on deck, an observant policeman recognized him from the description which had been issued and went on board to arrest him. However, a brawny bobby was an unusual and conspicuous sight in such surroundings and his intended prey was alerted instantly. Kelly had no idea what the constable wanted, but he did not wait to find out. Without further ado, he was down another gangway and running for all he was worth.

It had been a close shave – far too close – and Kelly was well aware that the alarm would now be renewed at all ports. It seems that he abandoned his plans to leave the country, and made for somewhere where he could be reasonably sure of safety.

Kelly never revealed where he stayed and his reticence indicates that he was shielding somebody. In the past, on his own admission, he had 'always stayed with friends', and if he ever needed a friend he did then. The likeliest explanation is that he headed straight for the East End of London, and his old lodgings with the Lamb family in Collingwood Street. Walter Lamb had been a good friend, and Kelly had always been on good terms with his family. More importantly, the police knew nothing of any previous connection there.

That, however, is all speculation. The fact of the matter is that we just do not know where Kelly stayed after slogging the seventy-odd miles back to London, nor precisely when in 1888 he arrived there. Naturally uncommunicative about his movements, he was to be even more secretive about this particular period of his life.

All that we know for certain is that Kelly reappeared in the East End of London during the first half of 1888. He had some money, but we do not know how much, how long it lasted, or how he supported himself when it ran out.

In the early days of his return he would have needed to be extremely circumspect. There would have been no question of his visiting John Merritt or the Briders. He would have realized that the police might suspect that he would lie low in London after his narrow squeak at Harwich, and that all his known haunts would be watched. Also, the possibility that his description had been circulated so widely would have deterred him from working at his old trade. All that he could do during those first weeks was to husband his meagre resources and avoid the streets as much as possible during daylight hours.

We shall consider later what Kelly might have done over the next few months. What we know is that later that year he was virtually penniless and that, completely unprepared, he left London precipitately and fled to France.

Despite his haste to leave the country, his lack of money and the need for caution debarred him from public transport. He therefore walked the eighty miles to Dover, and managed to work his way to Dieppe on a cross-Channel steamer.

In his usual way, when anything which he may have said could have incriminated him or others, Kelly was to draw a veil over what exactly he did next. All we are told is that, for whatever reason, he hugged the coastline of northern France, between Dieppe and Boulogne, during the ensuing months. Once, at Boulogne, he 'got a little help from some sporting characters', but apart from that we have no idea how he existed.

Then, in a change as abrupt as his departure from London, Kelly walked to Paris. He had a hard time there, most of which he felt was due to a hatred of the English. Eventually he could endure his privations no longer and decided to return to his own country.

By that time he was completely destitute, and was therefore driven to desperate acts. Using one of his aliases, he applied to the British Consul for aid, but was refused. A similar request to 'another agency' was rejected also, because he was unable to produce any identification papers. It was a clergyman's son who came to his rescue by lending him a sovereign (£1 – about £40 by today's value), and, somehow Kelly arrived back in England at the end of January 1892. (He was to say later that he repaid the loan by sending a postal order for £1 to the Young Men's Christian Association.)

At this point we have the choice of believing one of two tales which

Kelly related. It is said that a liar should have a good memory, but obviously he was deficient in that respect.

In his first version of what he did next, he stated that he found employment in the Midlands after returning from France, and that by the spring of 1892 he had saved sufficient to pay his fare from London to New York, on the *Zaandan*.

However, a later, and much more probable alternative, had it that he borrowed £3 10s. 'from friends', and bought a ticket from a Mr Hetherington at a shipping office 'in the Strand'. He then sailed from Rotterdam to New York on a German steamer – called the *Zaandam*, with an *m*.

Now that puzzled me for a time. I just could not understand why he should have decided to buy a ticket in London in order to sail to America from Holland. It was only when I was looking at a map of Liverpool that the penny dropped. There, running alongside the docks, between Waterloo Street and Wapping, I realized that Kelly's home city had its own Strand.

Suddenly, pieces of the jigsaw began to fall into place.

Kelly said that he received the £3 10s. with which to buy his ticket from 'friends'. Now that amount was equivalent to about £140 in today's values, and they would have needed to be very good friends indeed, and quite affluent, to have 'lent' such a sum to a man who was about to disappear – probably for ever. However, as my eyes travelled the map I saw that Water Street leads off the Strand and continues into Dale Street, and that is where Kelly's solicitors were located.

We know that the question of where he obtained the £3 10s. was a very sensitive one for Kelly; so much so that he gave two entirely different versions. Obviously he was protecting somebody. Might that 'somebody' be Mr Sampson?

It would make sense if it was. Rather than the unlikely scenario of Kelly borrowing such an amount from working-class friends, what more probable than that the cash came from the monies being held for him? (Had that, in fact, been the case, then another matter is explained – why Kelly went to Liverpool immediately he escaped. Again he would be looking for money from Mr Sampson.)

Kelly could have strolled from the solicitor's office to the Strand in

Liverpool, whereas it had always been difficult to imagine him laying his hands on £3 10s. in the East End and then courting the dangers of travelling to the Strand in the heart of London.

If my hypothesis is correct, Kelly did not linger long in London when he returned permanently from France, but went to Liverpool where, after having collected more than £3 10s. from Mr Sampson, he looked for an inconspicuous way to get to America. He would have discovered that just over a hundred miles away, on the opposite coast from Liverpool, was the port of (Kingston-upon-) Hull, and that ships went from there to Rotterdam from whence he could take direct passage to the USA.

What could have been easier? He may even have called in see the Motlers en route, which would explain how, three years later, John Motler was able to describe the adult Kelly when, supposedly, he had not seen him except as a youth some seventeen years before.

For Mr Sampson, there would, presumably, have been a conflict of ethics between his duties as an officer of the court and the confidentiality owed to a client. I am no legal expert, and therefore cannot say which takes precedence. If, however, an apparently rational Kelly had told him that he needed the money to begin a new life in America, Mr Sampson may have seen little wrong in making an advance. It could not, of course, have been debited as such to Kelly's account, but may well have been 'lost' in the books under 'Administration Costs' – which would go some way to explaining the high amount claimed later in the Court of Chancery.

From New York, Kelly made his way to Pennsylvania, where he spent the next eighteen months. By the autumn of 1893 he had had enough. The change of climate and the mosquitoes had caused him to become very ill, and he yearned to get back to England. Somehow, he managed to cross into Maryland, and there he secured a berth in a cattle ship which was leaving Baltimore for London. He worked his passage home, finally arriving in Deptford – which is the only known occasion during his various sojourns in London that he was south of the Thames.

In 1895 there was a rumour that Kelly had been seen in Liverpool, and it may have reached the ears of the Motlers. Certainly *something* caused John Motler to think of his cousin during that year because, in November 1895, Dr Nicholson received the following letter:

> Dear Sir,
>   There is a small sum of money left to my brothers and myself by Will and you will greatly oblige us by informing of one James Kelly who was convicted for manslaughter in London for killing his wife, as near as I think about 1880 which I understand after serving a term in prison was conveyed to the prison lunatic asylum. If he is living or dead the executor of the estate wrote you. The reply was he made his escape in 1888.
>   But there are a great many James Kelly no doubt who are committed for similar offences and there may possibly be a mistake.
>   If he is of slight build, small nose, dark hair, dark eyes and would be about this time thirty-five years of age and his origin was from Liverpool.
>   Any assistance from you as to his whereabouts will greatly oblige,
>   Yours truly,
>   John Motler

Scrawled across the bottom of this letter, in crayon, is: 'Say that the Superintendent is unable to give any further information on this matter.'

In fact, by then Kelly had worked his way back to the States.

By a combination of walking and 'stealing rides on trains', he made his way down through California to Los Angeles. He then crossed Arizona and New Mexico before arriving at El Paso on the border between Texas and Mexico or, as Kelly put it, 'El-paso on the desert'. From El Paso he went to Dallas, and it was there that he found regular work and recuperated before resuming his travels.

The next leg of his journey took him into Louisiana and to New Orleans, and it was there that he decided, once again, that he wanted to go home.

On January 27th, 1896, Kelly walked into the British Consulate in New Orleans and gave himself up. He was interviewed by the Vice-Consul, a Mr A. Donnelly, and then made a long statement which related his history to date, of course with his customary omissions. For instance, he told Mr Donnelly that he had been in the USA ever since landing from the *Zaandam* – omitting all mention of his return to London in 1893. His account ended with his hopes 'for a pardon and my liberty . . .' as he thought that he had already suffered sufficiently.

The British Consul, Mr C. L. St John, forwarded the statement to the Foreign Secretary, the Marquis of Salisbury, with a covering letter. It was then passed to the Home Office, from where a Charles S. Murdoch wrote to Broadmoor on February 14th.

My dear Nicholson,

What kind of a man was Kelly, and what do you think we ought to do?

Dr Nicholson replied as follows:

My dear Murdoch,

Kelly, at the time of his escape, had no doubt recovered from active indications of insanity. He was a decent enough young fellow, melancholic rather, he ought certainly to come back to Broadmoor again, but in telling him this it might be added (what is practically told to every inmate) that if he gets on well every consideration will be given to the circumstances of his case.

However, there was no extradition treaty for criminal lunatics, and the Home Office seems therefore to have been undecided about what to do, despite the fact that Kelly was himself asking to come back to England.

For four weeks he waited patiently whilst the British authorities dithered, but still no instructions arrived for the Consul. Eventually he took matters into his own hands and told Mr St John that he would 'see the thing through' himself, if the Consul would use his influence to enable him to work his passage home. That was arranged, and Kelly was escorted to the steamer SS *Capella*, of the Harrison Line, which was due to arrive in Liverpool on or about March 27th. He signed on in the name of 'John Miller'.

As soon as the *Capella* had left harbour, the Consul telegraphed the news to the Foreign Office, from which the following letter was written:

To The Under-Secretary of State, Home Office.
March 18th, 1896.
Sir,

   With reference to your letter A 30336/21, of the 25th ultimo, I am directed by the Marquis of Salisbury to inform you that a telegram has been received from Her Majesty's Consul in New Orleans reporting that the convict James Kelly will arrive at Liverpool, by the Harrison Line steamer *Cappella*, [*sic*] on or about the 27th.

Broadmoor and Scotland Yard were notified of Kelly's impending arrival, and the Liverpool police were asked to confirm the date of berthing of the *Capella* with the shipping office. It was arranged that a party of attendants from the Asylum would be on the quay at Liverpool when the ship arrived, but the Liverpool police were also asked to provide an escort for Kelly lest the Broadmoor contingent be 'unexpectedly delayed'.

What followed could have been used as a script for the Keystone Kops.

When the Liverpool police made their inquiries at the shipping office they made no request to be notified should there be any alteration in the supposed dates of arrival of the *Capella*, neither did they make any subsequent inquiries about the ship's progress. They were two unfortunate blunders because, in the event, it berthed on March 26th, and none of the authorities knew!

Kelly, of course, had expected to be arrested as soon as the steamer tied up, and he was therefore surprised when nothing happened. He loitered on board for a while and then, to pass the time and earn some cash, he agreed to smuggle some duty-free tobacco ashore for a crew-mate. What, after all, had he to lose were he caught?

Off he went, through the docks gates and into his home city. After delivering the tobacco as directed, he wandered back to the *Capella*. There, having received his reward for the errand, he once again sat around awaiting his welcome party. However still nothing happened, and finally he changed his mind about giving himself up, especially as he now had money in his pocket. He disappeared down the gangway, and was long gone by the time the two escort parties arrived on the following day.

The whole operation had been a complete fiasco, and although the Liverpool police and the party from Broadmoor ran around in circles for a time, Kelly was not to be found.

A call was made upon his solicitors and, as a result, they sent the following letter:

The Superintendent,
Dartmoor [*sic*] Asylum.   27th March, 1896
Dear Sir,
              Re James Kelly.
   Principal Attendant Hamilton has called upon us today with reference to the above but we have heard nothing of Kelly for a number of years, in fact since his escape from your institution.

It was generally supposed that Kelly would have lost little time in getting to London and therefore, on Friday and Saturday, March 27th and 28th, various house calls were made by the Metropolitan Police who wrote to Dr Richard Brayn, the then Medical Superintendent at Broadmoor. This small handwritten letter is unsigned and undated, but it bears the 'Broadmoor Received' stamp for March 30th. It reads:

On Friday and Saturday last, I went with Sergeant Morgan, C.I.D., to the following addresses:

Mrs Brider,
21, Cottage Lane.

Mr and Mrs Merritt,
40, Clarendon Square.

Mr Evans, Solicitor,
13, Bouverie Street,
Fleet Street.

Mr Smith,
66, Osnaburgh Street,
Regent's Park.

None of the above people have seen or heard anything of James Kelly for several years. They said if they heard anything they would communicate with Sergeant Morgan, who said in that case he would at once put himself in communication with you.

For the rest of March and April, the various authorities flooded the Home Office and each other with letters and reports giving their various excuses as to why Kelly had not been apprehended. Meanwhile, he had not gone very far at all.

James Kelly would have guessed that the authorities would expect him to head for London, but in Liverpool he was on equally familiar territory and he decided to stay there.

We are not told who sheltered and aided him when he absconded from the *Capella*, but within a very short time he had found work across the Mersey, in Birkenhead – not far from Dr Hurworth's Academy. He remained there until he thought that the hue and cry had died down, but then he was drawn back to the East End of London.

For whatever whimsical or other reasons, then he left London in a south-westerly direction, retracing the route of his escape from Broadmoor as far as Guildford. There, only about thirteen miles from the Asylum, he obtained work as a coach trimmer. There is some indirect evidence that he remained in that area for at least two or three years, but then his wanderlust got the better of him once again. He returned to Liverpool and subsequently secured a berth in a sailing ship, the *Beechdale*, which was leaving for Canada. After an arduous voyage via Cape Horn, the ship arrived at Vancouver, and there Kelly left her. He found work with the Hudson's Bay Company as an upholsterer, and later carried out a task which afforded him great satisfaction.

Edward VII ascended the throne in 1901, and in that same year his second son, George – Duke of Cornwall and York, and later to become George V – paid a brief visit to Vancouver.

Accompanied by his wife, Mary of Teck, the soon-to-be Prince of Wales arrived in the *Ophir* on September 30th, amidst scenes of great excitement. Although it was known that the Duke was to be in Vancouver for but one day, the preparations for his short stay were not skimped, and that was where Kelly came in. According to his own account, he 'undertook to do all the best work decorating the town'. He went on to say that 'With pardonably [*sic*] pride I must say I did the most good and permanent work. It was a surprise to all.'

It could be that it was the sight of his future king that stirred thoughts of home but, for whatever reason, it was in 1901 that Kelly again decided that he would return to England and give himself up. He therefore paid a visit to another British Consul – in Vancouver this time – and told his story all over again. The Consul communicated with England, but the authorities took no action and so, after a wait this time of about three months, Kelly once more worked his passage back to Liverpool. During the voyage, however, he had another change of mind about surrendering himself and 'thought he would have another run for his money'.

This time he did not loiter when he arrived in Liverpool, but made straight for London.

His stay there was as brief as his previous one, however, and in 1902 he again found himself drawn to his Broadmoor escape route. On this occasion he stopped at Godalming, about twenty miles from Crowthorne, where he resumed his now adopted trade of coach trimmer.

He remained in Godalming for somewhat longer than his usual time in a place, and that may have been because he suffered some of his episodes of active insanity during that period. Certainly we know that his curious behaviour made him the butt of his workmates.

Eventually he moved on, and travelled around England for a time, but we have no details of his activities during those years. It is quite likely, however, that he returned to the USA. In all, he travelled backwards and forwards across the Atlantic about seven times, and it may well be that one or two of those voyages occurred during this lengthy gap in his tale.

The next sighting which we have of him was in 1906, and knowledge of it was brought about by the publicity surrounding a legal dispute over the money from his inheritance which was still being held in his name.

On January 22nd, 1906, Kelly's solicitors, Messrs Sampson, Williamson, Inglis and Edgecombe, brought an action in the Chancery Court of Lancashire for payment out of Court of the sum of £351 'in the matter of Sarah Allan deceased'.

At the hearing, which took place in the imposing St George's Hall in Liverpool, the applicants were represented by a Mr John Rutherford, and the Motlers, who were disputing the claim, by a Mr Cochrane.

Mr Rutherford told the Vice-Chancellor, Mr Leigh-Clare, that there was a question as to whether the residuary legatee was a James Kelly 'who disappeared under such circumstances as the Court could not be asked to presume his death'.

Mr Sampson, the applicant, was a mortgagee of costs incurred in connection with the administration of the will of Mrs Allan and Kelly's defence on the murder charge. The claim would nearly absorb the amount in Court.

For his part, Mr Cochrane contended that the terms of the will precluded the paying out of Court of the sum named.

As we have seen, Kelly was worth more than £11,000 in present-day values when he entered Broadmoor. Obviously that sum had attracted interest over the intervening years, and now the figure stood at the equivalent of over £18,000 of which some £14,000 was now in dispute. The solicitors had already received the equivalent of over £13,000 in costs and administration fees, and naturally the Motlers were not prepared to see the remainder of the money go the same way.

Evidently, everything hinged upon whether the Vice-Chancellor would make a presumption of Kelly's death. However, after hearing both sides in full, he said that he was not prepared to do so at that stage.

The ruling caused a flurry of activity by the plaintiffs, of which the following letter to Broadmoor from the solicitors formed a part:

Dear Sir,
  Re Sarah Allen [sic] deceased, and re James Kelly.
Our predecessor, Mr T. E. Sampson, in July 1883, acted for a man named James Kelly who was tried at the Central Criminal Court upon a charge of murdering his wife. Kelly was then sentenced to death, but respited and confined in the Broadmoor Asylum and escaped from there in 1888. So far as we have been able to trace, he has not since been heard of. [In fact, they knew full well that he had landed from the *Capella* ten years before.]

Kelly was entitled to a sum of £351 recently paid into the Chancery Court here, and in respect of which you had in August last some communication with Messrs Norton, Clare and Higgins, solicitors of this city. [They presumably represented the Motlers.]

Mr T. E. Sampson has a claim upon the moneys in Court in respect of a charge given to him by Kelly and took out a Summons for payment out to him which came before the Vice-Chancellor on Monday the 22nd inst.

The facts were stated in Court, and it was also stated that Kelly had been seen in Liverpool in the year 1895 but this statement was not in any way verified. The Vice-Chancellor, however, adjourned the matter for a fortnight in order to enable further enquiries to be made as to Kelly's whereabout [sic] before making an order presuming his death.

This case was reported in the Liverpool papers, and as a result thereof an anonymous letter has been received by Detective Pierpoint of the Liverpool police stating that James Kelly (or Jim Allen, which was the name he went by,) was living in London and giving his present name and whereabouts, and we understand that the Head Constable of Liverpool is to communicate with you upon this matter.

It is necessary for our purposes to serve him with a Summons if he is still living and our object in writing is to ask you to let us know whether you have been able to trace him or not. We shall be glad, therefore, if you will kindly let us hear from you on the matter in the course of this week as the case will be mentioned to the Vice-Chancellor on Monday next.

The anonymous handwritten letter referred to was posted in Liverpool, with a penny stamp, and is franked '6.15 p.m. 25.1.06'. The small envelope, marked 'Important', is addressed to 'Detective-Sergeant Pierpoint, Dale St, Liverpool'.

The letter reads:

I see by Liverpool Exchange on the escape of Liverpool murderer (22.1.06)

All that I can say is that the authorities haven't looked much for him as he is and has been for some time in London living on the Caledonian Road under the name of John Miller and following his trade when he can of an upholsterer.

Two months ago he was seen for a dead certainty in East Ham. He is a bicycle rider and still at that time had his bicycle.

That is the truth and can be proved in 2 or 3 months time from now, but before that you ought to find him. You will find him still crazy and dangerous and mad as a hatter on certain points and better off under lock and key than he is now.

He had his violin until this last few years, perhaps he has one now for all I know. He has rooms furnished by himself.

For a man in your position he is as easy to find as St Georges Hall in Liverpool or Cleopatras Needle on the Embankment and still haunts the neighbourhood of his crime.

Several Liverpool people that know him from early days noticed that account in the papers, although he was called James Kelly in the Echo, recognized him as Jim Allen and now John Miller living on or off the Caledonian Market.

Caledonian Road is in north London. It begins at the bottom of Pentonville Hill, down which Sarah Kelly used to stroll to meet her husband from work, and is under a mile from Cottage Lane. Caledonian Market was at that time off the western side of Caledonian Road.

The gist of the anonymous letter was sent to Broadmoor and relayed to Scotland Yard, but the latter, in marked contrast to all their excitement about him in 1888, displayed very little interest in trying to apprehend the fugitive. They issued a circular giving the facts of Sarah Kelly's murder, and Kelly's escape from Broadmoor. It continues:

. . . said now to be living in the neighbourhood of Caledonian Road, to be an upholsterer born in Liverpool in 1860.

Height 5' 7"
Complexion, Hair and Eyes dark.
Spare in build.
Last heard of on his return from New Orleans in March 1896.

Not to be arrested but, if traced, immediate inf. to this office. Report 14th.

The circular is attached to a report which reads:

CRIMINAL INVESTIGATION DEPARTMENT,
NEW SCOTLAND YARD
6th February, 1906

REPORT

Referring to the attached, I have to report that the anonymous letter posted in Liverpool gives the information that James

Kelly has been for some time in London, living on the Caledonian Road under the name John Miller and following his trade as an upholsterer when he can. He is living on or off the Caledonian Road in rooms furnished by himself.

He was in East Ham two months ago.

James Kelly was born at Liverpool in 1860 and was brought up as an improver in upholstery. He was an illegitimate child and has no relatives or friends who know him now and also prior to 1883.

This report is unsigned and there is no addressee, but it may have formed the basis for a long, also undated, report which also begins with an account of Kelly's sentencing and escape, and then continues:

On 27.1.96 he went to the British Consul in New Orleans through whom he sent petitions to the Home Office for pardon and for permission to return to England.

He was seen on board S. S. *Capella* of the Harrison Line, due to arrive in Liverpool 26th March 1896, and he worked his passage in the name of Miller.

Arrangements were made to arrest him on his arrival at Liverpool, but the ship arrived earlier than she was expected and he landed without let or hindrance. No trace of him has been found since.

In 1888, he was described as follows:

Height 5′ 7″, Complexion dark (olive), hair black (heavy moustache) eyes dark, build spare, face pale and thin.

Police have no photograph of the man and, as he was last in the hands of the police 23 years ago, there is scarcely likely to be an officer serving who could recognize him.

I respectfully submit that, considering the meagre and unreliable information given, there is little chance of tracing this man by enquiry in the neighbourhood of the Caledonian Road or East Ham and suggest that a special enquiry might be called for; upholsterers, description of the man etc. for what it is worth.

These papers sent out for the information of Superintendents
G K & Y Divisions.
  Supt. Hare countersigns and recommends.
      Signed: Chas. Arrow, Chief Inspector
      A. Hare, Superintendent.

This report was extraordinary. Beyond stating that Kelly had 'worked his passage in the name of Miller', it made no mention of Kelly's known aliases, and the circular issued by Scotland Yard did not even mention 'Miller'.

In addition to those omissions, neither document included the clues which would have been invaluable to a constable familiar with his beat, i.e. that Kelly:

a) Was living in the *Market* area of Caledonian Road.

b) Rode a bicycle.

c) Played the violin.

One positive statement that Arrow *did* make was that the Metropolitan Police had no photograph of Kelly but, unless they had lost it, that was untrue. In any event, it is evident that no inquiries were made to see whether Broadmoor had one – and they *did*.

Arrow also wrote that there was 'scarcely likely to be an officer serving who could recognize Kelly', but no effort was made to find out if that was the case.

The circular made it quite clear that if Kelly was traced he should *not* be arrested.

What on earth could have been the reason behind that instruction? Both the Home Office and Broadmoor wanted Kelly safely behind bars, but Scotland Yard was saying that he should *not* be apprehended. If one takes that fact and combines it with all their other deficiencies over the docking of the *Capella*, and with the air of defeatism exhibited by both Arrow and Hare, there are sinister implications which cannot be avoided.

At the end of his report, Arrow suggested that a special enquiry at upholsterers might be called for, but the logical step of asking at the two London branches of the Amalgamated Union of Upholsterers does not seem to have crossed his mind. His phrase 'for what it is worth' sums up the whole attitude of the Metropolitan Police. It appears to have been a case of: 'It's doubtful whether Kelly can be traced, but if you do happen to stumble across him, despite our having withheld vital information from you, don't arrest him, just tell us and we'll allow him to escape again.' The impression given was that Scotland Yard did not want Kelly caught.

Whether or not any special enquiries *were*, in fact, carried out, on February 16th a letter was sent to the Home Office, reporting: 'A special enquiry has been made at upholsterers. Enquiries have been made in the G, Y & K Divisions, but no information has been obtained regarding Kelly.'

That is all.

The police hunt for James Kelly, if in fact there ever was one, proved fruitless, and during the following year Broadmoor formally disowned him. That was done by means of a Notice of Discharge, dated April 26th, 1907, which reads:

Name: James Kelly – Male.
Mental state:
Date of admission: 24th August, 1883.
Date of escape: 23rd January, 1888.
Mental state when discharged:
As this patient has not been recaptured, he has been written off the Asylum books.

John Baker – Deputy Superintendent.

During the succeeding years Kelly went back and forth to America a few times. Upon one of his returns to England he yet again headed south-west from London and found work as a coach trimmer. On that occasion he settled in Aldershot, Hampshire, where he was a mere eight miles due south of Crowthorne. It was closer than he had been at either Guildford or Godalming, and obviously he felt some increasing nostalgia for Broadmoor which was, after all, the only place where he had ever received any personal care and attention.

On another of his stays in England, his trade society found him employment as a coach trimmer in various motor works, including one in Luton.

The Great War came and, in 1917, Kelly went totally deaf – it is not known whether the two events were connected in any way. His deafness, coupled with his periodic episodes of unusual behaviour, made him the target of much abuse, and sometimes he was treated quite brutally. Then, in 1924, his general physical health began to fail and he was no longer able to command the good wages which he had enjoyed. The Amalgamated Union of Upholsterers, with which his former trade society had been merged, found him less demanding work, again in Luton, but the pay was much lower and he was treated even more badly by his new fellow workers. He was convinced that 'sinister influences' were working against him, and became even more peculiar in his ways. That notwithstanding, he continued to work, and was able to support himself until around August 1925, when he became unemployable as an upholsterer.

Kelly was then sixty-five, and for the next eighteen months he struggled to survive. He had returned to the East End and, although he was sometimes forced to walk the streets at night, he managed to exist by earning a few pence here and there doing odd jobs. However, even after all the years which had elapsed since 1888, he, in his own words, lived in 'constant fear' that he 'might be pounced upon' by any policeman he passed.

Eventually, feeling that old age was closing in, and that 'the struggle was hopeless', he took a decision which he had been considering for some time and set out for Crowthorne.

On the afternoon of Friday, February 11th, 1927, 'a wizened little man with grey hair and wrinkled face, footsore, and half-starved,' – as the *News of the World* described him – appeared at the main gate of Broadmoor.

He explained who he was and pleaded for shelter in the place to which he declared himself 'bound by fetters, fetters of gratitude on his side and fetters of kindness on the side of the authorities'. After wandering around the world he wanted to die amongst friends, and his most cherished wish was 'to set his conscience at rest'.

The attendant on the gate listened incredulously to his long, rambling discourse, made worse by Kelly's inability to hear any questions, and finally he summoned Dr H. P. Foulerton, who was the third Medical Superintendent since Dr Brayn. Dr Foulerton interviewed Kelly at length and then, pending identification – although he thought there was 'every possibility that his statements were correct' – he telephoned the Wokingham police and asked them to remove a lunatic!

On the following morning the Superintendent sent a telegram to the Home Office advising them of the facts, and stating that if the man was identified as Kelly he proposed to readmit him to Broadmoor. Then he travelled the four miles or so to Wokingham Police Court in company with ex-Chief Attendant Pulham and ex-Principal Attendant Rich, who had been brought out of retirement for the purpose.

Kelly appeared before the local magistrates charged with being 'A mentally deranged person wandering abroad'.

The two former attendants identified him readily as the escaped inmate, and Dr Foulerton therefore informed the Home Office and requested instructions. He received a telegram saying that Kelly was to be returned to Broadmoor, and that he should submit a report on the patient's mental condition, and his history since 1888.

Once back at the Asylum, Kelly underwent the usual admittance routine and was given a fresh number. He was then returned to his old block, Block 4. Over the weekend he was questioned by Dr Foulerton who, on February 14th, wrote to the Home Office confirming the sequence of events since the Friday, but devoting only three lines to Kelly's history since his escape.

In his letter he stated that 'Kelly is now 67 years of age, and shows indications of mental enfeeblement, but is rational in conversation and quiet in demeanour. He expresses a wish that he be allowed to die in Broadmoor, as he feels unfit to cope with outside conditions any longer.'

On the very same day, however, the Superintendent submitted a 'Medical Report' giving his opinion that 'Broadmoor ought not to be regarded as an alms house or place where criminal lunatics may return to spend the waning years of life. Kelly seems more suitable for a workhouse infirmary than for Broadmoor Asylum, he would not be certifiable as insane.'

Dr Foulerton's views were ignored. He was instructed to do as he had been asked and submit a more detailed report on Kelly's movements since 1888. In addition, he was required, unusually, to make regular reports on the patient's mental condition.

Then, only three days later, without any of their officials having even seen him, and in direct contradiction of the Superintendent's professional opinion, the Home Office stated flatly that Kelly was 'now insane' and should be kept 'for a time in Broadmoor for observation again as noted'.

Dr Foulerton did as he was told but, meanwhile, what of Kelly himself? He wrote a few pages on how he had escaped in 1888, and on his adventures overseas, but that was all.

By the end of 1927, Kelly's mental condition was deteriorating rapidly. He was full of petty grievances, and felt that he was not receiving the attention due to him. Then, at the start of January 1928, he claimed that he was being 'dosed in order to make him an idiot'.

In May 1928, he was described as being 'delusioned and mentally enfeebled', although he continued in good physical health. By December, however, his bodily condition was 'weak', and he was said to be paranoid and showing signs of senile degeneration.

When 1929 arrived, Kelly decided that he had had enough of Broadmoor. He was not at all happy with what was being done for, or to, him, and on several occasions he tried to get out of the Asylum. However he was closely supervised, and in any event his rapidly deteriorating physical condition did not permit a repetition of his 1888 feat. (Indeed, it was now beyond the abilities of even the fittest inmates, as the boundary wall had been raised to 16 feet in 1892.)

Gradually his health worsened until, at 7.15 a.m. on Tuesday, September 17th, 1929, he died peacefully in Block 3 in the presence of the Deputy Medical Superintendent, Dr J. Stanley Hopwood, and Attendant Farr.

The subsequent post-mortem examination report stated that he had died of double lobar pneumonia and, at an inquest held on

September 19th, the Coroner, Mr Robert S. Payne, recorded a verdict of 'Natural Causes'. Then, on Friday, September 20th, 1929, James Kelly was slipped quietly into his grave at Broadmoor Cemetery at 2.30 p.m. He had taken his secrets with him, most notably the details of what he did and where he lived in 1888/9, the years in which, as he shall now see London was terrorized by Jack the Ripper.

4

Martha and Polly

THE EAST END SADLY was the setting of so many brutal murders in the nineteenth century that there has been much debate over which of those in 1888/9 were definitely attributable to 'Jack the Ripper'. I personally am convinced that the first of his victims was Martha Tabram, who was found murdered in George Yard Buildings.

George Yard Dwellings – to give them their correct title – had been built in 1875 to provide single rooms for the very poor. They were situated in George Yard, now called Gunthorpe Street, which was, and still is, a narrow thoroughfare which joins Whitechapel High Street and Wentworth Street.

At that time, a number of courts and alleys led from George Yard, in which, according to the *East London Advertiser*, 'some of the poorest of the poor, together with thieves and roughs and prostitutes, find protection and shelter in the miserable hovels bearing the names of houses.'

It was here that a woman's corpse was discovered at 4.50 a.m., on Tuesday, August 7th, 1888. She was lying in a pool of blood. Her clothing was completely disarranged, the bosom of her petticoat having been ripped away and her garments thrown upwards as far as the waist. There were thirty-nine wounds to various parts of the body.

The murder caused much speculation. Although homicides were not uncommon in Whitechapel, there was something different about this one. Neither the killer nor his victim had apparently made any sound, nobody knew who the woman was, and the sheer ferocity of the attack was unique.

The inquest began on the afternoon of Thursday, August 9th, in the library and reading room – known as the Alexandra Room – of The Working Lads' Institute in Whitechapel Road.

In charge of the proceedings was Mr George Collier, the Deputy Coroner for the South-Eastern Division of Middlesex. He was standing in for the Coroner, Mr Wynne Edwin Baxter, who was on holiday in Scandinavia. Mr Collier sat at a large table. The twenty jurymen were on his left, whilst to his right were Inspector Reid and the doctor who had first examined the body, Dr Killeen.

The first witness to be called was a young woman who was clothed plainly in a discoloured black dress and wore a black woollen shawl pinned around her shoulders. She was Mrs Elizabeth Mahoney, aged twenty-five, who lived at No. 47, George Yard Buildings and was employed in a match factory at Stratford where, she said, she usually worked from nine in the morning until about seven o'clock at night.

It was obvious that the poor girl was very nervous, and the few facts which she had to give were spoken in such a low voice that some of the jurymen complained that they could not hear what she was saying. Mr Collier therefore had her come and stand immediately next to them before she was allowed to continue.

Mrs Mahoney, still ill at ease but now audible, resumed her evidence by saying that her husband, Joseph, was a carman and that, as far as she could remember, they had occupied rooms in the building for about eight months. Monday, August 6th, having been a Bank Holiday, they were out all day and did not return until twenty minutes to two on the Tuesday morning. They had seen nobody about as they toiled up the stone steps in the dark.

She had taken off her hat and cloak when they reached their room, but then Joseph had decided that he was rather peckish and, in the true fashion of the East End male, he despatched his young wife into the night to buy something to eat.

It was about a quarter to two when she hurried off, no doubt rather apprehensively, to a chandler's shop in Thrawl Street where she bought some fish and chips (at a farthing a portion!) Five minutes later she was back in No. 47 where, after eating their belated supper, husband and wife retired wearily to bed.

Mrs Mahoney concluded her evidence by saying that she had not got up until 8.30 a.m., and that she had heard no noise or disturbance during the night.

The man who had found the murdered woman, John Saunders Reeves, cut a rather peculiar looking figure. A short young man, with a pale drawn face, he sported a dark beard and moustache, and he was wearing earrings. A shabby black overcoat concealed everything except the bottoms of his corduroy trousers.

Reeves stated that he was a stevedore living at No. 37, George Yard Buildings. On the morning in question he had left his room at a quarter to five. It was quite light, and as he reached the first floor landing he saw a female lying on her back in a pool of blood. There were also traces of blood on other parts of the landing. Although he had not examined the woman, he was quite certain that she was dead and he had fetched a policeman immediately. He did not know the woman at all. Questioning elicited the information that there was no blood coming from her mouth, and that although her hands had been clenched they did not appear to be holding any hair – or, indeed, anything else. All her clothes were disarranged, as if she had been in a struggle. There were no footprints on the steps, nor was there any sign of a weapon. Reeves thought it quite possible that people could have gone up and down the stairs in the dark without stumbling over or noticing the body.

Francis Hewitt, the superintendent of the Buildings, was not able to help matters along very much. He stated that his bedroom was almost at right angles with the spot where the body had been found, and that he and his wife had been sleeping only twelve feet from the step in question but he had heard nothing.

His wife had a little more to say, but it was equally unhelpful. She had heard a single cry of 'Murder!' during the early evening, but although it had echoed through the building it had not originated there. No notice had been taken because it was a rough area, and such cries were a frequent, if not nightly, occurrence.

Dr Timothy Robert Killeen said that he had been summoned at five o'clock on the morning in question and had arrived at the scene half an hour later. In his opinion the woman had been dead for about three hours. She was about thirty-six years of age, well nourished, five feet three inches in height, with a dark complexion and dark hair.

His external examination had revealed that her body was punctured in no less than thirty-nine places.

When he performed a post-mortem examination he found that the deceased was perfectly healthy, apart from a rather fatty heart with some blood in the pericardium. The thirty-nine wounds consisted of nine to the throat; sixteen to the breast – of which five had punctured the left lung, two the right and one the heart; thirteen to the abdomen – which included five punctures of the liver, two of the spleen and six of the stomach, in which there was partially digested food. In addition, there was one wound to 'the lower portion of the body' which was different from the rest. It was not a stab but a slash, three inches long and an inch deep. On opening the head, he had found 'an effusion of blood' between the scalp and the bone.

Dr Killeen then went on to describe exactly where the entry wounds had been made, and only then did it become clear that the breasts and the vagina had been the main targets of the killer's frenzied attack.

His next comments were to cause some surprise at the time: that an ordinary penknife could have caused most of the wounds, but there was one, to the sternum, that must have been made with some kind of dagger, or a sword bayonet.

There was a great deal of blood between the legs, which were separated, but there was no reason to suppose that recent intimacy had taken place and there were no signs whatsoever of a struggle. The cause of death was haemorrhage 'consequent upon the punctured wounds'.

The inquest was adjourned for a fortnight in order to give the police time to identify the victim and investigate the whole matter.

During the following two weeks, many sensational rumours and reports started to go the rounds once the newspapers had got hold of the story, and the authorities were hard put to it to deny them all. Dr Killeen's statement that a bayonet could have inflicted the wound in the victim's breastbone caused the police to make enquiries as to whether any soldiers had been seen in the area on the night of the murder.

As a result, they learned of several who had been loitering about in the company of women, but identity parades at the Tower of London and Wellington Barracks proved fruitless.

The police came in for much criticism about their reticence during this period, with the press complaining about their not being more open with the details of the case. It was argued that their lack of co-operation served merely to fuel the speculation, and that may well be the reason why this particular murder began to attract more publicity than the many which had preceded it.

In a highly critical article, of August 18th, the *East London Advertiser* claimed that 'the police seem to be as far from solving the mystery as they were on the morning the crime was committed'. It was hoped that 'this Whitechapel murder will not have to be placed upon the records of the police as one of those undiscovered crimes of which there have been far too many within the last decade'. Such forthright censure must have nettled the constabulary, and perhaps the editor was 'leaned upon' because the next issue of the newspaper was conciliatory in the extreme. Now it spoke of the police having exerted 'every energy to clear up the mystery, although success has not yet attended their efforts'.

With all the conjecture and public discussion, and in contrast with the lack of curiosity shown previously, it is hardly surprising that, on Thursday, August 23rd, a small crowd had gathered outside the Working Lads' Institute where the inquest was due to recommence at 2 p.m., with the Deputy Coroner, Mr Collier presiding.

The first witness was a working man of about forty-five, with a sallow complexion and iron-grey hair, moustache and imperial. In contrast with most of the other witnesses, he presented a smart appearance which was enhanced by his neat, dark-blue, serge coat.

Henry Samuel Tabram was his name, and he stated that he was a foreman packer in a furniture repository and lived at No. 6, River Terrace, East Greenwich.

On August 14th, he had identified the body in the mortuary as being that of his wife Martha, who was aged about thirty-nine or forty. The last time he had seen her alive had been about eighteen months previously, when he met her by chance in the Whitechapel Road. At that time she was, as far as he could judge, in her usual state of health.

Tabram said that he and his wife had been separated for thirteen years. The separation had not been by mutual consent. In the first instance he had left her because of her excessive drinking, and he had refused to live with her after that because she had taken out a summons against him for maintenance. He had paid her twelve shillings (60p, but equivalent to over £20 today) a week for about the first three years after their parting but, about ten years before, he had reduced that to half a crown (2/6) because of her behaviour in constantly accosting him in the street for money. Also, he had discovered that she was living with another man, and he did not see why he should continue to support her. That man, he said, was at that very moment waiting outside in the passage to give evidence. He said that he did not know whether his wife had had any occupation, and went on to say that he had learned of her death only through the newspapers, following which he had gone and identified the body.

Tabram was told that he could stand down. The way in which he had given his evidence had created a good impression, but it was obvious that he was shedding no tears over his wife's death.

The next witness was the man to whom Tabram had referred. William Turner was a short young man, with a pale face from which sprouted a light moustache and imperial. He was dressed in a light tweed suit, but his general appearance was both dirty and slovenly. Speaking very indistinctly, he said that he was now living at the Victoria Working Men's Home in Commercial Street. Although a carpenter by trade, he had been a street hawker for some years.

Turner told Mr Collier that he had lived with Martha, on and off, for about ten years until three weeks prior to her death. The 'off' periods had been when he was forced to leave her because of her drinking. He had had no family by her.

The last time he had seen Martha alive was at about 2 p.m. on Saturday, August 4th, when he had bumped into her in Leadenhall Street, near the Aldgate Pump. She used to sell 'things' in the street and therefore, when she told him that she had no money, he had given her 1/6d to buy some stock. Their meeting had lasted for approximately twenty minutes, and he had not seen her since. In all the time they had lived together any money which she had had been spent on drink.

The witness was then questioned about the hours Martha had kept, but he told the inquest that she was not in the habit of staying out late. They usually got home at about 11 p.m. when they were together, although it could be as late as midnight or 1 a.m. on Saturdays. On balance, he thought that around 11 p.m. was their usual time, but it had been an entirely different matter when she went off on a binge; then he had left her to her own devices. He himself was, as a rule, of sober habits, and when *she* was sober they usually got on pretty well. Even when she was drinking heavily he never quarrelled with her, but simply left until she was off the bottle.

In reply to further questions from the Deputy Coroner, Turner explained that he had not learned of Martha's death until the inquest opened on August 9th. Then some friends had told him of the proceedings, and later he had identified the body. He did not consider himself accountable for whether or not she walked the streets, but maintained that if she had done so whilst they were living together it was without his knowledge. However, when pressed, he was forced to contradict what he had said earlier and admitted that there were times when she stayed out all night. On such occasions she would sometimes say that it was because she had had a fit. She was subject to fits which were brought on by drink, and once she had told him that she had been taken to a police station whilst suffering one. As far as he knew, she had no regular companions, and it was only after her death that he had learned of her association with a woman called 'Pearly Poll'. He had seen her in the company of different men and women from time to time, but that, he said, was only to be expected as anyone who obtained their living from the streets got to know a lot of people.

Turner was finally allowed to go, and his place was taken by a nervous little woman who mumbled that her name was Mary Bousfield, and that she was the wife of William Bousfield, a wood cutter. She gave their address as No. 4, Star Street – which was off the Commercial Road and notorious as a slum inhabited by criminals. It was described at the time as being 'very low and miserable', with the entrance to its black and muddy road blocked by fruit stalls and loiterers.

Taking evidence from this witness was very difficult. On several occasions she had to be told to speak up as her voice was so indistinct; and she tended to wander off the subject with inconsequential remarks. Nevertheless, Mr Collier persevered and gradually her tale unfolded.

It transpired that the dead woman had lodged with the Bousfields and that whilst she was there she had used the name of 'Martha Turner'. The witness had known the deceased for about four months, but Martha had lodged with her for only about a fortnight and had then decamped owing rent.

According to Mrs Bousfield, her lodger had 'got her living by selling matches, needles, pins, menthol cones and suchlike'.

The questioning then turned to Martha's drinking habits and the witness stated that, as far as she could see during the four months she had known her, the deceased had been 'of temperate habits'. It was a reply which caused Mr Collier to remind her, somewhat sharply, that she had told police officers that the dead woman 'would rather have a glass of ale than a cup of tea'. Which, he asked sternly, was correct? He waited patiently for an answer, but to no avail. Obviously flummoxed, Mrs Bousfield stammered and stuttered that the deceased had not been a woman who habitually got drunk, and she had never seen her so.

Her credibility became even more strained when she told of what a retiring person Martha had been, and that she 'scarcely knew two people in the street'. To that she added the ambiguous observation that 'she never brought any female companions home with her'.

Next the jury heard of a conversation with Martha during which she had told Mrs Bousfield that she had been living with a man called

Turner prior to coming to Star Street. She had said that she picked up with Turner soon after the separation from her husband. He had been very good to her and, at one time, he had helped to support her two children. That was the first mention that had been made of the deceased having children, and Mr Collier was obviously interested. He asked whether the witness had ever seen them, but she had not.

By this time it had become obvious that very little more of use was going to be dragged out of Mrs Bousfield and she was told that she could go. However Inspector Reid intervened, saying that he would like to question her. In her replies, the witness repeated that the dead woman had done a moonlight flit, and had left No. 4, Star Street without giving any notice. That had not been very difficult as the only 'furniture' which she owned consisted of two grubby mattresses.

Mrs Bousfield departed, and the jury turned its gaze upon the next witness, a pale-faced woman whose pallor was accentuated by her being dressed entirely in black. Described as 'very respectable', she was Henry Tabram's sister, Mrs Ann Morris.

She began by stating that she was a widow living at No. 23, Fisher Street, Mile End, and that her husband's name had been Thomas. In reply to a question from Mr Collier, she cleared up one point by telling him that Martha had borne two children by her husband, both boys, and that one of them must, by then, have been about seventeen.

The last time she had seen her sister-in-law alive had been at about 11 p.m. on the Bank Holiday Monday night. Martha was alone and was entering a pub in the Whitechapel Road – she thought it was the White Swan.

Mrs Morris confirmed that the dead woman had drunk very heavily, and stated that she was 'a very bad woman in other respects'. She seemed to have no doubts whatsoever that Martha was 'on the streets'.

Apparently the two women were barely on speaking terms, and had seen very little of each other in recent times. The deceased had used to ask the witness for money, but not lately. Although Mrs Morris had heard that Martha was a street hawker, she had never seen her doing *anything* for a living. She had not been close enough to her on the Monday night to tell whether or not she was sober, and she could tell the inquest nothing about about the circumstances of Martha's death, not having heard of it until nearly a week later.

That was the sum total of her evidence, but when she had gone Inspector Reid was once again instrumental in providing some background information, and what he had to say explained the obvious animosity which had existed between the two women. He told the jury that the deceased had been under the impression that Mrs Morris had encouraged Henry Tabram to reduce her maintenance allowance. Martha had therefore harassed her sister-in-law and demanded money from her. As a result she had been charged three times with annoying Mrs Morris. When she had appeared before the magistrate on the third occasion he had apparently run out of patience with her because she received a sentence of seven days' hard labour.

Inspector Reid sat down, and there was a slight hiatus during which a distinct stir ran around the room as the name of the next witness was called. Mary Ann Connolly, better known as 'Pearly Poll', had been much talked of and everyone was agog to see her.

What they beheld was a big, somewhat mannish woman. Hatless, and with an old green shawl around her shoulders, her face reddened by drink, Poll's whole appearance proclaimed her profession. Aged fifty, she was some ten years older than Martha, and it was obvious that she would have been the more dominant of the two.

Before she was allowed to say a word, Inspector Reid asked that she be cautioned and Mr Collier was only too happy to oblige. He explained to her that she need not answer any questions but that, if she did, what she said would be written down and could be used against her in the future. Poll was not at all put out by that – no doubt she had heard it all before. She confirmed that she understood the caution, and that she was still quite willing to give evidence. That being so, she was sworn and things got under way again.

Speaking in a low, husky voice, which she explained was because her chest was 'queer', she stated that she was a single woman and an 'unfortunate' of no fixed address. She stayed at various lodging-houses, but had been at 'Crossingham's, at No. 35, Dorset Street' (of which we shall hear much, much more later) for the previous two months.

Pearly Poll said that she had known the dead woman as 'Emma', and that she had been acquainted with her for some four or five months but did not know what she did for a living. Her assertion that 'Emma' did not drink very much caused a raising of eyebrows and that incredulity appeared justified by what was to follow.

Describing the events of the Bank Holiday, the witness told of how she had started drinking with the deceased at around 10 p.m. They had picked up with two soldiers, a corporal and a private, in the Two Brewers in Brick Lane, and had continued to drink with them in various pubs before finishing up at the Blue Anchor (67A, Whitechapel Road). They had all left there at about a quarter to midnight, and then there had been a parting of the ways with 'Emma' taking the private up George Yard and the witness going into the parallel Angel Alley with the corporal. Before the separation, Pearly Poll had had an argument with the soldiers about money, but 'Emma' had not been involved and they had all parted good friends.

She and the corporal had finished their business by ten or fifteen minutes after twelve. They parted at the corner of George Yard, and the soldier went off in the direction of Aldgate whilst the witness headed back to the centre of Whitechapel. She had not seen 'Emma' after they had paired off with the soldiers, and she did not know what became of her. The first she had heard of the murder was on the following morning, that was to say the Tuesday after the Bank Holiday, and she had known at once that the dead woman was 'Emma'.

In answer to Mr Collier, Pearly Poll said that she had no idea to which regiment the soldiers belonged, and that she had not noticed whether they were wearing side-arms. All she *could* say was that they had a kind of white band around their caps. She had never seen the soldiers before that night, and had been unable to pick them out when a regiment had been paraded before her.

Questioned by Inspector Reid, she agreed that she had threatened to drown herself after the murder, but it was 'only a lark' and she had not been serious. Her threat may have caused some concern when she then disappeared for a couple of days, but she had actually gone off to stay with her cousin, a Mrs Shean, who lived at No. 4, Fuller's Court, off Drury Lane. Not knowing that she was being sought in order to attend a parade of the soldiers at the Tower, she had stayed at Fuller's Court for two days and two nights.

The Deputy Coroner then took up the questioning, and Pearly Poll told him that she and 'Emma' had been drinking for an hour and three-quarters on the Monday night. She had seen nothing of the private after he had gone off with her friend.

Pearly Poll went, and once again Inspector Reid took the floor to elaborate on the evidence. He told the jury that a large number of persons had made statements, and that in each case what they had had to say had been 'thrashed out'. Some of those who had come forward had said that they had seen the deceased with a corporal on the night before the Bank Holiday, i.e. the Sunday. They had therefore been taken to the Tower but, although all the corporals and privates who had been on leave that night had been paraded in front of them, no identification had been made. Constable Barrett, who had been the first police officer at the seene of the crime, had said that he spoke to a corporal at two o'clock on the morning of the killing. The soldier had been hanging around in Wentworth Street, and when asked by Barrett what he was up to he had replied that he was waiting for a mate who had gone with a girl. Because of that, Barrett had also attended an identification parade at the Tower, but with the same lack of success as the others.

Referring to Pearly Poll the inspector stated that, as a result of what she had said when interviewed, there had been another parade at the Tower, but she had been unable to identify anyone. It was only after that parade that she had volunteered the information about the white bands around the caps. That had suggested that the soldiers belonged to the Coldstream Guards, and so he went with her to the Wellington Barracks, in Birdcage Walk, and there she had positively identified two men. However subsequent police enquiries had established that both soldiers had alibis. Inspector Reid concluded by appealing to anyone who could identify the women's companions on the Monday night to come forward.

All the evidence had now been heard, and it was time for Mr Collier to sum up. He began by acknowledging the assistance which had been offered by the military authorities, and went out of his way to say that not the slightest aspersion should be cast upon the two soldiers picked out by Pearly Poll. To his mind, this was one of the most horrible crimes to have been committed for some time, and the person who had inflicted such revolting injuries could have been nothing but a fiend. It was his opinion that the jury could bring in no other verdict than that of 'Wilful murder'.

The jury agreed, and added a rider that they thought it wrong to allow the stairs and passages of 'these model lodging-houses' to be unlighted at night.

The verdict was noted, the jury discharged, and the proceedings terminated. That, however, was not to be the end of the matter by any means. Nobody present could possibly have foreseen that they had just heard the bloody details of the first in a series of murders which was to shock the country and the civilized world. Nor could poor Martha have dreamed that her name would go down to posterity as that of the first victim of a new kind of killer. 'Jack the Ripper' had appeared upon the scene, and it was to be only a very few days before the unsuspecting inhabitants of Whitechapel learned of another of his 'funny little games'.

There, can be no doubt that the Ripper's second victim, dark-haired and petite Mary Ann Nichols, known universally as 'Polly', had once been an attractive woman. Even now, at forty-two, she looked ten years younger, and her delicate features still bore witness to that earlier charm. However, the years had not been kind to her in other ways and now, like Martha Tabram, she had come down in the world and was an 'unfortunate' with a drink problem. Indeed, as we shall now see, there had been many other similarities in their lives.

Thursday, August 30th had been a good day for Polly. Clients had sought her favours, the drink had flowed, and somewhere along the way she had even acquired a new bonnet. By the evening she was quite happy with life, but continued to call at various pubs in search of jollity and more cash customers.

At around eleven o'clock, she was seen wandering alone on her beat in Whitechapel Road, heading in the direction of Aldgate, but by about midnight she was in The Frying Pan pub on the corner of Brick

Lane and Thrawl Street. She left at 12.30 a.m., and then she must have either picked up a client or wetted her whistle elsewhere – or both – because it was not until 1.20 a.m. that she arrived at a lodging-house at No. 18, Thrawl Street, which was only two doors from the Christian Community Mission Hall! It had been her home for some three weeks until August 24th, but since then she had been dossing at 'The White House', at No. 56, Flower and Dean Street, because there men and women were allowed to sleep together. That being the case, it is difficult to understand why she had now appeared at her former address, but whatever the reason her reception was cool, to say the least. The lodging-house deputy soon espied her in the kitchen and, upon discovering that she did not have the fourpence for her bed, wasted no time in tipping her back out on to the street. However, Polly was not, apparently, at all put out by that. Asking that a bed be saved for her, she told the deputy chirpily: 'I'll soon get my doss money; see what a jolly bonnet I've got now.'

Even so, she very quickly found that it was no joke being on the streets and penniless at that time in the morning. She trailed around in a fruitless attempt to find a customer, with the alcohol taking more effect as time went by.

Just before 2.30 a.m., she was discovered by a friend, Ellen Holland. Polly was leaning against the wall outside a grocer's shop at the corner of Osborne Street and Brick Lane, and she was very drunk. Ellen still lodged at No. 18, Thrawl Street, where she had previously shared a room with Polly and two other women, and she tried hard to persuade her friend to return there with her. What that would have achieved is hard to comprehend, unless Ellen intended to pay for her, but it was of no matter anyway because Polly would have none of it. She boasted that she had earned her doss money three times over that day, but had drunk it all away. Now she was off to earn it again but, obviously more peeved than she had shown at being ejected in Thrawl Street, she said that when she had the money she would go to 'The White House'. There was obviously nothing to be done with her, and so Ellen went to No. 18 whilst Polly tottered off along the Whitechapel Road towards Whitechapel Station. The clock of Whitechapel Church had struck half-past two during their conversation, and Mary Ann Nichols now had less than an hour to live.

The place in which she met her end was Buck's Row, now Durward Street. It lies to the north of, and parallel with, Whitechapel Road. In those days, it ran from Brady Street in the east to Baker's Row in the west, where it was quite wide, and only some 700 yards from George Yard Buildings. At roughly halfway along its length, however, a large Board School marked a division into two much narrower thoroughfares. There, between Buck's Row and Whitechapel Road, Winthrop Street came into being and continued east, and parallel with the other two, until Brady Street.

The part of Buck's Row with which we are concerned is, in fact, that same stretch from the school to Brady Street. It was quite a respectable little backwater. On the southern side, after the school, was Brown's Stable, and then came a row of small terraced houses as far as the beer-house on the corner of Brady Street. The northern side was occupied by large warehouses, some of which were known locally as wharves as originally they had been served by a canal. A busy, cheery street during the day, it took on an entirely different aspect at night when the one street lamp, at the far end, did little to dissipate the shadows cast by the towering warehouses.

Winthrop Street was very different. Probably it had always seemed an evil and disreputable little lane and, in 1888, its only dubious claim to fame was that it accommodated Barber's Yard, a slaughterhouse belonging to Harrison, Barber and Co. Ltd.

Police Constable John Neil's beat took him past the entrance to Barber's Yard at 3.15 a.m. on Friday, August 31st, 1888, and he continued up Winthrop Street and round the school into Buck's Row. He saw nothing untoward, neither did Sergeant Kerby, who was there at roughly the same time, nor PC John Thain who was passing at the Brady Street end.

Less than half an hour later, however, at about 3.40 a.m., Polly's body was discovered by Charles Cross, a carman, who was passing through Buck's Row on his way to work at Pickford's in Broad Street. It was lying on the other side of the street, against the gates leading into the yard of Brown's Stable, and at first Cross thought that it was a tarpaulin. Only as he approached it did he realize that it was the figure of a woman, but he had no time to examine it before he heard footsteps approaching.

They belonged to Robert Paul, another carman, who was also on his way to work, in Corbett's Court, Whitechapel. He was somewhat apprehensive at encountering another man in such a secluded place and made to pass by, but Cross tapped him on the shoulder and said: 'Come and look over here, there's a woman lying on the pavement.' The two men bent over the recumbent form, but it was so dark that they could not see what was wrong with the woman, although they noticed that her clothes had been pulled up almost to her stomach.

Paul thought that she was breathing slightly, and wanted to sit her up, but Cross thought they should leave her as she was and inform the first policeman they met. That turned out to be PC Jonas Mizen, who was on his beat at the corner of Old Montague Street and Hanbury Street, and they told him that the woman was either dead or drunk. Glad of something to relieve the boredom of an otherwise uneventful night, Mizen headed for Buck's Row. Rather surprisingly, he asked neither man to accompany him and so they continued on their ways to work, as they were now in danger of being late.

What none of the three knew was that the matter was already receiving police attention.

PC Neil had made his return trip along Buck's Row within seconds of the departure of Cross and Paul and, at 3.45 a.m., he too had discovered the body. Having the advantage of his lantern, he saw at once that the woman's throat had been cut and, hearing PC Thain returning past the bottom of the street, he signalled for assistance and told him to go for a doctor.

PC Mizen then arrived on the scene, and Neil sent him to Bethnal Green police station for more help and an ambulance which, in those days, was little more than a handcart.

It was shortly after that PC Thain returned with a doctor and discovered that Neil had been joined by three slaughterers from Barber's Yard. Dr Llewellyn was not at all pleased at having been called out, and he was even more unhappy when he saw the onlookers. He pronounced the woman dead, ordered the removal of her body, and then disappeared back to his bed saying that they knew where he was if they wanted him again.

By this time Sergeant Kerby and another police constable had appeared and it was they who, in company with PC Neil, wheeled the corpse of Polly Nichols through the gloomy streets to the same mortuary shed in which the body of Martha Tabram had lain so recently.

Constables Thain and Neil were the ones who had actually lifted the body on to the ambulance, and it was only then that a small pool of congealed blood was seen. It was about six inches in diameter, and had tended to run towards the gutter. Thain discovered that his hands had become covered with blood from the back of the body, and he assumed that it had run down from the neck.

Inspector John Spratling received news of the murder at 4.30 a.m., whilst he was in the Hackney Road. He went immediately to Buck's Row, but the body had been removed by the time he got there and a young man, James Green, was already washing down the pavement and brushing the blood away. Green worked in the stable at the entrance to which the corpse had been found. His mother was the tenant of the last house in the terrace, 'New Cottage', and would later testify that she and her daughter slept in the first-floor front bedroom, the window of which was only a few feet from being directly above where the body was found. Nevertheless, and despite being a light sleeper, she had heard nothing out of the ordinary during that quiet Friday/Saturday night until the police knocked on her door.

Spratling found that PC Thain was still there, however – quite happily watching possible clues go down the drain – and he was able to show his superior where the body had lain, and to point out the slight bloodstain which remained on the cobblestones.

The Inspector, with Thain in tow, then went off to the mortuary shed to have a look at the body. Upon arrival he found that it was locked up and, although it had been sent for, the key had not arrived. However, the body was on the ambulance in the yard and Inspector Spratling was able to start taking notes of its condition, a process which he continued once the mortuary attendant had arrived and the corpse had been moved inside. It was all a very routine procedure for him until he lifted the skirt to complete his description of the clothing. What he saw then made his gorge rise, and caused one of the constables to vomit at the sight of the appalling abdominal mutilations from which the intestines were protruding. Shaken by what he had discovered, the Inspector had no scruples about summoning Dr Llewellyn from his bed again. Then, at 5 a.m., he despatched a PC Cartwright to make a thorough search of the murder scene and the surrounding area.

Dr Llewellyn duly arrived, no doubt even more displeased by a second call-out. He saw that the woman had been almost completely disembowelled, but declared that there was nothing he could do then, and that he would make a full post-mortem examination later in the morning.

There was little more that anyone could do at the mortuary shed at that time, and so they all went about their various duties leaving Detective Sergeant Patrick Enright to watch over the body. Then, for some reason not made clear, he too deserted the scene. Later he was to say that he had told the mortuary assistant that the body was not to be touched, but whether he did, in fact, leave any such instructions remains open to doubt.

The attendant was Robert Mann, a pauper inmate of the Whitechapel Workhouse who was subject to fits. When DS Enright left, Mann saw nothing to hold him there either and so he too departed to have his breakfast. He returned at 6.30 a.m. with his mate James Hatfield, another Workhouse inmate, and they set about undressing the corpse prior to washing it.

Word of the murder was spreading. Detective Inspector Joseph Henry Helson, of the local CID, learned of it at 6.45 a.m. and went straight to the mortuary. He arrived as the two Workhouse inmates were stripping the body, but he appears to have been yet another policeman who was prepared to stand by whilst possible evidence was destroyed. Before departing for Buck's Row he did, however, manage to notice that one of Polly's petticoats was stamped 'Lambeth Workhouse, P.R. [Prince's Road]'. As a result, the matron was fetched from the Workhouse but she was unable to identify the dead woman.

Dr Llewellyn returned at 10 a.m. to make his full post-mortem examination, but by then, of course, any possible clues had been obliterated by the washing and laying out of the corpse.

The police investigations continued all day Friday, with particular emphasis upon discovering the identity of the victim. The 'Lambeth Workhouse' markings were followed up more closely, and this time they proved to be the key to the mystery. Armed with a description of the deceased, the police unearthed a young woman, named Mary Ann Monk, who said that it sounded like someone whom she had known in the Workhouse. Monk was taken to the mortuary at 7.30 on the Friday night and she was able to make a positive identification. That enabled Polly's family to be traced and, early in the afternoon of Saturday, September 1st, her husband and one of her sons confirmed the identification.

The inquest into the death of Mary Ann Nichols was opened on that same Saturday afternoon, and only some thirty-six hours after the discovery of the body. Once again the Working Lads' Institute was called into service, but this time, in contrast with a certain apathy displayed at Martha Tabram's hearing, there was great competition for the few public seats.

Another notable difference was that Mr Wynne Edwin Baxter, the somewhat flamboyant Coroner, was now back from his holiday and was to preside. Mr Baxter was well known for his probing qualities, and the police may have been rather apprehensive because they were certainly well represented. Not only were Detective Inspector Helson, Detective Sergeants Enright and George Godley watching the inquiry, but with them was Detective Inspector George Abberline of the Scotland Yard CID.

The jurymen were sworn in. They elected a Mr Horey as their foreman and then, as was usual, they were taken to view the body.

Upon their return, the Coroner heard the detailed evidence of two men, the father and husband of the deceased.

Polly's father was Edward Walker, a grey-haired, grey-bearded man of some sixty years of age. A former locksmith, he told the jury that he was now unemployed and living at No. 16, Maidsworth Road, Camberwell.

Her husband was William Nichols, who was also full-bearded. A pale, rather pompous little man, he stated that he lived at No. 12, or 20, Cobourg Road (accounts differ), off the Old Kent Road. He was a printer's machinist, employed by Messrs Perkins, Bacon and Company of Whitefriars, just off Fleet Street.

Nichols appeared at the inquest in hired clothes, and looked somewhat ill at ease in his full mourning outfit of black frock coat, black tie, dark trousers and black silk top hat. To complete the effect, he had possessed himself of a black umbrella. He really was something of a humbug. When viewing the body, and no doubt very conscious that his words would be reported, he had stated in solemn tones: 'Many's the hard words I've said about her, but I forgive her for everything she did now I find her like this.'

Both father and husband gave evidence of identification, and between the two of them, albeit one after the other, there emerged a tale which could have come straight from the pages of a Victorian morality play.

Polly had been born on August 26th, 1845, in Dean Street, which linked Fetter Lane with Great New Street. As we know, her father was Edward Walker and her mother's name was Caroline. She married Nichols at St Bride's Church, Fleet Street, on January 16th, 1864, and over the next fifteen years she presented him with five offspring, three boys and two girls, Edward John, Percy George, Henry Alfred, Alice Esther and Eliza Sarah. However, at some time along the way she acquired a taste for alcohol and began to drink heavily. That led to rows, and on several occasions she left the marital home for short periods.

Only a year after the youngest child had been born, matters finally came to a head and there was a permanent parting of the ways, with Nichols keeping all the children except the eldest, Edward John, who left with his mother. Nichols made her a weekly allowance of 5s. (25p) a week which, even in those days, was not a lot of money. Even so, she might have got by had she stopped drinking and taken up some sort of work – in other words, if she had stopped being Polly! However, Polly she was, and it was no time at all before Edward was living with his grandfather whilst, for the following three years, his mother earned what she could on the streets and spent most of it, and the maintenance money, on drink.

In 1882, Nichols stopped her meagre allowance when he learned what was going on. At that time Polly was in the Lambeth Work-house, and presumably the authorities relieved her of Nichols's money as a contribution towards her keep. Therefore when it stopped, and she became a total charge on them, the Guardians of the Parish of Lambeth were not at all pleased. They had Nichols summoned to explain why he should not continue the allowance, but it did them no good. The magistrates dismissed the case out of hand after he had told them his reasons.

Polly was in and out of the Lambeth Workhouse during the next twelve months, but in March 1883, in an effort to pull herself together, she went to live with her father and eldest son. She was no doubt brimming over with good intentions at the time, but it was foreseeable that they would not last. There was a series of arguments with her father about her excessive drinking and she left in May.

Replying to questions, Edward Walker, in probably the under-statement of the year, testified that his daughter was 'not a particu-larly sober woman', but he had not thought her 'fast' with men. He stated that there was no question of his having turned her out; it was simply that they had had words and she had left.

Within a fortnight of her departure, Polly had, somehow, picked up with a man with whom she was to have a more or less stable relationship over the next four years. He was Thomas Stuart Drew, a blacksmith with a house and shop at No. 15, York Mews, York Street, Walworth – a parish sandwiched between Lambeth and Camberwell.

Naturally, Polly carried on drinking whilst she was with Drew but, generally speaking, she appears to have kept it under control and to have conducted herself quite properly.

For reasons unknown, but which can be guessed at, the association with Drew ended late in 1887, and for the next six months she was in and out of various workhouses. Then, around April 1888 – and only God knows how – she became a domestic servant with a respectable and teetotal couple. They were Samuel and Sarah Cowdry, of

'Ingleside', Rose Hill Road, Wandsworth, and it was from that address that she wrote the following letter to her father:

> I just write to say you will be glad to know that I am settled in my new place, and going all right up to now. My people went out yesterday and have not returned, so I am left in charge. It is a grand place inside, with trees and gardens back and front. All has been newly done up. They are teetotallers and religious, so I ought to get on. They are very nice people, and I have not much to do. I hope you are all right and the boy has work. So goodbye now for the present – From yours truly,
>   Polly.
> Answer soon please, and let me know how you are.

Her father said that he *did* reply, but he never heard from his daughter again.

Old habits die hard, and it took less than three months for any resolutions Polly may have made to go out of the window. On July 12th, and probably dying for a drink, she absconded from those 'very nice people', taking some of their clothing with her.

It was estimated that the clothes were worth 'in excess of £3.10.0', and no doubt the pawning of them kept Polly nicely in drink and other necessities for the next few weeks. However, by the end of July she was destitute, and on August 1st she spent the night in the Holborn Union Workhouse, off Gray's Inn Road.

In her situation, penniless and with the likelihood of being arrested for the theft of the clothes, it was almost inevitable that she should have turned her steps in the direction of that thieves' kitchen, better known as Spitalfields, which was only just over a mile down the road.

It would be new territory for her but, from what she had been told, only there would she find anonymity and the means of making a living. She had no way of knowing that she was about to take the first step on a road which would bring her to a bloody end at the hands of a crazed killer.

Dr Llewellyn described her fate in detail. First, he told of having been called by the police from his house at 152, Whitechapel Road.

Although he had noticed only about a wineglass and a half of blood beside the body, he was convinced that the woman had been killed where she was found.

His post-mortem examination had revealed that there was no blood on the upper [meaning 'the front'] parts of either the body or the clothing. Five of the victim's front teeth were missing, there was a slight laceration of the tongue, and bruising was found along the lower part of the jaw on the right side of the face. In his opinion, that could have been caused by a blow from a fist or pressure from a thumb. On the left side of the face was a circular bruise which could have resulted from the pressure of fingers.

Dr Llewellyn then proceeded to describe the gory mutilations, and began with those to the neck. He said that he had found an incision of approximately four inches long running from a point about an inch below the jaw, and directly below the left ear. Roughly an inch below that cut, but beginning an inch in front of it, there was another, some eight inches long, which went right round the neck and ended at about three inches below the right jaw. That longer incision had severed the major arteries on both sides of the neck, and all the tissues down to the spine – in other words, the killer had almost cut off Polly's head.

The doctor went on to say that he had found no injuries to the body proper until he had examined the lower part of the abdomen. Then he had discovered a very deep jagged wound, running from the left side, which had cut through all the tissues. In addition, there were several light slashes across the abdomen – three or four down the right side – and two deep stab wounds to the genitals. All the injuries were from left to right and downwards, and had been 'deftly and fairly skilfully performed' in four or five minutes. They had been inflicted, with great violence, by the same instrument, which he thought was a moderately sharp long-bladed knife, perhaps similar to those used by corkcutters and shoemakers.

Dr Llewellyn was of the opinion that the killer had attacked from the front. That led him to deduce, from his ideas of how the facial bruising had been caused, that the murderer was left-handed.

That was all the doctor had to say, and Mr Baxter decided to hear no more evidence that day. Polly Nichols was buried on September 6th in Public Grave No. 49500, Square 318 in the City of London Cemetery at Manor Park. Thousands, in respect, thronged the streets as the hearse went by, past Bucks Row where, only a week before, Polly had staggered, tired, cold and homeless.

The inquest was reconvened on September 3rd and September 17th, and then concluded on September 22nd. It heard evidence from all the police involved, from those who found the body, from Polly's friends and acquaintances, and from a succession of witnesses who lived or worked near the murder site, none of whom had apparently seen or heard anything suspicious that night. Chief among these was Walter Purkiss, the manager of Essex Wharf, the gates of which were almost opposite those of Brown's stable. Purkiss lived in a house that adjoined the Wharf gates and had its front door in Buck's Row. On the night in question he and his wife had retired just after 11 p.m. to their second-floor bedroom, from the window of which one could look down, across that narrow lane, directly on to the spot where Polly had been found. Mrs Purkiss being unwell, both had experienced a somewhat sleepless night. Purkiss testified that, although the night had been unusually quiet, he had awoken several times, while his wife had actually been walking around the bedroom at about the time, 3.30 a.m., that the murder was thought to have taken place. Neither had heard a thing.

Summing-up, Mr Baxter made reference to certain similarities between the murder of Polly and an even more horrific killing that had now been committed in their midst. In both cases there were bruises about the head, which was nearly severed from the body, and there were other dreadful injuries which had been performed 'with anatomical knowledge'.

Having completed his rather lengthy say, Mr Baxter allowed the jurymen to consider their verdict. For some inexplicable reason, it took them twenty minutes before they came to the obvious conclusion that poor Polly had been the subject of wilful murder by some person, or persons, unknown.

The inquest was then closed, and the police were free to give their undivided attention to the third victim in what was now recognized as a series of horrific killings.

5

Annie

THE AREA AROUND Nicholas Hawksmoor's masterpiece, Christ Church, Spitalfields, was without doubt the most lawless and vice-ridden in the district. A contemporary report described some of the streets: 'Such passages as Edward-street, nearby Hanbury and Princess-streets, Flower and Dean-street, between Brick Lane and Commercial-street, which in daylight only strike one as very unwholesome and dirty thoroughfares, appear unutterably forlorn and dismal in the darkness of night.' The streets named were all busy and lighted, however poorly, and so the writer was probably wise to leave to his readers' imaginations what was to be found in the myriad of stinking and unlit courts, and the labyrinth of evil alleys which connected them.

One of the streets named, Hanbury Street – formerly Brown's Lane – ran, and indeed still runs, through the heart of Spitalfields. Beginning at Commercial Street, in the west, it crossed Brick Lane and traversed 'one of the frowsiest quarters of the East End' before terminating at Baker's Row, not far from the start of Buck's Row.

No. 29, Hanbury Street was an old three-storeyed house which, even in 1888, had seen far better days. It was one of the hundreds which were owned by absentee landlords who, through agents, leased their properties for high rents but carried out little, and usually no, maintenance. In order to pay those rents and still make a profit, it was necessary for the lessees to sub-let every available square inch for as much as the market would stand, and it was that state of affairs which accounted for much of the squalor and misery in the East End.

The fact that the next murder was committed on those particular premises has ensured that a permanent record exists which not only emphasizes the points just made, but also provides a vivid illustration of the habits and ways of life of a typical cross-section of the more respectable working-class denizens of the neighbourhood.

No. 29 was let to a Mrs Amelia/Emilia Richardson, a widow who lived in the first floor front room with her fourteen-year-old grandson. Mrs Richardson owned a packing-case making business which was carried out from the cellar and the backyard.

Mrs Harriet/Annie/Mary Hardyman/Hardiman/Hardman/Handerman (reports differ widely) and her sixteen-year-old son occupied the ground-floor front room, which doubled as a cats' meat shop from which she sold pieces of horse flesh, on skewers, at a farthing or a halfpenny each depending on size. Her son went out selling the meat also. The room behind was Mrs Richardson's kitchen/parlour, in which she sometimes held prayer meetings.

The first-floor back, that is to say the room behind Mrs Richardson's, was tenanted by a Mr Walker/Waker, a maker of lawn-tennis boots, and his 27-year-old, feeble-minded, son Alfred – said to be 'very inoffensive'.

There is some mystery about just who rented the room above them – the second-floor back. Most reports assert that it was a Mr and Mrs Copsey/Copely, cigar makers, but one newspaper had it that the tenants were two sisters named Huxley of, perhaps, the same occupation.

In the second-floor front were Mr and Mrs Robert Thomson/Thompson and their adopted daughter. Mr Thomson is generally described as having been a carman or carter working for Goodson's of Brick Lane.

An old lady named Sarah Cox, kept by Mrs Richardson 'out of charity', had the rear garret.

Next door to Sarah Cox, the Davis/Davies family was packed into the front garret. The pater familias was John Davis, an elderly carman who worked out of the Leadenhall Market, off Gracechurch Street in the City. He, his wife and three adult sons had lived in the house for only about a fortnight, and it was a move which he would have cause to regret as he was to suffer an experience which would haunt him for the rest of his life.

The door to Mrs Hardyman's cats' meat shop opened directly off the pavement in Hanbury Street. To the left of it, as one looked at the house, was another door, which gave entrance to a passage, twenty-three feet nine inches long and three feet wide. The passage gave access to a staircase to the upper floors and, past that, to the kitchen. At the far end was a stable-door into the flagstoned backyard, which was about two feet and six inches lower than the passage. Short of scaling the various fences, there was no way out of the backyard except by the passage, the front and rear doors to which were always left unlocked.

When the stable-door was opened, outwards and to the left, it passed over a recess, about three feet six inches wide, between the three steps down to the yard and the five-foot-six-inch-high fence. To the right of the door, looking out, were covered steps which led down to a door to the cellar, which was kept padlocked when not in use.

The yard proper covered an area of approximately twenty square yards, with fences on all sides. Opposite the back door, but slightly to the left, was a small shed in which was kept the wood used to make the packing cases. In the other, far right, corner was the privy which served the whole household – the condition of which was the probable reason why some of the men preferred to urinate in the recess or against the fence! Nearby, against the right-hand fence, was a stand-pipe with a tap which provided the only supply of water to the whole house.

It was, in fact, a rather urgent call of nature which compelled John Davis to the yard just before six o'clock on the morning of Saturday, September 8th. (Davis would report later that he had been awake from 3 a.m. to 5 a.m.) He hurried down the three flights of stairs and the passage, unfastening his belt as he went, but what he saw when he flung open the back door drove all else from his mind.

Lying in the recess to his left was the body of a woman. She was flat on her back, with her knees raised and apart, and her clothes up about her thighs, but what made Davis suck in his breath was the appalling spectacle presented by the upper half of her body. The head appeared to have been cut off, and some of her intestines seemed to be draped over her shoulder. That was enough for him. He did not venture down the steps for a closer look, but ran back along the passage and into the street, seeking help.

News of the latest atrocity travelled fast and invoked a wave of horror. In what seemed no time at all, a crowd had gathered in front of the house and another around the entrance to the yard in which what passed for a mortuary was situated. Eventually the body was to be removed in the same 'shell' – a light coffin – used for Polly Nichols, and into the hands of the same Workhouse inmate, Robert Mann. On all sides there was loud criticism of the police, for both their inefficiency and lack of numbers, and many were asking why no reward had yet been posted.

One thing upon which everybody seemed to agree was that such barbarous murders and mutilations could not possibly have been perpetrated by an Englishman; they were obviously the work of 'some ill-bred and ill-nourished foreigner from the lowest dens of vice in Europe'. All foreigners came under suspicion, but as the Jews were, by far, the largest alien element in the local population, they took the brunt, and anti-Semitism escalated. The police were very much alive to what was being said and warned foreigners, and especially Jews, to keep away from the murder sites until passions had cooled.

Increased anti-Semitism was, however, but one symptom of a phenomenon of which the authorities were becoming increasingly aware. By now it was obvious that the terror, apprehension and sense of outrage felt by the underprivileged East Enders were causing the more affluent Londoners concern about the possible reactions.

As a result, there was far more activity after this murder than had succeeded the others, and even the police seemed galvanized into action – although that consisted mainly of running faster in ever-decreasing circles – with Inspector Abberline being instructed to combine enquiries about this killing with the Nichols investigation.

Rumours spread throughout the district like wildfire, sold newspapers, and kept the crowds coming. The occupants of No. 27, Hanbury Street and their neighbours, as with all East Enders then and now, saw a business opportunity and seized it. They charged an admission fee of a penny to those wishing to view the actual spot where the body had lain, and over Saturday and Sunday thousands of respectably dressed sightseers flocked to the Hanbury Street area, while half-a-dozen costermongers did a brisk business in refreshments and fruit. Sometimes the road became so congested that the police were forced to make several charges in order to keep it clear, and no fewer than five of their number stood guard outside Nos. 27 and 29 to ensure that only tenants gained admission. There was much grumbling about this from both inside and outside the houses. People appreciated that the murder site proper should be protected, but neither the entrepreneurs nor their would-be customers could understand why they should be prevented from looking out of upstairs windows.

The *Star* was the first newspaper on the streets on Saturday evening. In a long editorial, highly critical of the police, it stated, amongst other things, that:

London lies today under the spell of a great terror. A nameless reprobate – half beast, half man – is at large, who is daily gratifying his murderous instincts on the most miserable and defenceless classes of the community.

The ghoul-like creature who stalks through the streets of London, stalking down his victim like a Pawnee Indian, is simply drunk with blood, and he will have more.

Whitechapel is garrisoned with police and stocked with plain-clothes men. Nothing comes of it. The police have not even a clue. They are in despair at their utter failure to get so much as a scent of the criminal.

The editorial advocated the setting up of Vigilance Committees which would arrange for the streets to be patrolled, and ended with the exhortation: 'Up citizens; then, and do your own police work!'

At the same time, the London correspondent of the *New York*

Times commented: 'The London police and detective force is probably the stupidest in the world.'

Stung to the quick by the many public criticisms, the police sprang into action, but it was action for action's sake – reacting to everything and initiating nothing. Over 200 doss-houses were visited, and scores of people were questioned. Some were detained at various East End police stations, twelve being taken to the Commercial Street 'nick' alone. All were eventually set at liberty, except for one who was certified as insane.

On Sunday evening, Scotland Yard sent the following telegram to every station throughout the metropolis and suburbs:

Commercial Street 8.30 p.m.

Description of man wanted, who entered a passage of the house at which the murder was committed with a prostitute at 2 a.m., the 8th.

Age 37; height 5 ft. 7 in.; rather dark beard and moustache; dress, short dark jacket, dark vest and trousers, black scarf, and black felt hat; spoke with a foreign accent.

It would be interesting to know whether the police had a secret witness, or whether the description of this suspect was merely a figment of someone's fevered imagination. Even if they had, why should the constabulary have been so interested in what happened at 2 a.m.? They were apparently convinced that she was murdered much later. Did they know something which we do not, and which fits in more closely with an earlier murder time?

On the day before the murder, i.e. Friday, September 7th, Detective Inspector Helson had reported that a search was being conducted for a Polish Jew named John (Jack) Pizer, nicknamed 'Leather Apron', in connection with the killing of Polly Nichols. Apparently the man had a criminal record, and had 'for some considerable period been ill-using prostitutes in this, and other parts, of the Metropolis'.

The search bore fruit and, very early on Monday, September 10th, Pizer was arrested off the Whitechapel Road. He was taken to Leman

Street police station. Word of the arrest sent the public excitement up to fever pitch, and did nothing to ease the high feelings which were running against the Jews. However, he was able to supply satisfactory alibis for the nights of the two recent murders and therefore, on the Tuesday evening, he was released.

Monday the 10th was a busy day all round, with the *Daily Telegraph* setting the scene as well as any other newspaper: 'The latest deed of ferocity has thrown Whitechapel into a state of panic . . . We are certainly led . . . to imagine the existence of some baleful prowler of the East-end streets and alleys who . . . knows every bye-place well, who is plausible enough in address to beguile his victims, strong enough to overcome them the moment homicidal passion succeeds to desire, cunning enough to select the quiet spot for his furious assaults, and possessed of a certain ghastly skill in using the knife . . .'

Stimulated by such articles, the crowds continued to throng the area, and two 'prominent members of the peerage' visited the murder site. Alarmed by the increasing anti-Semitism, Samuel Montague, the Jewish Member of Parliament for the Whitechapel Division of Tower Hamlets, offered a reward of £100 for the capture of the murderer, and asked the police to issue notices to that effect. The Jewish community, as a whole, also announced its intention of offering a reward.

A meeting of ratepayers was held in the Crown public house, No. 74, Mile End Road, and there was much criticism of the police. It was decided to form the Mile End Vigilance Committee, and the officers appointed were Mr George Akin Lusk, a builder and decorator, as President; Mr John Cohen, No. 345, Commercial Road, Vice-President; Mr Joseph Aarons, licensee of the Crown, Treasurer; and Mr B. Harris, No. 83, White Horse Lane, Secretary. One of the first duties undertaken by the last named was to have posters pasted up all over the neighbourhood which read:

Finding that, in spite of murders being committed in our midst, our police force are still inadequate to discover the author or authors of the late atrocities, we, the undersigned, have formed ourselves into a committee, and intend offering a substantial reward to anyone, citizen or otherwise, who shall give such information that will bring the murderer or murderers to justice.

The proprietor of the *Illustrated Police News* also offered a reward of £100.

Meanwhile, as all this frantic and unprecedented activity was in progress, the body of the poor woman who had been the catalyst for it was identified by Timothy Donovan, the deputy of Crossingham's common lodging house, at No. 35, Dorset Street, Spitalfields (where Pearly Poll was living). His identification was confirmed by a young man named Frederick Simmons, who also lodged at Crossingham's. They said that she was 'Dark Annie', a prostitute, who also hawked goods in the street at Stratford – some three miles away – on market days.

Simmons added that when he had last seen Annie, which was only a few hours earlier, she had been wearing three rings, one a wedding ring and two chased, but they were now missing.

The identifications were also confirmed by several others, at least two of whom knew her real name – Anne Chapman.

To be more precise, she was Eliza Anne Chapman, née Smith, aged forty-seven. Exactly five feet tall, she had been a buxom, but well-proportioned, woman with dark brown wavy hair, blue eyes and a fair complexion. Having a very fine set of teeth, with only two lower molars missing, her smile had been one of her most attractive features, and had offset her large and prominent nose.

Annie Chapman was a pleasant enough little woman, who had been making the most of her miserable existence, but her history was virtually identical to those of Martha Tabram and Polly Nichols.

She was born, out of wedlock, in Paddington, in September 1841, but her mother, Ruth Chapman, married the father, George Smith, a Lifeguardsman, the following year. There were other children of the marriage, both boys and girls. In 1856, the family moved to Windsor, but on May 1st, 1869, Annie, then aged twenty-seven, and very much older than the average marrying age for a woman of those times, was wed in Knightsbridge, in the West End of London. The bridegroom was one John Chapman, a relative of Annie's mother, who seems to have been much older than his bride. It was said that at the time of the marriage he was the valet of a nobleman living in Bond Street, a situation which he was to lose in 1881, allegedly because of Annie's dishonesty. There must, however, be some doubts about all of that. John and Annie set up home at No. 1, Brook Mews, Bayswater, but by 1873 they were living at No. 17, South Bruton Mews, off Berkeley Square, Mayfair. That address would suggest that John, as is usually stated, was in fact a coachman.

In 1881, Annie, John and their, by now, three children, were back in the Windsor area; with John working as head domestic coachman for a farm bailiff named Josiah Weeks, at St Leonard's Mill Farm Cottage, Clewer. The couple were not very fortunate with their children; there were two girls and a boy: Emily Ruth, Annie Georgina and John. The son was deformed, and Emily Ruth died of meningitis in 1882. Those may have been two of the reasons why Annie turned, increasingly, to the bottle for solace, although she was never to become an alcoholic. Even occasional binges were expensive for a woman in her situation, however, and there is some evidence that she was not above prostituting herself when money was short.

The marriage suffered, and finally failed. The pair separated in 1884, with John retaining custody of the children. However, the parting appears to have been amicable enough, because John allowed Annie a nominal ten shillings a week by way of Post Office orders payable at the Commercial Street post office. The payments were sometimes irregular but, even so, they were more generous than those allowed to Polly Nichols by her prig of a husband.

It may be wondered why Annie made for Spitalfields. To go from sedate Windsor to such an infamous locality in one bound does, on the face of it, seem rather mysterious and somewhat foolhardy. The reason, however, was simple and straightforward. Annie's third, and favourite, sister was married and living in Oxford Street, Whitechapel – just behind the London Hospital. What more natural, therefore, than that Annie should have turned her steps in that general direction?

Footloose and fancy-free, Annie usually stayed in common lodging-houses in the Spitalfields area. There she was not too far from her sister, but far enough away to be able to do as she wished without the family knowing what she was up to. For a short time, she lived with a friend, Amelia Palmer, in a lodging-house at No. 30, Dorset Street, and that is where, in 1886, she picked up with a sievemaker. The man was known as 'Jack Sievey' – not, surely, his true surname but derived from his occupation. Their liaison was not a particularly lengthy one, but it lasted long enough for Annie to be known as 'Mrs Sievey'.

After the Christmas of 1886, Annie did not receive her weekly ten shillings. She made enquiries, and discovered that John Chapman had died on Christmas Day, at the age of only forty-four.

As if that were not enough, Jack Sievey left Annie at about the same time and went to live in Notting Hill. Whether or not the two events were simply coincidental is not known, but perhaps Annie was not so attractive to him without her ten bob a week!

With no regular, or even irregular, income, and no protector – for whatever he may have been worth – Annie was hard put to it to get by. She would share a bed with any man who could pay for it, and sometimes she sold matches, flowers and her own crocheted anti-macassars in the streets. After the disappearance of 'Sievey', the most regular seeker after her favours was a man known as 'The Pensioner', so called because he was believed to be an ex-soldier drawing a pension from the Essex Regiment. On the weekends that he felt in need of female companionship, they would usually sleep together in any of the lodging-houses which permitted such cohabitation. However, for the four months prior to her death Annie had lodged at one particular doss-house, Crossingham's, and that caused a minor problem. It seems that 'The Pensioner' was also partial to the charms of another resident, Eliza/ Elizabeth Cooper, who became jealous of Annie.

Crossingham's doss-house figured prominently in the evidence presented on the first day of the inquest. This was held on Monday, September 10th, that is to say, two days after the discovery of the body. Once again the Working Lads' Institute was called into use, and Mr Baxter presided.

Timothy Donovan, the deputy manager of Crossingham's, stated that he had known the dead woman as a prostitute for about sixteen months, but she had lived at Crossingham's for only the previous four months. She was usually the worse for drink on Saturdays, but not on other days of the week.

At about three or four o'clock on the afternoon of Friday the 7th, she had turned up at the lodging-house and asked permission to go down to the kitchen, saying that she had been in the infirmary but still felt unwell. He had allowed her in. He had not seen her again until half-past one or a quarter to two on the morning of Saturday the 8th. He had seen her come into the lodging-house by the front door and go downstairs to the kitchen without so much as a 'by your leave'. She was eating a baked potato, and had obviously had enough to drink, although she was 'walking straight'.

Donovan was not having that, and without further ado he had sent down to ask if she had the money for the double bed which she usually occupied. The next he knew, she had reappeared and, at first, she had asked him if he would trust her for the money. That he declined to do, whereupon, almost echoing Polly Nichols, she told him: 'I haven't enough, but don't let it, Tim, I shan't be long before I'm in again.' The deputy was completely unsympathetic to her plight; he had heard it all before. He told her that that was all very well but 'you can find money for beer, but not for your bed'. Placed on the defensive, Annie had replied that she had 'only been to the top of the street; to "Ringer's".' Ringer's was The Britannia, a 'beer shop' on the corner of Dorset Street and Commercial Street, run by Mrs Ringer.

The witness continued by stating that he had not seen the deceased in company with any man that night. She had been in the habit of bringing a man to the house who was said to be a pensioner and was of soldierly appearance. He did not know the man's name or address, but he was about forty-five years old, about 5 feet 6 inches or 5 feet 8 inches tall, and of rather dark complexion. Sometimes he was dressed like a dock labourer, but at others he had quite a gentlemanly appearance. He had stayed at the house with the deceased on the night of Sunday the 2nd.

Apparently, Annie's paramour, obviously a man of double standards, was of a jealous disposition. Donovan said that he had been given instructions that he was not to allow her into the lodging-house if she was with any other men. She had, on occasion, brought different men back with her but, in accordance with 'The Pensioner's' instructions, Donovan had refused them admittance. What the witness did *not* say was by how much his palm had been greased to provide such a unique service.

In reply to questions from Mr Baxter, he went on to say that the deceased was always on very good terms with the other lodgers, and he never had any trouble with her. However, during the last week but one – on Tuesday, August 28th – to be precise, she had had 'a bit of a row' with another woman, in the kitchen, and had received a 'clout'. He had no knowledge of any other arguments. Shown a handkerchief, Donovan said he recognized it as one which the deceased used to wear. Annie had bought it from another lodger a week or two previously, and was wearing it when she left Crossingham's on the Saturday morning. She wore it 'three corner wise' around her neck and tied in a knot. There was a black woollen 'sort of scarf' underneath.

The next person to give evidence was John Evans, the night watchman at Crossingham's. He was an elderly man who seems to have had a closer, and more sympathetic, relationship with the lodgers than Donovan.

He told the inquest that it was he who had carried Donovan's message down to Annie when she was in the kitchen. She had told him that she had been to Vauxhall to see her sister, and that she had just been out for a pint of beer. When he asked her if she had the money for her bed, she told him what she was to repeat to Donovan – that she had not got enough, but would soon get it. Her last words to him had been: 'I won't be long, Brummie. See that Tim keeps the bed for me.' He had seen her off the premises, and then watched as she went up Little Paternoster Row towards Brushfield Street.

Questioned by the Coroner, Evans said he knew that Annie had been leading a rough life but, with the exception of 'The Pensioner', he did not know any man she was associated with. He did not know 'The Pensioner's' name or address but, on the morning that the body was discovered, he had called at Crossingham's and asked for the deceased. When Evans told him that Annie had been murdered, he went straight out of the house without saying a word. The witness had never heard any of the women in the house say that they had been threatened, or asked for money, by strangers.

The last witness, at what was really only a preliminary session of the inquest, was William Stevens. He had been described variously as a painter or a printer, but the former is probably correct. Stevens testified that he lodged at Crossingham's, and had seen Annie in the kitchen there at about ten past midnight on the morning of Saturday the 8th. He, too, had thought her the worse for drink. She had taken a box of pills from her pocket, but the box broke and she therefore wrapped the pills in a piece of torn envelope from the mantelpiece. Annie had then left the kitchen, and he had assumed that she was going upstairs to bed.

That concluded the evidence for the day and the hearing was adjourned, although groups of people lingered outside for hours discussing the murder.

The next day, when Inspector Chandler was preparing a detailed street map of No. 29 and the neighbouring houses, a small girl named Laura Sickings showed him what appeared to be bloodstains in the backyard of No. 25. There was a trail of them, running for some five or six feet up the path to the yard door, and on the fence adjoining No. 27 was a curious mark somewhere between a smear and a sprinkle. A piece of newspaper, absolutely saturated in what appeared to be blood, had already been discovered in the yard of the Black Swan pub at No. 23, where Joseph and Thomas Bayley had a packing-case business. Speculation therefore arose that the killer had climbed over the two fences from No. 29, had wiped his hands on the newspaper and thrown it over the fence, into No. 23, and had then entered Hanbury Street from No. 25. An alternative theory was that he had scaled three fences, to No. 23, and had merely dropped the paper there before leaving the premises. In the event, nothing came of those discoveries. The stains on the newspaper proved, on analysis, to be of human blood – and were never explained – but the others were of urine, which said more about the habits of the tenants than anything else!

The inquest was resumed at just after 3 p.m. on Wednesday the 12th.

One of the first witnesses was Mrs Amelia Richardson.

Mrs Richardson, said to have been 'of an advanced age', was not offered a chair during what was to be a lengthy examination, and it was to become increasingly obvious that standing for such a long time was causing her great distress.

She was a short woman, and was dressed entirely in black. Despite her age, she was clear and precise when giving her evidence. Firstly she told the inquest that she was a widow, and then went on to state that she rented No. 29, from which she carried on a packing-case making business with the help of her son, John, and a hired hand named Francis Tyler, who had worked for her for eighteen years.

On the 8th, her grandson, who lived with her, got up from bed at 6 a.m. and she sent him to find out why there was so much noise in the passage. He had returned with the news that there had been a murder, and so she went down immediately and saw the body lying in the yard. She had then returned to her room to attire herself properly, after which the police had taken possession of the house.

The witness told the Coroner that she had gone to bed at about half-past nine on the previous evening, but was very wakeful for half the night. She had heard no noise during the night, although she was awake at 3 a.m. and only dozed after that. At ten or fifteen minutes to four she had given Mr Thomson his usual early morning call, and had said 'Good morning' to him when he left the house at about 4 a.m. She had heard him leave the house, and could say quite definitely that he had not gone into the backyard.

Questioned by the jury, Mrs Richardson confirmed that she had property in the house and yard, but she was not concerned about the doors being left merely on the latch as she had never heard of any robberies.

Mr Baxter then took up the questioning again:

Q: 'Were the front and back doors of No. 29, Hanbury Street *always* left open?'

A: 'Yes, all the houses along the street leave their doors open. They are all let out in rooms, and people are coming in or going out at all hours of the night.'

Q: 'Did *you* ever see anyone in the passage at No. 29?'

A: 'Yes, about a month ago I heard a man on the stairs. I asked Mr Thomson, my second-floor tenant, to investigate, but the man said he was waiting for the Market to open.'

Q: 'At what time was this?'

A: 'Between half past three and four o'clock.'

Q: 'Coming now to the early hours of Saturday morning, the 8th of September, did you hear anyone go through the passage at that time?'

A: 'No. There is always a great bustle and noise on market mornings, but even so I would have heard even if someone had gone through later on, say about half past eight, although it wouldn't have attracted my attention as much.'

Q: 'You heard no cries?'

A: 'None.'

Q: 'Supposing a person had gone through at half past three, would that have attracted your attention?'

A: 'Yes.'

Q: 'You always hear people going to the backyard?'

A: 'Yes, people do frequently go through.'

Q: 'People go there who have no business to do so?'

A: 'Yes, I dare say they do.'

Q: 'But you still adhere to your statement that on Saturday morning no one *did* go through?'

A: 'Yes. If they *did* go through they must have kept purposively quiet.'

That caused a juryman to ask whether such people went there for an immoral purpose, but the reply he received was evasive: 'I would not allow such a thing if I knew about it.'

To her great relief, Mrs Richardson was allowed to go; her place being taken by Mrs Hardyman.

She said that she occupied the ground floor at No. 29, but had heard no noise at all during the night in question. Although she had often heard people going through into the yard she had never gone to see who they were. The dead woman was unknown to her and, as far as she was aware, she had never seen her before.

Next came Mrs Richardson's son, John, aged thirty-seven. His evidence was to cause a flurry at the time and has been a source of contention ever since. For a time, he had been regarded with suspicion by the police, both because of what he had told them and their finding of a leather apron in the backyard when the 'Leather Apron' hysteria was at its peak.

In a rather husky voice, he stated that he lived at No. 2, John Street, Spitalfields. He was a porter at Spitalfields Market, and also helped in his mother's business.

On one occasion he had discovered a man and a woman up to no good on the stairs at No. 29. As a result, he had adopted the habit of checking the building occasionally, when on his way to work at the Market, to make sure that prostitutes and their customers were not using it. He had increased the frequency of his visits after the cellar was broken into twice.

The questioning then turned to the morning of the 8th, and Richardson told Mr Baxter that he had called at No. 29 at between 4.40 and 4.45 a.m., his usual time for doing so on market days. The front door had been closed, and he had lifted the latch and gone along the passage. He had opened the back door and glanced to his right, to see if the padlock on the cellar door was intact. A piece of loose leather inside one of his boots had been making walking uncomfortable, and he had decided that then was a good time to sit down and remove it.

It is the following part of his evidence that has led to so much speculation and debate, because the reports of what he said he did next vary so widely. In order to cut off the offending piece of leather, he is stated, variously, to have 'sat on the step', 'stopped on the steps', 'sat down on the yard steps', 'stopped at the entrance to the yard', 'sat down on the top step with his feet on the flags of the yard', and 'stood on the steps'. So many differing accounts have been published, and that is frustrating, to say the very least, because what he *actually* did is vital when trying to establish the time of Annie's death. Richardson always maintained that he could not have failed to notice the body had it been there, but other evidence suggests that it was. In order to clear up this point once and for all, therefore, let us pick up from where the witness had glanced towards the cellar door. Mr Baxter is carrying out the questioning:

Q: 'What did you do next?'
A: 'I cut a piece of leather off my boot with a table knife.'
Q: 'What is the size of that knife?'
A: 'About five inches long.'
Q: 'Do you usually carry this knife with you?'
A: 'No, usually I keep it at home in John Street, but this morning I had been cutting up carrots to feed my rabbit, so I just slipped the knife into my pocket. I don't know what made me do it.'
Q: 'What did you do after cutting the leather from your boot?'
A: 'I put the knife back into my pocket and left for work.'
Q: 'Did you close the back door?'
A: 'No, *it closed itself*. [My italics.] I shut the front door, however.'
Q: 'How long were you there?'
A: 'Not more than two minutes at most.'

Richardson went on to say that it had not been light, but was getting so and he could see 'all over the place'. He could not have failed to notice the body had it been lying by the steps.

Q: 'Did you sit on the top step?'
A: 'No, on the middle step, so that my feet rested on the flags in the yard.'
Q: 'You must have been quite close to where the deceased was found?'

A: 'Yes.'

Q: 'Have you ever seen any strangers there?'

A: 'Yes, plenty, at all hours, both men and women. I have often turned them out. I have even found them on the first-floor landing.'

Q: 'Do you mean that they go there for an immoral purpose?'

A: 'Yes they do.'

The Coroner observed that he did not seem to have taken much trouble to see that the cellar *was* all right, but the witness replied that he could see the padlock was on the door.

Richardson went on to say that, in Spitalfields Market, a man called Pearman had told him that there was a murder in Hanbury Street. He had gone to see what was what, but found the police on guard at No. 29 and had therefore gone into the yard at No. 27. From there he had seen the body 'two or three minutes before the doctor came'.

There were no more questions, but the Coroner was not quite finished with the witness. He thought that he, the jury, and the police should see the knife with which Richardson said he had tried to trim his boot. The witness was therefore sent off home to fetch it.

Some of his evidence had been so much at odds with that given by his mother that Mrs Richardson was recalled in an effort to clarify the discrepancies. The jury was also eager to learn more about the leather apron which, some of the members had discovered, had been found in the backyard. News of that find had been withheld by the police because of the hue and cry about 'Leather Apron' at the time, but now it was to be made public.

Mrs Richardson began by repeating what she had said earlier about not being afraid of leaving the doors unlocked because she had never heard of any robberies. At that, she was confronted with the contradictory evidence given by her son and, for a moment, she appeared rather disconcerted. Then, recovering herself, she explained that it had been 'a long while ago' that she had missed a hammer and a saw from the cellar after it had twice been broken into early in the morning. Until then, she used to lock the cellar door, but after it was 'put to' it had been padlocked. She knew that her son was in the habit of visiting the house to see that everything was all right.

Mr Baxter then asked her whether, at any time, she had suspected that a part of the house was used for an immoral purpose. Mrs Richardson replied that she had not, and was quite indignant at the suggestion, and the also, by now, widespread rumour that it was: 'I am greatly shocked by this murder,' she said, 'for my rooms are regularly used for prayer meetings, and both me and my landlord are very angry that a slur should have been put on the respectability of the house.' The words absolutely rattling out by now, she protested vehemently that she had no knowledge of women having been found on the first-floor landing, and denied that her son had ever mentioned such a thing to her.

From what she had said, it was apparent that the owner of the house had not been at all pleased to discover that it seemed to be common knowledge that his property was being used regularly by prostitutes. Perhaps fearful of losing her lease, and with it her business, Mrs Richardson was bound to have denied knowing of the 'goings on', but it is difficult to believe that she did not know.

That point out of the way, the witness was shown the leather apron which had been found in the backyard. She identified it as belonging to her son, adding that he wore it when working in the cellar. Needless to say, the Coroner had some questions:

Q: 'It is a rather dangerous thing to wear, is it not?'
A: 'Yes.'
Q: 'Can you explain to us how the apron happened to be under the water tap in the backyard when it was found by police?'
A: 'Yes, I can. Last Thursday I found the apron in the cellar, where it had got mildewed – my son hadn't used it for a month – so I put it under the tap intending to wash it, and left it there.'
Q: 'The apron remained there from Thursday to Saturday?'
A: 'Yes. On the Saturday morning, the police found it in exactly the same position as I had left it, and took it away together with an empty nail box. On the Friday night, there

was a pan, full of water, by the tap, and that was also found
in the same place on the Saturday morning.'

Q: 'Was the tap used?'

A: 'Yes, by all of us in the house. The apron was on the stones.'

When John Richardson returned with the knife which he had been
sent to fetch, it turned out to be a much worn, and quite blunt, dessert
knife. It came as no surprise, therefore, when Richardson told the
Coroner that it had not been sharp enough to trim the leather in his
boot properly, and that he had been forced to borrow a sharper one at
the Market to complete the job. Nevertheless, Mr Baxter decided that
the police should have it, and handed it to Inspector Chandler.

Questioned about his previous evidence, Richardson unhesitat-
ingly contradicted his mother about the nocturnal visits of men and
women to No. 29, which she had said she would not have allowed
had she known of them: 'My mother has heard me speak of people
having been in the house. In fact she has heard them herself!'

With that, Richardson was allowed to go on his way, no doubt to
face a tongue lashing from his irate mother.

Mr Baxter eventually adjourned the inquest, telling the jury: 'The
doctor will be here first thing tomorrow.'

Contrary to what Mr Baxter had said, the doctor was *not* there first
thing on the morning of Thursday the 13th. Instead it was the hapless
Inspector Chandler who faced the somewhat hostile jury and the
inquisitive and at times merciless Coroner.

He began his evidence by explaining that he had been the Duty
Inspector at Commercial Street police station on the morning of
Saturday the 8th, and told of how John Davis had come running in at
ten past six shouting: 'Another woman has been murdered!' Having
heard his blurted tale, Chandler had immediately sent two constables
to No. 29, and had followed very shortly after, leaving word of what
was going on for his superiors. When he arrived at Hanbury Street –
he had run all the way – he found a number of people in the passage,
but there was nobody in the yard.

There he found a woman 'lying on her back, dead, left arm resting on left breast, legs drawn up, abducted, small intestines and flap of the abdomen lying on right side above right shoulder, attached by a cord with the rest of the intestines inside the body; two flaps of skin from the lower part of the abdomen lying in a large quantity of blood above the left shoulder; throat cut deeply from left and back in a jagged manner right around the throat.'

One of the constables was despatched straightaway to fetch the divisional police surgeon, whilst the other was sent back to the station to fetch assistance, and to arrange for telegrams to be sent to Detective Inspector Abberline 'and to several other officers'. Inspector Chandler remained in charge of the yard and the body.

As soon as he had the police help for which he had sent, he had the passage cleared of onlookers and covered the body with a piece of sacking acquired from a neighbouring house.

The doctor and his assistant arrived at about 6.30 a.m. He declared life extinct, and said that the woman had been dead for at least two hours.

After the body had been removed to the same mortuary shed which had housed the corpses of Martha Tabram and Polly Nichols, the Inspector and Dr Phillips had made a careful search of the yard. About eighteen inches from the ground on the back wall of the house, and behind where Annie's head had been, they had discovered 'six patches of blood varying in size from a sixpence to a point'. There were some more patches and smears of blood on the wooden fence nearby, about fourteen inches from the ground and immediately above the blood which had flowed from the neck.

Close to where the head had been was a small portion of an envelope which contained two pills. The words 'Sussex Regiment' were embossed in blue on the back. On the address side was the letter 'M', in a man's handwriting, with 'Sp' lower down – the rest having been torn away. There was a postmark 'London, August 20 [or 23 or 28 – reports vary] 1888'.

Lying near where the feet had been, they found a piece of coarse muslin, a small toothcomb and a pocket comb in a paper case. They also discovered a flat piece of steel, which was identified by Mrs Richardson as a spring belonging to her, an empty nail box and, about two feet from the water tap, the Inspector had found a leather apron which he had shown to the doctor.

Continuing, Inspector Chandler stated that there were no signs of a struggle having taken place. The woman's clothes had been old and dirty, and consisted of:

A long black figured jacket
A silk neckerchief
A black skirt
Two cotton petticoats
Two bodices (one brown)
Red and white striped stockings
Lace-up boots

The jacket was hooked at the top and buttoned down the front. There were bloodstains inside and outside of the collar, and two or three spots of blood on the left arm. He noticed a little blood on the outside of the back of the skirt, but the petticoats were hardly stained and the bodices had blood only around the neck. No blood was found on the stockings.

Annie's clothes had not been cut or torn, but the large pocket, which she wore under her skirt and tied round her waist, had been torn down the front and the side and was empty.

Replying to the Coroner, the witness said that, in his opinion, it would have been quite possible for anybody to open the back door partially, and glance in the yard, without being aware that a body was lying behind it.

That completed the Inspector's evidence and he stood down, at which the foreman of the jury, Mr Thorpe, took the opportunity to say that he would like to raise the question of a reward. He said that although rewards were being offered locally, he thought that 'something might be found out' were the government to offer one, and for a more substantial sum. Mr Baxter told him that, although he was speaking without any real knowledge of the situation, he had been informed that the government had decided not to give rewards in the future. That decision applied to murders generally, and was not directed at this case in particular.

There then followed some minor police evidence, of a purely formal nature, following which, and at last, the police surgeon was called.

Dr George Bagster Phillips, MRCS, declared that his surgery and residence were at No. 2, Spital Square, Spitalfields, and that he had been the police surgeon for 'H' Division for twenty-three years. A pompous man, he was determined to safeguard the police interests and assert his authority.

It all started off quietly enough. The doctor said that he had been summoned by a constable at 6.20 a.m. on the 8th. When he arrived at No. 29, he found the police guarding the body of a female which was to the left of the steps in the backyard.

The left arm was placed across the left breast, and the legs were drawn up, with the knees turned outwards and the feet resting on the ground. He discovered the face to be bruised and swollen, and turned on its right side, with the tongue, which was very swollen, protruding between the teeth but not beyond the lips. Upon touching the corpse, he found it to be cold, except under those intestines which still remained in the body. Stiffening of the limbs had begun, but was not marked.

There were terrible mutilations, with the throat having been severed deeply by jagged incisions which reached right around the neck.

In reply to questions from Mr Baxter, the witness stated that, in his opinion, the same instrument had been used for all the mutilations. It must have been a very sharp knife, with a thin narrow blade and at least six to eight inches long. He did not think that a bayonet or a sword-bayonet had been used; what was more likely was an instrument such as a medical man would use at post-mortem examinations, although ordinary surgical cases might not carry such an instrument. There was the possibility that a well-ground slaughterman's knife had been used, but he did not consider that one as used in the leather trade would have been long enough in the blade.

Dr Phillips's next comments caused a noticeable stir of excitement. He said that the whole of the body was not present, and the way in which the missing parts had been severed from the abdomen showed signs of 'anatomical knowledge'.

He thought that the woman had been dead for at least two hours, and probably longer, before he examined her at 6.30 a.m. However, it was only fair to say that it had been a fairly cool morning, and the body was likely to have cooled more rapidly because of the loss of so much blood.

There had been speculation that Annie may have been killed elsewhere and her body merely dumped in the backyard. Mr Baxter, as usual, was determined to lay such rumours to rest and therefore asked the doctor the question directly. He was told that, in the opinion of the witness, the deceased had been alive when she entered the yard.

With that out of the way, Dr Phillips resumed his tale of events by saying that he had carried out a search of the yard. He told of the finding of the articles and bloodstains already mentioned by Inspector Chandler, but added that the items at the foot of the body appeared to have been 'arranged in order'.

The questioning then turned to the doctor's post-mortem examination, which he had begun at 2 p.m. on Saturday the 8th. Before giving his findings, however, he made a vigorous protest about having to conduct such examinations in an inadequate shed instead of a proper mortuary, and was highly critical of the fact that the body had been 'attended to', and probably washed, before his arrival. In making his complaint about the 'mortuary', Dr Phillips knew that he would have the support of the Coroner because he himself had made a similar plea for better facilities at the conclusion of Polly Nichols's inquest. What he could *not* have foreseen is that his remarks about the body having been 'attended to' would rebound upon the very people whose interests he was determined to protect. Although it necessitates taking events out of sequence, it is probably logical to recount the outcome now.

Following the criticism of the slipshod mortuary arrangements revealed at Polly's inquest, and the public disquiet at the idea of male paupers stripping and washing the bodies of females, the Parish Guardians had decreed that in future only nurses would be employed on such duties. Dr Phillips must therefore have assumed that someone in authority at the workhouse infirmary had issued the instructions in this particular case, and would have felt quite safe in making his complaint.

He had, however, underestimated Mr Baxter's intense curiosity, and his almost intuitive detection of the slightest hint of police inefficiency. Determined to get to the bottom of the matter, if only to ensure that there was no such carelessness in the future, he had had enquiries made of the Clerk to the Parish Guardians. Those enquiries revealed that the Clerk had indeed appointed the nurses, Mary Elizabeth Simonds and Frances Wright, and the Coroner therefore had the senior of the two, Nurse Simonds, summoned as a witness.

When she appeared before him, she gave an account which completely justified whatever suspicions Mr Baxter may have had. Annie's corpse had arrived at the mortuary at between 7 and 7.30 a.m., and from then on police and officials had been in and out all day. It was quite true that the Clerk had told the nurses of the murder, and had instructed them to attend at the mortuary but, said Nurse Simonds, when they arrived there it was actually Inspector Chandler who told them that they could proceed with the laying-out! As one would expect, Inspector Chandler immediately, and indignantly, denied Nurse Simonds's allegation, but she had had no reason to lie, and there was no doubt who Mr Baxter believed.

The doctor now began to give the details of what he had discovered during his examination.

He had found the same protrusion of the tongue as he had seen earlier, and there was an old scar on the left of the forehead. The face was swollen and, in addition to general bruising, there was a bruise over the right temple and another on the upper lid of the right eye. There were two more bruises, each the size of the top of a man's thumb, on the front of the chest.

The fingernails and lips were turgid, and there was an abrasion over the first joint of the ring finger, with distinct markings of a ring or rings, probably the latter. On the right hand, there was a bruise over the middle part of the bone. By then, the stiffness of the limbs was well marked, and was more noticeable on the left side – especially in the fingers, which were partially closed.

Dr Phillips repeated his previous evidence about the way in which the throat had been cut, but added that the incisions seemed to have been made from the left. On the left side of the spine there were two easily discernible clean cuts; they were parallel, and about half an inch apart. There were indications that some attempt had been made to separate the bones of the neck in order to cut off the head.

At that point the doctor paused. He then told Mr Baxter that there had been other mutilations but, as he was satisfied that the cause of death arose from the injuries which he had just described, 'I think I had better not go into further detail of those mutilations, which can only be painful to the feelings of the jury and the public.'

Mr Baxter looked at him in amazement. Perhaps more than most coroners, he was very mindful of the duties of his office which, amongst other things, obliged him to enquire into the nature and size of *every* wound, and to ensure that they were all recorded. Dr Phillips was well aware of those requirements, and one can but wonder why he saw fit to say what he said.

The Coroner, however, for the time being, allowed the witness to have his way and Dr Phillips continued with his other evidence.

He was of the opinion that the woman's breathing had been interfered with previous to death, and that death itself had been caused by syncope, or failure of the heart's action in consequence of the loss of blood which had resulted from the severance of the throat.

Questioned by Mr Baxter, he replied that the dead woman was far advanced in tuberculosis of the lungs, and that the disease had even affected the membranes of her brain, but neither had anything to do with the cause of death. The stomach had contained a little food, but there was no sign of any fluid, and no appearance of the deceased having taken alcohol for some hours before her death. There were, however, indications of great deprivation, and he would say that she had been 'badly fed'.

The Coroner then turned his attention to the injuries which the deceased had sustained and asked whether any of them could have been self-inflicted, but Dr Phillips was adamant that they were not. As for the bruises which he had found, those on the face, and especially those about the chin and the sides of the jaw, were obviously recent. The others, on the front of the chest and the one on the temple, were much older and had probably been caused days before. He thought that the murderer had taken the woman by the chin and had then begun the incision from left to right. He did not consider that she had been gagged, the protruding tongue and swollen face being more indicative of suffocation, and therefore it was highly probable that she could have called out.

With that, Dr Phillips was allowed to leave, and the inquest adjourned. On the next morning, Friday, September 14th, Elisa Anne Chapman was laid to rest at Manor Park – like Polly Nichols in a common grave (No. 78, Square 148). At the family's request the arrangements were kept secret, and there was no procession.

At 3 p.m. on Wednesday the 19th, Mr Baxter was once more seated in his chair in the Alexandra Room, and Dr Phillips was recalled, to give details of the mutilations. Dr Phillips wasted no time in renewing his objections: 'I still think it is a great pity that I should have to give this evidence.'

That buttered no parsnips with the Coroner, who told him: 'Dr Phillips, whatever may be your opinion and objections, it appears to me necessary that *all* the evidence you have ascertained from the post-mortem examination should be on the records of the court for various reasons which I need not enumerate. However painful it may be, it is necessary in the interests of justice.' Mr Baxter did, though, make one concession to Dr Phillips's supposed sensibilities: 'I see, however, that there are several ladies and boys in the room, and I think that they might retire.'

In the event, the Press responded to Mr Baxter's indirect appeal that all the gory details should not be published, but they *were* printed in the *Lancet* of September 29th, 1888.

'It appears that the abdomen had been entirely laid open; that the intestines, severed from their mesenteric attachments, had been lifted out of the body, and placed by the shoulder of the corpse; whilst from the pelvis the uterus and its appendages, with the upper portion of the vagina and the posterior two-thirds of the bladder, had been entirely removed. No trace of these parts could be found, and the incisions were cleanly cut, avoiding the rectum, and dividing the vagina low enough to avoid injury to the cervix uteri.'

Having finally obtained the information which he had been determined to have, Mr Baxter proceeded to subject the hapless doctor to what was virtually an exhaustive cross-examination, and the answers to his questions make interesting reading.

Dr Phillips said that the missing parts had obviously been removed by an expert, or one who, at least, had enough anatomical knowledge to remove the pelvic organs with one sweep of the knife. In his opinion, the instrument, like the one which had divided the neck, must have been very sharp and at least five or six inches long – or probably longer. He did not think that he could have carried out all the injuries and mutilations, even if the victim had not struggled, in less than fifteen minutes. Had he performed the cutting in the deliberate manner of a surgeon, it would probably have taken him the better part of an hour.

He was allowed to stand down, and we may be sure that both he and the Coroner were heartily relieved to see the back of each other.

Next to be questioned was Elizabeth Long, sometimes named as Elizabeth Darrell/Durrell, of No. 32, Church Street.

The witness told the court that she was married to James Long, a park-keeper. On the morning that Annie was killed, Mrs Long had been walking along Hanbury Street on her way to Spitalfields Market. She was on the same side of the street as No. 29 and, as she approached the house, she saw a man and a woman on the pavement near the shutters of Mrs Hardyman's shop. Both were half turned away from her, the man's back being towards Brick Lane and the woman's towards the Market, but she saw the woman's face quite clearly. She had never seen her before, but later, in the mortuary, she had identified her as the deceased. Mrs Long said that she came alongside the couple just as the brewery clock struck half-past five, and heard the man say: 'Will you?', to which the woman had answered: 'Yes', but she heard nothing more.

In reply to Mr Baxter, Mrs Long stated that the man was 'very dark', probably over forty years of age, and looked like a foreigner. He was a little taller than the woman, and wore a brown deer-stalker hat and what the witness remembered vaguely as being 'a dark coat'. Her general impression of him had been one of 'shabby gentility'.

The appearance of the next witness caused quite a little stir. Most people who knew anything at all about Annie's killing had heard of her mysterious lover, 'The Pensioner', and the police had made the finding of him one of their priorities. Nevertheless it will come as no surprise to readers to learn that they had been unsuccessful, although it would transpire that he lived only some 350 yards from Dorset Street – and much closer to the murder site – was moving about openly, and was even known personally to some members of the jury! Their problem was solved for them when, on the evening of Friday the 14th, 'The Pensioner' himself walked calmly into Commercial Street police station and said he understood that they wished to interview him. They did indeed, and Inspector Helson lost no time in taking down a statement.

'The Pensioner', it turned out, was one Edward ('Ted') Stanley, and now everyone in the Alexandra Room waited to hear what he had to say for himself.

He was a tall, upright man of military appearance, and was described as being 'superior to the ordinary run of those who frequent the lodging-houses of Spitalfields'. It came as something of a surprise, therefore, when he began his evidence by stating that he was a bricklayer's labourer. Stanley gave his age as forty-seven, and said that he lived at No. 1, Osborne Place, off Brick Lane.

Answering the Coroner, he confirmed that he had known the dead woman. They had been acquainted for about two years, and he had visited her at Crossingham's 'once or twice, and at other times elsewhere'.

Apart from the obvious reason for wanting to question Stanley, the police had been interested in him because, being by reputation an army pensioner, they wondered if there was any connection between him and the piece of envelope bearing the crest of the Sussex Regiment. Obviously they had primed Mr Baxter about this, and no doubt he too was interested in the supposed military background of the witness. As was his way, he did not beat about the bush in trying to satisfy his curiosity and his probing questions made Ted Stanley decidedly uncomfortable:

Q: '*Are* you a pensioner?'
A: 'Am I bound to answer that question?'
Coroner: 'You have to answer *all* questions affecting this case.'
A: 'No, I am not a pensioner.'

Q: 'Did you belong to the Essex regiment?'
A: 'No, neither that nor any other regiment.'

As far as 'The Pensioner' was concerned it was all too humiliating for words. For years he had told people that he was a former soldier drawing a pension from the Essex Regiment, and now his world of pretence was shattered. Only too well aware that his reputation would be ruined if the news got out, he was driven to pathetic protest: 'What I say will be published all over Europe,' he lamented. Then, indignation succeeding self-pity, he told the Coroner angrily that he had lost five hours' work to come and give his evidence, adding: 'When you talk to me, sir, you talk to an honest man.'

Actually, Stanley did have *some* military connections, although they were not what he had put out. He belonged to what we now call the Territorial Army: in his case, the 2nd Brigade, Southern Division, of the Hants. Militia. Coincidentally, he had been away with them to Fort Elson, Gosport, Hampshire, for the annual summer camp, from August 6th until just before he met Annie on September 1st.

That little mystery cleared up, Mr Baxter's questioning took a different tack. Stanley told him that the last time he had seen Annie alive had been between 1 p.m. and 3 p.m. on Sunday, September 2nd. [Donovan had testified that the couple stayed together at Crossingham's on that Sunday night, but all the evidence is that he was mistaken.]

Stanley concluded his evidence by stating that he knew of no one with whom the dead woman had been on bad terms, and he was then allowed to go. Off he went, glad to be out of the place, but almost certainly dreading the reception he would receive from those to whom he had bragged in the past. One cannot help but feel rather sorry for him.

The testimony of the next witness was to contribute another minor mystery to the riddle of precisely *when* Annie was killed.

He was Albert Cadosch/Cadoche/Cadosh, a 23-year-old carpenter who lodged at No. 27, Hanbury Street. The jury heard that he had arisen at 5.15 on the morning of the 8th, and had immediately gone out to the privy in the backyard. As he passed the dividing fence with No. 29, he heard a woman say 'No, no', but his call of nature had been rather urgent and he had not stopped. On his way back, 'a few minutes later', he had heard a sound as if someone had fallen heavily against the fence, but then there was silence and so he hurried off to work. He had not seen anybody about in Hanbury Street, and the time, as he passed Spitalfields Church, had been 5.32.

William Stevens was then sworn in. He was a painter who lived at Crossingham's – together, it would seem, with half of Spitalfields! The last time he had seen Annie was at 12.20 on the morning of her death. They were in the kitchen at Crossingham's and, according to him, she was *not* the worse for drink. He had watched as she took a box of pills from her pocket, but the box had broken and the pills had dropped out. She had therefore walked across to the mantelpiece over the fire, where various slips of paper were kept for use as spills and had taken a piece of envelope in which she wrapped the pills.

Replying to the Coroner, Stevens said that Annie had then left the kitchen saying that she would not be long out of bed.

That was all Stevens had to contribute, and it would appear that, by then, even the Coroner thought it time for the proceedings to be brought to a halt. Turning to the jury, he said: 'Well, that is all the evidence there is. Now it is a question for you to say whether you would like to close the inquest or have it adjourned.' He sat back and waited whilst the jurymen conferred, and then the foreman told him that they had decided upon an adjournment, 'to see if the police can get further evidence.' We can be quite sure that Mr Baxter had his own views on *that* likelihood, but it was all one to him and the inquest was adjourned for a week, until Wednesday, the 26th.

On the following day, Thursday the 20th, there was a conference between some of the detectives engaged on the case. It was prompted by the evidence given by Albert Cadosch, which seems to have come as something of a surprise to them, and resulted in yet another examination of the yard at No. 29.

This time it was discovered that there was an 'aperture' in the palings of the dividing fence, immediately above the place where Annie's body had lain. Through it, the body could have been plainly visible from No. 27, whilst anyone moving in the yard might easily have been seen. Obviously, those discoveries cast strong doubts upon what young Cadosch had said.

Even so, they had another conflict of evidence to explain: Dr Phillips had put the death at about 4.30, while Mrs Long had said she saw Annie alive at 5.30. This remained unsolved, and when the inquest was resumed on Wednesday the 26th, it came as no real surprise to anyone that the police had discovered nothing of value during the preceding week.

Neither was the verdict when it came, a surprise: 'Wilful murder against some person or persons unknown.'

Yet, without a shadow of a doubt, Dark Annie's murder caused more of a sensation, and had more far-reaching repercussions, than any other in the series. Murder was not uncommon in the East End, but most received little or no publicity. It was only with Annie's slaying, kept constantly before the public with the newspaper reports on the protracted inquest, that there came a general awareness that there had now been three similar killings in a month, each more brutal than the last. Even the national newspapers had taken an interest in what was going on, and their extensive coverage startled the whole country, if not the world. An editorial in the *Daily Telegraph* had brought the reality home to countless readers, and was in the vanguard of what was to become a public clamour for better conditions for the hitherto despised and ignored denizens of the East End:

> Dark Annie's' dreadful end has compelled a hundred thousand Londoners to reflect what it must be like to have no home at all except the common kitchen of a low lodging-house, to sit there, sick and weak and bruised and wretched, for lack of fourpence with which to pay for the right of a 'doss'; to be turned out after midnight to earn the requisite pence, anywhere and anyhow; and in the course of earning it to come across your murderer . . . 'Dark Annie' will effect . . . what fifty Secretaries of State could never accomplish.

More murders were to come, and far worse mutilations, but it was Annie Chapman's which caused the change in public opinion, and the outcry which resulted must have given even the killer pause for thought before, as we shall see, he ventured on to the dark streets again.

6

Long Liz

THE MURDER OF ANNIE Chapman created a panic in the East End, along with such a burst of activity from the police and vigilante groups that her killer must have been shaken. The increased awareness of the public in general and prostitutes in particular made the Spitalfields/Whitechapel area a dangerous place in which to continue his activities. So it surprised very few that the next murder was perpetrated to the south of the Whitechapel Road whereas all the others had been to the north.

It was in Berner Street, 'a narrow, badly-lit, but tolerably respectable' turning off Commercial Road, over half a mile from where Annie Chapman had breathed her last. It was taken up mostly with small terraced houses but, some 150 yards down, on the left, there was a large Board School on the corner with Fairclough Street.

On the other side of Berner Street, and only four houses up from the Fairclough Street intersection, was No. 40, an old two-storeyed building. Formerly a private dwelling, it had been converted in 1885 by some Jewish socialists to house the International Working Men's Educational Club. Although open to working men of all nationalities, it was patronized mainly by immigrant Jews. The Club was not popular with neighbours because of the noise which emanated from it, and the many rows which took place there necessitating police action.

No. 40 was quite large and could hold over 200 people. From the front door, a passage ran the length of the left side of the building and half-way along it were the stairs. The first room, to the right of the front door, was used as a dining room. Behind that, and along the passage to the rear of the building, was the kitchen which had a window in its passage wall. Beyond the stairs, and opposite the kitchen, was a side door which led into what was known as Dutfield's Yard and gave access to two outside water-closets. From the kitchen window it was possible to see who was using the side door, which had a fanlight above it from which there was a little illumination into the Yard at night. The stairs in the passage led up to the spacious meeting room, which had a small stage.

The main entrance to Dutfield's Yard was to the left of No. 40. It was guarded by two stout wooden gates, each 4 feet 6 inches wide. Although the gates were usually kept closed at night, there was a wicket in the right-hand one to allow access to the side door of the Club. This was used more than the one at the front where one had to knock for admittance.

Upon passing through the gates, the initial impression was of a narrow residential court about twenty-five yards long. For the first six yards, there was a dead wall on each side which meant that that section was in absolute darkness all night. The wall to the right was that of the Club which was, in all, about nineteen yards long. The whole of the left-hand side was occupied by three small dwellings tenanted by Jewish families, the members of which were mainly tailors or cigarette makers. From where the dead walls ended, there was some light at night from the cottages and from the kitchen and three upstairs windows of the Club.

At the far end of the court, facing the street, was the workshop of Walter Hindley, a sack maker. At first glance, it seemed that the workshop was all there was at that end, but that was an optical illusion. Just where the Club wall ended, there was a ninety degrees turn to the right, to an irregularly shaped area of the Yard which was twice as wide as the court section.

It contained an unused stable, which was next to Hindley's workshop, premises formerly occupied by 'Arthur Dutfield, van and cart builder', and abutting on to the rear of the Club but with no direct access to it, a brick-built, single-storeyed building which housed *Der Arbeter Fraint*, a Yiddish journal, *The Worker's Friend*.

Louis Diemschütz, a Russian Jew, was the steward of the Club, but his wife managed it during the day, when he was following his other occupation as a hawker of cheap jewellery. On Saturday, September 29th, he had decided to go quite far afield – to the market on Westow Hill, which was some ten miles to the south, by the Crystal Palace at Sydenham, in Kent.

On his return that evening, as he turned into Berner Street, he noticed the time by a clock in a baker's shop in Commercial Road, and was able to say later that it was about 1 a.m. that he drew into the entrance of Dutfield's Yard. After he had passed through the gates, his donkey shied a little to the left as the cart struck something on the ground. Diemschütz looked down and saw what appeared to him to be a heap of mud but, after prodding it it with the long handle of his whip, he realized that it was something else.

He jumped off the cart, struck a match and, in its flickering light, was shaken to discover the body of a woman stretched out on the ground, her feet towards the street. Not knowing whether she was drunk, unconscious or dead, he ran into the Club by the side door and first of all asked where his wife was 'because she is of a weak constitution and I did not want to frighten her'. He discovered her in the dining-room, enjoying herself with several members. Having told them of what he had found, he returned to the Yard with a candle.

A young member, Isaac Kozebrodski, a tailor's machinist, accompanied him, and the two men peered at the body. Just for a few seconds there was no sound from either of them as the horror of what they were seeing penetrated their minds. The woman's head seemed to have been almost severed from her body, and blood from her neck was running down the gutter almost to the side door. Then the spell was broken; Diemschütz and Kozebrodski ran off in the direction of Fairclough Street to find a policeman. Meanwhile, almost immediately after, two other members, Eagle and Isaacs, tore towards Commercial Road shouting 'Police!' at the tops of their voices.

The pace of events during that early morning of Sunday, September 30th, was to be fast and furious from that moment on. However, in order to appreciate the situation fully, it is now necessary for us to make our way to Duke Street, at the Aldgate end of Houndsditch, long known as 'The Jews' fruit market'. Midway along Duke Street was Church Passage, a dark, covered entry leading to the eastern corner of Mitre Square, which was just a couple of hundred yards within the boundary of the City of London.

Mitre Square was a gloomy place avoided by respectable people at night. Even PC Watkins, of the City of London police, must have had a slight feeling of apprehension every time his beat took him to its dismal precincts.

On the morning of Sunday, September 30th, he entered the Square from Mitre Street at 1.44, less than three-quarters of an hour after the discovery of the body in Dutfield's Yard. As was his custom, he began to look into the various corners and passages and started with the southern corner, to his right. He did not really expect to see anything unusual as he had passed the same spot less than a quarter of an hour before, and that is why he froze in his tracks, momentarily, when his lantern picked out a form lying on the ground. Warily he approached the inert figure for a closer inspection and found that it was the body of a woman, but one in such a condition as he had never seen in all his seventeen years on the force.

She was lying on her back in a pool of blood, with her clothes thrown up. Her throat was cut and her abdomen ripped open. Part of her intestines were over her right shoulder.

That was quite enough for Watkins; he ran across to a warehouse, found the nightwatchman and sent him for help. Then, albeit reluctantly, he returned to maintain a solitary and nerve-racking vigil over the mutilated corpse.

Far more people had been involved in the discovery of the first body and that, coupled with the fact that then, as now, the City was largely uninhabited at weekends, ensured that word of the Berner Street killing spread much faster than the news of the second. Hordes of would-be sightseers had descended upon the Berner Street area well before dawn on that Sunday morning, but they were to be frustrated. With the experience gained from the previous murders, and the addition of fifty uniformed officers to the two principal police stations, the police had ensured that all approach roads were guarded, and constables were stationed all along Berner Street itself and outside the mortuary.

Although news of the Mitre Square atrocity may have been slower in getting out, the crowds which were attracted were, if anything, greater than those near Berner Street. By ten o'clock, the adjoining streets were so densely packed that all traffic was brought to a halt. For the few denizens of the area the whole event was a mixed blessing. Their lives were completely disrupted, but, following the precedent set in Hanbury Street, they managed to turn the whole business to their advantage by charging high prices for seats at their windows. Others were also quick to make a profit, and costermongers and newspaper boys did a thriving trade.

Even amidst all the uproar, complaints about the inefficiency of the police were to be heard on all sides, and many of the frustrated spectators voiced the opinion that the 'coppers' would have been better employed in trying to track down the killer than keeping them back from the murder site.

Throughout the whole of that Sunday, a stream of people, some under police escort, visited the mortuaries to which the two bodies had been taken in the hope that the dead women could be identified. Curiously, nobody was able to put a name to the Mitre Square victim, but the police achieved a quick success in the case of the Berner Street victim when, early in the morning, two men, John Arundell and Charles Preston, both of No. 32, Flower and Dean Street, Spitalfields, named her as Elizabeth Stride, known generally as 'Long Liz', 'a frequenter of the Flower and Dean-street lodging-houses'.

Long Liz's background was very different from that of her fellow victims. She was born on November 27th, 1843, at Stora Tumlehed Farm in the parish of Torslanda, which was immediately to the north of Gothenburg, in Sweden. Her parents were Beata Ericsson (née Carlsdotter) and Gustaf Ericsson, and she had two brothers and an older sister. On December 5th, 1843, she was christened Elisabeth Gustafsdotter, and she was confirmed in 1859.

In 1860, Elisabeth left the farm and entered domestic service with a family in Gothenburg, but that came to an end when, in 1864, she was found to be pregnant.

That left her in a desperate situation because, unlike James Kelly's mother, she felt unable to turn to her family for help. Her mother had died of a chest complaint earlier in the year, and without her support Elisabeth was unwilling to go back to the farm to face the wrath of her father and the wagging tongues. Needless to say, there was no prospect of another job whilst she was in her condition and so, with no family and no means, she trod the path of so many girls before her in similar predicaments. By March 1865, she was registered by the police as prostitute No. 97, and on the 21st of the following month she gave birth to a still-born daughter.

In Sweden at that time, registered prostitutes were kept under strict medical supervision, and the periodic examinations resulted in Elisabeth being ordered into a hospital for venereal diseases on two occasions. She also received treatment for ulcers, the nature of which is not specified.

There can be little doubt that, at twenty-one, she was an attractive young woman. At that time she was described by the police as having a slender figure, an oval face, blue eyes, brown hair and a straight nose. Elisabeth was to retain her good looks; her mortuary photograph, when she was nearly forty-five, shows her to be the most attractive of the 'Ripper' victims to date.

Despite her attractiveness, and possibly because of her religious upbringing, her spell 'on the game' did not last for long and, on February 7th, 1866, she moved to London. Why she chose to go to England is not known, although it was said that she had relatives, on her mother's side, somewhere in Britain. Be that as it may, somehow she found her way to the East End of London and, on July 10th, 1866, she was registered as a member of the congregation of the Swedish Protestant Church, which stood in the centre of Prince's Square, off Cable Street, Stepney.

Probably through the good offices of the Swedish Church, it was not long before she was employed as a domestic servant by a family living near Hyde Park. She worked there for over two years and then, on March 7th, 1869, when she was twenty-five, she married a man nearly twice her age – John Thomas Stride, a 48-year-old carpenter.

We are not told why she should have married so much older a man. It may, of course, have been a love-match, but it is more likely that Elizabeth, as we must now call her, wanted British nationality and/or that she came to some kind of 'business arrangement' with Stride. Whatever the reason, it is a matter of fact that the couple's fortunes somehow took a dramatic turn for the better because within twelve months they were keeping a coffee shop in Poplar. It was there that Elizabeth first became known as 'Long Liz', which does not say much for the average height of the women of the East End – she was only five feet and five inches tall!

Two years later the Strides moved the business closer to the docks, and set up at No. 178, Poplar High Street – on the southern side of the East India Dock Road. They stayed there until 1874, but what happened after that is not clear. Elizabeth told her friends that her husband became a ship's carpenter at Sheerness, and that he and two of their children were drowned when she was a stewardess on the *Princess Alice*. However, this must be open to question.

When the *Princess Alice* sank in the Thomas in 1878, over 600 day trippers lost their lives. A relief fund was set up. The names of the claimants are known. The Strides were not among them. By then, in any case, for reasons unknown, the marriage had deteriorated to such an extent that Liz and her husband had separated. She was admitted to Poplar Workhouse on March 21st.

We do not know whether there were any children of the marriage whose welfare then had to be taken into consideration. 'Long Liz' claimed later that she was the mother of nine, two of whom had died on the *Princess Alice*. The others, she had said, 'were in a school belonging to the Swedish Church on the other side of London Bridge' or with friends of her husband. However, there were no schools in London connected with the Swedish Church.

Details of her life over the next four years are very sketchy. In 1878 she was said to be in very poor circumstances and received financial assistance from the Swedish Church. It is not known where she was lodging then, nor what she was doing for a living. Certainly her fortunes were at a very low ebb, and her mental state cannot have been helped when, in 1879, she received the news that her father had died a pauper on February 6th of that year.

The next reliable sighting of her which we have occurred on December 28th, 1881, when she was admitted to the Whitechapel Infirmary for a week, suffering from bronchitis. It would appear that she was then living at No. 35, Devonshire Street, where 240 families lived in only sixty four-roomed houses!

We are not told whether John Stride made an allowance to his wife after their separation. If he did, it seems unlikely that it continued for long as he was registered as a pauper when, on October 24th, 1884, he died from heart disease in the Poplar and Stepney Sick Asylum.

All the evidence tends to indicate that Elizabeth Stride was leading something of a double life from, at least, the beginning of 1882. In Devonshire Street she was apparently living quietly, earning a pittance from a little sewing and charring and attending the Swedish Church. In between times, however, she absented herself to lodge at No. 32, Flower and Dean Street, amongst other places, from where she went on drinking sprees and, at times, probably operated as a prostitute. However, it is only fair to say that there is no evidence for that supposition. Indeed there is no evidence, although we may suspect what we wish, that Long Liz had been immoral in any way after leaving Sweden until 1885. However, all that changed after John's death, either because of the cessation of any allowance or because his demise released her from her marriage vows – or both.

For the last three years of her life she cohabited with Michael Kidney, a waterside labourer, firstly at No. 35, Devonshire Street and then at No. 36. It is perhaps an indication of the nature of their relationship that once Liz was dead Kidney found it necessary to move to one of the cheapest lodging-houses in Spitalfields.

The inquest on Long Liz opened on October 2nd. Mr Wynne Baxter was the coroner in that case and so fireworks were expected.

Mr Baxter opened his inquest bang on time, at 11 a.m., in the Vestry Hall, Cable Street, St George-in-the-East, near Prospect Place. On this occasion, the mortuary was conveniently a hundred yards behind the Hall, in the public gardens surrounding St George's

Church, and therefore it did not take very long for the jury to view the body.

Local Inspector Edmund John James Reid, the newly appointed Head of 'H' Division, Whitechapel CID, was watching on behalf of the police.

William West, the first witness, told the court that he was the overseer of the printing office of *Der Arbeter Fraint*. Questioned about the events of Saturday the 29th, he explained that he himself was in the Club until about 9 p.m., at which time he went out to see an English friend home and did not return until about 10.30 p.m. Between a quarter and a half-past midnight, he went to the printing office to place some literature there and then left the Club by the street door, with his brother and another member, Louis Stanley, to go home. They went by way of Fairclough Street, and Grove Street.

Answering Mr Baxter, West stated that when he went to the printing office he had left the Club by the side door, and returned the same way. As he passed through the Yard on his way back, he had noticed that the gates were open, but there was nothing unusual to attract his attention.

Coroner:	'Can you say that there was no object on the ground?'
West:	'I could not say that.'
Coroner:	'Do you think it possible that anything can have been there without your observing it?'
West:	'It was dark, and I am a little short-sighted, so that is possible.'

West's place was taken by Morris Eagle, a Russian immigrant, who stated that he was a traveller in jewellery. On the evening of Saturday the 29th, he had chaired a discussion at the Club about the necessity for socialism amongst Jews. It had attracted an audience of some ninety persons. The discussion ended between 11.30 and midnight, and then most of the people left, by the street door, but some twenty or thirty remained upstairs, talking or singing, whilst around a dozen were downstairs. Between half-past eleven and a quarter to midnight, he had left to take his young lady home. They went out by the street door, but when he returned, at about twenty minutes to one, that door was closed and he had to go through the gates and gain entry by the side door.

Replying to the Coroner, he said that he thought he had walked through the middle of the gateway, and he had noticed nothing on the ground by the gates. It had been 'rather dark', however, and he could not say for certain whether anything was there or not. He could not remember seeing anyone in Berner Street on his way back to the Club.

He said that he had been singing in Russian with a friend when, after about twenty minutes, a member had rushed up and told them: 'There's a dead woman lying in the Yard!'

In Eagle's own words: 'I went down in a second and struck a match. I could then see a woman lying on the ground near the gateway, and in a pool of blood.'

He saw Diemschütz and another member hurrying towards Fairclough Street in search of a policeman. He, therefore, went in the opposite direction – to the Commercial Road – 'all the time shouting "Police!" ' – but it was not until he reached the corner of Grove Street that he discovered two Constables, and told them of the body.

Next came Louis Diemschütz, who related the events of his day right up to his running off in search of a policeman. He said that he had gone into the Club when the police reinforcements arrived, and stayed there. Nobody had been allowed to leave until they had been searched, and their names and addresses noted.

When the inquest was resumed at 2 p.m. the following day, the first witness was Constable Henry Lamb. He testified that he had been on duty in Commercial Road, between Christian Street and Batty Street, when, shortly before one o'clock, two men had come running towards him, shouting as they came. Lamb went to meet them and was told 'Come on, there has been another murder!' He asked where and, as the three men reached the corner of Berner Street, received the reply 'There'. 'I ran, followed by another constable 426 H.'

After sending Eagle for the duty inspector at Leman Street police station and PC Collins (426 H) for the doctor, Lamb had placed his hand on the woman's face and found it slightly warm, but he could detect no pulse. He had then blown his whistle for assistance.

The woman had been lying on her left side, her left hand on the ground; but the witness had not noticed if she was holding anything in it. Her right arm was across her breast, and her face was about five or six inches from the Club wall. There were no signs of a struggle, and the woman's clothing had not been disturbed; in fact only the soles of her boots were visible.

Questioned about the blood, Lamb replied that some was liquid and had run towards 'the kitchen door' of the Club, but he could not say whether it was still flowing from the woman's throat at that time. The little on the ground nearest to the body was slightly congealed.

Dr Blackwell had been the first doctor to arrive, but Lamb could only estimate that he had appeared on the scene some ten or twelve minutes after his own arrival because 'I had no watch with me'. Inspector Charles Pinhorn had followed closely on the doctor's heels.

Lamb did not know whether the body had been touched before he got there, but Dr Blackwell had scrutinized it, and the surrounding area, before Dr Phillips came some ten minutes later and made his own examination.

The gates had been wide open but, following the blowing of his whistle, several colleagues had appeared and Lamb had then had the gates closed whilst Dr Blackwell looked at the woman. Her feet had extended 'just to the swing of the gate', and so there was no disturbance of the body when the police closed them.

After stationing a constable at the entrance to the Yard, Lamb had gone into the Club. The fifteen to twenty members who were still inside were all on the ground floor. He had examined their hands and clothes, but had found no blood on them nor, indeed, anywhere in the Club.

Until then, Mr Baxter had displayed great patience during his thorough questioning of the witnesses. Now, however, he became quite acerbic with Lamb, the first policeman to give evidence:

Coroner: 'Was the steward present?'
Lamb: 'Yes.'

Coroner:	'Did you ask him to lock the front door?'
Lamb:	'I didn't; there was a great deal of commotion. That was done afterwards.'
Coroner:	'But time is the essence of the thing.'

Lamb was then forced to admit that he had not even tried the front door to see whether it was *already* locked, adding lamely that he had seen nobody leave.

Another sharp exchange followed, and by this time the hapless bobby must have been wishing that he was anywhere but under the merciless scrutiny of Mr Baxter.

Lamb:	'I afterwards went over the cottages, the occupants of which were in bed. I was admitted by men who came down partly dressed. As to the water closets in the Yard, one was locked and the other unlocked – but no one was there.' [He did not say how he could have been sure of that if one was locked!]
Coroner:	'There is a recess near the dustbin; did you go there?'
Lamb:	'Yes, afterwards with Dr Phillips. I examined the dustbin and the dung-heap.'
Coroner:	[One can hear the testiness in his voice.] 'But *I'm* speaking of at the time.'
Lamb:	'I did it subsequently.'
Coroner:	'Did you look over the wooden partition?'
Lamb:	'I don't recollect doing so,' [and then, in an effort to show he had done *something* right,] 'but I *did* examine the store belonging to Hindley's the sack makers, but I saw nothing there.'

Mr Baxter then asked whether the murderer could have escaped whilst he was examining the body and Lamb made the mistakes not only of failing to give a direct answer, but also of injecting a note of sarcasm into his reply: 'Several people were inside and outside the gate, and I should think that they would be sure to observe a man who had marks of blood.' He was wasting his breath; the Coroner had broken stronger men than him: 'But supposing he had *no* marks of blood?' Lamb surrendered, and gave the answer which he should have rendered in the first place: 'It was quite possible, of course, for a person to escape while I was examining the corpse. Everyone was more or less looking towards the body, and there was much confusion.' However he thought that the killer was more likely to have escaped *before* he arrived.

Frederick William Blackwell, a physician and surgeon living at No. 100, Commercial Road, testified that a policeman had come to his surgery at ten minutes past one on the Sunday morning and asked that he attend the scene of the crime. The witness had not been dressed at the time and therefore his assistant, Edward Johnston, had gone with the constable and the doctor had followed very shortly after.

Dr Blackwell said that he had looked at his watch upon arriving at the Yard, and the time was precisely 1.16 a.m. He added that Lamb must have been mistaken in his evidence, because the gates were closed when he got there.

The woman had been lying obliquely across the court, with her face towards the right wall. Her legs were drawn up, with the feet close to the wall and three yards from the gate. There was a rut, made by the wheels of carriages, which acted as a gutter. The victim's head had been resting beyond the rut, but her neck was directly above it and blood was running down it – away from the feet – and into the drain. There was, in fact, a stream of blood all the way to the side door of the Club, with 'about 1 lb. of clotted blood' close to the body. Her mouth was slightly open, but her facial expression was placid. There was a check silk scarf around her neck, with the bow turned to the left and knotted very tightly.

He had found the neck, chest and legs to be quite warm, whereas the face was only slightly so and the hands were cold. The blood-smeared right hand was open, and resting on the woman's chest, whilst the left, which was lying on the ground, was partially closed around a small packet of cachous wrapped in tissue paper. There were no rings, or marks of rings, on her fingers.

Moving on to the injuries which he had discovered, Dr Blackwell described an incision in the neck which started on the left side, 2½ inches below the angle of the jaw and in almost a straight line with it. The vessels on that side had been almost severed, whilst the windpipe was completely in two. The cut had ended 1½ inches below the right jaw, but had not damaged any vessels on that side. It corresponded exactly with the lower border of the scarf, which was slightly frayed, as if by a sharp knife. Answering the Coroner, the doctor said that he did not know whether the bloodstained hand had been moved before his arrival.

Coroner:	'Were there no spots of blood around?'
Blackwell:	'No, only some marks where blood had been trodden in.'
Coroner:	'Was there any blood on the soles of the deceased's feet?'
Blackwell:	'No.'
Coroner:	'No splashing of blood on the wall?'
Blackwell:	'No, but it was very dark, and what I saw was by the aid of a policeman's lantern and I have not examined the place since. I *did* examine the clothes, but found no blood on any part of them. I noticed she had a bunch of flowers in her jacket, and the bonnet of the deceased was lying on the ground a few inches from her head. Her dress was unbuttoned at the top.'

The doctor said that the clothes had not been wet with rain.

He thought it impossible that the injuries had been self-inflicted. In his opinion, the woman had been dead between twenty and thirty minutes when he arrived. She would have bled to death comparatively slowly because the vessels on only one side of the neck had been cut, and the artery had not been severed completely. There was absolutely no possibility of the deceased having been able to cry out after the throat had been cut.

The witness then described the arrival of Dr Phillips, some twenty to thirty minutes after his own, and then answered a question from a juror: 'Can you say whether the throat was cut before or after the deceased fell to the ground?'

Blackwell: 'I formed the opinion that the murderer probably
caught hold of the silk scarf, which was tightly
knotted, and pulled the deceased backwards, cutting
her throat in that way. The throat might have been
cut as she was falling, or where she was on the
ground. The blood would have spurted about if
the act had been committed while she was standing
up.'

Coroner: 'Was the silk scarf tight enough to prevent her calling
out?'

Blackwell: 'I could not say that.'

Coroner: 'A hand might have been put on her nose and mouth?'

Blackwell: 'Yes, and the cut on the throat was probably instantaneous.'

That concluded the evidence for that session and the inquest was
adjourned until 1 p.m. the following day.

In *The Times* that Tuesday, there appeared a letter which should
have given the authorities pause for thought. Dated October 1st, and
written by Edgar Sheppard, MD, from No. 42, Gloucester Square,
Hyde Park, London, W., it began:

Sir,
    I cannot help thinking that these Whitechapel murders point
to one individual, and that individual insane. Not necessarily an
escaped, or even as yet recognized, lunatic.

Dr Sheppard thought the killer could be someone with a delusion
that he had 'a mission from above' to destroy vice, and that was why
he was selecting prostitutes as his victims. He said there were many
such in the asylums.

The first witness on the next day of the inquest was Mrs Elizabeth
Tanner, a widow and the deputy at No. 32, Flower and Dean Street. It
was one of the many common lodging-houses used by prostitutes in
that truly awful sink of iniquity.

Mrs Tanner stated that she had recognized the body as being that of a woman 'who has lodged in our house, on and off, for the last six years. She was known by the nickname of "Long Liz".'

She and her lodger had been drinking in the Queen's Head, on the corner of Commercial Street and Fashion Street, until about 6.30 on the evening of Saturday the 29th. They then returned to the lodging-house, where the deceased had gone to the kitchen and the witness to 'another part of the building', and that was the last time Mrs Tanner saw Long Liz alive.

According to Mrs Tanner, Long Liz had left the man with whom she was living on Thursday the 27th. She had stayed at the lodging-house on the Thursday and Friday nights, but had not paid for a bed for the Saturday.

The deceased was described by Mrs Tanner as having been a very quiet, and sober, woman who sometimes stayed out late at night. On the Saturday evening in question, the deputy had paid her sixpence for cleaning two rooms, but she did not know whether Long Liz had any other money. There had never been any talk of her being frightened of anyone, or of having been threatened 'with injury'.

Michael Kidney, the Irishman with whom Long Liz had been living, now added further information on the mysterious victim.

Kidney stated that he was a waterside labourer, now living at No. 38, Dorset Street, Spitalfields. He had consorted with Elizabeth Stride for about three years.

Coroner:	'You had a quarrel with her on Thursday?'
Kidney:	'I didn't see her on Thursday.'
Coroner:	'When *did* you last see her?'
Kidney:	'On the Tuesday, and then I left her on friendly terms in Commercial Street. That was between nine and ten o'clock at night, as I was coming from work.'
Coroner:	'Did you expect her home?'
Kidney:	'I expected her home half an hour afterwards. I found out later that she'd been in and had gone out again, but I didn't see her again alive.'

Kidney went on to say that Long Liz had been perfectly sober when he last saw her, and he could give no reason for her sudden disappearance other than that she would occasionally go away. In total, she had done so for about five months during the three years he had known her, but she never gave any reasons for her absences.

Coroner: 'Do you know whether she had picked up with anyone?'

Kidney: 'I have seen the address of the brother of the gentleman with whom she lived as a servant somewhere near Hyde Park, but I cannot find it now.'

It was by no means a direct answer, and there was an implication in what he had said that should have been pursued. As it was, Mr Baxter told the witness sharply: 'That is not what I asked you. Do you think she went with anyone else?'

Kidney replied that he thought she liked him better than any other man, and he did not believe that she had left him on the Tuesday for a rival: 'It was drink that made her go before, but she always came back again.'

It then came out that the witness did not think the police were doing their job properly, and also that he had information that would enable a detective 'to discover the man at any time'. When questioned by Mr Baxter, he confirmed that on the night of Monday, October 1st, he had called at Leman Street police station, admittedly whilst drunk, and had requested the services of any young detective who was not known in the district. He already had *some* information, but 'the parties I obtained my information from know me, and I thought someone else would be able to get more from them'. Not surprisingly, the police had refused his request, especially after he had told them that if *he* had been the copper on the beat where Liz was murdered he would have killed himself!

Now, however, Inspector Reid intervened to ask: 'Will you give *me* the information directly, if you will not give it to the Coroner?' It was no good. What had gone before had been either drunken ramblings, out of which he was now trying to bluff his way, or else he did not wish to be branded publicly as a police informer. In any event, his answer was short and to the point: 'No, I will keep it to myself.'

Mr Baxter then turned to the subject of children, and Kidney said that Long Liz had had none by him. He then related the tale of the supposed nine children of the marriage.

Kidney was allowed to retire, but he had made a poor impression on those who saw him.

He was succeeded by Edward Johnston/Johnson, who stated that he lived at No. 100, Commercial Road, and was the assistant to Drs Kay and Blackwell.

He told the jury that he had been awakened by PC Collins at just after one o'clock on the Sunday morning. After rousing Dr Blackwell, he had accompanied the constable to Dutfield's Yard where, by the light of the policeman's lantern, he had seen a woman lying on her left side. There was an incision in her throat, but the wound had stopped bleeding. The body was 'all warm', except for the hands which were 'quite cold'. It was he who had undone the woman's bodice, in order to see if the chest was warm, but he had not moved any part of the body. There was very little blood near the neck, it having all run into the gutter and clotted. The woman's left arm was bent away from her body, whilst the right, also bent, was lying across it. Her bonnet was on the ground three or four inches 'beyond the head'.

Johnston said that the gates were closed shortly after his arrival, which was three or four minutes before Dr Blackwell appeared on the scene at precisely 1.16 a.m.

Not many people knew why the next witness, a mere lad, was there, but his evidence was to cause a minor sensation.

Young Thomas Coram gave his address as No. 67, Plumber's Row, and said that he worked for a coconut dealer.

On the evening of Sunday the 30th, he had gone to visit a friend living in Bath Gardens, Bath Street – off Brady Street. He had left his friend's house at nearly half-past midnight, and walked down Brady Street to the Whitechapel Road where he turned right, towards Aldgate. After a few yards, he had crossed to the other (the south) side of the road, and 'when opposite (in those days, the word 'opposite' was used to mean 'abreast of', as well as its present sense) No. 253, I saw a knife lying on the doorstep.'

Coroner: 'What is No. 253?'

Coram: 'A laundry. There were two steps to the front door, and the knife was on the bottom one.'

The knife was then produced and, to quote the *Daily Telegraph*, 'It was a knife such as would be used by a baker in his trade, it being flat at the top instead of pointed, as a butcher's knife would be.' The blade was discoloured by something resembling blood. It was 'quite a foot' long and an inch wide, whilst the black handle was six inches long and 'strongly rivetted in three places'.

Mr Baxter allowed the weapon to be examined and then, when the excitement had died down, Coram went on to say that he had not touched the knife, but when he saw a policeman approaching he told him what he had found.

The constable, PC Joseph Drage, then gave his version of events: 'As I went towards him, he beckoned and said: "Policeman, there's a knife lying here." I then saw a long-bladed knife on the doorstep and, when I picked it up, I found it was smothered with blood.'

Coroner: 'Was it wet?'

Drage: 'No – dry. There was a bloodstained handkerchief bound round the handle and tied with a string.'

Coroner: 'What did you do next?'

Drage: 'I asked the lad how he came to see it, and he told me: "I was just looking around and I saw something white." He said that the knife made his blood run cold because we heard of such funny things nowadays. I asked him what he did out so late and then, after I had taken down his name and address, he went to the police station with me.'

The constable added that he had passed the step a quarter of an hour before and, although he could not be sure, he did not think that the knife was there then. About an hour earlier, he had stood near the door and had seen the landlady let out a woman, but the knife was not there then. Later in the day, during the afternoon, he had given the knife and the handkerchief to Dr Phillips.

As it happened, Phillips was the next witness, and he could not have been too happy about appearing before Mr Baxter again.

He began his evidence by saying that he had been called to Leman Street police station at 1.20 on the morning of the murder. After being briefed, he had gone to Dutfield's Yard where he found Inspector Pinhorn and Acting Superintendent West with the body.

The woman was lying on her left side, with her face to the wall and her legs drawn up close to the wall and towards the street. Her left arm was extended, with the hand holding a packet of cachous, some of which had spilled into the gutter. The right arm was over the body, and the back of that hand and the wrist had clotted blood on them.

He had found that the body and the face were warm, and the legs 'quite warm', but the hands were cold. Producing the silk handkerchief which had been around the throat, Dr Phillips stated that the cut on it corresponded with the right angle of the jaw. The throat was deeply gashed, and there was an abrasion of about an inch and a quarter in diameter under the right clavicle.

At 3 p.m. on Monday, October 1st, he and Dr Blackwell had carried out a post-mortem examination in St George's Mortuary. Dr Reigate and Dr Blackwell's assistant, Edward Johnston, had been present for part of the time. The temperature in the mortuary was 'about fifty-five degrees'.

It was found that rigor mortis was still fairly marked. There was mud on the face and on the left side of the head, where it was matted in the hair. Decomposition of the skin had begun, and there were dark brown spots 'on the anterior surface of the left chin'.

Dr Phillips said that the body was 'fairly nourished'. Over both shoulders, especially the right, from the front under the collar bones, there was a bluish discoloration.

Upon removing the scalp they found no signs of bruising or bleeding between it and the skull-cap. The skull itself was about one sixth of an inch thick and of a dense texture, and the brain was 'fairly normal'. The deceased had not been wearing earrings, but the lower lobe of the left ear had at one time been torn through as if by the wearing of one, or its forcible removal, although it was now thoroughly healed. Her right ear was pierced for an earring, but it had not shown signs of similar damage.

There was a clean-cut incision in the neck, from left to right, of about six inches long. Beginning two and a half inches in a straight line below the angle of the jaw, it was three-quarters of an inch deep over an undivided muscle, but then it deepened to about an inch, dividing the membrane and the blood vessels. It then ascended a little, grazing the muscle outside the cartilages on the left side of the neck. All the vessels on the left side were completely severed in a line about one-twelfth of an inch deep, with the exception of the back of the carotid artery where the cut was not deep enough to divide it fully. The cut through the tissues on the right side of the cartilages was more superficial, and tailed off to about two inches below the right angle of that side of the jaw. Teeth on the left lower jaw were absent.

Regarding the rest of the body, Dr Phillips stated that there were no recent external injuries, although he had noticed some healing sores. He described the lungs as being 'unusually pale'. The heart was small, with the left ventricle firmly contracted but the right less so. There was no clot in the pulmonary artery, but the right ventricle was full of dark clot – the left being absolutely empty.

Upon examining the stomach, the doctors had found it to be large, with the lining congested. It contained the partly digested remains of the woman's last meal – bread, cheese and potatoes – but there was no trace of liquor.

There was a deformity in the lower fifth of the bones of the right leg, insomuch as they were not straight but bowed forward. The bones were straighter on the left leg, but there was a thickening above the ankle.

Dr Phillips stated firmly that death had been caused by the loss of blood from the partially severed left carotid artery, and the division of the windpipe. That led to questions about the blood in Dutfield's Yard to which the doctor gave much the same replies as his colleague, Dr Blackwell, but with the addition that, 'considering the stature and the nourishment of the body', he thought the flow of blood was 'unusual'.

There was much more that Mr Baxter wanted to hear from the witness, but the session had gone on for long enough. He therefore adjourned until 2 p.m. on Friday the 5th, making it quite clear to Dr Phillips that his presence would be required.

Day after day the newspapers received 'a vast amount of Correspondence upon the subject of these appalling crimes' and it contained a multitude of suggestions, comments and complaints. There were some recurring themes, amongst which the apathy of the Home Secretary, the inefficiency of the police, and the need for the latter to have their boots shod with rubber soles were popular. Another stemmed from the general opinion that only a foreigner, probably Jewish, could have been guilty of such terrible atrocities and that in the highly unlikely event that an Englishman was involved he must be mad. One of these letters appeared in the *Daily Telegraph* on that Wednesday. It was from 'X' of St Albans, and read:

> Sir,
>
> Just about twelve months ago, an inmate of the lunatic asylum at Leavesden, near Watford, escaped while out with others in the charge of keepers. He managed to get into the Bricket Woods, and has since evaded capture.
>
> The local paper warned females against being out at night in the neighbourhood, as this man was dangerous only to women. The question is, whether the authorities in London have had this lunatic's description, as the fearful crimes of the East-end point to such a person.

What the writer did not know was that even if 'the authorities in London' had been provided with a description the probability is that it would not have been brought to the attention of those actually engaged in hunting the killer. James Kelly's escape was more recent, but they did nothing to apprehend *him*. The Scotland Yard left hand just did not know what the right did.

The inquest reopened on Friday, October 5th, and the proceedings were watched by Superintendent Arnold and Detective Inspector Reid as the first witness, Dr Phillips, was recalled to say that he was convinced that the deceased had not swallowed the skin or seeds of a grape within 'many hours of her death'. (The significance of those remarks will be appreciated later.)

He then commented upon the discoloration on the right side of the neck which he had mentioned at the previous session. Apparently the staining had disappeared after having been washed, and the skin was found to be uninjured.

Mr Baxter questioned him about the knife which PC Drage had handed in and was told that it was a slicing knife, as would be used in a chandler's shop. It had indeed had blood on it – 'which was similar to that of a warm-blooded being'. Originally it had been a very sharp knife, but it had been blunted recently by the edge being turned – apparently by rubbing on a stone. Although it was not the weapon which the witness would have chosen, the knife *could* have caused the injuries. If, however, the doctor's theory about how the attack had taken place was correct, the knife was 'an improbable instrument'.

At that, he was pressed by the Coroner to say just what his theory was, but the doctor needed no encouragement: 'I have come to the conclusion that the deceased was seized by the shoulders, placed on the ground, and that the perpetrator of the deed was on her right side when he inflicted the cut. I am of the opinion that the cut was made from the left to the right side of the deceased, and therefore arises the unlikelihood of such a long knife having inflicted the wound described in the neck, taking into account the position of the incision.' He continued by saying that the injuries could have been caused in two seconds, and his reason for supposing that they had been inflicted whilst the woman was on the ground was partly because there was no blood except on the left side, and between that side and the wall.

Coroner:	'How long had the deceased been dead when you arrived?'
Phillips:	'Within an hour, she was alive.'
Coroner:	'Does the presence of the cachous in her hand show

	that it was done suddenly, or would it simply show a muscular grasp?'
Phillips:	'No; I cannot say. You will remember some of the cachous were found in the gutter. I have seen several self-inflicted wounds more extensive than this one, but then they have not divided the carotid artery. You will see by that, as in the other cases, there appears to have been a knowledge of where to cut the throat.'
Coroner:	'Was there any other similarity between this and Chapman's case?'
Phillips:	'There is a great dissimilarity. In Chapman's case the neck was severed all round down to the vertebral column, the vertical bone being marked, and there had been an evident attempt to separate the bones.'

Asked whether the murderer would have been bloodstained, the doctor replied that that would not necessarily have been the case. The beginning of the wound, and the injury to the blood vessels, would have been away from him, and therefore the stream of blood would have been similarly directed.

In answer to further questions from Mr Baxter, Dr Phillips stated that there was 'no perceptible sign' of an anaesthetic having been used, and that the victim may or may not have made a noise when attacked.

That concluded Dr Phillips's evidence and he was then allowed to depart.

Dr Blackwell was the next witness, and right from the outset he seems to have antagonized the Coroner by giving the impression that his being recalled was a waste of his time: 'I have little to say except to confirm Dr Phillips' statement.' However Mr Baxter had other ideas, and he set about his questioning by asking the witness whether he had removed the cachous from the dead woman's left hand. The doctor said he had, but added that, although the hand was nearly open, the packet had become lodged between the thumb and the fourth finger and was almost hidden: 'That accounted for its not having been seen by several of those around.' He believed that the hand relaxed after

James Kelly, aged 23 – the regulation photograph taken just before his admission to Broadmoor Criminal Lunatic Asylum in 1883.

The 'Horse and Groom', Curtain Street, Shoreditch. This Victorian public house, which has remained essentially unchanged over the last 100 years, housed the Lodge of the East London Upholsterers Trade Society, to which the young James Kelly used to come in search of work.

St Luke's Parish Church, Old Street, where James Kelly, aged 23, bachelor and upholsterer, married Sarah Ann Kelly, aged 21, spinster and envelope worker, on 4 June 1883.

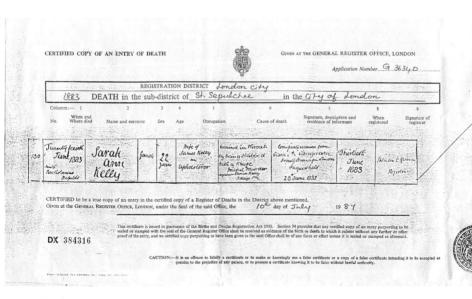

The death certificate of Sarah Ann Kelly, which records her death on 24 June 1883, from 'a wound in the throat by being stabbed with a knife', and the charge of the coroner's court of 'wilful murder against James Kelly'.

An aerial view of Broadmoor Criminal Lunatic Asylum, in 1958. The general layout has remained unchanged since James Kelly's escape in 1888. Block 4 can be seen on the left partially obscured by trees and the kitchen garden through which he escaped can be seen in the foreground of block 4.

In 1867, Broadmoor published pictures of life inside the Asylum, including this picture of an inmate playing the violin. James Kelly may have seen this picture on his admission. He requested a violin – and used the violin case to conceal the keys he forged and used in his escape.

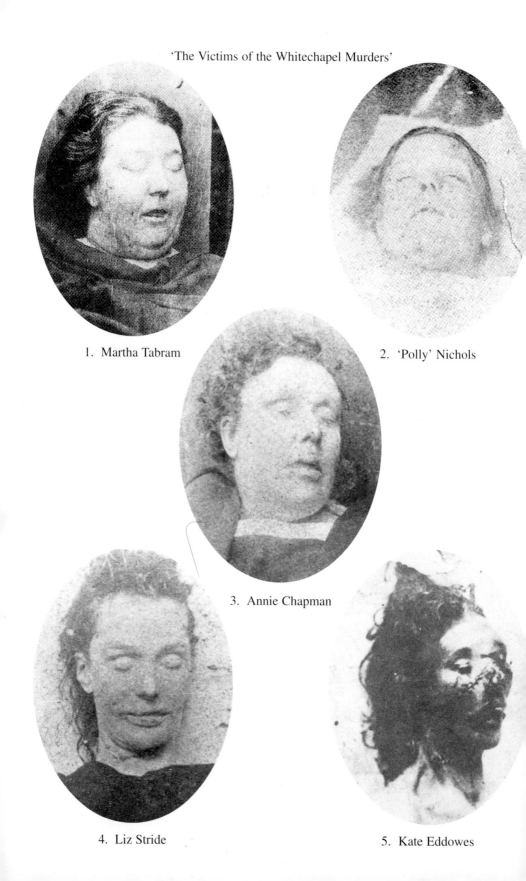

'The Victims of the Whitechapel Murders'

1. Martha Tabram

2. 'Polly' Nichols

3. Annie Chapman

4. Liz Stride

5. Kate Eddowes

6. Mary Kelly
(This is a police photograph of the victim, taken at Miller's Court, the
scene of the murder)

7. Alice McKenzie

8. Frances Coles

CERTIFIED COPY of an ENTRY OF DEATH
Pursuant to the Births and Deaths Registration Act 1953

HC 0843

	Registration District				Whitechapel			
1888.	Death in the Sub-district of Spitalfields				in the County of Middlesex			
Columns:— 1	2	3	4	5	6	7	8	9
No.	When and where died	Name and surname	Sex	Age	Occupation	Cause of death	Signature, description, and residence of informant	When registered	Signature of registrar
326	9th November 1888 1 Millers Court Christchurch	Marie Jeanette KELLY otherwise DAVIES	female	about 25 years	Prostitute	Severance of right Carotid artery Wilful murder against some person or persons unknown Violent	Certificate received from R Macdonald Coroner for Middlesex Inquest held 12th November 88	Seventeenth November 1888	W. Edwards Registrar.

Certified to be a true copy of an entry in a register in my custody.

....Superintendent Registrar

The death certificate of Mary Kelly. Like James Kelly's wife she died from 'wounds in the neck'.

George Yard Dwellings, now Gunthorpe Street – the site of what is generally accepted as the Ripper's first murder, that of Martha Tabram.

A unique photograph of the Purkiss house. It was taken by the author, from the spot where 'Polly' Nichols's body was found, just before the whole of Essex Wharf was demolished in 1990. Mr and Mrs Purkiss were in the second floor front bedroom at the time of the murder and heard nothing.

James Kelly at the age of 67, as photographed on his voluntary return to Broadmoor Asylum, 44 years after his escape.

This tool – known among upholsterers as a 'Ripping Chisel' – was used by James Kelly throughout his professional life.

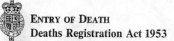

CERTIFIED COPY of an   ENTRY OF DEATH
Pursuant to the Births and   Deaths Registration Act 1953

HC 09608

	Registration District				EASTHAMPSTEAD				
1929 . Death in the Sub-district of				Sandhurst		in the County of Berks.			
Columns:— 1	2	3	4	5	6	7	8	9	
No.	When and where died	Name and surname	Sex	Age	Occupation	Cause of death	Signature, description, and residence of informant	When registered	Signature of registrar
270	Seventeenth September 1929 Broadmoor Criminal Lunatic Asylum, Crowthorne, Berks, R.J.	James Kelly	Male	69 years	Inmate of Broadmoor Asylum formerly an upholsterer	Double Lobar pneumonia Natural Causes (P. M. Exam)	Certificate received from Robert S. Payne, Coroner for Reading District of Berks Inquest held 19th September 1929	Twentieth September 1929	Edwin Henry Burnham Registrar.

Certified to be a true copy of an entry in a register in my custody.

.... M. Morris ....Superintendent Registrar.

.... 6th February 1987 ......Date.

James Kelly's death certificate, dated 17 September 1929.

The marble angel that presides over Broadmoor's 'Block 8', the cemetery that contains the unmarked graves of James Kelly and his fellow inmates at the asylum.

the injury had been inflicted, as death would have arisen from fainting owing to the rapid loss of blood.

There was, he said, no likelihood of this being a case of suicide, especially as no weapon had been found near the body. As for the knife which had been found, he agreed with Dr Phillips that although it *could* have inflicted the cut it was extremely unlikely: 'The murderer using a sharp, round-pointed instrument would severely handicap himself, as he could only use it one way. I am informed that slaughterers always use round-pointed instruments.'

It was most unfortunate that Dr Blackwell should have seen fit to add that last sentence. During this session of the inquest there had been no sparks flying between his colleague, Dr Phillips, and the Coroner, and perhaps that was what tempted Dr Blackwell to ramble on a little. If, however, he had thought that Mr Baxter was not up to his usual form he was swiftly disillusioned: 'No one suggested anything about a slaughterer! Is it *your* suggestion that this was done by a slaughterer?' The answer, when it came, was a meek 'No,' and, almost certainly to the doctor's relief, the questioning moved on.

He said that there were some pressure marks on the shoulders, but there was no abrasion of the skin. A juryman who asked how the marks had been caused was told: 'By two hands pressing on the shoulders.'

In reply to further questions, the doctor stated that he had not seen any grapes in the Yard, nor had he heard anybody say that they had seen grapes there.

Various people had claimed to have seen Long Liz in Berner Street on the Saturday night/Sunday morning, and now the jury heard from some of them.

First came William Marshall, a labourer in an indigo warehouse, who lived at No. 64, Berner Street.

Marshall told the Coroner that he had viewed the body in the mortuary during the evening of Sunday the 30th. He recognized it as being that of a woman whom he had seen in Berner Street on the night before, when he had been standing at the front door of his lodging. His vigil had lasted from 11.30 until around midnight, and it was at about 11.45 that he had noticed her talking quietly to a man. They were on the pavement opposite [i.e. outside] No. 58; which was three doors off from where he was standing, and between Fairclough and Boyd Streets. In the mortuary, he had recognized her both by her face and her clothing.

Coroner: 'Was she wearing a flower when you saw her?'
Marshall: 'No.'

Asked if he could describe the woman's companion, the witness replied that there was no lamp near, and he did not see the man's face distinctly. He seemed to be middle-aged, rather stout, and about five feet six inches tall. From the little he could see, he did not think that the man had any whiskers. 'Decently dressed', his clothing had consisted of a round cap with a small peak, 'something like a sailor would wear', a short black 'cutaway' coat and dark trousers. There was nothing in his hands, and he was not wearing gloves. He was a 'mild speaking' man, and seemed to be educated: 'I should say he was in some light business, and did nothing like hard work.' When pressed for a more graphic description, Marshall said that the stranger looked more like a clerk than anything else.

The witness was quite sure that the deceased was the woman whom he had seen. At first he had not taken much notice of the couple, but his attention had been attracted by the length of time that they had stood there, and the fact that the man was kissing and cuddling the woman. He had heard the man say: 'You would say anything but your prayers', and that had made the woman laugh.

Answering Mr Baxter, Marshall said: 'They went away after that, towards Ellen Street. They were walking in the middle of the road, and they would not have passed No. 40 on their way. Neither of them appeared to be the worse for drink.'

Questioned by Inspector Reid, the witness stated that the pair had been standing between his house and the Club. They were there for about ten minutes, and then passed him 'in the road'.

A juror: 'Did you see the man's face as he passed you?'
Marshall: 'No; the woman was next to me, and the man had his

arms around her neck. His face was turned towards me, but I did not take any notice of it, as I did not expect to come here.'

Other questions established that there was a gas-lamp over No. 70, which was on the corner of Boyd Street; that the couple had not been hurrying; and that it did not rain until nearly three o'clock.

The next witness, James Brown, a dock labourer of No. 35, Fairclough Street, told of how he had seen the deceased in the mortuary and was almost sure that she was the woman whom he had seen with a male companion at 12.45 a.m. on that Sunday morning. He was on his way from his house to buy some supper from a chandler's shop on the corner of Berner and Fairclough Streets and, as he crossed over Fairclough Street, they were standing against the wall of the Board School. Just as he passed them, he heard the woman say, 'No, not tonight – some other night.' That had caused him to look back at them. Both appeared to be sober. The woman had her back to the wall, and the man was facing her with his hand on the wall. Brown had not noticed whether the woman had any flowers in her dress.

Asked to describe the man, the witness said that the place where they were standing was rather dark, but he would think that the woman's companion was about his own height, five feet seven inches. He appeared to be 'stoutish built', but it was difficult to tell because he was wearing an overcoat which was so long that it came 'very nearly down to his heels'. Brown had seen 'nothing light in colour about either of them', and he was unable to say whether the man had been wearing a hat or cap.

Another who said that he had seen Long Liz was a young constable, PC William Smith. Compared with those of some of his colleagues, he had a large beat. It went from the Commercial Road corner of Gower's Walk along Commercial Road as far as Christian Street; then down Christian Street until the Fairclough Street intersection. From there, he patrolled east along Fairclough Street to Grove Street, then reversed his steps alongth the entire length of Fairclough Street to Back Church Lane, and thus back to Commercial

Road. He was also responsible for all the thoroughfares within that perimeter, including Berner and Batty Streets.

Smith began his evidence by stating that it usually took him between twenty-five and thirty minutes to go round his beat. On the Sunday morning in question, he had been in Berner Street at around 12.30 or 12.35. The next time he was there was at 1 a.m., and he saw a crowd outside No. 40. He had heard no cries of 'Police!', and had not been called to the spot; he was there merely as part of his 'ordinary round'. Constables Lamb and Collins were already on the scene.

The witness had looked at the woman on the ground and had found that she was dead. Dr Blackwell's assistant had arrived just as he was leaving to fetch the ambulance from the police station.

Coroner:	'When you were in Berner Street the previous time, did you see anyone?'
Smith:	'There was a man and a woman.'
Coroner:	'Was the woman anything like the deceased?'
Smith:	'Yes, I saw her face. I have seen the deceased in the mortuary, and I feel certain it is the same person.'

She and the man had been on the pavement on the other side of the street from Dutfield's Yard, and a few yards up from it. The woman was wearing a flower in her jacket, and the constable had noticed that the man was carrying 'a newspaper parcel' which was about eighteen inches long and six or eight inches wide. Asked to describe him, Smith said that he was about twenty-eight years old, around five feet seven inches tall, and had no whiskers. His overcoat, trousers and hard felt deerstalker hat had all been dark in colour.

The couple had not been acting suspiciously.

Further questions elicited the information that there were some courts in the middle of Berner Street which led to Back Church Lane, and which the witness patrolled on occasion. This time, however, he had gone straight up Berner Street to Commercial Road. As far as he could remember, it had rained very little after 11 p.m.

| Foreman: | 'Do you see many prostitutes, or people hanging about, in Berner Street?' |
| Smith: | 'No; very few.' |

Detective Inspector Reid then asked Smith whether he had seen the couple more than once. The constable replied that he had not, but nevertheless he had recognized the dead woman immediately when he saw her in the Yard.

Michael Kidney then made a reappearance. He was to participate in a rather curious little exchange which makes one wonder just what the Coroner and the police suspected or knew that they should have made an issue over such an apparently minor detail.

He was shown a hymn-book, and was asked if he had seen it before. 'Yes. I recognize it as one belonging to the deceased. It used to be in my place. I found it in Mrs Smith's room, next to my own. Mrs Smith said the deceased gave it to her to take care of when she left on Tuesday.'

| D.I. Reid: | 'When you and the deceased lived together, I believe you had a padlock on the door?' |
| Kidney: | 'Yes; there was only one key, which I had, but she got in and out somehow. The hymn-book was taken from the room on Wednesday week – the day after she went away. That was done during my absence.' |

Kidney was then allowed to retire and passed into oblivion. All that is known of him subsequently is that, during the following year, he was treated in Whitechapel Workhouse Infirmary for syphilis, lumbago and dyspepsia.

The last witness for the day was Inspector Reid, who stated that he had been at the Commercial Street police station when, at 1.25 a.m., he had received a telegram informing him of the murder. He went immediately to Dutfield's Yard, where he found that he had been preceded by Chief Inspector West, Inspector Pinhorn, several sergeants and constables, Drs Blackwell and Phillips, various residents and some members of the Club.

When he arrived the doctors were examining the woman's throat. Hard on his heels had come Superintendent Arnold and 'several other officers'.

Reid then told of how the Yard, and the houses and other buildings in it, had been searched and, yet again, of the examination of onlookers and members – twenty-eight people in total.

All the rooms in the houses had been searched, and in doing so a loft was found to be locked on the inside. The door was forced, and the loft searched, but nothing was found.

A description of the body was telegraphed to the local police stations, and inquiries were made at houses in Berner Street.

The Inspector said that he had examined the wall near where the body was found, but could find no traces of blood. The corpse was then removed to the mortuary at 4.30 a.m., and he had then gone to Mr Baxter's home and informed him of the murder. It was then daylight, and he had returned to the Yard, but found that the blood had been removed. He had examined all the walls, but had been able to find no signs that anybody had scaled them. After that he had gone to the mortuary and compiled a correct description of the dead woman and her clothing and effects.

His evidence concluded the evidence for that session, and Mr Baxter adjourned the proceedings until Tuesday, October 23rd.

As was, by now, usual, the correspondence columns of the newspapers were taken up with letters about the killings. There was also a continuation of the new concern for the inhabitants of the East End, and the 'upwards of 15,000 homeless and shelterless wanderers' in London every night. Many writers expressed hopes that the movement toward providing night shelters would not fade 'as soon as the momentary excitement shall have subsided'.

Suggestions as to the possible identity of the killer, and ideas for his apprehension, continued to be many and varied but, although the police seem to have taken up some of them, they were no nearer catching him than they had been at the start. The total lack of intelligent direction and original ideas from the top left the senior officers on the ground largely to their own devices. They, never having experienced such a situation, relied instinctively upon well-tried but unimaginative methods which were virtually useless.

On October 9th, Chief Inspector Swanson reported that, following the Berner Street killing, 80,000 leaflets had been distributed in 'H' Division asking the occupiers of houses to give information to the police about any suspicious lodgers. House-to-house enquiries and searches had been made, and 2,000 common lodging-houses visited.

Swanson also stated that the Thames Police had made enquiries on board ships in the docks and on the Thames, and had 'extended enquiry as to Asiatics present in London'. Eighty people had been detained at various police stations whilst their statements were taken and verified, and the movements of over 300 were checked as a result of 'communications received'. Seventy-six butchers and slaughterers had been visited.

It all sounded very impressive, but those were merely *re*actions, and in any case doubts must remain about how efficiently they were carried out. The overwhelming impression is that the police were casting their nets in every conceivable direction in the vain hope that somehow they would snare the killer.

The inquest was duly resumed, and the jury returned a verdict of 'Wilful murder against some person or persons unknown'.

That, then, would have appeared to have been that, but there was a great deal of evidence which had *not* been heard. There were a few minor matters, such as that Long Liz had had eight convictions for drunkenness in her own name, and possibly one under the alias of 'Fitzgerald', and that, in April 1887, she had charged Michael Kidney with assault, but had not appeared in court to press her accusation, causing the charge to be withdrawn. Far more importantly, however, there were witnesses with seemingly vital information whom the police had not seen fit to bring forward.

For instance, there were two men who said that they had seen the dead woman at the Bricklayers Arms in Settles Street (across Commercial Road, opposite Christian Street), just before 11 p.m. on September 29th. They were two labourers, J. Best, of No. 82, Lower Chapman Street, and John Gardner of No. 11, Chapman Street.

Talking to reporters, they said that Long Liz was in the company of a short man – about five feet five inches tall – of respectable appearance. He had a black moustache, and wore a black billycock hat with a black morning suit and coat.

The couple had finished their drinks, and had been on their way out of the pub as the men came in. However they were forced to shelter in the doorway from the heavy rain. Best and Gardner were somewhat surprised at the way the man was hugging and kissing his companion in public, and began to pull his leg. They told the woman 'That's Leather Apron getting round you,' and made other jocular remarks until the man could stand it no longer and moved off with his woman friend just after 11 p.m.

Another potential witness had been Matthew Packer, an elderly man who lived at No. 44, Berner Street, only two doors down from the Club. He carried on a small business as a greengrocer and fruiterer from the front room of his terraced house, serving customers on the pavement through the lower half of the sash-window. At night, the only light was from an oil lamp in the window.

During the course of his house-to-house enquiries, Sergeant Stephen White had interviewed Packer, his wife, and their two lodgers at about 9 a.m. on the day of the murder. Not one of them admitted to having seen or heard anything suspicious, and Packer said that there was nobody about in Berner Street when he closed at 12.30 a.m.

That, however, was not the end of this story. Mile End Vigilance Committee had engaged two detectives. They were from the firm of Le Grand and Company, of No. 283, Strand, which, apparently, had also accepted a retainer from at least one newspaper, the *Evening News*. On the morning of October 2nd, Mr Le Grand himself and a Mr J.H. Batchelor visited Berner Street to make their own enquiries, and spoke to many of the residents. They interviewed a Mrs Rosenfield and her sister, Miss Eva Harstein, both of No. 14, and were most interested when the women told them that they had seen a 'blood-caked' grape stalk, and some white petals, in Dutfield's Yard before the police washed it down. That led them to speak to Matthew Packer and, in two or three interviews, he said that he had sold some grapes to a man and a woman on the night of the murder. 'At what time?' was the next, and crucial, question, to which Packer, uncertain but willing to please, and probably sensing that fame could be his, had replied: 'Between midnight and half-past.'

All this was reported back to the Vigilance Committee and the *Evening News*, and it was decided that Packer's story should be tested.

On October 3rd he was asked if he would go to the mortuary to see if the body was that of the woman whom he had served. Packer agreed but, to test his reliability, he was taken to view the victim of the Mitre Square murder and asked if she was the woman. To everybody's relief, he said that she was not and arrangements were then made to take him to the correct, St George's-in-the-East, mortuary on the following afternoon.

Naturally, news of all this came to the ears of the police, and Chief Inspector Henry Moore, to his credit, despatched Sergeant White to have another word with Packer. What happened then is best described in White's own words, contained in a report countersigned by Superintendent Arnold and Detective Inspector Abberline:

On fourth inst, I was directed by Inspr. Moore to make further inquiry and if necessary see Packer and take him to the Mortuary. I then went to 44 Berner Street and saw Mrs Packer, who informed me that two detectives had called and taken her husband to the Mortuary. I then went towards the Mortuary where I met Packer with a man. I asked him where he had been. He said, 'This detective asked me to go to see if I could identify the woman.' I said, 'Have you done so?' He said, 'Yes, I believe she bought some grapes at my shop about 12 o'clock on Saturday.' Shortly afterwards they were joined by another man. I asked the men what they were doing with Packer and they both said they were detectives. I asked for their authority. One of them produced a card from a pocket book, but would not allow me to touch it. They then said they were private detectives. They then induced Packer to go away with them. About 4 p.m. I saw Packer at his shop. While talking to him the two men drove up in a hansom cab, and after going into the shop they induced Packer to enter the cab, stating that they would take him to Scotland Yard to see Sir Charles Warren.

From inquiry I have made there is no doubt that these are the two men referred to in the attached newspaper cutting who examined the drain in Dutfield's Yard on the second inst. One of the men had a letter in his hand addressed to Le Grand & Co., Strand.

Packer had identified Long Liz as the woman he had seen, and the *Evening News* was jubilant at having secured evidence missed by the police. Once the story had been written, it was decided that the information should be passed to the police, but not to the 'locals' – it would make far better headlines if they went straight to the Metropolitan Police Commissioner.

As we have seen from White's report, the two detectives told him that they were taking Packer to tell his story to Sir Charles Warren, and that is what they did. Confirmation of that comes from a statement taken from Packer by the Commissioner himself in an almost illegible form of personal shorthand. Dated 4.10.88, it reads:

Matthew Packer
    Keeps a small shp in Berner St – has a few grapes in window. Black & white. On Sat night about 11 pm a young man from 25–30 – about 5.7. with long black coat buttoned up – soft felt hat, kind of hunter hat rather broad shoulders – rather quick in speaking. rough voice. I sold him ½ pound black grapes 3d. A woman came up with him from Back Church end (the lower end of street) she was dressed in black frock & jacket, fur round bottom of jacket a black crape bonnet, she was playing with a flower like a geranium white outside & red inside. I identify the woman at the St George's Mortuary as the one I saw that night – They passed by as though they were going up Com Road, but instead of going up they crossed to the other side of the road to the Board School & were there for about ½ an hour till I shd say 11.30 talking to one another. I then put up my shutters. Before they passed over opposite to my shop they went near the Club for a few minutes apparently listening to the music.

I saw no more of them after I put up my shutters. I put the man down as a young clerk.

He had a frock coat on – no gloves.

He was about 1½ inch or 2 or 3 inch [the next words are *completely* illegible. They *could* be 'a little bit' or '. . . ? . . . but'] higher than she was.

The statement is initialled 'C. W.'

That evening, the *Evening News* burst into print with its sensational story alleging that Packer had spoken to the murderer, and endeavouring to denigrate the police by quoting Packer, mostly in capital letters, as saying:

Except a gentleman who is a private detective, NO DETECTIVE OR POLICEMAN HAS EVER ASKED ME A SINGLE QUESTION NOR COME NEAR MY SHOP TO FIND OUT IF I KNEW ANYTHING ABOUT THE GRAPES THE MURDERED WOMAN HAD BEEN EATING BEFORE HER THROAT WAS CUT!!!

His statement was, of course, true, but only as far as it went. There was absolutely no evidence that Elizabeth Stride had been eating grapes on the evening in question, and therefore there was no reason why Sergeant White, at nine o'clock on the morning of the murder, should have asked Packer about grapes – and the latter had not seen fit to volunteer any information about the couple he had, allegedly, served.

Packer was an unreliable witness. He gave several different times for the alleged events, and later in October, and in November, he was to make further sensational claims. In those subsequent interviews he stated that he had seen the man who bought the grapes on several occasions, both before and after the day of the murder. He would also allege that yet another man had told him that the killer was his, the man's, cousin who now lived in America!

Great significance has been read into the fact that Packer was interviewed by no lesser person than the Commissioner, but Warren really had little alternative once Packer was brought to him and he was told of the story which was to be printed. Having agreed to see the fruiterer, we may be sure that Sir Charles was searching in his interrogation. During their meeting, Packer gave times an hour earlier than those which he had mentioned to Sergeant White, and the Commissioner queried that in the margin of Packer's statement, but Sir Charles must have been convinced that the times which *he* took down were correct because he left them unaltered.

The police were almost certainly correct in their view that, as reported by Chief Inspector Swanson, Packer had made so many different statements that any evidence which he may have given at the inquest would have been 'almost valueless'. Nevertheless it should have been tested there as it may be taken for granted that Mr Baxter would soon have elicited the truth.

Another and far more significant witness who was never called to give evidence was a Hungarian Jew named Israel Schwartz, of No. 22, Ellen Street.

On the day of the murder he visited Leman Street police station accompanied by a friend who, as Schwartz spoke no English, was to act as interpreter. The story which he had to tell, and about which he was questioned closely by Inspector Abberline, was regarded as being so important that it was eventually the subject of a report by Chief Inspector Swanson.

It seems that on September 29th Schwartz had gone out for the day, leaving his wife to effect the move from their lodgings in Berner Street to fresh ones in Ellen Street. On his return from wherever he had been, he had decided to walk down Berner Street, en route to his new address, just to make sure that his wife had, in fact, made the move. This was at 11.45 p.m.

When he turned into Berner Street, from Commercial Road, he saw, some distance in front of him, a man lurching along as if slightly drunk. Then, according to Swanson's report, he saw the man, having got as far as the gateway where the murder was committed:

stop and speak to a woman, who was standing in the gateway. The man tried to pull the woman into the street, but he turned her round and threw her down on the footway and the woman screamed three times, but not very loudly. On crossing to the opposite side of the street, he saw a second man standing lighting his pipe. The man who threw the woman down called out, apparently to the man on the opposite side of the road, "Lipski", and then Schwartz walked away, but finding that he was followed by the second man, he ran so far as the railway arch, but the man did not follow so far.

Schwartz cannot say whether the two men were together or known to each other. Upon being taken to the Mortuary Schwartz identified the body as that of the woman he had seen. He thus describes the first man, who threw the woman down: age about 30, ht. 5ft. 5in. comp. fair, hair dark, small brown moustache, full face, broad shouldered; dress, dark jacket and trousers, black cap with peak, had nothing in his hands.

Second man age 35, ht. 5ft. 11in. comp. fresh, hair light brown, moustache brown; dress, dark overcoat, old black hard felt hat, wide brim, had a clay pipe in his hand.

'Lipski' was a derogatory term which came to be directed at Jews after a notorious murder at the lodging-house at No. 16, Batty Street, which was the next street to the east from Berner Street and ran parallel with it.

On June 28th, 1887, a relative had discovered a young woman, six months pregnant Miriam Angel, dead in her bed. Another lodger, a twenty-two-year-old Jew named Israel Lipski, was charged with her murder, found guilty and hanged. It was a controversial case which did nothing to lessen the anti-Semitism in the area.

The other Israel – Schwartz – was tracked down by a reporter from the *Star*, ten days after he had spoken to Swanson, and gave an interview in which he changed some of the details in his police statement. Now he said that the second man had just come out of the doorway of a pub 'a few doors off', that he had a knife in his hand, and that his 'moustaches' were red. He also stated that it was the second man who had shouted 'Lipski', and that he had rushed forward as if to attack Schwartz.

Chief Inspector Swanson told the Home Office that he considered

Schwartz's statement to be reliable, but it was doubted that the man seen attacking Long Liz was her killer. That may or may not have been the case, but it is obvious that, whatever the police thought, Schwartz should have appeared before Mr Baxter.

Another person who should have been called to the inquest was a Russian Jew named Joseph Lave. A printer and photographer by trade, Lave lived in the United States but was in England on a short visit and was staying at the Club whilst he looked for lodgings.

Lave told reporters that he had left the Club for some air, because the concert room was so hot, about twenty minutes before the body was found. The occupants of the cottages had gone to bed, and therefore the only light into the Yard was from an upstairs window of the Club.

He had stayed outside for five minutes or more, and had gone as far as the street. It was so dark, however, that he had been forced to feel his way along the Club wall and there was definitely no body there then. In fact nothing in the Yard or the street had attracted his attention, everything being very quiet after the recent heavy rain.

Obviously, what he had to say was at odds with the statement given by Schwartz, but there is no evidence that Lave was ever questioned by the police, and it is a great shame that both men were not summoned to the hearing and the matter thrashed out.

Two other people too should have been there, who were keeping a look-out in Berner Street that early morning. Charles Letchford lived at No. 39, and he said that he had walked to his house at half-past twelve and everything seemed 'to be going on as usual'. His sister had been standing at the door at ten to one and had seen nobody pass.

Best, Gardner, Packer, Schwartz, Lave, the Letchfords, and goodness knows how many others, all had apparently important, if not vital, information, but all were kept well away from the probings of Mr Baxter. One wonders why?

Unlike the other murders, in this case we have a plethora of alleged sightings of the victim with a man during the two hours prior to her death. Unfortunately, no two descriptions of the man agree in all respects, and therefore several conclusions may be drawn.

It may well be that Long Liz picked up with more than one man, or that the descriptions of just one man were inaccurate, or that there was at least one woman resembling Liz in Berner Street with a man that night. Indeed it could be that permutations of those possibilities are responsible for the continuing mystery.

7

Kate

SO, THE MURDER OF Elizabeth Stride had been investigated, the inquest held, and the expected verdict returned – but nothing had emerged to bring the Metropolitan Police one step nearer to finding the killer. It should, however, be remembered that the Berner Street slaying was but one of two perpetrated during the early hours of Sunday, September 30th.

As we have seen, the second had taken place within the jurisdiction of the City of London, and the police and authorities there had been just as busy as their counterparts in the East End. However, as the two inquiries were concurrent, we shall now need to return to the morning of the 'double event' in order to follow their activities.

When we last saw PC Watkins he was in the darkest corner of Mitre Square waiting for the help for which he had despatched the night-watchman, George Morris. The latter, after one look at the terribly mutilated body, had run off up Church Passage blowing his whistle with all his might.

Those shrill blasts heralded a series of events unparalleled in the history of the City Police but, just for the moment, Ted Watkins was alone and apprehensive. Fortunately for his state of mind, he did not have to wait very long.

A constable on an adjoining beat, PC Harvey, had heard the

whistle and intercepted Morris, who gabbled out what was amiss. That was enough to send Harvey off post-haste and, sighting a colleague, PC Holland, on the other side of the street, he urged him to follow.

Coincidentally, a team of three City detectives, Daniel Halse, Edward Marriott and Robert Outram, had been patrolling in the area and, at 1.58 a.m., they were comparing notes at the corner of Houndsditch and Aldgate High Street – by St Botolph's Church and only some 175 yards from Mitre Square. They went to the scene immediately upon learning of the murder, and Halse gave instructions to his companions to search the neighbourhood and examine every man they came across. For his own part, he returned to Aldgate High Street, took the first left into Middlesex Street and continued as far as Wentworth Street. He encountered two men there, but they were able to give satisfactory replies to his questions and, as they were the only persons whom he had seen, he gave up the search and returned to Mitre Square – passing through Goulston Street at 2.20 a.m.

PCs Harvey and Holland had, of course, preceded him to the murder scene, and once they had seen the ghastly sight which awaited them they had acted with commendable promptitude. Holland went off for the nearest doctor and was soon back with a Dr Séquêria who lived in nearby Jewry Street. They entered Mitre Square at just about the same time that Dr Phillips was arriving in Dutfield's Yard. Meanwhile, Harvey had sent 'private individuals' for more assistance and as a result the news was received quickly by Inspector Collard, the duty inspector at the Bishopsgate Street Without police station. He in turn lost no time in telegraphing his superiors at the City Police headquarters at No. 26, Old Jewry, and ordering a constable to fetch the police surgeon, Dr Brown. Then, in company with a Sergeant Jones, he hurried off to Mitre Square.

Once there they had a good look at and around the corpse and, on the left side of the dead woman, they saw a small metal button, a common thimble and, more importantly, a small mustard tin containing two pawn tickets. They were all left in situ until the body had been examined, but then Sergeant Jones picked them up and handed them to

Inspector Collard together with three small black buttons which had been revealed after the body was removed. The Inspector stayed by the body until Dr Brown came, but in the meantime he ordered his subordinates upon an immediate search of the neighbourhood.

Very shortly after the doctor, there were more arrivals in the forms of Superintendent Alfred Lawrence Foster, from Old Jewry, and Inspector James McWilliam, who was in charge of the City Police CID, and some of his detectives. Hard on their heels came the Acting Commissioner of the City Police, Major Henry Smith, who was in charge whilst the Commissioner, Sir James Fraser, was on leave. For some reason, Major Smith had been sleeping on a camp bed in the Cloak Lane police station when he was given the news, but a hansom cab had conveyed him to the scene without delay.

With the top brass present, police activity was intensified and detectives were sent in all directions to search the streets and lodging-houses.

Meanwhile, the doctors had been going about their examination of the body, and Dr Brown had drawn its exact position. However, it was only when they had finished, and the dead woman was being lifted into a shell, that a most curious sight was observed. On the flagstones there were clear white outlines of where the legs and feet had lain – almost as if someone had chalked round them. The effect was so striking that it was decided that a photograph should be taken, but the marks disappeared before that was possible. Later it was explained that the phenomenon had been caused by the warmth of the body having absorbed moisture from the wet pavement, but those present were rather shaken and no time was wasted in having the corpse wheeled off to the City Mortuary, over a mile away in Golden Lane, Barbican.

In view of his involvement in some of the previous murders, Dr Brown had sent for Dr Phillips to see the body before it was moved but, for the moment, Phillips was otherwise engaged in Berner Street.

Despite his absence, there were, in fact, quite a few spectators present when, under the instructions of the doctors, the mortuary keeper – a Mr Davis – began stripping the corpse. They had been aghast at what they had seen in Mitre Square, but now, as the full extent of the injuries was gradually revealed, even the most hardened were appalled at the mutilations. It can therefore be imagined that it may have been the finishing touch for some when a piece of a human ear fell from some of the clothing as it was being handed to the police!

It soon became clear that the deceased had been, as the phrase goes, of no fixed abode. Such women had, perforce, to wear or carry about with them everything which they owned, and this one was so typical that it is worth listing what she carried in her pockets.

'1 large white handkerchief, bloodstained. 1 white cotton pocket handkerchief with red and white bird's eye border; 1 pair of brown ribbed stockings, feet mended with white; 12 pieces of white rag, some slightly bloodstained; 1 piece of white coarse linen; 1 piece of blue and white shirting (3 cornered); 2 small blue bedticking bags; 2 short clay pipes (black); 1 tin box containing tea; 1 ditto sugar; 1 piece of flannel and 6 pieces of soap; 1 small-tooth comb; 1 white handled table knife & metal tea spoon; 1 red leather cigarette case, with white metal fittings; 1 tin match box, empty; 1 piece of red flannel containing pins and needles; 1 ball of hemp; 1 piece of old white apron.'

Apart from the terrible wounds and mutilations, about which we shall hear more later, two things about the dead woman stood out. In spite of her obviously having been an itinerant lodging-house dweller, her hands were 'small and of a delicate cast', and that was taken as a sign that she had known better days. Then there were the initials 'T.C.' tattooed in blue ink on the dead woman's forearm. I can find no mention of them in the official documents, but they were reported by the newspapers and could hardly have been an invention because the *Daily Telegraph*, at least, could not have known of their significance when they were mentioned in its edition of October 1st.

The doctors had done all they could until they had permission to conduct a post-mortem examination. That had to be obtained from the City of London Coroner, Mr Samuel Frederick Langham, whose Officer finally found him in church on that Sunday morning and obtained his signature to the necessary order. (Mr Langham had been promoted from Deputy Coroner, since conducting the inquest on Sarah Kelly.) It was then decided that the examination would be conducted during the afternoon, and Dr Phillips, who had arrived at the mortuary earlier from Leman Street police station, was invited to attend.

As for the police, most of them returned to Mitre Square where they found that there was already a growing number of would-be sightseers. Let us leave them there for the moment, because we need to turn our attention to what was happening in a street about a third of a mile away – that very Goulston Street, in fact, down which DC Halse had passed at 2.20 a.m. To do so had meant crossing the demarcation line between the City and Metropolitan police forces by some seventy-five yards and, unknowingly, he had strayed on to the beat of PC Alfred Long, who was one of the reinforcements brought in from other Metropolitan divisions.

It was a wonder that the two policemen did not, literally, bump into each other because Constable Long had also been in Goulston Street at 2.20 a.m. – at least, that is what he said – but somehow their paths had not crossed and it was to be thirty-five minutes before Long passed that way again.

Long was very much on the alert, as not only was he in the dark on a strange beat but, since his last time around, he had been told of the Mitre Square killing and had heard uncertain rumours of another. It was therefore with perhaps more care than hitherto that he flashed his lamp into the gloomy lobby which led to the staircases serving the tenants of Nos. 108–119 of the new Wentworth Model Dwellings. There had been nothing there on his previous visit, so it came as something of a surprise when he saw a sizeable piece of rag inside against the wall.

Closer examination revealed it to be a portion of a woman's apron. Originally it had been white, but now it was very dirty and part of it was wet. What excited Long, however, was the fact that it was spotted with blood and smeared with what seemed to be faecal matter. Straightening up, he shone his lantern around more carefully and it was then that he made another discovery.

The lower sections of the brick walls of the vestibule were painted black and the upper white. At the top of the black bricks, on the black dividing fascia and just above where he had found the piece of apron, there was some writing and, looking closer, Long saw that it was a message in white chalk which read:

> The Juwes are
> The men That
> Will not
> be Blamed
> for nothing

It was written in 'a schoolboy's good round hand', but the letters were not large – it being estimated later that the capitals were only about three-quarters of an inch high, and the others in proportion.

Somewhat startled by the two finds, and thinking that he might have yet another murder on his hands, Long made an immediate search of the six or seven staircases to the top of the building. There was nothing untoward to be seen, but he realized that his discoveries might be important and so he summoned a colleague, No. 190 H, from an adjoining beat to watch the building and then went off to Commercial Street police station with the piece of apron.

It would appear that it was then taken to Leman Street police station where it was handed to Dr Phillips who, in answer to Dr Brown's request, was on his way to Golden Lane Mortuary. When he arrived there, Dr Brown fitted it against the piece found on the body, and the excitement may be imagined when it was immediately obvious that they were parts of the same garment.

By the time Dr Phillips had reached the mortuary, Major Smith and Detectives Halse and Hunt had departed. They had waited to see whether the stripping of the body revealed any clues, and had then returned to Mitre Square. It was there that they heard of the Goulston Street finds and they lost no time in hurrying to Leman Street to learn more. They had all noticed the piece of apron which the dead woman had been wearing and were eager to see the portion which had been found. Unfortunately, Dr Phillips had left with it by the time they arrived, but the description which they received was enough to convince them that it had been taken from Mitre Square by the killer, and must have been discarded by him en route to his den.

It was a vital clue, and Major Smith was off like a shot. Detectives Halse and Hunt, however, stayed to hear the details of how and when Long had made his discoveries, and the precise wording of the chalked message. Only then did they hurry to Goulston Street to see for themselves.

As was to be expected, they found quite a gathering of their Metropolitan colleagues at the scene. Superintendent Thomas Arnold was in charge and, fearful that the words might spark another wave of anti-Semitic violence, he had an inspector standing by with a wet sponge ready to erase them. It was a prospect which appalled DC Halse. As far as he was concerned, it was evident that the murderer had been frustrated in his intentions by the arrival of Diemschütz, had taken out that frustration, with a vengeance, on the poor creature in Mitre Square, and had then fled via Goulston Street. Now, at last, there were what could be two valuable clues, and he just could not believe that arrangements were in hand to destroy one of them.

Obviously he had no authority outside the City, but he managed finally to persuade Superintendent Arnold that it would be in the interests of all parties at least to have the writing photographed before it was wiped away. He sent DC Hunt to obtain the necessary authorization from Inspector McWilliam, and all would have been well – and a lot of subsequent speculation avoided – had it not been for the untimely arrival of Sir Charles Warren, the Commissioner of the Metropolitan Police.

Warren was the complete authoritarian, and would have been annoyed at what he probably regarded as unwarranted interference from some junior whipper-snapper of another force. He had no hesitation in supporting Superintendent Arnold's original intention, and it was he who finally gave the order to wipe away the chalked message. In vain did DC Halse plead for it to remain until Major Smith had seen it or, at the very least, that only the top line should be erased; Warren's order was carried out and a permanent record of the words was lost to posterity.

For those days, and certainly in sharp comparison with some of his colleagues in the 'Met', Halse seems to have been something of a rarity – a policeman with initiative. At forty-nine, he was not a young man and would appear to have deserved a higher rank. Having lost the battle over the chalking, and disregarding completely the fact that he was outside his bailiwick, he and Hunt then undertook a task which was long overdue. The two detectives knocked on every door of that block of the Dwellings, and interviewed all the, mainly Jewish, tenants. Sadly, however, their zeal went unrewarded – nobody had seen or heard anything out of the ordinary.

In the meantime, the man whose support Halse had needed, Major Smith, was galloping around the streets like a man demented. Following what he supposed to be the killer's line of flight, he had set off northwards, and way out of his territory, into the heart of Spitalfields.

According to what he was to write later, he was hot on the murderer's heels all the time. He even claimed to have arrived at a little-known sink, set back in a close off Dorset Street, in time to see bloody water gurgling down the plug-hole from where the fugitive had paused to wash his hands – all that quite ignoring the fact that his quarry would have left Goulston Street at least half an hour before Smith even arrived there!

Those dark hours of Sunday morning, September 30th, witnessed police activity, the mingling of forces, and a disregard of boundaries on a scale that was unprecedented. However, all those involved were only too aware that the coming of dawn would bring no respite, because so many things remained undone.

As always seemed to be the case, the immediate problem was to establish the identity of the victim, but at least there were some clues this time.

For a start, there were the two pawn tickets in the mustard tin found near the body. They had been issued by Mr Jones of No. 31, Church Street, Spitalfields, and the first, dated August 31st, was in the name of Emily Burrell, No. 52, White's Row, for a man's flannel shirt which had been pawned for 9d. The other, dated September 28th, had been issued to Jane Kelly, No. 6, Dorset Street, and concerned a pair of man's boots upon which 2/6d had been loaned.

Other leads were the tattooed initials 'T.C.', and the fact that the deceased had so obviously been a lodging-house dweller, but there was to be a quite unforgivable delay before the City Police realized that another clue was in their own files.

By lunchtime on that Sunday it must already have seemed a long day to those most closely connected with the 'double event'. We have witnessed the comings and goings in Berner Street, and there were no fewer in connection with the second killing. Every available police-man was brought in, but the situation was not helped by the crowds around Mitre Square which tied up valuable manpower.

Nevertheless, Inspector McWilliam was able to institute many inquiries and courses of action throughout the day, although his men were to experience some difficulties where they had probably been least expected. This was because, as the murders increased, and also as it became obvious that the victims were being restricted to one particular class, the local inhabitants were becoming wary of getting involved – and none more so than women of similar standing. No one could be sure where the killer might strike next, but the general feeling was that those who helped the police could be increasing the odds against their own safety.

Such caution was not limited to dealings with the police. Reporters were experiencing even less co-operation and, with the increasing awareness that the murderer was probably living amongst them, most residents talked freely only when they were sure of their companions.

One of the manifestations of this nervousness encountered by the City detectives was the reluctance of possible identifiers to view the body. By that time they knew that they could be called as witnesses at the inquest, and their names and addresses published, and few wanted that. It was therefore only by dint of strong 'persuasion' that the police succeeded in getting lodging-house deputies and others to the mortuary.

The police had a similar lack of success with their investigations in the immediate vicinity of Mitre Square, where Inspector Collard had organized house-to-house inquiries as soon as it was daylight. Most of the residents were German, Austrian or Russian Jews employed in the clothes trade or as cigarette makers, and their reluctance to become implicated was very apparent.

In Duke Street, and only a few yards from the entrance to Church

Passage, was the Imperial Club. It had been open until two o'clock on the fateful morning. At first, none of the members seemed to have any information, but when the inquiries began to be made farther afield a really promising lead was discovered.

At No. 1, Hutchinson Street, Mr Levy – a butcher – said that he had left the Imperial Club with two friends about ten minutes before the body was discovered, and that they had seen a man and a woman talking at the corner of Church Passage. Unfortunately he had not taken much notice of the couple, but he thought that his companions might have been more observant.

As will be appreciated, the City detectives could hardly believe their luck. For the first time since the murders began, it seemed that someone really *had* seen the killer. They lost no time in taking the names and addresses of the two other men.

The first man seen – on the Monday – was Harry Harris, a Jewish furniture dealer, but he had little more to say than Levy. However, the second man was far more helpful. He was Joseph Lawende, who lived in Dalston, over a mile and a half from Mitre Square, but worked as a commercial traveller for a cigarettes firm in St Mary Axe, just 300 yards from the murder site.

Lawende told the police that he had been walking a little apart from Levy and Harris after they left the Imperial Club and, probably for that reason, he seems to have noticed more. Certainly what he had to say resulted in the following description being printed of a man whom the police wished to interview: 'Shabby appearance. About thirty years of age and 5' 9" in height. Fair complexion and with a small fair moustache. Wearing a red neckerchief and a cap with a peak.'

It was vital information, and senior policemen could not have been too pleased when it was leaked to the press.

Another urgent, and equally promising, visit was made to the premises of Mr Jones the pawnbroker, but the results were disappointing because nobody could remember anything about the women who, supposedly, had pledged the items. Calls at the addresses on the two tickets were also fruitless; no Jane Kelly was known at No. 6, Dorset Street, and there was no such number as that given in White's Row.

Later in the day, the pawnbroker told the police that two women in his shop had said that the dead woman was known as 'Annie', and that she lived 'in a court near to Dorset Street'. One of them had gone on to say that the fair-haired 'Annie' was, like them, an 'unfortunate'. Furthermore, she had met 'Annie' in a pub in the City Road only a couple of hours before the murder.

Everyone must have heaved a sigh of relief when that Monday drew to a close. For the police it had been a hectic but completely unrewarding day. The most promising leads had come to naught, and even though half a dozen men had been arrested on suspicion of being the killer all were released after investigation.

As far as the local population was concerned, it had been a day of mixed emotions. Excitement was general, but for women, especially the 'unfortunates' or/and dossers, that excitement was tempered by apprehension. On the other hand, lodging-house deputies and their customers were heartily sick of being questioned and hauled off to mortuaries, and the criminal fraternity was equally upset by the unusual police attention, especially the reinforcements, with whom they had no rapport whatsoever.

On the Tuesday, even more police were drafted into the area, both uniformed and plainclothed, and a massive operation ensued. All empty properties were searched, and every tip acted upon. Nowhere was excluded, and even the most notorious thoroughfares and squalid courts and alleys – some of which had never before heard a bobby's tread – were now subjected to scrutiny and the inhabitants questioned.

Neither the murderer nor his den was discovered, but at least some progress was made towards discovering the identity of the Mitre Square victim. Several people had been found who seemed to recognize the dead woman's clothes from the published description. They were taken to Bishopsgate police station to see them, and then those who confirmed their identification had their personal details noted at the chief office of the City Police, in Old Jewry, before being taken to the mortuary. At Golden Lane, two women stated that they definitely knew the deceased, and that they had associated with her in the Spitalfields area. The only drawback was that they did not know her name or much else about her! All they could say was that she was sometimes without the money for her 'doss' and had then slept in a shed off Dorset Street, with up to a score of others in the same situation.

Then late on Tuesday evening the identity of the Mitre Square victim was established beyond doubt.

The sequence of events began a little earlier when an Irish labourer named John Kelly was sitting in the kitchen of Cooney's lodging-house, at No. 55, Flower and Dean Street, idly scanning an account of the murder. Much of what he had read was already known to him, but his heart skipped a beat when he came to the mention of the pawn tickets.

Without further ado he took himself off to Bishopsgate police station where, before even being shown the clothes, he was able to give a detailed description of them, and particularly of a boot which he had repaired. When the clothes were placed before him he had no doubts, and surprised those present by running his hand around the band inside the bonnet because, he said, that was where the deceased had kept her money!

Sergeant Miles then took him to the mortuary where he made a positive identification. He appeared to be 'very much affected' by the sight of the dead woman, and stated that he had lived with her for the past seven years. Her name was Kate Conway, and the initials on her arm were explained when Kelly told the police that she had a husband named Tom.

Major Smith and Superintendent Foster were informed and they hurried over from Old Jewry to question Kelly. He made a full statement and, when it was checked, further witnesses were discovered. Piece by piece the dead woman's history was uncovered.

She had been born on April 14th, 1842, at Graisley Green, Wolverhampton. Her parents were Catharine (née Evans) and George Eddowes, and she too was named Catharine. There are conflicting reports about her early days, but they do not differ overmuch and what seems the most likely version is that her father, who was a tinplate worker at the Old Hall Works, and her mother, a cook at a local hotel, took the family to London in either 1842 or 1843.

Their first address was No. 4, Baden Place, Bermondsey, but they moved later to No. 35, West Street, and finally to No. 7, Winters Square – both in the same borough.

Catharine attended St John's Charity School in Potters Fields, near Tooley Street. It was connected with the church of St John Horsley-down in nearby Fair Street. Her education was completed at the Bridge, Candlewick, and Dowgate Wards Charity School, in Old Swan Lane in the City of London – not far from London Bridge.

Catharine was one of eleven children when her mother and father died within a few months of each other in 1855. Two of her sisters were already in domestic service, and some of her other siblings were taken into the Bermondsey Workhouse and Industrial School.

For her part, Catharine was sent to Wolverhampton to live with an aunt and uncle, Elizabeth and William Eddowes, at No. 17, Bilston Street. The young girl was put out to work, almost certainly as a domestic like her sisters. It must have been a terrible time for a thirteen-year-old girl, and it is hardly surprising that those arrangements did not last. After only a few months, she robbed her employer and absconded to another uncle, Thomas Eddowes, who lived at No. 7, Court 5, Bagot Street, Birmingham.

Information about her movements over the next eight or nine years is sparse. All that is known is that she was about twenty when she met a soldier named Tom Conway, and was soon living with him. Catharine always said that she was married to Conway – 'my name was bought and paid for' – but there is no evidence to confirm that. Whatever the situation, she took his name and, in 1864 or 1865, their first child, Annie, was born. About three years later a son, George, arrived on the scene, and after another three years a second son completed the family.

Thomas Conway finished his army service in 1872 or 1873 and became a pensioner, but the amount he received did not go far in supporting a wife and three young children, and finding work was not easy for a man with no trade. Fortunately, both he and Catharine were intelligent and it was not long before they were able to augment their income by hawking the biographies and other chap [cheap]-books which Conway started to write.

He was said to have been 'almost a teetotaller', but for Kate, as we may now call her, an all too familiar pattern had developed. Somewhere along the way she had taken to the bottle, and that resulted in constant arguments during which, it was contended, Conway often hit her.

By 1880 they had had quite enough of each other. There was a parting of the ways, with Conway taking custody of the two boys. It has been said that Annie went with Kate, but that appears open to doubt in the light of subsequent events. By then, Annie would have been working and it is quite possible that she had a job where she was able to live in. Certainly it does not seem that she was with her mother a year later, because it was then that Kate moved in with John Kelly, whom she had met in the same lodging-house where he was to read of her death.

It was an opportune meeting. Their relationship was to last until Kate was murdered, and it appears to have been a happy one with a great deal of give and take. Quiet, inoffensive Kelly had more or less steady work as a porter around the markets, whilst lively Kate went charring 'amongst the Jews' and also hawked various bits and pieces in the street – and continued to drink.

After a while it became their habit, as with so many East Enders, to have an annual working holiday by picking hops in Kent. 1888 was no exception, and they were in Hunton, near Maidstone, until the Thursday before Kate's death. Whilst there, Kelly used some of his piecework earnings to buy a new pair of boots from a Mr Arthur Pash, in the High Street at Maidstone. Not to be outdone, Kate went to another shop nearby and treated herself to the fancy jacket in which she was to die.

That, however, must have been very early in their stay because later, according to Kelly, the couple 'didn't get on any too well' and were penniless. We are not told what brought that situation about, but whatever it was there was obviously no chance of making any more money and they decided to return to London earlier than planned. It was a story which, however vague, seems more believable than the reason which Kate is alleged to have given for their premature departure.

According to the superintendent of the casual ward at Shoe Lane [or Mile End – accounts differ] Workhouse, she told him that they had returned early because she thought she knew who 'the White-chapel murderer' was and hoped to earn a reward!

Whatever the cause, the fact remains that, at the crack of dawn on Thursday, September 27th, they set off to cover the forty miles back to London.

For part of the way they walked in the company of another couple who had worked with them in the same hop fields. We are not told whether they were married, but the woman was from the Spitalfields area and was the same Emily Burrell whose name was shown on one of the pawn tickets. Burrell and her companion were not, however, returning to London and so she gave Kate the pawn ticket saying, according to the *Yorkshire Post*, 'I have got a pawn ticket for a flannel shirt. I wish you'd take it since you're going up to town. It is only in for 2nd, and may fit your old man.'

They trudged along, chattering away in the early morning sunshine, but soon the couples had to separate. Kate and John turned more directly towards London whilst the other pair continued on to Chatham.

What a sight 'Mr and Mrs Kelly' must have presented as they toiled along that hot and dusty road. It is scarcely likely that they walked the whole way but we do not know whether they managed to beg any rides or whether they used some form of public transport for the middle part of the journey. What we *are* told (although this report is at odds with the one in which he is alleged to have said they were penniless) is that John Kelly stated that they did not have enough money to 'keep us going till we got to town'.

If they *had* possessed a little cash when they started out it was soon spent, and they must have been in a sorry state by the time they reached the casual ward in Shoe Lane, Holborn. It is not known why they made for that particular haven, although there is reason to believe that Kate had stayed there before. Perhaps it was a softer touch than some of the others.

They spent the night in Shoe Lane and then, after performing the customary chores to pay for their lodging, they made their way back to Spitalfields as quickly as possible. Kelly managed to find work for a few hours, whilst Kate may have picked up a penny or two as well, and so they were in funds when they met for a drink at lunchtime. Prudent and considerate Kelly then suggested that Kate should take fourpence of the sixpence which he had earned in order to pay for a bed at the lodging-house, whilst he would spend the night in the Mile End casual ward. Kate, however, would have none of it; she told *him* to keep the fourpence and said that *she* would go to Mile End. It was a good-natured argument which soon became quite irrelevant because as they talked they drank, and soon there was no fourpence anyway!

By then it was between three and four o'clock in the afternoon, and once more they were without a penny between them. Nevertheless help was at hand. We do not know from whom the suggestion came, but we may guess because Kelly was quite befuddled by that time. In a brace of shakes, he found himself standing barefoot outside the shop of Mr Jones the pawnbroker whilst Kate pawned his new boots!

Even with their cashflow problem solved, they decided to adhere to the second of the original ideas. Kate bought some food, which they appear to have eaten in the kitchen at Cooney's, and then, after giving Kelly his doss money, she left the lodging-house later that evening to make her way to Mile End.

Next morning Kelly was quite surprised when, quite by accident, he bumped into Kate in the street at the unusually early hour of eight o'clock. Later that morning the deputy saw them having breakfast in the kitchen, but by lunchtime they were drinking again and, for some unknown reason, making their way slowly towards the City. Just before 2 p.m. they were in Houndsditch, about half a mile from their lodging-house but a mere hundred yards from where Kate's mutilated corpse was to be discovered less than twelve hours later.

It was almost certainly in a pub in Houndsditch that their jaunt came to an abrupt end with Kate's announcement that the money was all gone, and that for the third time in as many days they were in their, by then, familiar predicament. However, the difference on this occasion was that their money-raising options were far more limited. There had been no work that day for Kelly, and Kate was loath to pawn her new jacket although that was their only possession of value. Various possibilities were discussed, but in the end Kate said that she would go over to Bermondsey to try to find her daughter Annie and borrow some money from her.

There is something quite touching about the picture which comes to mind of their fond parting on that warm autumn afternoon. As the pathetic pair stood on the pavement in Houndsditch making what they thought to be their temporary farewells, and presumably with Kelly still bootless, neither could have foreseen what Fate had in store for them. Promising to be back within a couple of hours, Catharine Eddowes turned on her heel and walked out of John Kelly's life for ever.

It is unlikely that he really expected her to be back as quickly as she had said. He knew her of old, and it was also well over a mile to Bermondsey. Nevertheless he must have become just a little concerned when she had not returned by her usual time of around nine o'clock. However, any anxiety was soon allayed when two women told him that Kate was locked up safely in Bishopsgate Street police station for being drunk. He knew that the custom was to release drunks the following morning, and so he went happily to bed – having been 'trusted' by the deputy for the price of his doss.

Next morning the neighbourhood was abuzz with news of the 'double event', but it does not appear to have bothered Kelly that Kate had still not come back to the lodging-house. He wandered out, probably hoping to meet her, and in one of the ironies of fate, having no luck, he became one of the curious onlookers at Mitre Square.

We know nothing of Kelly's intelligence or mentality, except that he seems to have been an easy-going individual, but what was to follow indicates that he must have been lacking in some respect. Even with the knowledge that two unidentified women had been killed, he made no enquiry at the police station when his 'wife' failed to appear on the Sunday, and what he did for money is anybody's guess. Even more astounding is that he was apparently just as unperturbed about her continued, and unusual, absence on the Monday and Tuesday. Certainly the police must have asked him about that, because he

would have saved them much running around had he gone to
Bishopsgate Street on the Sunday morning.

Once he *had* turned up, however, their main concerns were to
pursue the lines of inquiry suggested by his statement and to prepare
for the inquest, which was only some thirty-six hours away.

Meanwhile, the newspapers contained the usual crop of letters for
officials, jurymen, witnesses and spectators to mull over before
attending the inquest. Here, for instance, is just a small sample of
the 'vast numbers' which were arriving at the office of the *Daily
Telegraph* alone.

'Waterside' urged the police to pay close attention to the crews of
steamers leaving for the Continent, and 'out-ports', each Sunday
morning. He argued 'that many of the sailors have only too great a
reason to bear animosity to the class of woman from which these
unfortunate women came'. The fact that each successive murder had
occurred on Saturday night or early Sunday morning, and that the
murderer had 'immediately disappeared' was, to his way of thinking,
conclusive evidence that his 'abiding-place' was not far off.

Other correspondence included two letters which deserve to be
reproduced in full.

The first was from Dr Roderick MacDonald, the Coroner for
North-East Middlesex. We shall meet Dr MacDonald later but, in
view of the controversy surrounding his actions then, it is interesting
to learn what he had to say at this time.

Giving his address as No. 65, West Ferry Road, Millwall, East
London, he wrote:

Sir – A remarkable incident in connection with the above
[presumably he had headed his letter with some reference to
the murders] is that in no one instance has it been found that the
victim made any noise or cry while being done to death. My
assistant suggests a theory in reference to this very remarkable
fact, which strikes me as having something in it, and as such
ought to be made public.

The theory is that the murderer goes about with a vial of rum
or brandy in his pocket drugged with an opiate – such as a

solution of morphia, which is almost if not quite tasteless – that he offers a swig of it to his victims which they would all be likely to greedily accept when he meets them: that in about ten to twenty minutes the poison begins to do its work on constitutions well soaked with alcohol, and that then they are easily dispatched without fear of making any noise or call for assistance.

Having been out of town lately for my holidays, I have not followed the evidence at the inquests but there are two questions which I would require clearing up, if there is anything in this theory – First, Have the stomachs of most of them been ripped open to do away with the evidence of poisoning in this manner: and, second, has any analysis of the contents of the stomachs been made? – Yours respectfully . . .

Although MacDonald ascribed the theory to his assistant, he obviously supported it and it is useful to have an insight of the mind of the man who was later to be at the centre of an uproar. He could have made discreet enquiries of his fellow coroners and doctors, but instead he chose to publish the theory and that is remarkable coming from a man who was to be accused of abnormal reticence.

It was the second letter, however, which should have struck a few chords in various places. It was written by David Sime, MD, from Endymion Road, Finsbury Park, London, N4:

Sir – There can surely be little doubt that the mysterious demon who has worked such havoc in the East-end is a dangerous maniac. It cannot be that he has just escaped from any lunatic asylum: otherwise he could have been tracked ere now. It is possible, however, that he may have been some time ago 'dismissed' from such an institution as 'cured'. If so, could it not be ascertained from the journals of asylums whether any recently dismissed case ever at any time laboured under the appalling delusion with respect to prostitutes with which this dangerous madman is possessed. What if not only his delusion, but his insanity were due to a medical origin in the first instance? And hence his murderous attacks on this poor and most unfortunate class of women. This clue might prove of some service.

We cannot but admire the good doctor's faith in the constabulary when he avers that any escapee 'could have been tracked ere now'. James Kelly had not *just* escaped, he had been on the run for over eight months, and *he* had not been 'tracked'!

The inquest upon the death of Catharine Eddowes opened in Golden Lane at half-past ten on Thursday, October 4th.

Mr Samuel Frederick Langham presided. Also in attendance were Henry Homewood Crawford, the City Solicitor, Dr William Sedgwick Saunders, the City Medical Officer of Health and Public Analyst, Colonel Sir James Fraser, Commissioner of the City Police, Superintendent Foster and Detective Inspector McWilliam.

As usual, it was the doctor's evidence which was the most eagerly awaited, and there was the familiar stirring of anticipation as Dr Frederick Gordon Brown, the City Police Surgeon, was sworn.

Brown was a handsome man with a waxed moustache who had busied himself sketching the other witnesses whilst waiting to be called. He gave his address as No. 17, Finsbury Circus, and told of how he had been called out just after two o'clock on the Sunday morning and had arrived on the scene at about ten minutes past.

The dead woman was lying on her back, with her head turned towards the left shoulder and her arms by the side of her body 'as if they had fallen there'. Both palms were facing upwards, and the fingers were slightly bent. A thimble was lying 'off the finger' on the right side. The upper part of her dress had been pulled open a little way, but her lower clothing was completely drawn up leaving the abdomen exposed. A bonnet was at the back of her head. Her thighs were naked, and whilst the left leg was 'extended in a line with the body' the right was bent at the thigh and knee.

Dr Brown then proceeded to describe Kate's injuries.

Her throat had been cut across – a neckerchief being below the cut – and there was great disfigurement of the face, with the lobe and auricle of the right ear being cut through obliquely. The intestines, which were smeared over with some feculent matter, were drawn out 'to a large extent' and had been placed over the right shoulder. A piece of the intestines, about two feet long, was detached and had been placed between the left arm and the body.

Mr Crawford, the City Solicitor, interrupted at that point to ask whether the doctor's use of the word 'placed' had been intended to signify deliberate acts. The witness confirmed that interpretation and then continued to describe his findings.

There was a quantity of clotted blood on the pavement, by the left side of the neck and round the shoulder and upper part of the arm. Fluid blood-coloured serum had flowed under the neck to the right shoulder as the pavement sloped in that direction. Several buttons were discovered in the clotted blood after the body was removed. No spurting of blood was found 'on the bricks or pavement around'. The body was quite warm, and no 'death-stiffening' had taken place. In the doctor's opinion: 'She must have been dead most likely within the half-hour.' He and his colleagues had looked for superficial bruises but had found none. There was no blood on the skin of the abdomen, or anywhere below the middle of the body; and there was no secretion of any kind on the thighs.

A post-mortem examination was begun at 2.30 on the Sunday afternoon. The temperature of the room was fifty-five degrees. Rigor mortis was well marked, and there was a green discoloration over the abdomen, but the body was not cold.

After the left hand had been washed, a bruise, 'recent and red' and the size of a sixpence, was discovered on the back of the hand – between the thumb and first finger. There were also a few small older bruises on the right shin. The hands and arms were bronzed, as if from sunburning. No bruises were found on the scalp, the back of the body or the elbows.

As he had said previously, the face was badly mutilated. A cut of about a quarter of an inch completely divided the structures of the lower left eyelid; through the left upper eyelid there was a scratch through the skin near the angle of the nose. The right eyelid was cut through to about half an inch, and a deep cut ran over the bridge of the nose, extending from the left border of the nasal bone, across the right cheek and down to near the angle of the jaw on the right side. This cut went into the bone, and divided all the structures of the cheek except the mucous membrane of the mouth.

The tip of the nose was 'quite detached' from the nose by an oblique cut which ran from the bottom of the nasal bone to where the 'wings' of the nose joined the face, and a cut from this divided the upper lip and extended through the substance of the gum over the right lateral incisor tooth. There was another oblique cut about half an inch from the top of the nose.

At the right angle of the mouth there was a cut which appeared to have been made by the point of a knife, and which ran parallel to the lower lip for about an inch and a half. Each cheek bore a cut which 'peeled up the skin' forming triangular flaps of about one and a half inches. On the left cheek, which was slightly mudstained, there were two slight abrasions of the epithelium under the left ear.

The throat had been cut across for about six or seven inches. A superficial cut began about one and a half inches below, and two and a half inches behind, the lobe of the left ear and extended across the throat to about three inches below the lobe of the right ear. The sterno cloido mastoid muscle was divided: the cricoid cartilage below the vocal cords was severed through the middle and the large vessels on the left side of the neck were severed to the bone, with the knife marking the intervertebral cartilages. The sheath of the vessels on the right side was just opened. The carotid artery had a pin-hole opening, and the internal jugular vein, although not divided, was open for an inch and a half. The blood vessels contained clot.

All the injuries had been performed by some sharp, pointed instrument, such as a knife. Death had been immediate, and had been caused by the haemorrhage from the left carotid artery. The mutilations had been inflicted after death.

Dr Brown then turned to the wounds to the abdomen. He said that the front walls were laid open from the breast to the pubes, with the cut beginning opposite the enciform cartilage. The incision went upwards, not penetrating the skin that was over the sternum, and then divided the enciform cartilage which, being gristle, told the doctors how the knife had made the cut. It had been held so that the point was towards the left side and the handle towards the right, and the cut must have been made obliquely, at the expense of the front surface of the cartilage. Behind this, the liver was stabbed, as if by the point of a sharp instrument and, below that, there was another incision to the liver of about two and a half inches. Below that, the left lobe of the liver was slit through by a vertical cut. Two cuts were shown by a jagging of the skin on the left side.

The abdominal walls were divided vertically, in the middle line, to within a quarter of an inch of the navel, with the cut then taking a horizontal course for two and a half inches towards the right side. It then divided round the navel, on the left side, and made a parallel incision to the horizontal incision, thus leaving the navel on a tongue of skin. Attached to the navel were two and a half inches of the lower part of the rectus muscle – on the left side of the abdomen. The incision then took an oblique course to the right and was 'shelving'. It continued down the right side of the vagina and the rectum, for half an inch behind the rectum.

In the left groin there was a stab wound of about an inch which had been made by a pointed instrument and which penetrated the skin in only a superficial fashion. Below that was a cut of three inches which went through all tissues – wounding the peritoneum to about the same extent. An inch below the crease of the thigh was a cut extending from the anterior spine of the ilium, obliquely down the inner side of the left thigh and separating the left labium – thus forming a flap of skin up to the groin. The left rectus muscle was not detached.

There was another flap of skin formed from the right thigh, attaching the right labium and extending up to the spine of the ilium. The muscles on the right side, inserted into the frontal ligaments, were cut through.

The skin was retracted through the whole of the cut in the abdomen, but the vessels were not clotted – nor had there been any appreciable bleeding from the vessels.

The doctor had removed the contents of the stomach and placed them in a jar for examination. There had seemed to be very little in the way of food or fluid, but some partly digested farinaceous food had escaped from the cut end. The intestines had been largely detached from the mesentery, with about two feet of colon being cut away, and the sigmoid flexure was invaginated into the rectum very tightly.

The right kidney was pale and bloodless, with some slight congestion of the base of the pyramids. There was a cut from the upper part of the slit in the under surface of the liver to the left side, and another at right angles to this, which were about an inch and a half deep and two and a half inches long – the liver itself was healthy. The gall bladder contained bile. The pancreas was cut, but not right through, on the left side of the spinal column. Three and a half inches of the lower border of the spleen by half an inch were attached only to the peritoneum. The peritoneal lining was cut through in the left side, and the left kidney had been carefully taken out and removed; the left renal artery being cut through. The lining membrane over the uterus was cut through, and the womb was cut through horizontally leaving a stump three-quarters of an inch long – the womb having been taken away with some of the ligaments. The vagina and cervix of the womb were undamaged.

The bladder was healthy and uninjured, and contained three or four ounces of water. There was a tongue-like cut through the anterior wall of the abdominal aorta. The other organs were healthy.

From that point on most of the dialogue was between Mr Crawford and the witness.

Q: 'I think I understand you to say that, in your opinion, the cause of death was the cut in the throat?'

A: 'Loss of blood from the throat, *caused* by the cut. That was the first wound inflicted.'

Q: 'Have you formed any opinion that the woman was standing when that wound was inflicted?'

A: 'I believe she must have been lying on the ground.'

Q: 'Does the nature of the wounds lead you to any conclusion as to the kind of instrument with which they were inflicted?'

A: 'The wounds on the face and abdomen prove that they were inflicted by a sharp pointed knife, and that in the abdomen by one at least six inches long.'

Q: 'Would you consider that the person who inflicted the wounds possessed great anatomical skill?'

A: 'I believe the perpetrator of the act must have had considerable knowledge of the position of the organs in the abdominal cavity and the way of removing them.'

Q: 'Could the organs removed be used for any professional purpose?'

A: 'They would be of no use for a professional purpose.'

Q: 'You have spoken of the extraction of the left kidney. Would it require great skill and knowledge to remove it?'

A: 'It required a great deal of knowledge to have removed the kidney and to know where it was placed. It is easily overlooked as it is covered by a membrane.'

Q: 'Would not such knowledge be likely to be possessed by one accustomed to cutting up animals?'

A: 'Yes.'

Q: 'Have you been able to form any opinion as to whether the perpetrator of this act was disturbed when performing it?'

A: 'I think he had sufficient time. My reason is that he would not have nicked the lower eyelids if he had been in a great hurry.'

Q: 'About how long do you think it would take to inflict all these wounds, and perpetrate such a deed?'

A: 'It would take at least five minutes.'

Q: 'Can you, as a professional man, assign any reason for the removal of certain organs from the body?'

A: 'I cannot.'

Q: 'Have you any doubt in your mind that there was no struggle?'

A: 'I feel sure that there was no struggle.'

Q: 'Are you equally of the opinion that the act would be that of one man, one person, only?'

A: 'I think so; I see no reason for any other opinion.'

Q: 'Can you, as a professional man, account for the fact of no noise being heard by those in the immediate neighbourhood?'

A: 'The throat would be so instantaneously severed that I do not suppose there would be any time for the least sound being emitted.'

Q: 'Would you expect to find much blood on the person who inflicted the wounds?'

A: 'No, I should not.'

Q: 'Could you say whether the blood spots on the piece of apron produced were of recent origin?'

A: 'They are of recent origin. My attention was called to the apron. It was the corner of the apron, with a string attached. Dr Phillips brought on a piece of apron which had been found by a policeman in Goulston Street.'

Q: 'It is impossible to assert that it is human blood?'

A: 'Yes. On the piece of apron brought on there were smears of blood and apparently faecal matter on one side as if a hand or knife had been wiped on it. I fitted the piece of apron, which had a new piece of material on it which had evidently been sewn on to the piece *I* have and the seams of the borders of the two actually corresponding.'

Q: 'Have you formed any opinion as to the purpose for which the face was mutilated?'

A: 'Simply to disfigure the corpse, I should think.'

Q: 'Not much violence was required to inflict these injuries?'

A: 'A sharp knife was used, and not very much force would be required.'

A juryman, who had obviously read Dr MacDonald's letter that morning, then asked whether any drug had been administered to the deceased. The witness replied that, judging by her breath [sic], he did not think so – but he had not yet examined the contents of the stomach.

At that, Dr Brown having apparently been pumped dry of all possible evidence and every opinion which he may have had, the Coroner made one of his rare contributions to the proceedings and adjourned the inquest for a week. Even then, however, he was not allowed the last word. The indefatigable Mr Crawford popped up to say that it might be of interest for the jury to know that the Court of

Common Council had unanimously adopted the suggestion of the Lord Mayor that a reward of £500 should be offered for the detection and conviction of the murderer. The jury expressed satisfaction at the announcement and then, finally, they were allowed to depart.

Kate's funeral took place on October 6th. Her body was removed from the mortuary in Golden Lane at about 1.15 p.m., to be taken to the City of London Cemetery at Manor Park, E12, for interment.

It was a most impressive cortege. The first vehicle was an open glass hearse bearing a polished elm coffin, with oak mouldings and black 'furniture', upon which was a plate inscribed 'Catherine Eddowes. Died September 30, 1888. Aged forty-three Years.' in gold lettering. There was a wreath to each side.

Next came two coaches containing the principal mourners, who included John Kelly and four of Kate's sisters. They were followed by 'a large waggon crowded with women, the majority of whom were attired in a style not at all befitting the occasion'. Last of all was a carriage carrying reporters from local and national newspapers.

Thousands of people packed the streets, especially in the vicinity of Golden Lane, and the police were hard-pressed to contain the crowds and control traffic as the procession wended its slow way along the eight miles or so to the cemetery. At the beginning it was escorted by the City Police, commanded by Superintendent Foster himself. Then, at the City of London boundary, a force of Metropolitan Police, under Inspector Barnham, took over.

The cortege passed slowly along Old Street and Great Eastern Street into Commercial Street, but when it turned into Whitechapel High Street it was almost brought to a halt. There the pavements were absolutely choked with East Enders determined to pay their last respects to a woman whom they regarded as one of their own. Workmen removed their caps and women wept and bared their heads as the hearse passed at less than walking pace.

Nearly five hundred people were assembled at the cemetery when the vehicles arrived over two hours after leaving the City. Many of them were women carrying children. The brief service was conducted by the Rev. T. Dunscombe, the cemetery chaplain, who made no mention of the fact that the dead woman had been murdered, and then Kate was finally laid to rest. Despite the fact that the White-chapel Workhouse Infirmary authorities had her registered as a Roman Catholic, she was interred in the Church of England section. Her body was lowered gently into Public Grave No. 49336, which was in the same Square, 318, as the grave of Polly Nichols.

It had all been in stark contrast with the scant respect shown to Elizabeth Stride who had been slipped quietly, and almost secretly, into her pauper's grave – but then she was, after all, only a foreigner.

Kate's inquest was resumed at half-past ten on October 11th.

The first witness was the twenty-nine-year-old Dr George William Séquêria, who gave his address as No. 34, Jewry Street, Aldgate.

He told the jury that having been called out, he had arrived in Mitre Square at 1.55 a.m. on the 30th of September, and was the first doctor on the scene. The position of the body was exactly as had been described by Dr Brown.

Mr Langham was probably still noting that evidence when Mr Crawford darted in with his first question of the day. He wanted to know whether the doctor was acquainted with the locality and the positions of the lamps in the Square. Hardly surprisingly, as he lived less than 150 yards away, the witness said he was, and added that where the body was found was probably the darkest part. There would, however, have been sufficient light to enable the murderer to commit the deed. In his opinion, the killer had no design on any particular organ and possessed no great anatomical skill.

Q: 'Can you account for the absence of noise?'
A: 'The death must have been instantaneous after the severance of the windpipe and the blood vessels.'
Q: 'Would you have expected the murderer to be bespattered with blood?'
A: 'Not necessarily.'
Q: 'How long do you believe life had been extinct when you arrived?'
A: 'Very few minutes: probably not more than a quarter of an hour.'

Mr Crawford had finished with the young Dr Séquêria and he was allowed to depart. He was replaced by William Sedgwick Saunders, of No. 13, Queen Street, Cheapside, who stated that he was a Doctor of Medicine, a Fellow of the Institute of Chemistry, a Fellow of the Chemical Society, and the Public Analyst for the City of London.

'I received the stomach of the deceased from Dr Gordon Brown, carefully sealed with his own private seal. The ends of the stomach had been carefully tied, but the contents had not been interfered with in any way. I carefully examined the stomach and the contents, more particularly for poisons of the narcotic class, but with negative results, there not being the faintest trace of these or any other poisons.'

It was brief and to the point, and answered both Dr MacDonald's letter and the juryman's question.

Before the next witness could be called, Mr Crawford addressed the Coroner:

'The theory has been put forward that it is possible for the deceased to have been murdered elsewhere, and her body brought to where it was found. I should like to ask Dr Gordon Brown, who is present, what his opinion is about that.'

Mr Langham obviously had no objection, because Dr Brown was recalled and, when the question was put to him directly, he replied that he could see no foundation for such a theory: 'The blood on the left side was clotted, and must have fallen at the time the throat was cut. I do not think the deceased moved in the slightest after that.'

James Byfield, the Station Sergeant at Bishopsgate police station, then told of how Kate had been 'brought in' at 8.45 p.m on Saturday the 29th. She had been placed in a cell until 1 a.m. when, as she appeared to be sober, she was discharged.

One of Sergeant Byfield's subordinates that night had been PC George Henry Hutt, the City Gaoler. He now appeared and described how he had brought her into 'the office' for discharge. On the way, she had asked what time it was and Hutt had told her: 'Too late for you to get any more drink.' Kate, however, had persisted: 'Well what time *is* it?' and was told 'Just on one.' To that she had replied: 'I shall get a damned fine hiding when I get home then.' She had received no sympathy from the witness, who had told her: 'Serves you right; you've no right to get drunk.'

Sergeant Byfield had discharged her, and then Hutt had pushed open the swing door leading to 'the passage', and said: 'This way, missus,' at which she had gone down the passage to the door to the street.

'I said to her: "Please pull it to" and she said: "All right, goodnight, old cock." Kate had pulled the door to within six inches of being closed, and he had then seen her turn left, towards Houndsditch. He had noticed that she was wearing an apron, which he believed to be the one produced. In his opinion, it would take eight minutes of 'ordinary walking' to get from the station to Mitre Square.

The evidence given by some of the next witnesses was to demonstrate the apparent speed and stealth with which the killer had carried out his murderous intent.

First came George James Morris, a former policeman and now the night-watchman at Kearley and Tonge's warehouses in Mitre Square, who said that he had been at work there on the Saturday night from seven o'clock.

At 1.45 a.m. he had been inside sweeping the steps down to the outer door, which was ajar. He had come to within about two yards of the door when it was knocked, or pushed. Morris had opened the door fully, and had found himself confronted by an alarmed PC Watkins who blurted out: 'For God's sake, mate, come to my assistance! There is another woman cut to pieces.'

Morris told the Coroner that he had heard no noise in the Square before he was called out by Watkins. Had there been any 'cry of distress' he would have been bound to have heard it.

PC James Harvey was next. He said that he had gone on his beat at 9.45 p.m. on the Saturday, and at 1.40 a.m. on the Sunday, he had gone from Duke Street into Church Passage, and down it as far as, but not into, Mitre Square. He saw nobody and heard nothing. Then, when he was in Aldgate, on his way back to Duke Street, he heard a whistle and then saw Morris who told him that a woman had been 'ripped up' in Mitre Square.

Harvey concluded by saying that, having no watch, he could 'only speak with certainty as to time with regard to the Post Office clock'.

George Clapp told the inquest that he was the caretaker for the premises of Messrs Heydemann and Company, who were commission merchants at No. 5, Mitre Street, Aldgate, the rear of which overlooked Mitre Square.

He and his wife slept on the second floor, and they retired to bed at about 11 p.m. on the Saturday night. The only other person on the premises that night was a Mrs Few, who was a nurse in attendance on his wife. She slept on the third floor – at the top of the house.

None of them had heard anything during the night, and the first the witness had known of the murder was at between five and six o'clock on the following morning.

The next witness was a young man who must have spent the rest of his life regretting that he had not suffered a bout of insomnia on the night in question. He was Richard Pearce, a City policeman, who had the unique distinction of being the only private resident in the Square.

Pearce was the tenant of No. 3, Mitre Square, where he lived with his wife and family. He had gone to bed at 12.30 a.m. on the Sunday, and had heard no noise or disturbance of any kind until 2.20 a.m. when he was called by a colleague who told him of the murder. The witness told the inquest that he could see the murder spot quite clearly from his window.

It will be recalled that, soon after the murder, the City police had interviewed Joseph Lawende, who had left the Imperial Club near Mitre Square only minutes before the body was discovered.

He now told of being at the Club with his two friends. At 1.30 a.m., when they came to leave, they had discovered that it was raining and so they sat and waited for a few minutes, until it stopped, and then departed.

For some reason or other, Lawende was walking 'apart' from his companions when he espied a man and a woman standing at the corner of Church Passage and Duke Street.

Mr Langham wanted to know whether the couple had been talking, but the witness ignored his question and, surprisingly, the Coroner did not repeat it. The only reply which he received from the witness was that the woman was standing with her back to him, facing the man, and had her hand on his chest. Lawende had not been able to see her face.

Further questioning revealed that the man was taller than the woman, whom the witness considered to be about five feet in height. She had been wearing a black jacket and a black bonnet, and Lawende believed that they were the same as those he had been shown at the police station.

Coroner: 'What sort of a man was this?'
A: 'He had on a cloth cap, with a cloth peak and . . .'

– and that was as far as he got because Mr Crawford had leaped to his feet to interrupt: 'Unless the jury particularly wish it, I have a special reason why no further description of the man should be given now.'

He looked at the jury, as did the Coroner after pushing his spectacles up to his forehead, and both waited whilst the foreman had a brief word with his colleagues before stating that they did not 'desire it'. Mr Langham, however, was not prepared to leave it at that, and it was only after he had satisfied himself that Lawende had given a full description to the police that the subject was dropped.

Then the Coroner wanted to know something much more to the point: 'Would you know the man again?'

Lawende: 'I doubt it. The man and woman were about nine or ten feet away from me.'

Lawende said he had 'fixed' the time by the Club clock and his own watch: 'I have no doubt it was half-past one o'clock when we rose to leave the Club, so that it would be twenty-five minutes to two o'clock when we passed the man and woman.'

That brought Mr Crawford, obliquely, to the question from the Coroner which Lawende had ignored: 'Did you hear anything that either said?'

A: 'No.'

Lawende elaborated upon his reply by saying that the pair did not appear to be quarrelling – they seemed to be conversing very quietly. There was nothing about either of them which particularly attracted his attention, save that the man had looked rather rough and shabby. When the woman had placed her hand on her companion's chest she had done so gently, and not as if to push him away. The witness had not been curious enough to look back to see where they went.

The jury duly returned a verdict of 'Wilful murder by some person unknown.'

On October 19th, the *Police Gazette* was to carry the following descriptions of the persons sought by the police:-

At 12.35 a.m., 30th September, with Elizabeth Stride, found murdered at 1 a.m., same date, in Berner-street – A MAN, age 28, height 5 ft 8 in., complexion dark, small dark moustache; dress, black diagonal coat, hard felt hat, collar and tie; respectable appearance. Carried a parcel wrapped up in newspaper.

At 12.45 a.m., 30th, with same woman, in Berner-street – A MAN, age about 30, height 5 ft 5 in., complexion fair, hair dark, small brown moustache, full face, broad shoulders; dress, dark jacket and trousers, black cap with peak.

At 1.35 a.m., 30th September, with Catherine Eddows, in Church-passage, leading to Mitre-square, where she was found murdered at 1.45 a.m., same date – A MAN, age 30, height 5 ft 7 or 8 in., complexion fair, moustache fair, medium build; dress, pepper-and-salt colour loose jacket, grey cloth cap with peak of same material, reddish neckerchief tied in knot; appearance of a sailor.

Information to be forwarded to the Metropolitan Police Office, Great Scotland-yard, London, S.W.

Those descriptions are based upon those given by PC Smith, Israel Schwartz and Joseph Lawende, yet in spite of all the descriptions, the thousands of words spoken, and the hundreds of inquiries made by two police forces, the killer was no nearer to being caught – and the worst was yet to come.

8

Mary

THE ALTERNATING INQUEST sessions, police pronounce-
ments, journalists' tales, funeral reports, false confessions, abortive
arrests and the hundreds of letters to newspapers provided ideal
breeding conditions for the innumerable rumours which now swept
the area and ensured that fear and excitement were kept at fever-
pitch. Nothing, however, was to match the impact of a letter that had
arrived at the Central News Agency on September 27th.

Written in red ink, and in a good hand, it was addressed to: 'The
Boss, Central News Office, London City', and read:

25th Sept. 1888

Dear Boss,

    I keep on hearing the police have caught me but they wont fix
me just yet. I have laughed when they look so clever and talk
about being on the *right* track. That joke about Leather Apron
gave me real fits. I am down on whores and I shant quit ripping
them till I do get buckled. Grand work the last job was. I gave
the lady no time to squeal. How can they catch me now. I love
my work and want to start again. You will soon hear of me with
my funny little games. I saved some of the proper *red* stuff in a
ginger beer bottle over the last job to write with but it went thick

like glue and I cant use it. Red ink is fit enough I hope *ha.ha*. The next job I do I shall clip the ladys ears off and send to the police officers just for jolly wouldnt you. Keep this letter back till I do a bit more work then give it out straight. My knife's so nice and sharp I want to get to work right away if I get a chance. Good luck.

yours truly
Jack the Ripper

Dont mind me giving the trade name

wasnt good enough to post this before I got all the red ink off my hands curse it. No luck yet. They say I'm a doctor now ha ha

The second postscript, written sideways, is said to have been in red crayon.

The letter was regarded as a practical joke at the News Agency, and was not delivered to Scotland Yard until the 29th, nor made public until the 30th. However, on Monday, October 1st, it was followed by a postcard which was delivered with the first post. The card, which was franked for that day, October 1st, was much besmeared with either red ink or blood, but was written in what, again, appeared to be red crayon.

Bearing a 'London E.' postmark, and addressed to 'Central News Office, London City EC', it was in the same handwriting as the letter and read:

I was not codding dear old Boss when I gave you the tip, youll hear about saucy Jacky's work tomorrow double event this time number one squealed a bit couldnt finish straight off had not time to get ears for police thanks for keeping last letter back till I got to work again

Jack the Ripper

The postcard was also handed over to Scotland Yard, where the hierarchy professed to attach no importance to the two communications. They noted that the postcard revealed no special knowledge; reports of the 'double event' had been circulating all over London since dawn on September 30th. That notwithstanding, they had facsimiles made and sent to the press, in the hope that somebody would recognize the handwriting when they were published. Nothing came of this, but the chilling nickname had arrived to stay.

By then, not even the most exclusive suburbs of London, nor indeed the rest of the country, were immune from the near hysteria, but it is only to be expected that it should have been greatest in the East End, where the anticipation of further horrors increased daily.

A mathematical progression of the dates of the murders indicated that another could be expected during the weekend which would begin on Friday, October 5th, and therefore more police reinforcements were drafted in, the vigilance committees stepped up their patrols – and the population held its breath.

Tradesmen had already been complaining bitterly about the drop in after-dark business, but now they found that their takings were slumping even more as females refused to venture even a few yards from their homes once the evening darkness had descended.

Yet, ironically, the very women who were most at risk were forced on to the murky and menacing streets. 'Ripper' or no 'Ripper', the doss money had to be earned and they had only one way to earn it. Most were fatalistic about their chances but, even so, they were inclined to eye potential customers cautiously, and to avoid the darkest and most secluded alleys and courts.

As it happened, there was not a murder that weekend, nor the next, and there was a slight relaxation of the tension. Then, on the evening of Tuesday, October 16th, an event occurred which brought back all the fear and apprehension in double measure.

George Lusk, President of the Mile End Vigilance Committee, received a small brown paper parcel. It bore two one-penny stamps, and a postmark of which only the letters 'OND' were visible – undoubtedly part of the word 'LONDON'.

When Lusk unwrapped the package he discovered it contained a small cardboard box, roughly three and a half inches square, and a letter which read:

From hell
Mr Lusk
    Sor
    I send you half the Kidne I took from one women prasarved it for you tother piece I fried and ate it was very nise I may send you the bloody knif that took it out if you only wate a whil longer
    signed   Catch me when
                                                        you can
                                                 Mishter Lusk

Lusk opened the box and found, to his horror, that it did indeed contain half a kidney, but his initial reaction was that it was hoax. Only after giving the matter some thought the next day, during which he recalled the details of the Mitre Square mutilations, did he begin to think that it was something far more serious.

The Treasurer of the Vigilance Committee, Joseph Aarons, suggested that it be taken to a local doctor, Dr Frederick Wiles, who lived nearby at No. 56, Mile End Road. The doctor was absent, but his assistant, Mr F. S. Reed, examined the disgusting object and expressed the opinion that it was human, had been divided longitudinally, and had then been preserved in 'spirits of wine'.

It was obvious that the matter should be reported to the police, and so the vigilantes trooped off to Leman Street police station and handed the parcel to Inspector Abberline. As the inference was that the revolting scrap of meat was connected with a City case he, very wisely, lost no time in having it delivered to his colleagues across the boundary.

Chief Inspector Swanson reported to the Home Office that the medical opinion was that it was 'the kidney of a human adult, not charged with a fluid, as it would have been in the case of a body handed over for purposes of dissection to an hospital, but rather as it would be in a case where it was taken from the body not so destined. In other words similar kidneys might and could be obtained from any dead person whom a post mortem had been made from any cause by students or dissecting room porter.'

On the other hand, Mr Sutton, one of the senior surgeons of the London Hospital, and one of the greatest authorities living on the kidney and its diseases, said he would pledge his reputation that the kidney 'had been put in spirits within a few hours of its removal from the body – thus effectually disposing of all hoaxes in connection with it. The body of anyone done to death by violence is not taken direct to the dissecting-room, but must await an inquest, never held before the following day at the soonest.'

The newspapers were on to the story very quickly, and were instrumental in causing a Miss Emily Marsh to come forward with a possible clue as to the identity of the sender of the package.

Miss Marsh worked for her father, a leather trader, who had a shop at No. 218, Jubilee Street, at the top of which the Crown pub made a corner with the Mile End Road. She stated that during the early afternoon of Monday, October 15th, i.e. the day before Lusk received the parcel, a tall man dressed in 'clerical costume' had entered the shop. Pointing to a Vigilance Committee reward poster in the window, he had asked for Lusk's address. Emily, obviously an obliging girl and an asset to her father's business, had disappeared into the back room and fetched a newspaper. She had made to hand the paper to the man, in order that he could copy the address therein, but he would not take it. Instead, he had asked Emily to read it to him and had written it in his pocket-book. Then he had thanked her and left, just avoiding Mr Marsh who was about to enter the shop.

The whole episode had disturbed the young lady so much that she had sent the shop boy, John Cormack, to watch which way the man went.

A newspaper description of him reads:

'The stranger is described as a man of some forty-five years of age, fully six feet in height, and slimly built. He wore a soft felt black hat, drawn over his forehead, a stand-up collar, and a very long black single-breasted overcoat, with a Prussian or clerical collar partly turned up. His face was of a sallow type, and he had a dark beard and moustache. The man spoke with what was taken to be an Irish accent.'

Despite this disturbing incident, however, there was no gainsaying the fact that a sense of calm was beginning to prevail again and, on October 22nd, Superintendent Arnold reported that there was very little excitement in the area.

November arrived, things remained quiet, and the East Enders were only too pleased to allow their minds to stray to an event dear to their hearts, the Lord Mayor's Show.

This year the Lord Mayor, the Right Honourable James White-head, had arranged for 3,000 of the poorest inhabitants of East London to be provided with a tea in the Great Assembly Hall, Mile End Road, on the evening of his inauguration day.

Each pauper was to be allowed half a pound of bread and butter, a similar weight of cake, a large pork pie and two apples. Unfortunately, and quite unlike his guests at the Guildhall, the poor were not to be provided with any alcoholic beverages – a quart of tea apiece being deemed quite sufficient.

It looked, therefore, as if November 9th was indeed going to be a memorable day, and even the 'unfortunates' were looking forward to what, for them, could be a profitable weekend.

Had they but known what was to come, their happy anticipation would have been short-lived because the Right Honourable James Whitehead's day was to be marred, and his headlines stolen. The demented being living in their midst had merely been biding his time. He had his own plans for the 9th, and soon he was to sate himself with an orgy of blood-letting beside which his previous abominations were to pale into insignificance.

Only about three-quarters of a mile, as a rather sooty crow would have flown, was to separate the next murder scene from the streets which were to witness so much pageantry on the ninth, but the cultures of the two areas could not have been more different.

The City of London, heart of the richest country and greatest empire in the world, was a very far cry from the dilapidated and filthy dwellings which housed the poor, desperate and villainous inhabitants of Spitalfields. Yet even in that notorious district one thoroughfare predominated in squalor, vice, violence and crime – Dorset Street.

It will be recalled that it was from Crossingham's lodging-house in Dorset Street that poor Annie Chapman wandered off into the night to suffer her fate only 300 yards away. Bounded by Crispin Street and Commercial Street, it was widely regarded as one of the most dangerous roads in London.

In 1888, as now, the imposing Convent of Mercy, in Crispin Street, kept vigil at the western end and gazed frowningly at the graveyard of Christ Church, in Commercial Street. Nevertheless, and seemingly in defiance of such reminders of the Last Judgement, most of the inhabitants of Dorset Street eked out existences of unimaginable debauchery and depravity.

There were three pubs: the Horn of Plenty made the corner with Crispin Street; then, about sixty yards on the left hand side, walking east, came the Blue Coat Boy (Wm. Jas. Turner, Prop.); and finally, on the Commercial Street corner, was the Britannia (Ringer's).

For a street of a mere 130 yards, it is somewhat surprising that not only were there a couple of stables but also three grocery, or chandler's, shops from which, somehow, Barnett Price, John McCarthy and Alfred Coates all contrived to make a living. In the main, however, Dorset Street was renowned for the number of common lodging-houses, registered and unregistered, crammed into it, and the multitude which they accommodated – 300 men and women, and sometimes more, in Crossingham's alone!

As a result, Dorset Street was rarely referred to as such – 'Dossers' or 'Dosset' Street being popular corruptions. It was also known as 'The Do As You Please' – a colloquialism which was graphically descriptive of its reputation of being an evil place into which even the police hesitated to venture.

It was in this sink of iniquity that the young woman known as Mary Jane Kelly ended her rather rapid fall from grace and, in her dying, presented us with more mysteries than all the other killings put together.

There is scarcely a single 'fact' about her of which we can be sure, not even her real name. From what she was alleged to have said, Mary Jane Kelly, or 'Marie Jeanette' as she affected, was about twenty-five years old at the time of the murders, and that vague age was to be entered on her death certificate. She was variously described as being 'a good-looking young woman of fair and fresh-coloured complexion'; 'about 5 feet 7 inches in height, and of rather stout build, with blue eyes and a very fine head of hair, which reached nearly to her waist'; 'a pleasant little woman, rather stout, fair complexion, and rather pale'; 'tall and pretty, and as fair as a lily'. Various nicknames have been attributed to her: 'Fair Emma', 'Ginger' and 'Black Mary', although, if true, the last is more likely to have been a reference to her temperament, as the overall impression is that everything in her physical appearance was fair. Generally speaking, she was considered to be quite pleasant when sober, but inclined to black moods and violence when in drink.

Unlike the previous victims, Mary Kelly made no pretence of being anything other than what she was, and that is probably why she is the only one to have the word 'Prostitute' on her death certificate.

She occupied a single room, roughly twelve feet square, at the ground-floor rear of No. 26, Dorset Street, which was a common lodging-house kept by a John McCarthy – one of the chandlers mentioned above, whose shop and home was next door at No. 27. Unlike the other rooms in No. 26, there was no access to her room from inside the house as the internal door to it had been nailed up or boarded over. Instead, it was approached from Dorset Street by means of a covered flagged passage – three feet wide and some twenty feet long – which was between Nos. 26 and 27, and was the only means of access to Miller's Court. As one emerged from that damp and gloomy entry, Mary Kelly's door was immediately on the right. Then, also on the right, was a yard about fifteen feet square which was overlooked by the two windows of her room, and which contained the communal dustbin, tap and what was known as 'the shed'.

Miller's Court extended for roughly forty feet and was about ten feet wide. On the left, beginning opposite Mary's door, was a building which was divided into four, and on the right – beyond the yard – was another partitioned into three. The first three divisions on each side were 'one-up, one-down' cribs, whitewashed to the first floor, which had been converted into twelve individual rooms. Their numbering began with No. 1 on the left opposite Mary's door, and went up and down the Court ending with No. 12 on the far side of the yard from Mary's windows. That, of course, left her in the unfortunate position of being the tenant of No. 13, as it had been designated when it was separated from the rest of the Dorset Street house.

John McCarthy was the landlord of Miller's Court also, and the thirteen rooms were known collectively as 'McCarthy's Rents'. Some had it that the term applied equally to the female tenants, many of whom appear to have been prostitutes living either alone or with temporary partners. Be that as it may, McCarthy was in a good position to keep a close eye on what his tenants were up to. All their mail was delivered to his shop, the door to which had to be passed by those coming from Commercial Street and from the back room window of which he could see directly down the Court. The window was at right angles with the door of No. 1, above which was a gas lamp attached to the wall, and the only room which could not, therefore, be watched was No. 13.

The day of the Lord Mayor's Show was a Friday. Saturdays were generally regarded as 'pay-days' by those of the working-class who *were* working, and it appears to have been McCarthy's routine to have his rents paid then. On the 9th, however, he made a particular exception with Mary Kelly because he was intent upon getting some money out of her. She rented her room 'furnished' at 4s. 6d.(22½p) a week, but she was now twenty-nine shillings in arrears and it was a state of affairs that could not be allowed to continue. Knowing the habits of his tenants, McCarthy left it until a quarter to eleven on the morning of the 9th, and then despatched one Thomas Bowyer to No. 13 to see what he could collect.

Bowyer, an Indian Army pensioner, served in McCarthy's shop and seems also to have been a general odd-jobs man. With the East Enders' penchant for never calling anybody by their correct name if another could be invented, he was known locally as 'Indian Harry'.

Leaving the chandler's, he turned left into the dreary passage and approached the small squalid room that Mary Kelly called home. What happened next is best described in his own words:

'I went and knocked at the door and got no answer. I knocked again, and got no answer. I went round the corner by the gutter where there is a broken window. There was a curtain. I put my hand through the broken pane and lifted it and looked in. I saw two lumps of flesh laying on the table close against the bed. The second time I looked I saw a body of someone laid on the bed and blood on the floor. I at once went very quickly back to my master, Mr John McCarthy, and we then stood in the shop and I told him what I had seen. We both then went directly to the police station, but before doing so I and my master went and looked in the window.'

It was to the station in Commercial Street that they had gone, and the duty Station Inspector to whom they blurted out their tale was Inspector Walter Beck. His statement sums up his subsequent actions succinctly: 'I was the first police officer called to Miller's Court by McCarthy. I sent for the doctor and closed the court to all persons.'

Fortunately, forty constables were being held in reserve at Commercial Street station to cope with any disturbances at the Lord Mayor's Show, and that enabled Beck to ensure that all loiterers were cleared from the street and that it was guarded at both ends.

Inspector Beck had been called out just after 11 a.m., and the doctor for whom he had sent arrived at Miller's Court at 11.15. As this was yet another 'H' Division murder, the doctor in question was none other than the ubiquitous George Bagster Phillips, who was to say at the inquest:

'I was called by the police on Friday morning last about eleven o'clock and proceeded to Miller's Court which I entered at 11.15 a.m. I found a room, the door of which led out of the passage next to 26, Dorset Street, and having two windows. I produce a photograph I had taken.

'There are two windows in the Court. Two of the panes in the window nearest the passage were broken and, finding the door locked, I looked through the lower broken pane and satisfied myself that the mutilated corpse lying on the bed was not in need of any immediate attention from me, and also came to the conclusion that there was nobody else on the bed or within view to whom I could render any professional assistance.'

Inspector Abberline had arrived at 11.30 a.m. in company with Inspector Reid and a small army of plain-clothes detectives. He was asked by Phillips 'not to force the door, but to test the dogs if they were coming'.

This reference was to two bloodhounds, Barnaby and Burgho, who were owned by a Scarborough breeder, Mr Brough. The Chief Commissioner of the Metropolitan Police, Sir Charles Warren had given instructions that they were to be taken to the scene of any future murder, and that the body was not to be touched until they had been given the scent.

Mr Brough had returned to Scarborough, leaving the canines in the care of a friend pending the conclusion of the negotiations with the police to buy them. However, because he received no firm offer from Scotland Yard, the owner had the dogs returned to him forthwith.

Unfortunately, however, nobody had thought fit to countermand Sir Charles's orders, and not even Superintendent Thomas Arnold, the man in charge of 'H' Division, knew that they were no longer effective. So it was gone one o'clock before any further word about the dogs arrived from Scotland Yard, and it was not what had been expected. In yet another example of the left hand of the headquarters of the Metropolitan Police not knowing what the right was up to – and it was not to be the last, by a long chalk – it had taken them some two hours to detect the true situation with regard to the blood-hounds. Now the Superintendent was informed that they were *not* being sent after all!

Arnold lost no time in imparting the news. He arrived at Miller's Court at 1.30 p.m., and it was no doubt with a sense of relief that those assembled learned that their long wait was over.

The inhabitants of Dorset Street would also have been pleased. They had been confined indoors in order that the road be kept clear for the dogs to follow any scent, but now they were allowed to go about their business. Nevertheless, the police cordons were maintained at each end of the street, and those in Miller's Court remained restricted to their rooms.

It had taken no time at all for word of the latest atrocity to spread, and even the Lord Mayor's Show had been disrupted by the 'Read all abaat it!' shouts of the newspaper boys. Soon hundreds had flocked to the neighbourhood, and the lines of constables came under heavy pressure from the crowds trying to get to the murder site. As always, the street vendors were not slow in making an appearance and their hoarse cries were overtones to the quiet deliberations now taking place outside the windows of No. 13.

Having been told that the door was locked, Superintendent Arnold told McCarthy to fetch something with which to break it open. By now Dr Anderson, the Assistant Commissioner, CID, had arrived and he and the rest of the little group watched as the landlord inserted the tip of a pickaxe between door and jamb and gently effected an entrance.

Determined to be first inside, Dr Phillips now stepped forward and we shall hear later about his entering No. 13 and what he found there. However, far more information was to be contained in a confidential report submitted to Dr Anderson by Dr Edward Bond. (Anderson, concerned by the contradictory opinions on how much surgical skill the killer possessed, had recruited Bond to provide another opinion. It is to that, therefore, that we must turn for the full details of the horror Phillips beheld:

Notes of examination of body of woman found Murdered & mutilated in Dorset St.

Position of body.

The body was lying naked in the middle of the bed, the shoulders flat, but the axis of the body inclined to the left side of the bed. The head was turned on the left cheek. The left arm was close to the body with the forearm flexed at a right angle & lying across the abdomen. The right arm was slightly abducted from the body & rested on the mattress, the elbow bent & the forearm supine with the fingers clenched.

The legs were wide apart, the left thigh at right angles to the trunk & the right forming an obtuse angle with the pubes.

The whole of the surface of the abdomen & thighs was removed & the abdominal cavity emptied of its viscera. The breasts were cut off, the arms mutilated by several jagged wounds & the face hacked beyond recognition of the features. The tissues of the neck were severed all round down to the bone.

The viscera were found in various parts viz: the uterus & kidneys with one breast under the head, the other breast by the Rt foot, the liver between the feet, the intestines by the right side & the spleen by the left side of the body.

The flaps removed from the abdomen & thighs were on a table.

The bed clothing at the right corner was saturated with blood, & on the floor beneath was a pool of blood covering about 2 feet square. The wall by the right side of the bed & in a line with the neck was marked by blood which had struck it in a number of separate splashes.

Postmortem examination.

The face was gashed in all directions the nose, cheeks, eyebrows & ears being partly removed. The lips were blanched & cut by several incisions running obliquely down to the chin. There were also numerous cuts extending irregularly across all the features.

The neck was cut through the skin & other tissues right down to the vertebrae the 5th and 6th being deeply notched. The cuts in the front of the neck showed distinct ecchymosis. The air passage was cut at the lower part of the larynx through the cricoid cartilage.

Both breasts were removed by more or less circular incisions, the muscles down to the ribs being attached to the breasts. The intercostals between the 4' 5' & 6' ribs were cut & the contents of the thorax visible through the openings.

The skin and tissues of the abdomen from the costal arch to the pubes were removed in three large flaps. The right thigh was denuded in front to the bone, the flap of skin including the external organs of generation & part of the right buttock.

The left thigh was stripped of skin, fascia & muscles as far as the knee.

The left calf showed a long gash through skin & tissues to the deep muscles & reaching from the knee to 5in. above the ankle.

Both arms & forearms had extensive & jagged wounds.

The right thumb showed a small superficial incision about 1 in. long, with extravasation of blood in the skin & there were several abrasions on the back of the hand & forearm showing the same condition.

On opening the thorax it was found that the right lung was minimally adherent by old firm adhesions. The lower part of the lung was broken & torn away.

The left lung was intact. It was adherent at the apex & there were a few adhesions over the side. In the substances of the lung were several nodules of consolidation.

The Pericardium was open below & the Heart absent.

In the abdominal cavity was some partly digested food of fish & potatoes & similar food was found in the remains of the stomach attached to the intestines.

The police made plans of the premises, and an inventory of the contents of No. 13, but unfortunately they seem to have disappeared. For that information we are therefore dependent upon newspaper, and other, reports, and the ageing memories of police officers – all of which are unreliable. Nevertheless, there appears to be general agreement that Mary's room contained only four pieces of old furniture; a hefty wooden double bed, two tables – one larger than the other – and a kitchen chair.

As one entered the room, the door opened to the right but was prevented from moving beyond ninety degrees because of the proximity of the smaller table. That was hard against the bed which in turn was close to the wall separating the room from the rest of No. 26.

Facing the door, in the middle of the wall at the far end of the room, was the chimney-breast and fireplace with an alcove each side. Over the mantelpiece were stuck a couple of cheap engravings. The right-hand alcove housed a cupboard about four feet high, the top of which did service as a wash-stand. It was found to contain a few pieces of pottery, some ginger-beer bottles and a piece of bread on a plate.

The larger table was to the left-hand side of the room, not far from the unbroken window. On it was a broken wine glass containing a candle – a 'farthing dip' – of which less than half had been consumed. Some of Mary's clothes were draped over the foot of the bed, whilst others were folded neatly on the nearby chair. Her boots were before the fireplace, as if to dry. There was a man's navy-blue overcoat in the room, said to have been hanging over the broken window panes.

In the grate there was evidence of a large fire, and close by stood a cheap tin kettle which had been subjected to such extreme heat that the solder of the spout had melted. It was said that the ashes of the fire were still warm, and contained a piece of a velvet skirt and what little remained of the rim and wirework of a woman's burnt felt bonnet. On the whole, it was probably an above average room for Spitalfields, and especially Dorset Street.

It took some two hours for the doctors to complete their preliminary examination, and then came the question of the removal of the remains – a subject about which there can be little doubt that Bagster Phillips and the police had already reached agreement.

As we have seen, Dr Phillips had protested vigorously at Annie Chapman's inquest about the poor conditions which prevailed in the shed that did service as a mortuary for Whitechapel. He had considered it to be a totally unsuitable place in which to carry out a post-mortem examination, and the Coroner, Wynne Baxter, had agreed with him. Now, with a body that was in pieces, Phillips did not relish the thought of having to undertake a detailed investigation in such cramped and insanitary conditions. He had therefore considered the possibility of using more suitable premises – but those which were chosen in this instance were not selected solely on medical grounds.

Both Phillips and the police had had their fill of what they considered to be the humiliations heaped upon them by Wynne Baxter, and certainly the dapper little Coroner was not everybody's cup of tea. Some thought him over-zealous in his duties, but he was very conscious of his responsibilities and his natural curiosity had caused him to probe deeply into every aspect of the previous murders. The effects of those attributes, combined with an unwillingness to tolerate inefficiency, had, however, been to make the doctor squirm and the police embarrassed, and none of them wished to have the experiences repeated. There was, therefore, unanimous agreement to the suggestion that the corpse be taken to Shoreditch Mortuary, just over half a mile away. That would effectively kill two birds with one stone. Not only would Phillips enjoy better facilities, but Shoreditch came under the jurisdiction of a far more amenable coroner.

Transport was ordered and, at 3.50 p.m., a carrier's cart with the usual tarpaulin cover was drawn slowly into Dorset Street by a solitary horse. It came to a stop at the entrance to Miller's Court, and police assisted in the removal of a long shell which was carried into No. 13. If anything, it was even dirtier and more scratched than those used for the previous victims, and epitomized the whole sordid nature of the killing.

Word that the body was being taken away brought people running to the scene from every nook and cranny in Dorset Street. Determined not to be outdone, the crowd in Commercial Street surged forward in a concerted attempt to break the police cordon, but to no avail.

Nevertheless, the makeshift hearse – which was usually used as a furniture van – soon became surrounded, and the throng increased as the shell was manhandled along the narrow passage. Covered only by a piece of coarse canvas, but with its straps fastened, the appearance of the coffin caused much distress amongst the normally hardened onlookers. Women cried, and men removed their caps as it was slid gently into the cart and disappeared from view.

It was only with great difficulty that Sergeant Badham and several constables cleared a path out of Dorset Street and escorted the cart up Commercial Street and Shoreditch High Street. All the way they were followed by a great crowd, and even more were waiting to see the shell transferred when they reached their destination.

One newspaper reported that as soon as Dorset Street was no longer the focus of attention a detective was seen to emerge from Miller's Court carrying a pail covered with newspaper. Allegedly, it contained 'portions of the woman's body', and was taken to Dr Phillips's house in Spital Square.

Gradually those who had been present in the Court dispersed. The doctors had received permission to conduct their full post-mortem examination the following day, and the inquest was arranged for Monday the 12th. Evidently no time was being wasted.

At half-past five, the police cordons at each end of Dorset Street were withdrawn and those who had been confined to the other rooms in Miller's Court were allowed their freedom. They emerged to find the windows of No. 13 whitewashed and boarded over, the door padlocked, and constables stationed at the street end of the passage.

As evening drew into night, the scenes of frenzy and near hysteria continued unabated. Adding to the crowds were the reporters who descended in droves and interviewed everyone in sight. As a result, there was the usual rash of dubious tales from those anxious to see their names in the papers, and those fantasies were then embroidered into the wildest of speculations.

The Metropolitan police force also found itself caught up in rumour and speculation, albeit of an entirely different nature. Word had spread that its Commissioner, Sir Charles Warren, had resigned the day before and that Dr Anderson was his temporary replacement. It was said that the new Commissioner was likely to be James Monro, who had been Assistant Commissioner, CID, until he fell out with Warren and was replaced by Anderson. Monro was considered an excellent detective and was popular with the man on the beat; therefore, although nobody seemed to know the truth of the matter, hopes ran high that the grapevine was correct.

The inquest was opened at Shoreditch Town Hall on Monday, November 12th, with the Coroner for North-Eastern Middlesex, Dr Roderick MacDonald, presiding.

The plan hatched between Dr Phillips and the police was working fine and they were not to be made to endure the intensive questioning, and the criticisms, of Wynne Baxter. Instead, they had a much more compliant coroner; and one who, to say the least, was no friend of the man who had been such a thorn in their flesh.

The enmity – and I do not think that too harsh a word – between the two coroners stemmed from the year before, when the election for a coroner for East London and Tower of London had taken place. Baxter, a solicitor with a London practice, had already held two deputy coronerships, and was supported by the Conservatives.

MacDonald, on the other hand, was a Radical and the MP for Ross-Shire, where he was known as 'the crofters' MP'. Although he had practised medicine in the East End and was, at forty-seven, three years older than Baxter, he did not have the same experience in the office as his rival for the post. Nevertheless, he was more popular than Baxter in the Whitechapel and Spitalfields Wards and had the covert support of the police as, being the Metropolitan Police surgeon for 'K' Division, they considered him one of their own.

It was a very acrimonious election, with MacDonald and his supporters accusing Baxter and his party of all manner of irregularities. In the event, however, Baxter's popularity in the Stoke Newington and Hackney Wards proved overwhelming and he won the coronership from an embittered MacDonald.

Less than a year later, the East London and Tower Division was divided to form North-East and South-East Middlesex, and both men received a coronership. Curiously, each was given the post covering the wards in which he had received the least support during the election but, putting that to one side, MacDonald at last had the office which he had coveted. Now he was to conduct the inquiry into by far the worst of the murders, and the one which was surrounded by more minor mysteries than any of the others.

Superintendent Arnold, Inspector Abberline and Inspector Nairn arrived to represent the police, while in the passage outside, half-a-dozen 'wretched-looking' women took their places and waited to be called as witnesses – they were to be there for a long time.

Dr MacDonald took his seat precisely on the hour of 11 a.m., and the Coroner's Officer, a Mr Hammond, called upon the jury to rise. When they had answered to their names they were asked to select a foreman, but before that could be done one of their number – 'a gentleman with black gloves and a good coat' – addressed the Coroner. Determination written all over his face, he said: 'I do not see why we should have the inquest thrown upon our shoulders when the murder did not happen in our district, but in Whitechapel. We are summoned for the Shoreditch district. This affair happened in Spitalfields.' Another juror, emboldened by his colleague's protests, now decided that he would put *his* oar in: 'This is not *my* district,' he said vehemently.' *I* come from Whitechapel, and Mr Baxter is *my* coroner.'

The mention of Baxter's name was akin to waving the proverbial red flag in front of an Angus bull, and MacDonald could hardly contain himself: 'I am not going to discuss the subject with jurymen at all,' he blustered. 'If any juryman says he distinctly objects, let him say so.'

There was a pause, and in the silence which ensued Coroner and jury stared at each other. For a moment it appeared that an impasse had been reached, but then MacDonald addressed the good men and true in a more conciliatory manner: 'I may tell the jurymen that jurisdiction lies where the body lies, not where it was found.'

Another silence followed, as jury and spectators alike tried to fathom what he meant. Most of them were in no doubt as to the district 'where the body was found'.

There is no telling how long this silent puzzling would have continued had it not been for the intervention of the trusty Mr Hammond: 'Will you choose a foreman please, gentlemen?' he asked briskly and, with that, and in the face of MacDonald's obvious anger, the revolt collapsed.

It had not been a good start, and the row looked likely to draw unwelcome attention to the cosy arrangement which had been worked out – but worse was to come.

For the moment however, the procedures appeared to have got back to normal. Pursued by a crowd which had gathered outside, the jury followed Inspector Abberline to the small brick mortuary. Inside lay Mary's corpse. The face was so mutilated that it was impossible to say 'where the flesh began and the cuts ended', and the jurymen must have been relieved to regain the open air. Then, surrounded by the crowd, they made their way down Commercial Street to Dorset Street, only to find an even greater throng waiting to gawp at them. Frowsy women, some with babies in their arms, drunken men, and 'a whole regiment' of children, stared open-mouthed and pointed as the procession made its way into the dismal passage to No. 13.

They gazed around them in silent horror as Abberline, by the light of a candle stuck in a bottle, showed them the appalling sights and repeated the gory details of the finding of the body. He pointed out

the bloodstains on the wall, the filthy bloodstained bed, and the pools
of blood which had soaked through the mattress. It was a disgusting
and squalid scene, and nobody could have lingered longer than was
absolutely necessary because they were all back outside again within
twenty minutes. They filed out of the passage, past the two constables
on duty, and once again found themselves confronted by the staring
crowd, part of which followed them all the way back to Shoreditch
where a grim-faced MacDonald awaited their arrival. All in all, they
had been gone for an hour.

The first witness to be called was a Joseph Barnett.

His evidence forms such an integral part of the Mary Kelly legend,
because he is the source from which nearly all the known 'facts' about
Mary Kelly have been derived, that we should hear it in full. At first,
Barnett was a prime suspect. He was detained by the police for some
four hours before being released; so perhaps we should begin with the
statement which he made to Abberline:

Marie Janet Kelly.   Friday 9th
                                         9th November 1888
Statement of Joseph Barnett now residing at 24 and 25 New
Street Bishopsgate (a common lodging house)

I am a porter in Billingsgate Market, but have been out of
employment for the past 3 or 4 months. I have been living with
Marie Jeanette Kelly who occupied No. 13 room Millers Court.
I have lived with her altogether about eighteen months, for the
last eight months in Millers Court, until last Tuesday week
(30 ulto) when in consequence of not earning sufficient money
to give her and her resorting to prostitution, I resolved on
leaving her, but I was friendly with her and called to see her
between seven and eight pm thursday (8th) and told her I was
very sorry I had no work and that I could not give her any
money. I left her about 8 o'clock same evening and that was the
last time I saw her alive.

There was a woman in the room when I called. The deceased
told me on one occasion that her father named John Kelly was a
foreman of some iron works and lived at Carmarthen or

Carnarvon that she had a brother named Henry serving in 2nd Battn Scots Guards, and known amongst his comrades as Johnto, and I believe the Regiment is now in Ireland. She also told me that she had obtained her livelihood as a prostitute for some considerable time before I took her from the Streets, and that she left her home about 4 years ago, and that she was married to a collier, who was killed through some explosion, I think she said her husband name was Davis or Davies.

His evidence at the inquest was a little more detailed. (The following record is taken from the Coroner's notes.)

It began with his saying that at present he was working as a labourer, but that he had been a fish porter. Until 'Saturday last' he had lived at No. 24, New Street, Bishopsgate, but now he was staying at his sister's at No. 21, Portpool Lane, Gray's Inn Road.

He had lived with the deceased for a year and eight months. Her name was Marie Jeanette Kelly – Kelly being her maiden name and the one she always went by.

'I have seen the body and identify her by the ear [that is what MacDonald recorded, but obviously he had misheard 'ear' for 'hair'] and eyes. I am positive it is the same woman. I have lived with her at 13 room Miller's Court eight months or longer. I separated from her on the 30th of October.'

Coroner:	'Why did you leave her?
Barnett:	'I left her because she had a person who was a prostitute whom she took in and I objected to her doing so. That was the only reason; not because I was out of work. I left her on the 30th October between five and six p.m. I last saw her alive between half-past seven and a quarter to eight on the night of Thursday before she was found. I was with her about one hour.'
Coroner:	'Were you on good terms?'
Barnett:	'Yes, we were on friendly terms. I told her when I left her I had no work and nothing to give her, of which I was very sorry.'

Coroner:	'Did you drink together?'
Barnett:	'No, she was quite sober.'
Coroner:	'Was she, generally speaking, of sober habits?'
Barnett:	'She was as long as she was with me, but she has got drunk several times in my presence.'
Coroner:	'Was anyone else there on the Thursday evening?'
Barnett:	'Yes, there was a female with us on Thursday evening when we were together. She left first, and I left shortly afterwards.'
Coroner:	'Have you had conversation with the deceased about her parents?'
Barnett:	'Yes. She has often told me as to her parents. She said she was twenty-five years of age and that she was born in Limerick. From there she went to Wales when very young. She told me she came to London about four years ago.

The witness continued:

Her father's name was John Kelly; he was a ganger at some iron works in Caernarvonshire. She told me she had one sister who was a traveller with materials from market place to market place. She also said she had six brothers at home, and one in the army; one was Henry Kelly. I never spoke to any of them.

She told me she had been married when very young, in Wales; she was married to a collier. She told me the name was Davis or Davies, I think Davies, and that she was lawfully married to him until he died in an explosion. She said she lived with him two or three years, up to his death. She told me she was married at the age of sixteen years.

She came to London about four years ago. After her husband's death, she said she first went to Cardiff, and was in an infirmary there for eight or nine months and followed a bad life with a cousin whilst in Cardiff.

She said that when she left Cardiff she came to London and was first in a gay house in the West End of the town. A gentleman there asked her to go to France. She described to me how she went to France but, as she told me, as she did not like the part she did not stay there long. She lived there about a fortnight. She did not like it, and returned and lived in Ratcliffe Highway for some time – she did not tell me how long.

Then she was living near Stepney Gas Works – Morganstone was the man she lived with there. She did not tell me how long she was there, but she said that in Pennington Street she lived at one time with a Morganstone, and with Joseph Flemming. She was very fond of him. He was a mason's plasterer who lived in the Bethnal Green Road.

She told me all this, but I do not know which she lived with last. Flemming used to visit her.

I picked her up in Commercial Street, Spitalfields. The first night we had a drink together and I arranged to see her the next day, and then on the Saturday we agreed to remain together and I took lodgings in George Street, Commercial Street, where I was known.

I lived with her from then till I left her the other day.

She had on several occasions asked me to read about the murders. She seemed afraid of someone, but she did not express fear of any particular individual except when she rowed with me, but we always came to terms quickly.'

Despite many questions which just cried out to be asked, the jurymen had nothing to say. MacDonald, however, seemed delighted with their reticence. He almost beamed upon Barnett as he told him: 'You have given your evidence very well indeed,' and allowed him to return to the shadows from which he had come.

However, although we know what actually was *said*, absolutely nothing is known for a fact about 'Mary Kelly' before she came to London, if indeed she did arrive in the capital from elsewhere.

There is, however, some slight confirmation in newspaper articles of the story about her having been in a 'gay house' in the West End.

Reporters following up this story were told that Mary Kelly had said that upon her arrival in London she had made the acquaintance of a French lady living in the Knightsbridge area. That woman, according to Mary, had led her to pursue a degraded life. She had admitted, however, that she had enjoyed the luxuries which accompanied it, such as driving around in a carriage and making several trips to Paris.

Were that true, Mary's fortunes must have taken a sudden, severe and mysterious turn for the worse, because she had apparently gone straight from that life to one of degradation in the neighbourhood of the Ratcliffe Highway – one of the very worst areas of the East End.

The story goes that, in the first instance she lodged with, and some say worked for, a Mrs Buki, 'in one of the thoroughfares off Ratcliffe Highway, now known as St George's Street'. One of Mary's first actions upon arriving there was to enlist Mrs Buki's support for a return visit to the brothel in Knightsbridge. Apparently the landlady was only too pleased to oblige, and when they arrived in the West End she vigorously backed Mary's demands for the release of 'a box' which belonged to her and which contained 'numerous dresses of a costly description'.

Unfortunately that budding friendship did not last. Mary's drinking increased, probably from the proceeds of sale of the dresses, and she was asked to move on. It was then that she had gone to lodge with a Mrs Carthy.

That good lady told the journalists that Mary had eventually left her to live with a man 'in the building trade' who sounds very much like the Joseph Flemming mentioned by Joe Barnett.

Mrs Carthy does not appear to have mentioned the man Morganstone, but she told the Press that 'some short time ago' she had been awakened by Mary Kelly at two o'clock in the morning. Mary was with a strange man, and had asked for a bed for what remained of the night. The landlady had taken the opportunity to ask if she was still with the man 'in the building trade', but Mary had said that she was not and had 'explained her position'. That was the last time she was seen in that neighbourhood.

We know that Mary met Barnett one evening whilst she was living at Cooley's common lodging-house in Thrawl Street, Spitalfields, and soliciting in nearby Commercial Street. Unfortunately, however, at least two Joseph Barnetts have been identified as living in that area at that time, and therefore his antecedents cannot be verified.

It is said that Whittlowe's, in the Spitalfields George Street, was his favourite lodging – and that was almost certainly where he first lived with Mary – but that he occasionally used others in Thrawl Street and Brick Lane.

On Sunday, November 11th, Barnett had made one of his many statements to the Press. He told the reporter: 'I first met the deceased last Easter twelve-month, and lived with her from that time until last Tuesday week. I was in decent work in Billingsgate Market when I first met her, and we lived along quite comfortably. She was twenty-two years of age, fresh-looking and well-behaved, though she had been walking the streets some three years previously.'

Barnett and Mary had lived in George Street at first, but they had then moved to Paternoster Court, off Dorset Street. They were evicted from those lodgings 'because we went on a drunk and did not pay our rent'. From then they had gone to lodgings in Brick Lane, but they were not there for long. Soon, we are told, they were in rooms in George Yard Buildings, but they left that accommodation some five months before Martha Tabram's body was discovered on one of the landings.

The couple's last move had been from George Yard to Miller's Court, where they had lived 'comfortably' until Mary had allowed a prostitute named 'Julia' to stay in their room. Barnett told the journalist that he had objected to that, and when 'Mrs Harvey' succeeded Julia he had left. He had told Mary that he would go back to her if she went to live elsewhere.

He had last seen Mary alive at 7.30 p.m. on Thursday the 8th, when he had stayed talking to her for a quarter of an hour. Next day he had heard that there had been a murder in Miller's Court, and had been on his way there when he met his sister's brother-in-law who told him that the victim was Mary.

'I then went to the Court and there saw the police inspector, and told him who I was, and where I had been the previous night. They kept me about four hours, examined my clothes for bloodstains, and finally, finding the account of myself to be correct, let me go free.'

Barnett said that Mary had never solicited whilst he had lived with her.

After the perplexing Barnett had left the inquest, still hugging the solutions of many mysteries to his bosom, there was a pause whilst MacDonald studied a letter which had just been delivered. Then, turning to the jurymen, he told them: 'The doctor has sent a note asking whether we shall want his attendance here today. I take it that it would be convenient that he should tell us roughly what the cause of death was, so as to enable the body to be buried. It will not be necessary to go into the details of the doctor's evidence: but he suggested that he might come to state roughly the cause of death.'

It was, of course, completely improper for the Coroner even to have considered such a notion, as the law required that *all* injuries and wounds should be described in detail and noted by the coroner. Unfortunately, though, the jurymen were *not* aware of this, and therefore they acquiesced meekly in what he proposed.

Having disposed of that little matter to his satisfaction, Mac-Donald summoned Thomas Bowyer to give his evidence. The only difference between that and his statement to the police is that in the latter he said that he 'threw the *blinds* back' before looking through the window, whereas he now told the jury that there was a *curtain* which he pulled aside.

At the end of his evidence, 'Indian Harry' stated that he had seen Mary drunk only once. He then answered a couple of questions from a juror. One merely concerned the precise situation of McCarthy's shop, but the other had a more pertinent bearing upon the matter in hand:

Juror:	'When did you last see her alive?'
Bowyer:	'On Wednesday afternoon, in the Court, when I spoke to her.'

Now that was a rather different tale from that which apparently, he had given to a *Western Mail* reporter the previous day. Then, he had stated that he had seen Mary talking to what sounds like a James Kelly lookalike on the Wednesday *night*. He described the man as being twenty-seven or twenty-eight years of age, with a dark moustache and 'very peculiar eyes'. His appearance had been 'rather smart', and noticeable features of his attire had been that he was wearing very white shirt cuffs and had a rather long collar, the points of which 'came down in front over a black coat'.

Regrettably – and how often we are forced to use such adverbs in connection with the investigations of these killings – Bowyer was never to be questioned about his newspaper interview.

The next witness was John McCarthy, Mary's landlord. He began by stating that he was a grocer and lodging-house keeper, living at No. 27, Dorset Street, and went on to describe sending Bowyer for the rent from the woman he had known as Mary Jane Kelly.

Coroner:	'How long had the deceased lived in the room?'
McCarthy:	'For ten months, with Joe, both together; they lived comfortably together, but once broke two windows. The furniture and everything in the room belongs to me.'
Coroner:	'What rent was paid for this room?'
McCarthy:	'It was supposed to be four and sixpence a week, but the rent was twenty-nine shillings in arrears.'

Questioned about Mary's character, he replied: 'I very often saw the deceased worse for drink. When sober, she was a very quiet woman, but noisy when drunk.'

McCarthy was allowed to stand down and then came the first of the women who had been waiting to say their piece. What follows now is a combination of her statement to the police and her evidence at the inquest, and that is a procedure which will be followed with succeeding witnesses.

She was Mary Ann Cox, who stated that she was a widow living at No. 5 room, Miller's Court, 'the last house on the left-hand side of the Court'. Mrs Cox made no bones about her occupation: 'I get my living on the streets as best I can,' she told MacDonald.

Asked about the deceased, she replied: 'I have known the female occupying No. 13 room eight or nine months. She was called Mary Jane. I last saw her alive about a quarter to midnight on Thursday night. I came into Dorset Street from Commercial Street and I saw

Mary Jane walking in front of me with a shabbily dressed man. He was about thirty-six years old, and about five feet five inches high. His complexion was fresh, but I believe he had blotches on his face. He had a thick carroty moustache and small side whiskers, but his chin was clean. He wore a longish dark coat and a hard billy-cock black hat, and was carrying a quart pot of beer.

'They turned into the Court, and as I entered the Court they were going into her room. I said: "Goodnight, Mary Jane", but she was very drunk and could hardly answer me, but she said: "Goodnight, I'm going to have a song", and then the man banged the door. He had nothing in his hands but the pot of beer.'

Mrs Cox continued by saying that when she reached the top of the Court she heard Mary singing 'A violet I plucked from mother's grave when a boy'. She had remained in her room for about a quarter of an hour only, and the deceased was still singing when she went out again shortly after midnight.

Business must have been slow on that cold wet night because Mrs Cox returned at 'about one o'clock' to warm her hands. Mary was still singing, both then and when the witness went out again 'shortly after one o'clock'.

However when, at three o'clock, Mrs Cox finally gave up for the night and came home, the light in No. 13 was out and all was quiet. Apparently the widow was 'upset', probably at having done no business, and rent day approaching and all, because 'I did not undress at all that night. I heard no noise, it was raining hard. I did not go to sleep at all. I heard nothing whatever after one o'clock.'

Much later, though, she had heard several men going 'in and out' to work in the market. At a quarter to six, which was too late for the market, she had heard someone else leave the Court, but she was unable to tell MacDonald from which 'house' he had come because she heard 'no door shut'. She was able to say only that the man had not passed her window.

Further questioning revealed that Mary had been wearing what MacDonald noted as 'a red pillorine' and a dark shabby skirt. (The word should, of course, have been written 'pelerine' – a woman's long narrow cape or shoulder covering.) She had not been wearing a hat.

Mrs Cox's statement to Abberline shows slight variations. That records her as having said that the 'dead woman's clothing consisted of a linsey frock, red knitted crossover around her shoulders, had no hat or bonnet on'.

In reply to a juror, the witness said that there was a light in No. 13 when Mary was singing, but 'I saw nothing, as the blinds were down.' She confirmed that she would know the man again.

Then, to MacDonald, Mrs Cox stated that she would have heard any cry of 'Murder!', but she had heard nothing at all. Another question brought the reply that she had very often seen Mary drunk, and that brought her evidence to a close.

She was followed by Mrs Elizabeth Prater, who described herself as a married woman although her husband, a boot machinist, had deserted her five years previously. MacDonald recorded her address as 'No. 20 room, Miller's Court up stairs'.

The first thing that Mrs Prater did was to enlarge upon this by saying: 'I live in the room over where the deceased lived.' Then she went on to describe her movements on the evening of Thursday the 8th, and here we run immediately into a discrepancy. In her police statement she said that she went out at about 9 p.m., but now, to MacDonald, she stated that it was 5 p.m. Both accounts agree that she returned at about one o'clock on the Friday morning, but then we have another divergence. The statement records her as having said that she then 'stood at the bottom of Miller's Court [meaning the Dorset Street end] until about 1.30. I was speaking for a short time to a Mr McCarthy . . .' At the inquest, however, she stated: 'I stood at the corner by McCarthy's shop till about twenty minutes past one. I spoke to no one. I was waiting for a man I lived with, he did not come.'

Mrs Prater said that if Mary had a light in her room she would normally see a glimmer through 'the partition' as she went upstairs. She could not, however, recall having seen such a glimmer on the night in question although, having had 'a drink', she might not have noticed one had it been there! Answering MacDonald, she said that the partition was so thin that she would have heard any noise from Mary's room.

Once she had staggered into Room 20, Mrs Prater had 'put two tables against the door'. She had fallen asleep immediately, and had slept soundly until she was awakened by her kitten walking across her neck, about 3.30 or 4 a.m. 'I noticed the lodging-house light was out, so it was after 4 probably. I heard a cry of oh! Murder! as the cat came on me and I pushed her down, the noise was in a female voice.'

The cry had appeared to come from 'close by', in the Court, but such cries were common and Mrs Prater, hearing nothing more, had merely turned over and gone back to sleep.

She arose at 5 a.m. and 'was up again and downstairs in the court at 5.30 a.m.'. Then she went across to The Ten Bells pub which stood, and stands, on the corner of Commercial Street and Church (now Fournier) Street, and was in there by 5.45 a.m. 'for some rum'.

On her way, she had seen nobody except two or three carmen harnessing their horses in Dorset Street, and there had been no strangers in the pub. When she had had her 'hair of the dog', she had tacked her way back to No. 20 and slept soundly until about 11 a.m.

She told MacDonald that Mrs Cox *could* have gone down 'the entry' between one and half-past without her seeing her, but she had heard no singing from No. 13. The Coroner's notes have her saying: 'I should have heard any one if singing in the deceased's room – at one o'clock, there was no one singing.'

As nobody had any more questions for her, and it was quite obvious that she had been more than a little fuddled on that Friday morning, Mrs Prater was allowed to depart.

The next witness was a woman whose evidence was the subject of much speculation at the time, and has continued to be so.

She was a Mrs Caroline Maxwell, of No. 14, Dorset Street. Her husband was Henry Maxwell, the deputy of 'The Commercial' lodging-house, which was almost opposite the entrance to Miller's Court.

Mrs Maxwell said that she had known the dead woman for the past four months; she knew her as 'Mary Jane', and she also knew Joe Barnett. She believed that the deceased was 'an unfortunate girl', and certainly she had obtained her living in that way since Barnett had left her.

It was all very straightforward up to that point, but then came another of the contradictions which plague this murder.

Her police statement reads: 'I was on speaking terms with her [Mary Kelly] although I had not seen her for three weeks until Friday morning, 9th instant, about half-past eight o'clock, she was then standing at the corner of Miller's Court in Dorset Street.' However MacDonald wrote: 'I took a deal of notice of deceased *this evening* [my italics] seeing her standing at the corner of the Court on Friday from 8 to half-past.'

It was at that juncture, that MacDonald intervened and addressed her sharply: 'You must be very careful about your evidence, because it is different from other people's. You say you saw her standing at the entry to the Court?'

Mrs Maxwell: 'Yes.'
Coroner: 'Did you speak to her?'
Mrs Maxwell: 'Yes, I said "Why Mary, what brings you up so early?" She said "Oh! I do feel so bad! Oh Carry! I feel so bad. I have the horrors of drink upon me, as I have been drinking for some days past."'

Here, according to the *Daily Telegraph*, MacDonald interrupted the witness to ask, pertinently: 'And yet you say you had spoken to her only twice previously – you knew her name and she knew yours?'

Mrs Maxwell: 'Oh yes: by being about in the lodging-house.'

It was a mysterious reply, but unfortunately it was not queried and therefore we shall never know what it meant. Instead, the witness was allowed to continue the telling of her alleged conversation with the deceased: 'I said to her "Why don't you go to Mrs Ringer's, meaning the public house at the corner of Dorset Street called The Britannia, and have half a pint of beer?" She said: "I have been there, but I have brought it all up again." As she said this she motioned with her head and I concluded she meant she had been to 'The Britannia' at the corner, and at the same time she pointed to some vomit in the roadway. I saw it. I left her, saying I pitied her feelings, [and] went to Bishopsgate on an errand.'

Mrs Maxwell told the police that she returned to Dorset Street 'about 9 a.m.', but at the inquest she said it was 'about twenty minutes to half-an-hour later – about a quarter to nine'. Whatever the time, she had then noticed Mary talking to a man outside The Britannia.

Coroner: 'What description can you give of this man?'
Mrs Maxwell: 'I could not describe the man and I am doubtful whether I could identify him. I did not pass them. I went into my house. I saw them in the distance.'

At that point Detective Inspector Abberline interrupted briefly to tell MacDonald: 'The distance is about sixteen yards,' but Mrs Maxwell was in full flow and, sixteen yards or no sixteen yards, she told the Coroner: 'I am certain it was the deceased.' As it happens, it was about *thirty-five* yards.

She described him as having been about thirty, stout and about five feet five inches tall. 'He was dressed as a market porter, in dark clothes and a sort of plaid coat. I could not say what hat he had on.'

Coroner: 'What sort of dress had the deceased?'
Mrs Maxwell: 'She wore a dark skirt, velvet body, and maroon shawl and no hat.'

Then a juror had a rather peculiar query which must have had its origins in the legend that was being born. He wanted to know whether the man whom Mrs Maxwell said she had seen with Mary was wearing a silk high hat!

It was a silly and unnecessary question. The witness had already said that she could not describe the man's headgear, and that he was dressed as a market porter. Perhaps the juror's knowledge in such matters was limited, but porters wearing top hats must have been extremely rare – especially in combination with a plaid coat! Nevertheless, Mrs Maxwell appeared to take it seriously, although one can detect a trace of sarcasm in her reply: 'I did not notice; if it *had* been so I should have noticed it I think.'

By then it is more than likely that the Coroner's thoughts were elsewhere. Mrs Maxwell's evidence conflicted so much with the time of death estimated by the doctors that he had probably dismissed in advance anything she was likely to say. Whether he was wise to do so is something about which we shall ponder later.

Mrs Maxwell departed, and her place was taken by a Mrs Sarah Lewis, a laundress, of No. 24, Great Pearl Street, Spitalfields. Mrs Lewis said that she was friendly with Mrs Keyler, who lived at No. 2, Miller's Court (which was on the first floor opposite the door of No. 13, above No. 1) but she had not known the deceased. She had had 'a few words' with her husband during the early hours of the 9th and, as a consequence, had left him to go and stay with the Keylers.

It must surely have been more than a few words to have sent her out on a cold, drizzly morning, and on to those dark eerie streets where the 'Ripper' could have been lurking in every shadow, but go she did. As she passed Spitalfields Church she glanced up at the clock and saw that it was nearly half-past two and then, thankfully, it was only a minute before she arrived in Dorset Street.

Just as she was approaching the passage, she noticed a man standing alone opposite the entrance to Miller's Court, 'by the Lodging-House' (The Commercial?) In her statement to Abberline, on that very same day, Mrs Lewis had said that she was unable to describe the man, but now she told MacDonald that: 'He was not tall – but stout – [and] had on a wideawake [broad-brimmed soft felt] hat – I did not notice his clothes.' Another, rather young-looking man had passed along with a woman, the latter being 'in drink'. The man standing in the street was looking up the Court as if waiting for someone to come out.

Mrs Lewis had gone up to their room and roused the Keylers, but they were occupying the only bed and she had therefore resigned herself to dozing in a chair for what remained of the night. At first there was no noise in the Court and she had gone to sleep, but she awoke just before half-past three and had then heard the clock chime the half-hour. She was to remain awake for the next hour and a half and, just before four o'clock, she had heard 'a scream like that of a young woman'. There was but the one scream, and it seemed to be from not very far away, 'from the direction of deceased's room'.

Rather surprisingly – but then she did have her own marital problems to worry about – Mrs Lewis had taken no notice whatsoever.

It would appear that she had slept soundly when she finally went back to sleep, because she was still at No. 2 when the murder was discovered. Then, of course, she was trapped, as the police did not allow anybody out of the Court until around 5.30 p.m.

MacDonald noted all that she had said, and then he turned his attention to the second part of her statement to the police: 'Have you seen any suspicious persons in the district?'

Mrs Lewis:	'Yes, on Wednesday night, at eight o'clock, I was going along the Bethnal Green Road with another female and a gentleman passed us. He turned back and spoke to us – he asked one of us to follow him into an entry.'
Coroner:	'Did he want both of you?'
Mrs Lewis:	'No, only one, he didn't mind which. We refused and he went away, but he came back again and said that if we would follow him he would "treat" us. He had a black bag with him and he put it down saying: 'What are you frightened of?' He then undid his coat and felt for something and we ran away.'
Coroner:	'Was he a tall man?' (MacDonald seems to have had tall men on his mind – he had asked Mrs Maxwell the same question.)
Mrs Lewis:	'No, he was short, pale-faced, with a black moustache, about forty years of age. The bag was about a foot or nine inches long. He had on a round high hat – a high hat for a round one – a brownish long overcoat and a short black coat underneath, and pepper and salt trousers. On our running away we did not look after the man.'

Coroner:	'Have you seen him since?'
Mrs Lewis:	'Yes, on the Friday morning, at about half-past two, when I was coming to Miller's Court, I met the same man. He was with a female, in Commercial Street near Mr Ringer's public house near the market. He had no overcoat on, but he had the bag and the same hat, trousers and undercoat. I passed by them and looked back at the man. I was frightened. I looked again when I got to the corner of Dorset Street. I have not seen the man since, but I should know him if I did.'

Mrs Lewis's evidence had been very interesting, and was to become more so over the next few days, but the next witness, Dr Phillips, was the one for whom everybody, especially the journalists, had been waiting. The medical details of the previous murders had been horrific enough but, if the sensational newspaper reports were to be believed, those about to be revealed would be the goriest yet.

The doctor began by telling of how he had been called out. He then described his entry to No. 13: 'On the door being opened it knocked against a table, the table I found close to the left hand side of the bedstead and the bedstead was close up against the wooden partition. The mutilated remains of a female were lying two thirds over towards the edge and from my subsequent examination I am sure the body had been removed subsequent to the injury which caused her death, from that side of the bedstead which was nearest to the wooden partition. The large quantity of blood which was under the bedstead, the saturated condition of the palliasse, pillow, and sheet at that top corner nearest the partition leads me to the conclusion that the severance of the right carotid artery, which was the immediate cause of her death, was inflicted while the deceased was lying at the right side of the bedstead and her head and neck in the top right hand corner.'

He concluded by announcing grandly: 'That is as far as I propose to carry my evidence today.'

It was something which was not totally unexpected in the light of MacDonald's earlier address to the jury, and MacDonald swiftly added that it would *not* be necessary for the doctor to go into any further particulars then. If it was necessary, they could recall him 'at a subsequent period'. That seemed very reasonable and, on that understanding, the jury put no questions to Phillips and he was allowed to depart. Very few people knew that there would never be another word about this murder from Phillips, and that what he had just said was to be all that the public learned officially.

The next witness was Mrs Julia Venturney, who lived at No. 1, Miller's Court – which meant, of course, that her door was almost opposite that of No. 13, and that her room was immediately below the Keylers'.

Mrs Venturney, a charwoman, stated that she was a widow but lived with a man named Harry Owen. She had known 'the female' occupying No. 13 for about four months, and had understood from her that her name was Kelly and that she was a married woman. Until recently, the deceased had lived with a man called Joe Barnett, and the witness had heard him say that he did not like her going out on the streets. He frequently gave the dead woman money, and was very kind to her, but he said that he would not live with her while she led 'that course of life'.

Julia Venturney had told Abberline that the deceased 'used to get tipsy occasionally', but at the inquest that became 'she frequently got drunk'. She had broken the window 'a few weeks ago' when she was drunk.

Mary had told Julia that she was very fond of another man named Joe who, the witness thought, was a costermonger. He used to come and see her and give her money, although he had often ill-used her because she cohabited with Joe Barnett.

The last time she had seen Mary alive had been on the day before her death when, at about 10 a.m., she was having breakfast with another woman in No. 13. On the evening of that same Thursday, the witness had gone to bed about eight o'clock, but she had not been able to get off to sleep and had merely dozed all night.

Coroner: 'Did you hear any noises in the Court?'
Mrs Venturney: 'I did not. I heard no screams of "Murder!", nor anyone singing.'

She had heard Mary singing on other occasions though: 'I knew her songs. They were generally Irish.'

It was obvious to all that, despite what she thought and said, the witness *had* slept that night, and quite soundly at that. It just was not possible for her to have been awake and not heard all the comings and goings, doors shutting, the singing, the screaming and Sarah Lewis's arrival and her knocking up of the Keylers in the room above. Nevertheless, she was not pressed on the issue and she departed leaving a faint impression that, whilst she had thought quite highly of Barnett, she had had little time for Mary Kelly.

The woman who followed her was Maria Harvey, of No. 3, New Court, Dorset Street. We are not told her marital status officially, but newspaper reports called her 'Mrs Harvey' and there is no reason why we should not afford her the same courtesy. Although she described herself as a laundress, we may be reasonably certain that she augmented her income by prostitution.

Mrs Harvey said that she had known the deceased as Mary Jane Kelly, and had slept with her, in No. 13, on the Monday and Tuesday nights before her death. She had then taken a room at the address which she had given.

She went on to state that she and Mary had been together 'all the afternoon on Thursday', but we are not told *where*. What we *do* know is that she was in No. 13 when Barnett arrived and, there being no love lost between them, she had made herself scarce immediately. That was brought out during the following exchange:

Coroner: 'Did you know Joe Barnett?'
Mrs Harvey: 'Yes.'
Coroner: 'Were you in the house when he called?'
Mrs Harvey: 'Yes, it was about five minutes to seven when he called, and I went away. I left my bonnet there together with an overcoat – a black one, a man's –

	two men's dirty cotton shirts, a boy's shirt, a little girl's white petticoat, a black crepe bonnet bound with black strings and a ticket for a shawl in for two shillings.'
Coroner:	'Have you seen any of these articles since?'
Mrs Harvey:	'I have seen nothing of them since, except the overcoat produced to me by the police.'
Coroner:	'Did the deceased ever speak to you about being afraid of any man?'
Mrs Harvey:	'No. Although I was her friend, she never told *me* of being afraid of any one.'

With that, the woman who probably knew more of the truth about Mary Kelly than any living soul – including Joe Barnett – was allowed to go! There is little doubt that she could have resolved many of the mysteries surrounding Mary Kelly and her murder, but her evidence was amongst the shortest given, and the jurors had no questions.

Inspectors Beck and Abberline then described how they had been called to the murder scene, and what they found. Abberline added, 'I have since gone through the ashes in the grate and found nothing of consequence except that articles of women's clothing had been burnt, which I presume was for the purpose of light as there was only one piece of candle in the room.'

MacDonald limited himself to just one question: 'Is there anything further the jury ought to know?', and Abberline, right on cue, replied: 'No. If there should be, I can communicate with *you*, sir.'

Then turning to the jurors, MacDonald told them: 'That is all the evidence I propose to take today . . . It is for you to say whether at an adjournment you will hear minutiae of the evidence, or whether you will think it is a matter to be dealt with in the police-courts later on, and that, this woman having met her death by the carotid artery being cut, you will be satisfied to return a verdict to that effect.'

The foreman went through the motions of consulting his colleagues, but their decision was a foregone conclusion because all the spirit had gone out of them. It was no surprise to anyone when the foreman told MacDonald that the jury had quite sufficient evidence before it upon which to give a verdict, and that their verdict was 'Wilful murder against some person or persons unknown.'

It was very brief – and very unsatisfactory.

We can only assume that the police wanted to reveal as little as possible – not that it would do them any good. As a result, though, we are left with a number of inconsistencies that were never explained.

The first concerns the fire.

For a start, we have no idea when it was last alight, when the solder on the kettle was melted, nor the heat of the ashes when the room was entered. We do not know who lit it, or why it was built up, or when.

Let us begin with what we know. There had been a fire and some clothing, including women's, had been burned. It had almost certainly been lit by Mary Kelly, because the idea of the killer clearing the ashes, finding paper, kindling wood and possibly coal, and then standing around until the fire was established is ludicrous.

The night of November 8th/9th was cold and wet. When it was not drizzling it was raining heavily. Mrs Cox had had the foresight to light a small fire, and Mary Kelly no doubt did the same. I think that we may take it for granted that the clothes which were burned were those that Mrs Harvey left behind, but why, and was anything else disposed of?

Abberline, and many others after him, thought that the killer had burned the clothes in order to see what he was doing, but that is ridiculous. Woollen clothing melts upon being lit; it may burn, but only with an extremely feeble light of no general benefit whatsoever. Cotton will flame, but, again, only a very weak light will be produced, and it would take a pile of cotton clothing to give even a useless glimmer of light for some five minutes.

In any case, why should the murderer have needed light on this particular occasion? He had managed very well without it before – in fact darkness had been his principal ally.

Even supposing that illumination *was* needed, surely the candle, placed on the bedside table, would have been more effective and more easily doused in an emergency, than a fire at the far end of the room obscured by the killer's shadow?

It is always assumed that it was the killer who burned the clothes, the reasoning being that Mary was hardly likely to have done so – especially as they did not belong to her. But to whom *did* they belong?

Maria Harvey had brought them to the room, but we do not know when. She purported to be a laundress, and the inference is that the clothes had been given to her for washing, but when?

She had departed for New Court on the Wednesday morning after sleeping at No. 13 on the Monday and Tuesday nights. Had the clothes been in her possession then she would, presumably, have taken them with her when she moved. She had spent the Thursday afternoon with Mary, and so two possibilities arise. Either she came back to retrieve the clothes which she had left behind, or she had collected them from her customer on the Thursday and had them with her when she called in at No. 13.

In the event, we know that she bolted from the room when Barnett appeared on the scene. She went so quickly that she left her bonnet behind. However none of that answers the question of why she took the clothes to Mary's room if she was on her way back from collecting them. She lived only about forty-five yards from Miller's Court, so why had she not taken them there rather than go visiting with a large bundle of dirty laundry? We must also remember that a man's coat was included in the pile, and it is very unlikely that she had been given *that* to wash. Of course there is always that possibility, but let us consider another.

What if, as part of a long-established routine, Harvey had stolen the clothes, either after having been given them to wash or in some other way, and she and Mary had intended to pawn or sell them. One of them had already 'popped' a shawl for two shillings, and they may have intended to take turns in pawning the remainder at different places. It was an old dodge, especially for itinerant laundresses, and one which they may have worked for some time.

Let us, however, consider another possibility. Supposing Harvey *had* stolen the clothes and had then discovered that the police were on to her? She would not have dared to leave them in her room at New Court, and so what more natural than to take them to her old friend, Mary, for safe-keeping. However wiser counsel could have prevailed once inside the nearby No. 13. Everyone locally knew they were friends, and that they had been living together until only recently. The trail would have led straight from New Court to Mary. There would have been only one thing to do, dispose of the evidence – and to burn the clothes may have seemed an ideal solution. Just then, however, Barnett had arrived and Harvey beat a hasty retreat, but she returned later to retrieve her bonnet and the pawn ticket, and the two women then burned all the identifiable clothing.

After Mary's death, Harvey would have had little choice but to admit 'ownership' of the clothing. Barnett would have seen it in No. 13, and would have guessed, or Mary could have said that Harvey had left it there. Had Abberline made inquiries about the clothes, all that Harvey would have needed to say was that it was some laundry which she had left in Mary's room temporarily, following her move to New Court, until she had time to deal with it. As it is, we are not told whether the police asked her what she was doing with the clothing, as surely they must have done.

The second inconsistency concerns the time of Mary Kelly's murder.

As far as we are aware, only Dr Bond ventured an opinion and that, according to my information, was wildly inaccurate.

After admitting that it was difficult to say 'with any degree of certainty' how long Mary had been dead, he put forward a probable time of death of one or two o'clock in the morning. That opinion was based upon the temperature of the body at 2 *p.m.*, the stage which the rigor mortis had reached, and the state of digestion of the dead woman's last meal.

The temperature of the body was described as being 'comparatively cold' at 2 p.m. It was hardly a scientific observation and is meaningless.

Dr Bond also stated that rigor mortis had set in, but increased whilst the body was being examined. He continued by saying that 'the period varies from six to twelve hours before rigidity sets in' which, I am told, is just not true.

One of my best friends was the late Dr F. D. M. Hocking, a forensic scientist who, early in his career, worked with Sir Bernard Spilsbury.

A chemist, biologist and toxicologist, he was eminent in the field of pathology. For over fifty years he was the County Pathologist for Cornwall, during which time he conducted more than 40,000 autopsies and also appeared in many notable murder trials.

Denis Hocking told me that rigor mortis commences between *two and four hours* after death: a statement based upon his personal observations and confirmed by *Gradwohl's Legal Medicine*, which is a leading American text book on forensic medicine, and the English edition of which was edited by Professor Francis E. Camps, and *Taylor's Principles and Practice of Medical Jurisprudence*, the standard text book on forensic medicine, which was edited by Professor Keith Simpson.

Gradwohl's states: 'The delay in the appearance of rigor mortis after death can vary considerably. Ordinarily it is about 2–4 hours. It is complete in another 3–4 hours, and is generally fully established about nine hours after death.'

Taylor's confirms that: 'Rigor mortis generally commences within two to four hours after death.'

With regard to Mary Kelly, Dr Hocking told me: 'Dr Bond reports that rigor mortis was commencing. This post-mortem change commences in the upper part of the body, extending downwards to the lower limbs. From his statement, I gather that when he saw the body at about 2 p.m. rigor mortis had affected the upper limbs, and later this had extended downwards, hence his statement that rigor mortis was increasing.

'Dr Bond states that the period of onset of rigor mortis is from six to twelve hours, and therefore he comes to the conclusion that death had occurred some twelve hours before his examination, i.e. in the early hours of November 9th.

'He is not correct in his estimate of the time that rigor mortis occurs. If Kelly had been killed in the early morning, rigor would have been fully established when the doctors saw her at 2 p.m. and not, as Dr Bond describes, 'commencing' and increasing. If rigor mortis was commencing at about 2 p.m., then death would have occurred at about 9 a.m., instead of the much earlier hour that he estimates. I take into consideration that there could have been some delay in the onset had the body been exposed to cold, but this is doubtful in the case of normally nourished human beings and in this particular instance delay would not be operative had the room been well warmed by the fire.'

With regard to the state of digestion of Mary's last meal, Dr Hocking stated: 'Dr Bond reports that there was some partly digested food of fish and potatoes in the stomach. No useful deduction can be made from this finding. It is generally recognized that any conclusion as to the time of death based on the degree of digestion of food in the stomach is inordinately inaccurate. People vary widely in their rate of digestion.

'Generally speaking, fish and potatoes are easily digested. I would put partial digestion at 1–2 hours after eating, and not Dr Bond's 3–4 hours. The partial digestion and the state of rigor mortis can be roughly related. Digestion will go on after death, whilst the body is cooling, but will slow down. 'Partial digestion' is rather a wide term, but in my opinion, the finding is consistent with the meal having been taken around 8 a.m. – and not about midnight.'

I sought Dr Hocking's expert opinion largely because of Mrs Maxwell's evidence. Most people, both at the time and since, have pooh-poohed what she said about having seen Mary alive at between eight and half-past on the morning of the 9th, and we can be sure that the police took her evidence with a pinch of salt as well. They probably gave Mrs Maxwell something of a rough ride to boot, as did MacDonald on their prompting, and yet her story never wavered.

Abberline took her statement on the very same day that the body was discovered, and it is therefore unlikely that she was confused about events which had occurred only a few hours earlier. It is also very doubtful that Mrs Maxwell was an imbecile, a known drunk, or a congenital liar, otherwise Abberline would not have had her appear at the inquest. Why, then, is there no record of any investigation having been made by the police into the verifiable facts of her statement?

Apart from checking her avowed movements on that morning, one would have thought that Abberline, on being told by her of Mary's vomiting in the street, would have said: 'Show me.' It is unlikely that Dorset Street was cleaned from one year to the next, and surely *some* traces of the vomit should have been there – perhaps even enough to establish whether it contained fish and potatoes – if some stray mongrel had not found it first.

Either the police had an incredible faith in their doctors, and were even more incompetent than usual, or else they *did* investigate Mrs Maxwell's claims and discovered evidence which they thought it best to conceal. Were the latter the case, they may well have decided to have Mrs Maxwell's evidence derided publicly at the inquest in order that the murderer should not be alarmed.

9

Alice & Frances

MARY KELLY'S INQUEST was a fiasco and a sham which lasted virtually only half a day. It had been marred by disagreements between Coroner and jury, and no effort had been made to establish many of the facts required by law. Everything was over quickly, and far too quickly as it transpired because, at six o'clock on the evening of that very same Monday the 12th, a man of military appearance strolled into Commercial Street police station with seemingly vital information.

He was George Hutchinson, a casual labourer who had been unemployed for some weeks, and he told Sergeant Badham that he had something to say in connection with the death of Mary Kelly. This is the statement which he signed:

Commercial Street
Metropolitan Police.
H Division
12th November 1888
Murder
At 6 p.m. 12th George Hutchinson of the Victoria Home Commercial Street came to this Station and made the following statement:

About 2 a.m. 9th I was coming by Thrawl Street, Commercial Street, and just before I got to Flower and Dean Street. I met the Murdered woman Kelly, and she said to me Hutchinson will you lend me sixpence. I said I cant I have spent all my money going down to Romford. she said good morning I must go and find some money, she went away towards Thrawl Street. a man coming in the opposite direction to Kelly tapped her on the shoulder and said something to her they both burst out laughing. I heard her say alright to him, and the man said you will be alright, for what I have told you. he then placed his right hand around her shoulders. He also had a kind of a small parcel in his left hand, with a kind of a strap round it. I stood against the lamp of the Queens Head Public House, and watched him. They both then came past me and the man hung down his head with his hat over his eyes. I stooped down and looked him in the face. He looked at me stern. They both went into Dorset Street I followed them.

They both stood at the corner of the court for about 3 minutes. He said something to her. she said alright my dear come along you will be comfortable. He then placed his arm on her shoulder and gave her a kiss. She said she had lost her handkerchief. he then pulled his handkerchief a red one out and gave it to her, they both then went up the Court together. I then went to the court to see if I could see them but could not I stood there for about three quarters of an hour, to see if they came out they did not so I went away.

Description. age about 34 or 35. height 5 ft 6 complexion pale, dark eyes and eye lashes slight moustache curled up each end, and hair dark, very surly looking dress long dark coat collar and cuffs trimmed astracan, and a dark jacket under. light waistcoat, dark trousres dark felt hat turned down in the middle button boots and gaiters, with white buttons, wore a very thick gold chain. white linen collar, black tie with horse shoe pin. respectable appearance. walked very sharp. Jewish appearance can be identified

George Hutchinson
E Badham Sergt
E. Ellisdon Insp
Submitted – FG Abberline Insptr. T Arnold Supdt
Circulated to A.S.

Abberline must have been awed by such a marvellously detailed statement, which certainly put the reports of some of his detectives to shame, and more was to be added when Hutchinson repeated his story to reporters. Obviously he lost no time in doing so, because it was to be carried by almost every newspaper in the country over the following six days, with minor embellishments.

It was reported that Hutchinson's statement had been taken by special messenger 'to the headquarters of "H" Division where Detectives Abberline, Nairn and Moore set about an immediate investigation.' Abberline expressed the opinion that the statement was both true and important, but that is hardly significant because by then the police were ready to clutch at almost any straw.

The impact of Mary Kelly's horrific murder had been greatly increased by the lull in the Ripper's activities which had preceded it, and consequently the criticism of the police was renewed with an even greater clamour.

Most of the newspapers thought them completely useless, and considered that the only possible way that the killer might be apprehended would be as the result of 'information received', or some accidental discovery, rather than by sound detective methods.

Then, as if such public castigation were not enough, no less a personage than Queen Victoria stepped into the fray.

On November 10th, she sent a telegram, in cipher, to her Prime Minister, the Marquess of Salisbury, stating that: 'This new most ghastly murder shows the absolute necessity for some very decided action. All these courts must be lit, and our detectives improved. They are not what they should be. You promised, when the first murder took place, to consult with your colleagues about it.'

Then, only three days later, she wrote to Henry Matthews, the Home Secretary:

The Queen fears that the detective department is not so efficient as it might be. No doubt the recent murders in Whitechapel were committed in circumstances which made detection very difficult; still, the Queen thinks that, in the small area where these horrible crimes have been perpetrated, a great number of detectives might be employed and that every possible suggestion might be carefully examined, and, if practicable, followed.

Have the cattle boats and passenger boats been examined?

Has any investigation been made as to the number of single men occupying rooms to themselves?

The murderer's clothes must be saturated with blood and kept somewhere.

Is there sufficient surveillance at night?

These are some of the questions that occur to the Queen on reading the accounts of these horrible crimes.

It was a devastating letter for a Home Secretary to receive from his sovereign, and was made worse by the fact that only a couple of days before he had been given a rough time in the Commons – although his announcement of Sir Charles Warren's resignation was greeted with loud cheers.

Finally he was forced into the admission that: 'I have already for some time had under consideration the whole system of the Criminal Investigation Department, with a view to introducing any improvement that may be suggested.'

There can be no doubt that, given half a chance, Matthews would have resigned under the barrage of criticism to which he was subjected, but Lord Salisbury would have none of it. All that the hapless Home Secretary could do, therefore, was to apply pressure downwards, and the ensuing panic at Scotland Yard spread to all those investigating the murders.

Small wonder, then, that the police mounted a show of frenetic action, and that Abberline was only too eager to have something – anything – to send to his superiors.

It was not only the police and the Home Secretary who had to contend with a wave of criticism, however, because, on the day after the inquest had been terminated so abruptly, Roderick MacDonald received his fair share.

The *Daily Telegraph*, for instance, made the valid point that had the inquest been adjourned witnesses could have been examined whilst their evidence was still fresh in their minds. It pointed out that the Attorney-General had the power to apply to the High Court to hold a fresh inquest, but thought it improbable that that would happen.

Altogether, it was an unusually trying time for the residents of the murder area also, and they were at a loss to know what to do or whom to believe. They too had been lulled into a sense of false security by the long interval between killings, but now all the former fears and apprehension had returned. Rumours abounded, and were embroidered with each telling. Arrests were made but, as usual, the suspects were eventually released, sometimes simply on the grounds that they lived where they said they did! Nothing was happening to inspire confidence in the police, and once more the feeling was abroad that the Ripper was merely biding his time before striking again in what was now recognized as his designated territory.

What puzzled many people at the time, the Queen amongst them, was the complacency of the police after the night of the 'double event'. After only a few weeks without another atrocity, they appeared to have heaved a collective sigh of relief and gone back to sleep. Even the various vigilance committees were affected by the same unjustified optimism, but now they too began to revise their opinions. It was announced that the Whitechapel Vigilance Committee, 'who had recently relaxed their efforts to find the murderer', had met at the Paul's Head Tavern, in Crispin Street, on the night of Tuesday, November 13th. The members had considered what steps they could take to assist the police, but we are not told what conclusions they reached.

The Rev. Prebendary William Rogers, of St Botolph's Church, summed up the feelings of the local population very well in his letter to *The Times* which was published on November 13th. He wrote that: '. . . at this crisis I share with my neighbours in the horror of the situation. "Our hearts are disquieted within us, and the fear of death is fallen upon us," and we ask, What is to be done? Murder succeeds to murder, and for a time we are staggered. A number of people are arrested who ought to be let alone, but gradually the excitement passes off.' He hoped that the latest murder would not be allowed to 'pass off' so quietly. In his opinion, it was not so much the murders, ghastly as they were, which 'saddened and appalled' as the disorderly and depraved way of living which they had revealed.

Having referred to Liverpool Street as 'the focus of harlotry', Mr Rogers proceeded to make a couple of suggestions, both of which were impracticable, and neither of which would have served to alleviate the disquiet which so concerned him. He suggested that all prostitutes should be registered and, if need be, licensed, and that there should be some kind of house-to-house visitation 'carried out by devoted men living in these districts', which would 'throw light into those dark dwellings'. His second suggestion would not have been welcomed by the people of the East End as the very last thing which they wanted was to have yet more do-gooders intruding upon them. They wanted the Ripper caught so that everyone could return to their former ways of life without the police poking everywhere.

A peculiar, and very telling, incident had occurred during the early hours of the 14th.

Mr Galloway was a clerk in the City. He was said to have been walking home along the Whitechapel Road when he passed a man who strongly resembled the one seen with Mary Kelly by Mary Ann Cox.

According to Galloway, the man was 'short, stout, about 35 to 40 years of age. His moustache, not a particularly heavy one, was of a carroty colour, and his face blotchy through drink and dissipation. He wore a long, dirty brown overcoat, and altogether presented a most villainous appearance.' Apparently he had a frightened look, and had glared at Galloway as they passed.

We are not told what Galloway was doing out in the early hours of a week-day morning, nor is it explained how somebody who looked 'most villainous', and was glaring at him, could, at the same time, have appeared frightened. Another mystery is how, after only a fleeting glance, Galloway had been able to diagnose the cause of the poor man's blotchiness as being due to 'drink and dissipation'!

Be that as it may, however, Galloway had been so suspicious of the stranger that he had followed him into Commercial Street. There the man had attempted to accost a woman, but had appeared rather disconcerted when a policeman appeared on the scene. He seemed undecided as to what to do next, and Galloway thought he was going to try to avoid the constable, but he did not and continued up Commercial Street.

At that, the intrusive Mr Galloway had gone to the bobby and told him of his suspicions, but he was disappointed and, one suspects, not a little put out, by the reception which he received. Apparently the officer refused point-blank to take any action, saying that he was looking 'for a man of *a very different appearance*'.

Nevertheless arrests continued to be made, and many were as direct results of the increased activities of the vigilance committees. All had convened after Mary's death, and within ten days they were patrolling the streets all night and making almost hourly reports to the police of suspicious movements by various individuals. Such actions were, of course, highly commendable and gave the public an added sense of security but, as is invariably the case with similar civilian organizations, there was always the danger of overzealousness by a few members.

The police were regarded with odium by many East Enders, and were the subject of ridicule elsewhere. Many inhabitants of Spitalfields and Whitechapel felt that had the police been doing their job properly Mary Kelly would have been seen with the man described by Hutchinson, and her ghastly end averted. As it was, her killer had gone undetected, and was still at large, whilst her terribly mutilated corpse still awaited burial because no relatives or friends had come forward. Eventually it was announced that her funeral would take place on November 19th, and the police braced themselves for a major demonstration.

Mary's remains still lay in the little mortuary by St Leonard's Church, and from an early hour on that Monday an enormous crowd completely blocked Shoreditch High Street near the junction with Old

Street and the Hackney Road. The police were out in force, but they stood little chance of controlling such numbers.

At noon, the bells of St Leonard's began tolling their mournful message, and that was a signal which brought out all the local residents to swell the already vast concourse. Women predominated, but it was a cause of comment that, contrary to usual custom, so few wore any form of head-covering.

Shortly after half-past twelve, the coffin appeared at the main gates of the Church, borne on the shoulders of four men. It was a sight which affected the crowd greatly, and the police found it very difficult to keep order as those men and women nearest to the coffin struggled desperately to touch it.

The pathetic sight stirred the crowds into a quite remarkable demonstration of grief, with emotions 'natural and unconstrained'. An account in the *East London Advertiser* described the scene: 'Women with faces streaming with tears, cried out "God forgive her!", and every man's head was bared in token of sympathy.'

Behind the hearse, which was drawn by two horses, were two mourning coaches, the occupants of which had been fortifying themselves for the long journey to come at a pub near the church gates – most likely The Conquerer in Austin Street. There were three mourners in the first: Joe Barnett, someone representing John McCarthy and a person unnamed. The second appears to have held Maria Harvey and Mesdames Cox, Prater, Lewis and Venturney.

It took over an hour and a quarter for the procession to cover the four and a half miles or so to St Patrick's Roman Catholic Cemetery at Leytonstone, where it arrived just before two o'clock. There, after a brief ceremony performed by Father Columban Ellison, the body of 'Mary Kelly' was finally laid to rest in Common Grave Number 16–67.

Mary may have been at peace, but her killer was still lurking somewhere, and her sisters in misfortune still faced the same daily struggle for survival which had dogged her miserable life. Her death, and the memories of it awakened by her funeral, had revived all their old fears and anxieties, but what were they to do? A few more moved out of the district, but the majority seemed in some way bound to their familiar haunts, and every evening they ventured out on to those dark and dangerous streets with their hearts in their mouths.

The new year of 1889 was greeted with hope, thankfulness and relief by East Enders and police alike. Two months had passed without another murder, and this time it really did seem that the Ripper had gone away.

In January, the number of constables on plain-clothes duties was reduced to 102; by February another fifty-five had gone back into uniform, and in March they were disbanded altogether and the vigilance committees wound down their operations.

Great play has been made of the fact that so much activity ceased so quickly. Many are convinced that by then the killer was either dead or incarcerated somewhere, and have used those suppositions to support various theories, but it must be remembered that the police did not terminate their activities overnight, as would have been the case had they been sure that the killer was dead or locked away somewhere. It was a gradual process which, as we have seen, took place over some four months, but that in itself prompts the question of why they were stopped at all if an unidentified Ripper was still at large.

There are two possibilities, which could be applicable individually or in combination.

The first, as ever, is money, because those additional plain-clothes men were expensive. Since December they had received an extra allowance of a shilling a day and, as time went by with no further murders, the Home Office was badgering Monro to limit the expenditure.

As for the other possibility, it may well have been that the police, or some of them at least, were convinced of the identity of the killer but, as their inquiries continued, they were driven to the conclusion that he had left the country.

Whatever the reasoning, the cessation of the patrols appeared to have been justified as the year wore on. There were no more murders, and by the summer of 1889 the Ripper was almost forgotten and everything was back to normal. The fine weather and lighter nights brought more people out for longer; the pubs were doing a roaring trade – boosted by the increased spending power of the 'unfortunates' – and the shops and stalls found that their takings had increased. In short, the East End was its old gaudy and bawdy self – until it was stunned by the news that the Ripper was back!

The latest victim was discovered in Castle Alley, Whitechapel, during the early hours of Wednesday, July 17th, 1889.

It was a dingy place, flanked by Goulston Street to the west and New Castle Street to the east. Access was by means of a gloomy arched passage, little more than a yard wide, between Nos. 124 and 125, Whitechapel High Street.

Castle Alley was about 135 yards long; at its northern end there was a right-angled bend and from then on it became Old Castle Street for a further 105 yards or so to Wentworth Street. To all intents and purposes, the two were one thoroughfare, and they were regarded as such by those familiar with them.

Although the High Street entrance to Castle Alley was narrow, it broadened somewhat thereafter. However, it was blocked, day and night, by tradesmen's carts and wagons and costermongers' barrows, which provided ample cover for anyone lurking with evil intent.

Because of the very sharp bend, a stranger viewing the lanes from their entrances would have supposed them to be cul-de-sacs. They were therefore ignored by those unfamiliar with the neighbourhood. What *The Times* called 'the respectable portion of the population' also steered clear of them, especially Castle Alley, unless it was completely unavoidable. The same newspaper described it as being 'probably one of the lowest quarters in the whole of East London'. It went on to state that 'a spot more suitable for the terrible crime could hardly be found, on account of the evil reputation borne by this particular place, and an absence of any inhabitants in the immediate vicinity.'

There were four street lamps; one, on the left, nearly twenty-three yards from the High Street entrance to Castle Alley, and another, also on the left, some fifty-eight yards further on. At the bend there was a third, opposite a pub – the Three Crowns – which, although standing close to the bend, actually fronted on to

New Castle Street. The fourth was in Old Castle Street, about fifty-eight yards north of the bend, on the right. They did not shed much light, however, and Castle Alley, in particular, was a dark and lonely place at night.

To the east of New Castle Street, and leading from it, was New Castle Place. For the inhabitants of both, the only route north to Wentworth Street and beyond was a right-angled extension of New Castle Place, which entered Old Castle Street at a point roughly thirty-five yards north of its junction with Castle Alley.

PC Joseph Allen had passed through Castle Alley several times on the unusually quiet night of Tuesday, July 16th, 1889. At about twenty minutes past midnight on the 17th he entered it again, from Whitechapel High Street, and stopped under the lamp nearly two-thirds of the way up for a hasty bite of late supper. He was on the move again in five minutes, and as he passed the Three Crowns he noticed that the landlord, Myer Jacobs, was shutting up. Glancing at his watch, he saw that it was 12.30 a.m.

Allen made his way into Old Castle Street and then into Wentworth Street, where he turned right towards Commercial Street. When he was about a hundred yards from Old Castle Street he met another constable, Walter Andrews. They exchanged a few words, and then Allen continued on to Commercial Street whilst Andrews went towards Goulston Street.

For some unspecified reason, Andrews popped into Old Castle Street briefly but, like Allen, he saw nobody about. He continued on his beat, which took him down Goulston Street, up Middlesex Street, back along Wentworth Street and back down Old Castle Street where, in his own words – according to *The Times* – 'About ten minutes to one this morning I saw Sergeant Badham at the corner of Old Castle Street, leading into Castle Alley. That was on the opposite corner of the public house.'

After enquiring whether everything was all right, and having been assured that it was, Sergeant Badham went up Old Castle Street to Wentworth Street to visit another constable on an adjoining beat. Andrews carried on 'up Castle Alley and tried the doors on the west side of the alley'.

He had been on that beat for only a fortnight, but already it was pretty much routine. Suddenly, however, any feelings of boredom vanished because, only a couple of feet from the lamp under which Allen had eaten his snack, he came across the body of a woman.

She lay across the pavement between a brewer's dray and a scavenger's wagon, which were chained together outside Messrs Ernest and Harold Hora's van and omnibus works, and five feet from the premises of Messrs David King and Sons, who were builders. The woman's feet were towards the builders' yard, and her head on the edge of the kerbstone – almost underneath the wagon. Her clothes were raised almost to her chin, exposing her abdomen and genitals, and at first Andrews thought she was drunk, but when he took a closer look with his lamp he saw that blood was running from the left side of her neck. Gingerly he touched the woman's face, and found that it was quite warm, then, with thoughts of the Ripper uppermost in his mind, he gave two urgent blasts on his whistle.

For just a split second there was an eerie silence, then, from the direction of the extension of New Castle Place, he heard footsteps going away from him up Old Castle Street. Ignoring Standing Instructions to stay by the body, Andrews gave chase immediately and very soon overtook a rather startled man who was standing with a plate in his hand.

'Where have you been?' puffed Andrews.

'I have been nowhere,' said the man indignantly. 'I am just going on an errand, and have just left my home.'

At that, Andrews told him that a murder had been committed and, quite properly, insisted that the man come with him.

It transpired that the man was Isaac Lewis Jacobs, a bootmaker, living at No. 12, New Castle Place, and that he was on his way to fetch his supper from, of all people, John McCarthy in Dorset Street! McCarthy's food must indeed have been something special to cause Jacobs to tramp the 500 yards to Dorset Street at that time in the morning, especially as there were two other chandlers' shops in New Castle Street, but, be that as it may, that was what he was doing.

Sergeant Badham had gone only about 150 yards from where they had met when Andrews blew his whistle. He rushed to the end of

Castle Alley and there met Andrews who said: 'Come on – quick!', and then ran back down the Alley with Badham following.

When he had seen enough, the Sergeant told Andrews to allow nobody to touch the body until the doctor arrived. Then off he went to the adjoining beats and recruited PCs Neve and Allen. He instructed the former to search the area, and told Allen to fetch the police surgeon and the duty inspector, and then to help with the search.

Badham then hailed a passing cab and sent a message to Superintendent Arnold. He returned to the murder scene to find that Inspector Reid had arrived together with several constables who were despatched immediately to make inquiries at lodging-houses, coffee houses and the like.

The police surgeon, of course, was Bagster Phillips. Allen called him out at one o'clock, and he arrived at Castle Alley ten minutes later when, as he recorded, it was raining 'sharply'.

He found the woman lying on her back with her face completely to the right. Her right forearm was flexed over her chest, and enclosed in a shawl which hung to the end of her fingers; the left arm was also flexed, and rested on her shoulder.

The left side of the throat had been cut, leaving a jagged wound from which blood had poured down the slanting pavement into the gutter. It had left a silhouette around the body, but there were no signs of arterial spurting. There was also a wound to the abdomen, but it did not appear to have opened the cavity.

That was enough for the moment. Phillips gave instructions for the body to be removed to the grandly named Whitechapel Mortuary, and as it was lifted on to the ambulance it was noticed that the ground beneath was dry. Inspector Reid was to say later that a broken clay pipe and a bronze farthing – both bloodstained – were also revealed.

Superintendent Arnold and Chief Inspector West had arrived by then, and it was in their company that Phillips followed the corpse to the mortuary, where he made a preliminary examination. He noted that the wound to the neck was 'cleaner cut than appeared at first sight', and then, as there was little more that could be done for the moment, Phillips and his companions departed for Leman Street police station. He left the dead woman in the custody of the police, with strict instructions that nothing should be touched.

By that time, no less than James Monro and Chief Constable Monsell were at the murder site. When PC Andrews first showed the body to Sergeant Badham he had said: 'Here's another murder!' and it would appear that, right from the outset, the police believed it to be another in the 'Ripper series', with the top brass taking an active part in the investigation. Had Dr Anderson not been on leave (again!), there is little doubt but that he, also, would have hastened to the spot.

Monro and Monsell conferred and then, having satisfied themselves that everything was in hand, they too left for Leman Street and subsequently had a mini-conference with Messrs Phillips, Arnold and West. Those left at the scene continued to scour the area for clues, but with no success.

Dawn broke and, inevitably, people were drawn to the spot. Because of the police calls at the lodging-houses, word of the murder had spread more rapidly than might otherwise have been the case, and there was considerable excitement in the neighbourhood. Although all the entrances to Castle Alley and Old Castle Street were guarded by the police, crowds built up steadily in Wentworth Street and Whitechapel High Street throughout the morning.

Naturally, the Coroner, Mr Wynne Baxter, was informed of the murder and, in customary fashion, he wasted no time. Quite early in the morning, he instructed Dr Phillips to make a post-mortem examination as soon as possible, and to be present at the inquest which he was convening at 5 p.m. that very day!

Such peremptory commands would not have pleased Phillips, who had been up half the night, but nevertheless he arranged for the autopsy to be held at 2 p.m., and advised 'the Ch. Surgn. [of the Metropolitan Police, Dr M'Kellar] and Mr Gordon Brown [the City Police Surgeon] who expressed a wish to be present'.

As the morning wore on, many lodging-house deputies were taken to the mortuary shed in efforts to identify the victim. Quite a few said that they knew her well by sight, but nobody was able to put a name to her until, at about 2 p.m., a deputy named her as Alice McKenzie. She also gave the police the name of Alice's paramour, and therefore they were able to gather witnesses for the inquest at a very early stage of their investigations.

Phillips knew nothing of the identification when he arrived at the 'Stone Yard' to conduct the post mortem. The police had to clear a way for him through the crowd which had built up at the entrances to the Yard, and that probably did little to improve his disposition.

The doctors found themselves looking at the body of a well nourished woman, five feet and five inches tall, aged about forty, with dark brown hair and a fair complexion. Rigor mortis was well marked, especially in the extremities, but had finished in the arms and face. (It is interesting that Phillips's observations on rigor mortis fit exactly those of Dr Hocking on p. 266.) All her clothing was old, and consisted of:

A Paisley shawl.
A white apron.
A red stuff bodice, with maroon patches under the arms and sleeves.
A brown stuff skirt.
A kilted [pleated] brown linsey petticoat.
A white chemise.
Odd stockings; one maroon, one black.
Pair of button boots.

Phillips supervised the attendants as they disrobed the body, but he was most displeased by something which happened in the process. In his own words: 'While removing the clothing one of the Attendants found a short pipe, well used, which he thoughtlessly threw on to the ground and broke it. I had the pieces put on one side meaning to preserve them but up to the time of writing this report they have not been recovered by me.'

One senses the extreme irritation felt by Phillips as he wrote of the incident: with the attendant for being so stupid in the first place, but mainly with himself. He had obviously forgotten to take the pieces away with him, and now he felt compelled to admit his omission.

It was found that the clothing had been fastened very tightly around the body, so much so that it could only be raised far enough to expose about a third of the abdomen. The rear of the undergarment was heavily bloodstained.

There were two jagged cuts in the throat, each about four inches long, which began on the left side of the neck, behind the sterno mastoid muscle, and finished above the larynx. The deeper incision had divided the left carotid artery and penetrated to the vertebrae, but the larynx and the windpipe were undamaged.

The cuts seemed to have begun as stabs, but it appeared that the knife had then been drawn forwards and upwards in the wounds, leaving a triangular piece of skin between them.

In addition to the two major incisions, there were four small jagged cuts over the angle of the left jaw where the blade of the knife had caught it as the larger wounds were made.

As we have seen, although the abdomen had been attacked, the abdominal cavity had not been opened, nor the muscles damaged. The main cut began seven inches below the right nipple. It was seven inches long, but was not in a straight line – inclining first to the right and then to the left. The wound was deepest where it began, the last three or four inches being only subcutaneous dissections.

On the right side of the abdomen, trailing towards the inner edge of the major incision but rising above it, there were seven scorings which merely divided the skin. Seven similar scratches descended below the larger cut, between it and the genitals, one on the mons veneris being distinctly deeper than the others.

There was some bruising on the upper chest and collar bone, and on the right side of the abdomen, but none to the back of the head or under the scalp. Various old scars and bruises were discovered, but the only noticeable feature was that part of the top half of the left thumb was missing.

No signs of coition were discovered, which may have been fortunate for somebody because Alice had syphilis.

The doctors found no evidence of a violent struggle, and the absence of any damage to the back of her head precluded any idea that she had been thrown to the ground. Nevertheless, the bruising on the upper chest, especially on the right side, indicated that the woman had been held down in some way. Although no sounds had been heard at the time of the attack, the gashes in the neck would not, in themselves, have prevented the victim from crying out.

Phillips concluded that the woman had died from loss of blood following the severance of the carotid artery. He thought that the cuts to the throat had been made whilst she was lying on the ground, and that the abdominal wounds had followed.

In his opinion, the knife had been a sharp one, and the incisions in the neck had been made from left to right by someone who knew the position of the blood vessels, or at any rate where to cut in order to ensure a speedy death. The long wound in the abdomen had, he thought, been caused by a sharp pointed instrument wielded from above and downwards. It had, however, been turned laterally and that tended to mask the true direction of the wound, which was actually from right to left. There was evidence which indicated that two thrusts of the knife had been made before it was withdrawn.

As to the various scorings and cuts on and near the genitals, Phillips did not consider them to have any sexual significance. Rather, he thought, they had been made by the killer trying to cut through the tight clothing. He also theorized that various marks and bruises which he had observed on the left side of the abdomen resulted from the pressure of the killer's right hand whilst he was attempting to cut the clothes with his left.

The latter theory did not, however, take into consideration the fact that the heavier bruising on the right side of the chest suggested that the woman had been held down with a left hand whilst the major cut, which was in a downwards direction, was performed with the right. Clearly, Phillips had given no thought to the possibility that the murderer may have changed his position during the onslaught.

True to his word, Wynne Baxter opened the inquest at five p.m. on Wednesday, July 17th, 1889, in the Working Lads' Institute. After they had been sworn in, the jurymen viewed the body in the little shed only some 350 yards away, then returned to hear the evidence. Superintendent Arnold and Detective Inspector Reid watched the proceedings on behalf of the Metropolitan Police.

The first witness was John McCormack, a fifty-year-old labourer who had been employed by Jewish tailors at Hanbury Street and elsewhere for about sixteen years. He stated that he lived in Mr Tenpenny's lodging-house at Nos. 52 and 54, Gun Street, Spitalfields.

McCormack told the jury that he had seen the body in the mortuary and identified it as being that of Alice McKenzie, with whom he had lived for six or seven years. She was aged 'about forty'. Answering Mr Baxter, he said that he had no doubts about his identification, having recognized her face, some scars on her forehead, and the deformed thumb which, he said, had been crushed by a machine – 'The nail was half off' – and her clothes and boots.

However, apart from the fact that Alice had told him that she came from Peterborough, he appeared to know very little about the woman with whom he had cohabited for so long. He could not even say whether she had any children. All that he seemed sure about was that she worked very hard as a washerwoman and charwoman 'to the Jews'. Their first meeting had been at Bishopsgate, and they had lived in common lodging-houses 'about Whitechapel' ever since.

The last time he had seen Alice alive had been between three and four o'clock on the afternoon of the previous day. He had given her 1s. 8d [8p], eightpence of which was to pay for their bed for that night, but the shilling was hers 'to do what she liked with'. She had gone off, perfectly sober, with the money.

Coroner: 'Did you have any words with the deceased yesterday?'

McCormack: 'I had a few words, and that upset her.'

Coroner: 'Did she tell you she was going to walk the streets?'

McCormack: 'No, she didn't. She told me nothing.'

Coroner: 'Did you not go down to the deputy and ask if the deceased had paid the money?'

McCormack: 'I did. That was between half-past ten and eleven o'clock.'

Coroner: 'What did the deputy say?'

McCormack: 'She told me she hadn't paid the rent.'

Coroner: 'Did you then say "What am I to do – go and walk the streets as well?"'

McCormack: 'That's what I did say.'

It was a little interchange which established that Alice *was* out late at night, and that McCormack had also lied about her telling him that she was going off soliciting. Not that that comes as any surprise; not one of the victims' 'husbands' ever admitted knowing that his partner was 'on the game'.

In the event, the deputy had told McCormack not to worry about the rent at that moment, and he had therefore gone back to bed until his normal rising time of 5.45 a.m.

Baxter followed up his previous question by asking McCormack whether he thought that Alice had gone out on the Tuesday evening 'looking for money', but it is difficult to understand what point he was trying to make. If Alice had had 1s. 8d in her pocket, why on earth should she have gone 'looking for money'? Of course it may well have been Baxter's way of saying that he believed McCormack's story of having given Alice money about as much as *I* believe that Michael Kidney supported Liz Stride!

McCormack may have sensed that the Coroner disbelieved him because, instead of giving a proper reply, he very wisely emulated an American pleading the Fifth Amendment: 'I can't say nothing about that,' he muttered.

The final piece of dialogue between Coroner and witness belongs properly in a Will Hay farce:

Q: 'Was the deceased a great smoker?'
A: 'Yes, she used to smoke, but I can't tell you what sort of pipe she smoked, all I can say is – she smoked.'
Q: 'Was it a clay pipe or a wooden pipe?'
A: 'It was always a clay pipe.'
Q: 'In bed?'
A: 'Yes – of course!'

Wynne Baxter had had his moment of humour. He allowed McCormack to depart, and off he shuffled – probably to find himself another 'old woman'.

His place was taken by a woman who identified herself as Elizabeth [Betsy] Ryder. She told the Coroner that she was the deputy of the lodging-house in Gun Street, and lived there with her husband John, who was a cooper.

Mrs Ryder had identified the body in the mortuary as being that of Alice McKenzie, who had lodged in her house for about twelve months, on and off, as the wife of John McCormack. The last time she had seen Alice alive had been at about half-past eight on the Tuesday evening. She was sober, and was passing from the kitchen to the street with some money in her hand. The deceased was wearing a light shawl, but she never wore a bonnet or a hat.

According to the witness, Alice had been drinking in the lodging-house all that day, and was drunk when McCormack came home. She believed that there had been 'a disagreement' between them then, but she had not heard what was said. The dead woman had been the worse for drink on previous occasions, but she rarely went out when she was in that condition.

Having disagreed with McCormack, who had said that Alice was perfectly sober when he came home, the deputy now closed ranks with him. She denied that the deceased was ever out late, and disavowed any knowledge of her having prostituted herself: 'She was generally in bed by ten o'clock. As far as I know, she got her living honestly and did not get money on the streets.'

She went on to confirm McCormack's evidence of their conversation on the Tuesday night, adding that she had tried to reassure him by saying that Alice would soon be home. Answering the Coroner, she also confirmed that Alice smoked, although she had seen her doing so only in the kitchen, using pipes which she borrowed from other lodgers 'which were short clay ones'.

Further questioning revealed that the lodging-house closed at 2 a.m. At 3.30 a.m. that day, Wednesday, she had gone into the kitchen to see whether Alice and another absent female lodger were there, 'but they had not come home'. The other lodger was a young woman named 'Mog' Cheeks, and she had still not returned. 'Mog' and Alice had not gone out together.

Coroner: 'Do you know where the deceased got the drink from?'

Mrs Ryder: 'No, but there's a public house [the Artillery Tavern] about two doors away.'

The witness said that she had not seen Alice with any men during the day and, indeed, had never seen her with *any* man other than McCormack. On the Tuesday, Alice had gone to meet McCormack at between three and four o'clock in the afternoon, and they had arrived back together. When they were not lodging with her 'they occupied a room at Crossingham's in White's Row'. She had often heard Alice mention that she had sons living abroad, but the witness did not know where.

Questioned about the elusive 'Mog' Cheeks, Mrs Ryder said that she had lodged with her for eighteen months, and was 'on the streets'. That brought an intervention from the foreman of the jury. Expressing understandable concern about the safety of the missing woman, he said that it was important that she be found. He was answered by Mr Baxter, who told him that he had no doubt that she would be, and Mrs Ryder observed that 'Mog' often stayed out all night if she did not have her bed money. Nevertheless it was worrying that of two women who had left the same lodging-house, on the same evening, one was still missing after the other had been found murdered.

Then PC Neve, in his answers to two questions from the Coroner, gave the lie to what both Mrs Ryder and McCormack had had to say about Alice's character. 'I have known her about the place for twelve months . . . It was my opinion that she was a prostitute. I have seen her talking to men. I have seen her in Gun Street, Brick Lane and Dorset Street.'

The last witness for the day was Mrs Sarah Frances Smith. She told the court that she lived at The Whitechapel Baths and Wash Houses in Goulston Street. Her husband, a retired police officer, was superintendent of the Baths, and she was 'the money-taker'.

Mrs Smith said that the Baths backed on to Castle Alley, and her bedroom window overlooked it close to where the body was found. She had gone to bed between 12.15 and 12.30 a.m., but she could not sleep. Even so, she had no idea that anything had happened until she heard a whistle blown and a knock at the door.

Coroner: 'If there had been a call for help in the Alley, would you have heard it?'

Mrs Smith: 'Yes, certainly. My bedstead is up against the wall next to Castle Alley.'

That concluded the proceedings for that session. Wynne Baxter adjourned the inquest until the following morning.

The night passed quietly enough, but all too soon it was daylight on that morning of Thursday the 18th, and those connected with the investigation arose to deal with their alloted tasks.

Bagster Phillips was not a happy man. Not only had he to appear at the inquest, but Dr Bond, in accordance with his brief from Dr Anderson, had informed him that *he* would like to examine the body. That Phillips was irked by Bond's 'request' goes without saying, but he had little choice in the matter and the examination was arranged for that evening.

For his part, Wynne Baxter had the resumed inquest to deal with and, at ten o'clock, he once more brought the Alexandra Room to order. Superintendent Arnold and Inspector Reid were again on hand to watch on behalf of the police and, as it happened, Reid was the first witness.

He told of being called to Castle Alley at about five past one, and of what he found when he got there. By that time, he said, 'the alley' was guarded by policemen at both the Wentworth Street and Whitechapel ends. After the doctor had examined the body it was placed upon the police ambulance, and it was only then that he discovered a short clay pipe, 'now produced', which had been covered by the corpse. The pipe was broken, there was blood on it, and unburnt tobacco in the bowl. It was very old, and was what was termed in the lodging-houses 'a nose warmer'. 'I also found a bronze farthing underneath the clothes of the deceased,' he added. That too had blood on it.

The Inspector took his seat and, at last, Dr Phillips was sworn. The jury heard of what he had seen in Castle Alley, and most of what was discovered at the post mortem. 'The cause of death was syncope, arising from the loss of blood through the divided carotid vessels, and such death was almost simultaneous.'

Whether Wynne Baxter had mellowed somewhat since the previous year, or whether he had since warmed to Bagster Phillips, we shall never know. Whatever the reason, the doctor was allowed to get away with what he had attempted at Annie Chapman's inquest. In words which were virtually a paraphrase of Bagster Phillips's own during the Mary Kelly inquest, the Coroner now declared: 'There are various points that the doctor would rather reserve at this moment.' It was a statement reminiscent of Roderick MacDonald, and highly unsatisfactory.

There was a slight stirring in the room when the next witness identified herself as 'Margaret Cheeks'. Here at last was the missing woman, and everyone wondered what vital evidence she had to contribute.

In fact, it transpired that she was unable to tell the inquest anything at all of moment, and it would seem that she had been summoned merely to demonstrate that she was still alive.

Questioning elicited the information that she had known Alice only from lodging in the same house. She had seen the deceased getting her 'husband's' breakfast on the Tuesday morning, but had not set eyes on her since. That was the whole of her evidence, and 'Mog' departed – having taken the inquiry not the slightest step forward.

What the next witness had to say was more interesting. She was a widow, Margaret Franklin, who gave her address as No. 56, which we also remember as 'The White House', in the notorious Flower and Dean Street with which Polly Nichols, Liz Stride and Kate Eddowes all had connections.

Mrs Franklin stated that she had known the dead woman for about fourteen or fifteen years 'in the neighbourhood', but only as 'Alice'. At about twenty minutes to midnight on the Tuesday, Mrs Franklin had been sitting on a doorstep at the top of Flower and Dean Street with two other women. They saw Alice, who was wearing a shawl, passing by 'in the direction of Brick Lane and Whitechapel'. 'I asked her how she was getting on. She said "All right, I can't stop now." She did not appear to have been drinking.'

Answering Mr Baxter, the witness declared loyally that she had never seen Alice talking with other men. 'She worked hard for the Jews, and they do not give much.'

Mrs Franklin finished by saying that it had just begun to rain slightly when Alice departed. She had not seen her since.

Mr Baxter adjourned until August 14th. He said he hoped that there would not be another 'affair of this kind' before then. His comments indicate that Baxter was of the opinion that Alice had been killed by the Ripper.

One man who did not agree with him was Dr Phillips who, at six o'clock that evening, held open the door to the shed in the 'Stone Yard', and ushered in Dr Bond for his examination of Alice's corpse.

Decomposition had begun, although not very markedly, and the body appeared to have been washed since the last examination. Short of reopening some of the incisions, it was therefore rather difficult for Phillips to give a proper description of the wounds as he had seen them. Nevertheless he did his best, and gave Bond his opinions.

It was a waste of time. Bond disagreed with Phillips on just about every point. For instance, he saw 'no sufficient reason' to agree that the killer had attempted to cut Alice's clothes with the knife in his left hand – in fact he believed precisely the opposite.

That was all very disconcerting for Phillips, who already felt insecure because the Assistant Commissioner had seen fit to bring Bond in to, as he saw it, check his work.

Bond did agree with Phillips on one thing – that the knife had been sharp-pointed; but whereas Phillips thought that 'the instrument used was smaller than the one used in most of the cases that have come under my observations in the "Whitechapel Murders"', Bond felt unable to express an opinion. Unfortunately, the two men were most opposed in their views on the point of major interest to the police.

Phillips wrote: 'After careful and long deliberation, I cannot satisfy myself on purely anatomical and professional grounds that the perpetrator of all the "Whitechapel Murders" is one man.' However, he then went on to hedge his bet by admitting that there 'may be almost conclusive evidence in favour of the one-man theory if all the surrounding circumstances and other evidence are considered'. Nevertheless, he held it as his duty to report only on the post-mortem appearance and express an opinion solely on professional grounds and his own observations.

Knowing that Bond's conclusions would contradict his, Phillips was trying desperately to have his cake and eat it, but it is doubtful whether anyone was deceived. He had not felt constrained to limit his opinions to 'anatomical and professional grounds' in most of the killings with which he had previously been involved – on the contrary, he had acted as an early Scenes of Crime Officer – so why should he begin now?

He submitted his report on Monday the 22nd, but Bond completed his four days earlier and Dr Anderson was able to read: 'I see in this murder evidence of similar design to the former Whitechapel murders, viz sudden onslaught on the prostrate woman, the throat skilfully & resolutely cut with subsequent mutilations. Each mutilation indicating sexual thoughts & a desire to mutilate the abdomen & sexual organs.

'I am of the opinion that the murder was performed by the same person who committed the former series of Whitechapel murders.'

That coincided with Monro's opinion, and is the precise reason why he had already increased the police presence. In the final analysis, Phillips's views counted for very little.

Within a week of her death, Alice was slipped quietly into her grave in the East London Cemetery at Plaistow. The London Evangelization Society and Common Lodging-house Mission had offered to pay the costs of her interment, but Mr Tenpenny 'and others interested in the deceased' declined the offer and defrayed the expenses themselves.

Her inquest was resumed on August 14th, but no fresh evidence was forthcoming and the jury returned the inevitable verdict of 'Murder, by a person or persons unknown'.

There were no more murders in 1889 which could, however remotely, be likened to the 'Ripper killings', and when the first three months of 1890 also passed without incident, there was again an atmosphere of relaxation, with the plain-clothes patrols being disbanded in April. The rest of 1890 was similarly quiet, and gradually things in the East End got back to normal, with the Christmas and New Year festivities exhibiting all their former gaiety and bawdiness. The streets were as busy as ever they had been, and the whores plied their trade without a single thought of 'Jack'. Then, early in 1891, came the news that another prostitute had been found with her throat cut, and a sudden chill descended upon the capital.

Just before 2.15 a.m., on Friday, February 13th, PC Ernest Thompson was on his beat in Chamber Street. Twenty-five-year-old Thompson had been in the Metropolitan Police Force for only just over six weeks, and this was his first unaccompanied beat duty.

He made his uneasy way along Chamber Street, in a westerly direction. When he had nearly reached the end, he turned left into an alley, under an arch of the London and Blackwall Railway, which led into the once pleasant little area known as Swallow Gardens and thence to Royal Mint Street.

It was a dark, dismal and narrow passage, and the young constable would have been relieved when he emerged into the comparative haven of Swallow Gardens proper. Just at that moment, however, two events occurred, almost simultaneously, which were to haunt him for the remainder of his life.

Behind him, but receding rapidly in the opposite direction towards Mansell Street, he heard the sound of a man's footsteps, then, horror of horrors, he almost stumbled over an inert body lying in the road.

Kneeling with his lantern for a closer look, Thompson was aghast at what he beheld. The figure was that of a young woman. Her throat had been cut from ear to ear, and was bleeding profusely. When he touched her face and hands he found them to be quite warm, and then he saw an eyelid flicker, causing him to think that she might still be alive.

All this happened in a matter of seconds, and Thompson found himself in an unenviable predicament. In the event of his discovering a body, his orders were to remain with it and summon assistance. On the other hand, the sudden commencement of the footsteps could have meant only that someone had concealed himself as Thompson passed, and was now leaving the scene. Should he stay with the woman and call for help, especially as there was a strong possibility of her being alive, or should he hasten after the mystery man and probably go down in history as the captor of Jack the Ripper?

A split-second decision was necessary, and discipline and concern for the woman prevailed. Unlike PC Andrews in Castle Alley,

Thompson blew his whistle and waited, forlornly, for someone to arrive.

Thompson did not have to wait for very long as two constables from adjoining beats, PCs Hyde and Hinton, were on the scene quite quickly. Hyde then went off to fetch Dr F. J. Oxley from nearby Dock Street, whilst Hinton sped the 300 yards or so to Leman Street police station.

Dr Oxley was in attendance in no time at all, but he found the woman to be dead. Inspector Flanagan, from Leman Street, came close on his heels and despatched a constable all the way to Spital Square to fetch Dr Phillips, and another to summon Superintendent Arnold, Chief Inspector Moore and Detective Inspector Reid. Telegrams were sent to surrounding police divisions advising them of the 'occurrence'.

As fast as men arrived, they were ordered to search the neighbourhood and 'make enquiries'. Constables Hyde and Hinton were questioned, but they had not seen or heard anything or anybody at the time when Thompson had heard the footsteps.

Superintendent Arnold appeared somewhat later than the others, and his contribution was to ensure that inquiries at common lodging-houses were put in hand. He then had a word with Dr Phillips, who told him that there were two cuts in the throat sufficient to have caused death, but that the body had not been mutilated in any other way. In his opinion, the 'posture and appearance of the body et cetera' were not in keeping 'with the series of previous murders which were accompanied with mutilation'. It was a typically pompous and dogmatic assertion by Phillips, and one made before he had even made a proper examination of the corpse. The body may not have been mutilated, but it was obvious that Thompson had disturbed the killer in the act, and before he could inflict further injuries, had that been his intention.

Whatever Phillips may have thought, Scotland Yard took this murder very seriously indeed. To them, it had all the hallmarks of a 'Ripper killing', and the possibility that 'Jack' was back in town brought not only Chief Inspector Swanson to the site but, later in the day, Anderson as well.

The body was removed to the Whitechapel mortuary shed and searched, but nothing of any seeming importance was discovered. Some of the local bobbies who viewed the body were able to say that the dead woman was known to them as a low-class prostitute, but no formal identification was forthcoming.

However the police inquiries soon turned up two promising leads.

One came from William Friday, known locally as 'Jumbo', who was a carman employed by the Great Northern Railway. He stated that about half an hour before the body was found he had been walking through Royal Mint Street, on his way to the Railway stables, when he had seen a man and a woman standing in a doorway. Although he had not seen their faces clearly, he had noticed that the woman was wearing a very distinctive round black bonnet, and when shown that worn by the deceased he declared it to be the one. Friday gave the police a slight description of the man who, he said, looked like a ship's fireman, but stated that he would not be able to recognize him again. Two brothers named Knapton, also carmen, made similar statements.

It was, however, the other avenue of inquiry which brought results, and again the bonnet was involved.

When Thompson came across the body a new black crepe bonnet was lying beside it, and later a much older one was discovered pinned under her dress. It was the combination of the two bonnets which led to the woman's identification, and then to the apprehension of a suspect answering the description of the man seen by the three carmen.

It transpired that the victim was named Frances Coles. She sometimes used the pseudonyms 'Hawkins' and 'Coleman/Colman', but was known to intimates as 'Carroty Nell'. She was twenty-six years old, a mere five feet tall, and was reported as having brown hair and eyes – although her nickname indicates hair of a reddish hue. I have seen her described as having been the prettiest of the murder victims, but her mortuary photograph shows nothing to support such a claim.

Frances was the daughter of a former bootmaker, James William Coles, who was in the Bermondsey Workhouse at the time of her death. Her only other immediate relative was a single sister, said to be 'very respectable', who lived at No. 32, Ware Street, Kingsland Road – which was about half a mile north of St Leonard's Church, Shoreditch.

At one time, Frances had been a respectable girl also, with a regular job corking bottles at a wholesale chemist's in or near the Minories. She had earned good wages, but did not like the work, especially as it caused callouses on her knuckles. By the time she was eighteen she had turned to prostitution, and solicited in Bow, Shoreditch, Spital-fields and Whitechapel. It seems that she preferred the doss-houses in the Commercial Street area, with one of the first at which she stayed, 'Wilmot's' at No. 18, Thrawl Street, remaining a favourite.

Right up to the time of her death, she told her father and sister that she was still working at the chemist's, and that she was lodging in Richard Street – which was the eighth turning on the right from Berner Street when walking eastwards along Commercial Road. She probably selected that area for her fictitious address because of the distance from her sister, but she was more than a little naive if she thought that her relatives did not know or suspect something of her true circumstances. Eight years is a long time to keep such a secret, especially when she was sometimes soliciting almost on her sister's doorstep, and, in addition to smelling of drink occasionally, she nearly always looked poor and dirty.

The man arrested for her murder was James Thomas Sadler, a bearded 53-year-old ship's fireman who was generally known as 'Tom'. He had been paid off from the SS *Fez* at 7 p.m. on Wednesday, February 11th, i.e. about thirty-one hours before the murder. He gave his address as what, in Swanson's report, looks like 'Davies Boarding House', East Smithfield – a house only some 250 yards from where Frances' body had been found. His story of what befell him over the next three days gives a vivid picture of the violent nature of the district.

He left the docks with probably in excess of £200, in present values, in his wallet. Before him was the prospect of a couple of weeks ashore and, with his wife and five children tucked away safely in Kent, the delights of the East End were his for the choosing. Off he went, up

Leman Street, to one of his favourite drinking spots – Williams Brothers, 'on the corner of Goulston Street'.

After a few gins, Sadler made his way along Wentworth Street to the Victoria Home in Commercial Street where, presumably, he stowed his gear. He did not linger there for long, and was soon esconced in the nearest pub, the Princess Alice, which was opposite the Home on yet another corner of Wentworth Street. There, luckily as he thought, he espied Frances, also on her own, and beckoned her over.

Sadler had first met her about eighteen months before. She had been soliciting in Whitechapel Road, and they had spent the night together in a lodging-house in Thrawl Street – almost certainly Wilmot's. Now they greeted each other like old friends, and were soon picking up where they had left off. Frances sensed easy pickings, but she wanted them all for herself. When Sadler asked her to have a drink she suggested that they go somewhere else, because 'when she got a little money, the customers in the pub expected her to spend it amongst them'.

That presented no problem for Sadler – to him one pub was much the same as another – so they left the Princess Alice and strolled the 200 yards up Commercial Street to The Britannia. However, no sooner had they made themselves comfortable than Frances encountered the same difficulty which she had anticipated in the Princess Alice. An acquaintance of hers, Annie Lawrence, joined them in the hope of a free drink, and Sadler would have been quite happy to have bought her one but Frances stopped him. She was not prepared to share him and his money with another woman, and lost no time in getting him out of the pub and the immediate area.

They went back down Commercial Street, and then began drinking their way eastwards along Whitechapel High Street and Whitechapel Road. One of their many ports of call was the White Swan – the same pub which Martha Tabram's sister-in-law had seen her entering. It was there that Frances prevailed upon Sadler to buy her a half-pint bottle of whisky before they continued on their, by now, quite merry way. Where else they went that night, and how many other pubs enjoyed their custom, is not known. Eventually, however, they finished up sharing a double bed in a lodging-house, known pretentiously as 'White's Row Chambers', at No. 8, White's Row, Spitalfields.

It was not until between eleven o'clock and noon the next day, Thursday the 12th, that they emerged and headed for Mrs Shuttleworth's eating-house – which was located in a section of Wentworth Street known as Ann Street.

After their meal they drank their way steadily along Wentworth Street and down Middlesex Street until they reached The Bell, where they stayed for about two hours, 'drinking and laughing', with Sadler becoming drunker by the minute.

Frances chose her moment carefully and then, when her companion was well into his cups, she raised the problem of her new bonnet. She told Sadler that a month previously she had placed a shilling deposit on a bonnet in a shop near Baker's Row, but had not been able to collect it because she was lacking the balance of half-a-crown (2/6 – 12½p). He, of course, did precisely what she had anticipated and insisted that they collect it forthwith. So off they tottered on a journey which developed into another pub crawl.

It was about seven o'clock, and quite dark, when they finally reached their destination, No. 25, Nottingham Street. We shall never know for certain what Frances was up to, but we can be sure that, somehow, she was making money out of the bonnet story because, after Sadler had handed over the half-a-crown, she insisted upon going into the shop alone. She returned to say that the bonnet was 'not ready' yet, as the woman was 'putting some elastic in it', and so, obviously, there was nothing for it but to repair to a nearby pub.

After a while, Frances made her unsteady way back to the shop. She returned with the bonnet, which she put on and displayed for Sadler's approval. He wanted her to throw the old one away, but Frances knew the value of a penny and insisted upon pinning it under her dress. In the event, her new bonnet was to do her as little good as Polly Nichols's had done for her.

From Nottingham Street they lurched over half a mile down Baker's Row and along Hanbury Street. Their destination was yet another pub, this time one much favoured by Sadler, the Marlborough's Head in Brick Lane. Just before they arrived there, he bought Frances a penny pair of ear-rings, to set off her new bonnet, at a 'little huckster's shop' on the corner of Brick Lane and Harbury Street. They were then only yards from where Annie Chapman's body had been discovered, but that was the last thing on their minds.

In the Marlborough's Head, Sadler met some former acquaintances and 'treated them'. However, by then, as he was to say later in a masterpiece of understatement, he was 'getting into drink' and the landlady began to object to the rowdiness. For some reason not disclosed, but probably because she was a known prostitute, the publican also objected to Frances being there. None of that disturbed Sadler though, because they were leaving anyway. He had arranged to meet a man named Nichols in Spital Square, just over a hundred yards away, and so he left to keep that appointment after arranging that, when she had finished her drink, Frances would go to another pub in which he would join her shortly. That was probably his undoing, because it would seem that she laid certain plans during his absence.

Sadler eventually arrived at the agreed rendezvous, and after another drink or two the pair tacked an unsure course in the general direction of White's Row. Coincidentally, or so it appeared, the most direct route was along Frances's familiar territory, Thrawl Street – and it was there that disaster struck.

In the shadows of that evil haunt of vice and crime, Sadler was suddenly hit violently on the head with a weapon wielded by a woman in a red shawl. He fell to the ground, and was then kicked almost insensible by several men who subsequently disappeared into various lodging-houses. Somehow he managed to get to his feet, but to his great dismay he found that his watch and all his money had been taken.

Sadler immediately rounded upon Frances, who had not even attempted to help him, and a violent row ensued. Blind drunk he may have been, but he knew all about the 'rolling' of sailors and he strongly suspected that she had 'set him up'. They parted at the very spot from which Hutchinson had seen Mary Kelly meet the myster-ious stranger, and a penniless Sadler staggered off into the night leaving Frances to her own devices.

She, in her drunken state – although by no means as far gone as he – appears to have been convinced that Sadler would soon rejoin her after their tiff, and she therefore continued on her way to No. 8, White's Row. There she persuaded the watchman, Charles Guiver, to allow her to wait in the kitchen until her paramour returned. Of course she had no means of knowing that he *would* come back, but she was three sheets to the wind, tired and probably penniless, and one tale was as good as another to gain an hour's sleep.

For his part, it is doubtful whether Sadler would have joined her willingly, but he had little choice. With his money gone, he realized that his only chance of getting a bed for the night was at the lodging-house where he had been almost an honoured guest only the night before. He arrived at the 'Chambers' only a very short time after Frances. His face was bleeding, his clothes were filthy, and he was very, very drunk.

Frances was sitting at the kitchen table with her head on her arms, and he asked her whether she had enough money to pay for their bed. When she replied that she had not, he told her that he had four pounds and eighteen shillings (£225 in 1997 values) still due to him from the *Fez*, and asked if she could 'get trust' for them for the night. Half stupefied, Frances did not even bother to try. She, at least, knew how strict lodging-house deputies were in applying the 'Cash Only' rule to casuals, and she told Sadler that she could not. He therefore approached Guiver himself. Swaying and slurring his words, he tried to explain about the money which he was due to 'lift' the next day, but he met with a blank refusal. Guiver took him out into the yard and helped him to clean himself up – and then turned him out. According to a lodger, Samuel Harris, that was at about 12.30 a.m., and Frances was evicted a few minutes later.

Tom Sadler picked his way carefully down White's Row, his sorry plight becoming more and more apparent to him. It was the early hours of the morning, and there he was, with not only enough drink inside him to make him almost incapable of speech, rational thought and controlling his actions, but injured and penniless to boot. He needed shelter, attention and a bed, and the only place that he could think of where they might be available was on board the *Fez*. His spirits lifted at the very thought. Not only would his immediate requirements be satisfied, but in the morning he would be on hand to collect the balance of the wages due to him. Setting a southerly course, he threaded his way down Commercial Street.

The SS *Fez* was tied up in the East Dock of St Katharine's Docks. It was a long way for him to walk in his condition – some three-quarters of a mile – but he finally reached the dock gates in Upper East Smithfield at about 1.30 a.m., thankful for the security which they represented. However his relief was very quickly transformed into a rage born of frustration when, so near to safety and comfort, he was refused admittance by an over-zealous sergeant of the Docks Police, backed up by a constable, because he was drunk. They must have been on a 'work to rule' exercise, or perhaps somebody else had upset them, because refusal of entry on such grounds was unheard of. Rarely did a seaman come back sober from a night ashore and, regardless of the rules, they were invariably nodded through the gates as long as they were capable of reaching their ships. It is understandable, therefore, that Sadler began to abuse the policemen in no uncertain terms.

There was a young Metropolitan PC nearby but, wisely, he took no part in the altercation and all might have been resolved satisfactorily had it not been for some dockyard labourers who were leaving after a late shift. One of them interfered and said something provocative to Sadler, who replied aggressively in words which were not to the docker's liking. Turning to the Metropolitan constable, he said that if he would 'turn his back' for a moment he would give Sadler 'a damned good hiding'.

It was an invitation that an older, wiser and more experienced bobby would probably have ignored, but foolishly the young policeman took the hint. He walked away to the far side of Nightingale Lane leaving Sadler to his fate. Then he and his two docks colleagues looked on as all the workmen piled in and attacked the drunken sailor. The one who had started it all knocked Sadler to the ground and kicked him mercilessly until one of his fellows intervened and stopped him.

All was silence for a moment after that, and then the labourers went off along Upper East Smithfield whilst Sadler rose painfully to his feet and then turned down Nightingale Lane to lick his wounds. He spent about a quarter of an hour there, recovering, and then he too made his way along Upper East Smithfield, towards the Tower of London, to the 'Victoria' lodging-house.

By then he presented a really sorry sight, and it comes as no surprise to learn that, although he was known there, he was refused admission by the night-porter – 'a stout fat man'. Despite explaining his predicament, and literally begging for shelter and a bed, he was turned away.

Sadler was nonplussed. He had set off on his journey to the docks full of optimism, but now he was even worse off. Slowly he racked his brains for a solution, but try as he would, and although he in no way fancied the long tramp, the only thing which came to mind was to return to White's Row. He had no means of knowing that Frances had been expelled from the lodging-house also and, in his muddled thoughts, he wondered whether she had, after all, been successful in obtaining 'trust'. Disconsolately, he began the slow haul back up Leman Street.

He arrived at White's Row Chambers just before 3 a.m. Frances, of course, had gone – in fact she had been dead for about three-quarters of an hour – and, instead of Charles Guiver, he was faced with the deputy, Sarah Fleming. Swaying drunkenly, but thinking that a woman might be more sympathetic to his plight, Sadler mumbled the story of the two assaults and asked to be allowed to sit in the kitchen until daybreak. However, it was all to no avail. Yet again he was turned away, and went wandering aimlessly down Commercial Street, into Whitechapel High Street and along Whitechapel Road.

Just opposite the London Hospital, he was stopped by another young policeman who told him that he looked 'in a pretty pickle', and asked him where he was going. Almost incoherently, Sadler poured out his woes and, to his amazement, found that he had at last reached a sympathetic ear. After searching him, the constable helped him across the road to the Hospital gates where, after some initial hesitation, the night-porter admitted the wounded man and led him to the Accident Ward.

After a cut in his head had been dressed, the porter allowed Sadler to lie down on a couch, where he slept until daylight. It was still quite early when he left the Hospital, and he therefore made his way to the Victoria Home and begged for a few pence until he could collect his wages. It did him no good of course, but then he had a bright idea. Miraculously, he still had with him, unbroken, the bottle which had contained the whisky that he had bought in the White Swan. There was a twopenny deposit on it, and so he slogged virtually all the way back from where he had come and redeemed his pennies. He spent them on beer, and then walked to the Shipping Office and collected the money due to him.

Sadler did not go far once he was in funds. He went to the nearby Victoria Lodging House, where he spent the day convalescing apart from venturing the few yards to The Phoenix pub.

What, though, did Frances do after she was turned out at White's Row?

As we have seen, Guiver evicted her at about 12.35 a.m. (Guiver himself thought that Sadler went just before midnight, and Frances over an hour and a half later, but his times appear unlikely.) The last time she was seen alive was at about half-past one, in Mrs Shuttleworth's eating-house. At that time she was alone, but there may be some truth in the rumours that she was seen with a customer after leaving White's Row. That would account not only for the missing hour, but would explain how she came to have a few coins in her pocket. Of course it may well be that she had them earlier, but that they did not amount to enough for a bed, but she had them now and bought herself three halfpence of bread and mutton. She was in Shuttleworth's for about a quarter of an hour and then, at around 1.45 a.m., she left in the direction of Brick Lane. Half an hour later, she was found dead over half a mile away.

From a remark which he was to make later, it would appear that, somehow, Sadler learned of Frances's death, but he took no steps to contact the police. He was content to rest, nurse his injuries and go drinking at the Phoenix, his philosophy being, as he told the police: 'I have not disguised myself in any way, and if you could not find me the detectives in London are no damned good.'

As was mentioned earlier, it was Frances's distinctive new bonnet which was instrumental in establishing her identity, and from that moment the trail led straight to Sadler. Curiously it was the same Samuel Harris – the lodger in White's Row – who finally tipped off the police about Sadler's whereabouts. How he came by his knowledge we do not know, but he led Sergeant John Wood and PC Gill to the Phoenix at about noon on the 14th, and pointed Sadler out to them from the doorway of the pub.

Sergeant Wood beckoned to Sadler to come outside, and then told him that he should come to Leman Street police station. A woman had been found with her throat cut, and it was alleged that he had been with her on the previous night. According to Wood, Sadler replied: 'I was expecting this,' and went on to say that he was a married man whose wife lived 'in the country', adding 'this will part me and my wife, you know what sailors are.' He confirmed that he had rowed with Frances 'because she saw me knocked about and I think it was through her'.

The police were jubilant at the arrest. Not only were they convinced that they had an open and shut case against Sadler for the murder of Frances Coles, they also felt there was a strong possibility that they had finally nabbed the Ripper.

Probably with the help of Samuel Harris, their excitement soon communicated itself to the local population, and a large crowd had gathered by the time the arresting officers arrived at Leman Street with their prisoner. Everyone seemed convinced that the 'Whitechapel Murderer' had finally been brought to book, and there was quite a scuffle as some tried to attack Sadler.

Once inside the station, he was handed over to Chief Inspector Swanson no less, and it is an indication of the importance attached to Sadler's arrest that his rambling, and sometimes incorrect, statement was taken by Swanson and witnessed by Superintendent Arnold.

On Monday, February 16th, 1891, James Thomas Sadler was charged with the murder of Frances Coles at Thames Magistrates' Court and then remanded to Holloway Prison 'pending further investigations'.

There were the usual 'leaks' to the Press, and as a result several inflammatory articles appeared which were highly prejudicial to Sadler. Some of them were so outrageous that questions about their propriety were raised in the House of Commons, leading the Home Secretary to express his regret that the newspapers concerned should 'seek to gratify public curiosity by tales of such nature'.

That was all very well, but Sadler began to become frightened at the way in which public opinion was being marshalled against him. All along he had steadfastly maintained his innocence and had thought that, with no evidence against him, that would be enough. Now, however, he realized that he was in urgent need of assistance. From Holloway, he wrote to the Secretary of the Stokers' Union, of which he was a member, and it rallied to his aid. The legal firm of Messrs Wilson and Wallace was engaged to act for him, and Mr Henry Wilson arranged for a QC to represent him at the inquest.

In the meantime, the autopsy had been performed by Bagster Phillips. He discovered that Frances had wounds to the back of her head, which suggested that she had been thrown to the ground before being killed. In his opinion, the murderer had then knelt at the woman's right-hand side and turned the body away from him, almost certainly to avoid bloodstains, before making the fatal cut. To do that, he had held the victim's chin with his left hand, the knife being in his right. Although there was only one incision, it appeared to Phillips that the killer had cut the throat with something of a sawing action, during which the knife went from left to right, right to left, and back again. The woman's clothing had not been disturbed, and there were no abdominal mutilations.

Dr Phillips detected no surgical skill, and he did not think that the knife had been very sharp. As far as he was concerned, the perpetrator was not the same person who had carried out the murders of 1888.

However the police were not so sure. They left no stone unturned in their efforts to pin not only the killing of Frances Coles on Sadler, but the 'Ripper homicides' as well.

Fortunately for the prisoner, the inquest was conducted by Wynne Baxter, and in his usual efficient manner. All the evidence was probed to the full, and it became increasingly obvious that there was absolutely nothing to connect Sadler with the death of Frances or any of the 'Ripper crimes'.

Henry Wilson must be accorded most of the credit for that. He had been extremely active on his client's behalf, and had located many witnesses whom he had produced. Three ship's captains spoke glowingly of Sadler's character, and rebutted completely newspaper stories of his fits of temper and 'wild staring eyes'. Other people had confirmed the prisoner's account of his movements and the sequence of events of the night of the 12th/13th, including the two assaults which he had suffered.

Wilson also discovered that the couple observed by 'Jumbo' Friday and the Knaptons were Thomas Fowles and Kate McCarthy. They not only knew the three men, but had seen and recognized them at the time.

Some of the most telling evidence, however, was provided by a Sergeant Edwards. He had seen Sadler near the Royal Mint at about 2 a.m. on the 13th, after he had been set upon by the dockers, and only a quarter of an hour before Thompson had discovered Frances's body. Edwards stated that Sadler had been very drunk and was staggering about, as indeed he was even an hour later when he spoke with Sarah Fleming. According to Dr Oxley, that ruled Sadler out completely as the killer. He did not see how a man so intoxicated could have controlled the muscles of his hand and arm sufficiently to have caused the wound. It was a telling comment which weighed heavily with the jury, as did the observation that, in such a condition, Sadler would have been incapable of departing the scene so quickly. On February 27th, it returned a verdict of 'Murder by some person or persons unknown'.

It was a damaging blow to the police, but still they were reluctant to admit that they were wrong, despite all their inquiries having failed to produce any convincing evidence against Sadler. They had even gone to the length of placing him in an identity parade to see if Joseph Lawende, the witness at Kate Eddowes's inquest, could identify him, and were disappointed when he could not.

Mind you, a very interesting situation would have arisen if Lawende *had* pointed Sadler out. When he was arrested, he had given the police a list of his sailings and discharges, going back as far as 1887, which was verified by the Shipping Office. One trip involved the SS *Winestead*, upon which he had sailed from Gravesend on August 17th, 1888, and from which he had not been discharged until October 2nd of that year. He therefore had the perfect alibi for the murders of Polly Nichols, Annie Chapman, Elizabeth Stride and Kate Eddowes, but even that may not have saved him had he not been represented so ably.

In the end the police gave up. The Home Secretary informed the magistrate that he had consulted the Attorney-General and it had been decided to drop the case.

Sadler was discharged on Tuesday, March 3rd, but still the police were not satisfied and continued to check on his movements. They were assisted greatly when, in December 1891, Chief Inspector Swanson was able to report that Mrs Sadler had been to see him to complain about her husband's conduct towards her. That gave him direct access to Sadler, and he appears to have warned him about his behaviour because a Sergeant Buswell reported later that Mrs Sadler now had no further cause for complaint.

A month later, Buswell submitted another report, stating that Sadler had acquired a shop that was doing good business and was a changed man. However, his assessment was a trifle premature because, only two months after, he had to report upon more domestic disputes. Then, in 1892, the zealous sergeant was able to inform his superiors that Mrs Sadler was summonsing her husband, and no doubt hands were rubbed in satisfaction at the prospect of having him convicted.

In the event, Sadler was bound over to keep the peace for six months, and the last we hear of him was when, in January 1893, he advised the police that he was, very wisely, leaving the area. He disappeared – his prediction that 'this will part me and my wife' having come true – and probably spent the rest of his life regretting the light-hearted impulse which had prompted him to offer Frances a drink.

For his part, Chief Inspector Swanson came to believe later that Frances was, in fact, a victim of the elusive 'Jack the Ripper'.

After her death there were no more murders in the area which bore any resemblance to those committed by the phantom killer. Seemingly he had disappeared never to be heard of again.

10

Portrait of a Killer

OVER RECENT YEARS, Offender, or Criminal, Profiling has made great advances, aided immensely by interviews with convicts. This scientific tool is only that, and is not infallible, but it has been extremely effective in the apprehension of serial killers and rapists. It would be tedious in the extreme to list all the criteria which have been published, but some common factors have emerged which demonstrate that a serial lust killer will usually:

1) Be a white man aged between twenty-five and thirty-five.

2) Have had a disturbed and female-dominated childhood, with an absent or weak father and a mother whose morals were questionable and whom he came to hate.

3) Have felt inferior because of his lack of a stable childhood, have had stunted emotions and have become a 'loner'.

4) Have had a low self-esteem.

5) Have had a strong sexual urge.

6) Have appeared quite ordinary and inoffensive.

7) Have been unmarried, or involved in a marriage which did not last for very long.

8) At some time in his adult life, have been in a situation in which he was sexually frustrated and spent a great deal of time in solitary brooding upon his hatred of women – his mother in particular – and

in fantasizing upon what he would like to do to them.

9) Live and work in the murder area, and have carried out his first killing in the proximity of his home or place of work.

Any reader who wishes to explore the subject – and there is some recommended reading in the bibliography at the end of this book – will, I think, come rapidly to the conclusion that James Kelly fits virtually every profile of a serial lust killer. In particular, *The Ripper Project*, by William G. Eckert, MD, and Colin Wilson's introduction to Donald Rumbelow's *The Complete Jack the Ripper*, provide fascinating correlations with Kelly.

As we have seen, James Kelly was a loner, born illegitimately to a young girl in whose family at least one member was insane. We have no knowledge of his mental state as a young child, but what we *do* know is that, when he was only fourteen, he received the kind of shock which has been sufficient to unbalance the sanest of minds. By the time he left Liverpool, at the age of seventeen, he was recognized generally as being 'crazy and dangerous and mad as a hatter'.

There is no evidence that Kelly had anything even approaching a meaningful relationship with a female until he met Sarah Brider. That may, in part, have been due to the fact that his curious behaviour made him unattractive to the opposite sex, an awareness of which would have done nothing to boost his already low self-esteem.

Prostitutes provided a partial solution. As long as he had money, they did not care whether a customer was peculiar if he was inoffensive. From Kelly's point of view, no pleasantries were needed and the outcome was guaranteed. However, the disadvantage of using whores was that each encounter lowered his self-esteem even further and increased the guilt engendered by his religious convictions.

For a man harbouring such misogynistic feelings as Kelly, contracting a venereal disease from a prostitute would have wreaked incalculable mental damage. Already unbalanced, his self-loathing would have been indescribable, and exceeded only by the intense hatred which would have been generated towards that class of woman in particular. Indeed, so traumatic would the experience have been for one of Kelly's religious susceptibilities that he may well have regarded it as a sign of divine displeasure and decided to mend his ways. That would account for the fact that, leaving all physical attraction to one side, he continued to make such a play for the respectable Sarah Brider, even whilst he was still treating himself secretly for the disease. Had she been more susceptible, and succumbed to his advances sooner, it is doubtful whether he would have continued to resort to prostitutes. It is, however, ironical that it was her eventual submission which caused all the doubts and suspicions which came to plague him about her.

Apart from the physical difficulties which were encountered, the mere fact that Sarah *had* finally allowed intercourse would have been enough to make him wonder about the girl whom he had placed on a pedestal. His thinking would have been that, as she had allowed *him* to have his way with her, she had probably bestowed the same favour on others. Innumerable men have had the same thoughts about the object of their affections, but not many have been in Kelly's mental condition.

Probably with more than a little help from Mrs Brider, he drifted into marriage, but the seeds of distrust and jealousy had been sown and, as the doors of his sanity began to close, they flowered into suspicions which could have had some basis in fact.

At his trial, the judge concluded that Kelly was the architect of his own misfortune because of his fevered imaginations about his wife in which there was no truth whatsoever – but is that really the case? Virtually all delusions spring from an original grain of truth, and in Kelly's case a couple of things do seem rather odd.

In evidence, Mrs Brider had said that on the evening of Monday, June 18th – Sarah's birthday – her daughter had been to Hackney Road on business for her father. However, Sarah herself told Kelly that she had been to Bethnal Green Road to fetch 'some bark to gargle his [Kelly's] throat'. So we have the two women contradicting each other in their attempts to explain why Sarah had come home late, and we have to ask ourselves where she had *really* been and why they felt compelled to lie about it.

Let us take the supposed 'business' for her father first. Sarah was the oldest child and also a married woman. Why, then, should *she* have been sent off on errands? Surely her sixteen-year-old brother would have been a more appropriate errand-boy.

Then there was the alleged buying of the bark in order that Kelly might 'gargle his throat'; but was there anything wrong with his throat? It was his ears that were hurting.

The excuses for Sarah being late seem even odder when one looks at a map, because both the Hackney and Bethnal Green Roads are nowhere near Sarah's route home. In point of fact, they are in precisely the opposite direction! It is not as if they were merely a step in the wrong direction either, because from De La Rue's to the *nearest* point of each road was three-quarters of a mile.

In the light of subsequent events, it is also worthy of note that both roads were in one of the roughest parts of the East End – the Spitalfields/Bethnal Green area! No father in his right mind would have sent a respectable young woman there at night and alone. As for the bark, that could have been bought at one of the many apothecaries which were much nearer Cottage Lane.

No, one is forced to the conclusion that those supposed errands were excuses thought up on the spur of the moment. They are, however, very revealing insomuch as both involved roads in such a notorious district. A spontaneous lie is often very revealing, and the obvious inference to be drawn here is that Sarah *was* in that vicinity, but not for the reasons given.

We can but speculate about what she was *really* doing there. Had she gone with some of her female friends from work for a birthday celebration? Did she have one drink too many, and was that why she felt 'very ill' when she came home? Or could it be that she had a beau there – perhaps someone from De La Rue's – with whom she had taken up since the rows with Kelly started? We just do not know, but Kelly, although a lunatic, was no fool! He knew that neighbourhood very well indeed and, amongst the many dark thoughts, fantasies and questions which bedevilled him, there must have been some which sought reasons for his wife to have been wandering around some of the roughest quarters of the East End at night and, supposedly, on her own. Whether or not she was innocent of any immorality, he certainly had sufficient grounds for the suspicions that were to haunt him into a very real sense of grievance. He came to believe that Sarah was a prostitute who, in collusion with her mother, had merely played a part with him in order to get her hands on his money. With hindsight, it all seemed so logical. Hitherto he had been rejected by women, but what he had thought to be a respectable girl, who was not unattractive, had accepted him – why? From that point on the forthcoming events were inevitable. What Kelly regarded as yet another betrayal at the hands of women intensified his hatred of them to such a degree that only violence would afford him any relief.

James Kelly certainly fits the profile of a serial killer, but we must now look a second time at the murders themselves to see if he also fits the, admittedly rather confusing, circumstances of the 'Ripper killings'. First, though, we should consider this: if James Kelly *was*, in fact, the Ripper, why then did the first murder not occur until over six months after his escape?

There are, I think, two possible answers to that question.

Time and time again it has been shown that sex crimes – which the 'Ripper murders' undoubtedly were – increase only when the basic needs of society and the individual have been satisfied. If a man is starving, homeless and afraid, his sexual needs will lie dormant until he has solved his more immediate problems.

This was certainly the case with Kelly. For the first few months whilst he was on the run after his escape, he was very short of money, constantly on the move and in great fear of apprehension. It was only when he returned to London that he began to lead anything approaching a normal life.

The other answer is that we just do not know whether any killings, or other attacks upon women, were perpetrated by the Ripper prior to August 1888. It is entirely possible that they were, but that they were not linked to the 'Whitechapel Murders'. Indeed, for instance, even today there are many who do not regard Martha Tabram as having been one of 'Jack's' victims.

For my part, I think that even if the killer had made previous attacks, Martha Tabram was his first homicide – a view shared by Dr Anderson, the Assistant Commissioner, CID, of the Metropolitan Police.

Although there were far more of them, one cannot fail to be struck by the similarity between what were almost certainly the first wounds inflicted upon Martha Tabram and the manner in which James Kelly killed his wife. Both had stab wounds in the neck, apparently made by a pocketknife, or penknife. In Martha's case, however, the killer had time to continue his frenzied attack. He needed to mutilate the vagina, the breasts and the abdomen in an outpouring of rage against those parts of the female body which he associated with his mother, his wife and the prostitutes for whom he felt such hatred and contempt.

There was one particular injury made during that violent assault which caused much comment at the time, and has been the subject of great speculation ever since. I refer to the massive blow which fractured Martha's breastbone, and which was made with a different instrument from that which had caused the other wounds. Contemporary thought, discounted by the Home Office, was that a dagger or sword bayonet had been used but, as we shall see later, I have my own ideas about what the weapon was and, if I am correct, another minor mystery is solved.

Next on the list of victims came Polly Nichols, and it should be noted that if Kelly was in fact living with the Lamb family at the time their house in Collingwood Street was a mere 250 yards, as the crow flies, from the murder site. That being the case, an item in the *Echo*, of September 20th, makes interesting reading:

'Inspector Reid, Detective Sergeant Enright, Sergeant Goadby and other officers then worked upon a slight clue given them by "Pearly Poll". It was not thought much of at the time: but from what was gleaned from her and other statements given by Elizabeth Allen and Eliza Cooper of 35 Dorset Street, Spitalfields, certain of the authorities have had cause to suspect a man actually living not far from Buck's Row. At present, however, there is only suspicion against him.'

Polly's murder was to set the pattern for those that followed. The killer had discovered that the mutilating of Martha Tabram's body had aroused him sexually, but probably not enough to bring him to a climax. After that he had had time to fantasize upon what more he could have done to her. The murder of Polly Nichols was therefore swift, and secondary to the now overpowering urge to mutilate.

It has been held that 'Jack' was disturbed by the arrival of Messrs Cross and Paul, but that is debatable. To my mind, he had achieved the ends over which he had fantasized during the previous three weeks or so, and had experienced complete sexual satisfaction in the process. Had that not been so, he would have continued until he had. The fear of apprehension is the last thing on a lust killer's mind when he is caught up in an overwhelming sexual frenzy, and it must be remembered that in Kelly's case *he had nothing to lose*. No prospect of the noose for him, the worst he could expect was to be sent back to Broadmoor, and that fact should always be borne in mind when considering the chances which the Ripper took.

Only eight days elapsed before the slaughter of Annie Chapman, but that was quite long enough for the killer to have relived Polly's killing over and over again, and it was probably during those episodes that he decided to take away a souvenir from the body of his next victim over which to gloat.

With Annie Chapman, he experienced for the first time the ultimate sexual gratification of plunging his hands deeply into the warm entrails of his victim's corpse, and then removing the easily identifiable womb – which exemplified all the hatred which he felt for his mother. It was a totally satisfying experience, but one that was short lived. Over the next three weeks there was another gradual build-up of his urges until the time came when he knew that he just *had* to kill again.

The early hours of Sunday, September 30th, witnessed what is usually described as 'the double event', but to my mind it was nothing of the sort. Certainly two women were found dead, but I do not think that 'Long Liz' was a victim of 'Jack the Ripper'.

Apart from the fact that her throat had been slit from left to right – the most common way of cutting a throat – Elizabeth Stride's killing bore none of the hallmarks of the other murders. No prostitute would have taken a customer to a place where there was the constant possibility of being disturbed and, for all his so-called 'daring', the murderer would not have allowed it anyway.

That, however, is by no means the only objection to this murder being one of the series. We must ask ourselves why, in the highly unlikely event that the victim and 'Jack' *had* gone to such a place, he stopped his activities after cutting her throat. Why did he not go on to mutilate her?

The popular notion that he was disturbed by Louis Diemschütz may, I think, be discounted, in view of Dr Brown's claim that the multiple mutilations of Kate Eddowes's body could have been completed in only five minutes. The killer would seem to have had more than enough time.

Then there is the geography of the murder site to consider. The slaying of Elizabeth Stride occurred well away from the territory which 'Jack' had come to regard as his own, namely the area north of a line from Aldgate to Whitechapel Road. That line appears to have constituted some form of psychological barrier for him in 1888, because there is absolutely no evidence that he ever crossed it.

No, I think that Long Liz was murdered by her lover, and probable pimp, Michael Kidney, who was a known drunk with a history of violence.

One gains the distinct impression that there was much about the relationship between Liz and Kidney which did not come out at the inquest and that, unless he was lying, Kidney did not know half of what Elizabeth got up to.

Violent and foul-mouthed, especially when in drink – he had been imprisoned for three days less than three months before the murder for being drunk and disorderly and using obscene language – he was eight or nine years younger than his mistress, although he professed not to know that. The question which springs to mind, therefore, is whether he was merely using Liz and living, if only partially, on her immoral earnings.

It is difficult to imagine that he did not know that she was 'on the game', and certainly there does not seem to have been much affection in the relationship. On the contrary, all the evidence demonstrates a lack of trust and respect on Kidney's part. He padlocked their room when he was out – although Liz lost no time in providing herself with a duplicate key – and, if her allegations were true, he was not above assaulting her.

On his own admission, in the three years that they had been 'together' Liz had spent a total of five months away from him. That is an average of seven weeks a year, and we must ask ourselves why she left and what she did during those periods. Did she leave when Kidney became *too* demanding and violent? When questioned by Mr Baxter, Kidney denied knowing the reason for her absences but then, almost immediately, he contradicted himself by saying that 'it was the drink that made her go', a rather ambiguous statement.

It is, of course, quite possible that Kidney was telling the truth, and that she went off on drinking sprees when she could no longer tolerate a humdrum life of semi-respectability. How she financed those excursions is a matter for speculation, but there can be little doubt that whoring played a part.

Did she leave Kidney on the Tuesday or the Thursday before her death? He was absolutely adamant that it was the Tuesday, and there is no reason to doubt him. However, she did not turn up at No. 32, Flower and Dean Street until the Thursday. Where was she in between?

According to Kidney, she let herself into their room on the Wednesday and, unlike on her previous absences, she appears to have removed all or some of her possessions – including the mysterious hymn-book. There is certainly something of an air of finality about that, and one suspects, even more, that Kidney did not tell the inquest all he knew.

During his recall, he said that he had found the hymn-book in Mrs Smith's room – which was next door to his own. Mrs Smith, he testified, had informed him that Liz had left it with her when she left on the Tuesday. Then, in almost the same breath, he stated that she took it from their room on the Wednesday. There must have been reasons why Mr Baxter made so much of the question of the hymn-book, and for Kidney's contradictory evidence on certain points. What the Coroner knew, or suspected, is open to conjecture, but Kidney's confusion was probably due to the fact that he was lying through his teeth.

If Liz *had* finally had enough and was leaving Kidney for good, did she tell him so in Commercial Street on the Tuesday evening, and were they the 'few words' about which she told Mrs Lane? Could the final break have come about because Liz refused to give Kidney any money, although he fully believed that she was 'not without a shilling' at the time? Had he sought her out that night for 'beer money'? He told the inquest that he met her in Commercial Street between nine and ten o'clock on the Tuesday evening as he was 'coming from work'. What was she doing there, but more importantly why was *he* in that area? Kidney was a waterside labourer but he was a long way from any water in Commercial Street, and it was rather late. In any case, to go to Devonshire Street via Commercial Street from the docks, if that is where he worked, is rather a long detour! It is probable, therefore, that he knew that Liz was plying her trade there and that he had gone to her for money.

Of course it may well be that she had none to give him, and was refusing to 'turn a trick' to earn some. We know that she received charity from the Swedish Church on September the 15th and 20th, and that indicates that for some reason – ill health perhaps – she had been unable to work at *anything*.

We must also ask ourselves how Kidney came to be in Mrs Smith's room when he found the hymn-book. Was he searching for Liz when she failed to turn up in the 'half an hour afterwards' that she had promised to be there? Why did she not wait for him to return? Could she have been afraid of a beating? Is that why she dropped out of sight until the Thursday? Everything points to a serious row which caused Liz to go immediately to their room and remove some, or all, of her possessions during the half-hour at her disposal before Kidney arrived from wherever he had gone since their meeting. When he *did* come home, and found that she had been and left, he is hardly likely to have been very pleased, especially if he was expecting that, somehow, she would have some cash for him. Liz may have suspected that he would then come looking for her, and that would explain why she disappeared from the immediate vicinity for a time.

All the circumstances point to the fact that Liz had had enough of Kidney and was intent upon leaving him for good. That she was frightened of him is beyond doubt, as is the fact that Kidney would not have been at all pleased to discover that his steady source of income had taken flight.

She dropped out of sight, but Kidney had no reason to suppose that she had gone far from their home in Devonshire Street and some of her usual beats. It is my opinion that he went drinking in the area on the Saturday night, hoping to find her and bring her back, and that he sighted her in Commercial Road – probably as she was turning into Berner Street.

Israel Schwartz stated that as *he* turned that corner, at 12.45 a.m., he noticed a man walking as if partially intoxicated. When the man reached Dutfield's Yard he spoke to a woman standing in the gateway. He tried to pull her into the street, but turned her round and threw her down on to the pavement. The woman screamed three times, 'but not very loudly'.

Now all that bears no resemblance whatsoever to the prelude to a 'Ripper killing' but makes complete sense if the man was Kidney – especially if Liz had detected that he was following her and had taken refuge in the gateway.

With the almost certain exception of Mary Kelly, all the Ripper victims led their murderer to the places where they were to die. Quiet, dark places where they were butchered in a trice without uttering a sound.

Here, however, we have a man coming across a woman, apparently by accident, and then proceeding to assault her publicly. It is also significant that although the woman screamed she did so 'not very loudly' – in other words, as if to protest but not enough to cause her assailant trouble.

In a nutshell, I consider that Kidney was looking for Liz, who may have noticed him trailing her and stepped into Dutfield's Yard to hide. He, however, saw what she had done and began to drag her out. She screamed, but not so loudly as to bring a crowd of people running to what was, after all, a domestic dispute. Nevertheless, the drunken Irishman became even more incensed by that and dragged her into the yard, probably by her scarf, and cut her throat.

It would have been all over within seconds, but by then Schwartz and the man across the road would have disappeared. That would have left the coast clear for Kidney to make off along Fairclough

Street – en route for Devonshire Street via the back streets – just as Diemschütz turned into Berner Street.

On the evening following the killing, Kidney turned up at Leman Street police station completely drunk, maudlin and blustering about the incompetence of the police. Then he lied through his teeth at the inquest, and also introduced the red herring of the brother of the 'gentleman' for whom Liz. had once worked. It was all very much the kind of behaviour which many a police officer has witnessed from a person discovered eventually to have been the actual killer.

Let us then convict Michael Kidney, *in absentia*, of the murder of Elizabeth Stride and hasten to Mitre Square.

The butchering of Kate Eddowes was typical of the being known at that time as 'The Whitechapel Murderer' or, less often, 'The Red Terror', and continued the progression in mutilations that one would expect from a serial killer.

This time the murderer really indulged himself and, in addition to removing the uterus, took a kidney and amused himself by performing the curious nickings of the cheeks and eyelids. Great play has always been made of the supposed fact that he knew where the kidney was located by those who cling stubbornly to the 'mad doctor' theories. They, however, assume that the killer set out deliberately to remove that organ – a view for which there is absolutely no justification. The doctors involved in the post-mortem examinations of the victims could never agree amongst themselves whether the perpetrator of the crimes possessed any anatomical knowledge whatsoever, and the commonsense reactions of policemen who actually saw the bodies indicate that, to them, the man was simply a butcher in the most basic sense of the word.

There is therefore no reason to suppose that the murderer was anything but a vicious individual who ripped and sliced and removed anything which took his fancy, and I consider it far more likely that the body parts which he took away as souvenirs were discovered quite accidentally during his disgusting rummagings. The only exception may have been Mary Kelly's heart. Perhaps it gave him great pleasure to make one of the sex which he regarded as heartless literally so.

We do not know whether, at that time anyway, James Kelly had had any experience in the killing of animals or whether he had witnessed any slaughterings. I have been unable to discover whether Broadmoor bred and butchered its own livestock, although it prided itself upon being self-sufficient. There is also no way of telling whether, before or during the murders, he had ever been employed on any of the cross-Channel cattle freighters, each of which usually carried at least one butcher.

It was immediately after the so-called 'double event' that the letter and postcard arrived bearing the signature which ensured the killer's place in the annals of infamy. On balance, the theory that the author was a journalist seems the most likely one, but something has niggled away at the back of my mind ever since I saw the Broadmoor file because there are several factors which could lead one to point an accusing finger at James Kelly.

I am no graphologist, but the first thing which struck me was the fact that, even allowing for the fact that it was written nearly forty years after, the handwriting in Kelly's 1927 statement bears a distinct resemblance to that in the two 1888 items, and his margins were observed just as meticulously. Then there are the Americanisms, which could be accounted for by Kelly's time on the American man-o'-war.

Another possible Kelly connection arises when one considers that Donald McCormick in his book, *The Identity of Jack the Ripper*, made mention of two supposed 'Ripper' letters which were posted in Liverpool. Nobody else has been able to trace those letters, but according to McCormick the first was dated September 29th, 1888, and read:

Beware, I shall be at work on the last. and second. inst. in Minories at twelve midnight, and I give the authorities a good chance, but there is never a policeman near when I am at work.
Yours,
'Jack the Ripper'

The second, date unspecified, is alleged to have read:

Prince William Street, Liverpool.

What fools the police are. I even give them the name of the street where I am living.

Yours,

'Jack the Ripper'

McCormick implies that those letters were in the same handwriting as the letter and postcard, and as the first of the Liverpool letters is dated September 29th, i.e. before the pseudonym was public knowledge, they were seemingly by the same author. As McCormick points out, it is hardly likely that a London journalist would have taken the trouble to travel all the way to Liverpool, twice, to post some letters, but there may, however, have been very good reasons why *Kelly* was in his home city on the relevant dates.

Finally there is the signature itself.

Kelly used the name of 'John Miller' frequently, and 'Jack' is a common diminutive of 'John'. He was an improver in the upholstery trade and, as such, one of the tools which he would have used most often, especially in renovation work, was a ripping chisel. So . . . was 'Jack the Ripper' the *'trade name'* – as the author emphasized – of *Jack* Miller, a ripper in the upholstery *trade*, and was the instrument which broke Martha Tabram's sternum a ripping chisel? Certainly such possibilities make one pause for thought.

Nearly six weeks were to elapse before the next killing, time indeed for the murderer to gloat over the souvenirs from Kate Eddowes' body, and to imagine how much more savagery he could wreak upon his next victim. Was it, perhaps, during that period that he decided that he would need more time for the atrocity which was to follow, and that therefore he would need to find a prostitute with a room of her own?

It may have been the close shaves which he experienced during his flight from Mitre Square which prompted such a long interval, but an alternative or additional possibility is that he decided to lie low because all the signs were that the police had a good idea of the area in which he was living. Nevertheless, the fact that the name of 'Kelly' had cropped up no less than four times in the investigations so far would have afforded him some puckish amusement, just as long as it did not remind the authorities that another was still at large!

Now we come to Mary Kelly, thought by many to have been the key to the whole riddle, especially as she and Kate Eddowes went by the same name and some believe the killings ended with the carnage in Miller's Court. However, I can find no justification for such a theory. Kelly was a common enough name – we have six or seven of them in this book alone – and who can say, with his hand on his heart, that Mary's was the last death in the series, or even that the body in No. 13 was hers at all?

Certainly more mysteries surround her demise than any of the others, but that, I feel, is mainly because she was murdered indoors and because Barnett and McCarthy lied or, at best, did not tell all they knew. Had she been found dead in a dark corner of, say, Paternoster Row, with a known ancestry and incontrovertible evidence of identification, she would now be merely number five or six on the list of victims, and everyone would be puzzling over why the killer stopped after Frances Coles!

Nevertheless, one cannot help but wonder whether there was, in fact, any connection between Mary and James. It is always possible, I suppose, that she could have been his wife's young sister. Mary Brider would have been of 'Mary Kelly's' supposed age. According to Barnett, Mary Kelly 'left her home about four years ago'; so did Sarah Brider's sister leave Cottage Lane after the tragedy there – perhaps because of her mother's part in it – and, for whatever reason, take to the streets using her sister's surname of 'Kelly' to avoid being traced by her parents? She had certainly left the family home by the time of the 1891 census.

Far-fetched perhaps, but stranger things have happened and, certainly something happened with this murder to send the police the very next day in search of James Kelly. It is the strangest of all the strange incidents that link Kelly and the Ripper, and we should study it in detail.

Dr Forbes Winslow, a man with vast experience of lunatics, had written to *The Times*, that in his opinion the slayings had 'been perpetrated by a lunatic lately discharged from some asylum'. Now he was interviewed about the latest atrocity and stated:

> It is the work of the same homicidal lunatic who has committed the other crimes in Whitechapel. The whole harrowing details point to this conclusion. The way in which the murder was done, and the strange state in which the body was left are not consistent with sanity.
>
> The theory I stated some days ago has come true to the letter. This was to the effect that the murderer was in a 'lucid interval', and would recommence directly this state had passed away. It appears that the authorities were forgetting this theory, and that someone had been persuading them that from the fact of so long a time intervening between the murders he could not be a homicidal maniac.
>
> I desire, as personally being originally responsible for this theory, to flatly deny that, and to state more emphatically than ever that the murderer is one and the same person, and that he is a lunatic suffering from homicidal monomania, who during the lucid intervals is calm and forgetful of what he has been doing in the midst of his attack.

Dr Winslow urged the authorities to heed his advice, and warned of more murders unless 'the proper steps' were taken.

Now it may well be that somebody in authority read that interview, and that it was instrumental in his decision finally to take action on something that had been gnawing at his mind over the past months.

The name 'Kelly' had been cropping up regularly since Kate Eddowes's death, and it is possible that, along the way, some memories in Whitehall had been stirred. As we saw in Chapter 3, it was, after all, only nine months earlier that James Monro, of all people, had written three letters to Broadmoor in as many weeks – all concerning James Kelly!

All were penned in February 1888. The first stated that the Metropolitan Police had not been able to trace Kelly, but that the inquiry would be continued. Then, on the 13th, Monro wrote: 'I have to acquaint you that observation has been kept on the residence of his [Kelly's] mother-in-law . . . but no information can be obtained respecting him', and that 'Inquiry has also been made at No. 31, Clarendon Square, St Pancras, and in the immediate neighbourhood, but no person named Merritt is known there.' Ten days later, Monro reported that John Merritt had been found but 'states he has not seen Kelly since he visited him in Broadmoor Asylum. He does not know of his present address.'

Monro's resignation from the post of Assistant Commissioner, CID, had taken effect from August 31st, the day upon which Polly Nichols was killed. Since that time he had, however, continued in his other role as head of the Secret Department (Section D), which specialized in political intelligence. As such, he was responsible to the Home Secretary and had direct access to him.

His office being in Scotland Yard, and human nature being what it is, the superintendents engaged on the Ripper investigations had continued to visit Monro, unofficially, both to confide in him and to ask his advice. That, of course, proves nothing, and whether or not he was therefore the catalyst is mere conjecture. What may be significant, however, is the interesting memorandum which the Home Secretary was to write on September 22nd to his Private Secretary, Evelyn Ruggles-Brise, asking that he: 'Stimulate the police about Whitechapel murders. *Monro might be willing to give a hint to the CID people if necessary*' [my italics]. Clearly Matthews and Monro knew something that the police on the ground did not, and the fact remains that the James Kelly penny finally dropped with the authorities on the day after Mary Kelly was murdered.

On that day, No. 21, Cottage Lane was raided by 'the Detective Police' and Mrs Brider, James Kelly's mother-in-law, was given a very rough ride indeed.

Needless to say, and if in fact he had actually been there, the bird had flown.

The police were not the only ones to have been put on notice either. What serves to increase suspicion that Monro was the informant is that the Home Office had also been alerted and was grinding into action.

On Monday, November 12th, somebody there with the initials 'CET' suddenly decided to get out James Kelly's file for the first time in eight months. On it he wrote the following minute:

> Would it not be well to make inquiry as to what steps have been taken to recapture thus man?
> It is not likely he is the Whitechapel murderer; but his offence was cutting his wife's throat, and he escaped last January, it would be well to know what has become of him.

'CM' received that note and, in good civil servant fashion, he lost no time in passing the inquiry down the line. After adding the terse instruction 'To Dr Nicholson for report', it was off his desk in a brace of shakes and arrived at Broadmoor the following day.

It was all a classic piece of Whitehall farce.

Neither the Home Office nor Broadmoor could possibly have known that Scotland Yard had also been tipped the wink; and Dr Nicholson was certainly unaware of the action taken by the police because his immediate reaction was to write to Mrs Brider!

His letter, dated the 13th, reads:

> I should be much obliged to you if you would inform me whether you have seen anything of James Kelly, who escaped from this Asylum on the 23rd January last, or whether you have had any communication from him, or have any knowledge as to where he is at the present time.

Living up to its proud reputation, the Royal Mail delivered that to Mrs Brider on the same day. Whether she was genuinely angry or merely protesting too much the result was the same. No sooner had she read Nicholson's inquiry than she had donned her coat and bonnet and was off on the tram to her solicitor.

The result was a letter, a copy of which I have before me. It reads:

Thomas. O. Evans,
Solicitors,
13, Bouverie Street,
Fleet Street,
London

To Dr Nicholson,
Broadmoor

Re: *James Kelly*

Mrs Brider has handed me your letter with instructions to reply thereto and to inform you that she has neither seen or heard of the above since his escape, nor does she know of his whereabouts, neither can she give you any information at all about him.

You will recollect the facts of the case for which Kelly was committed to your charge. On Saturday last Mrs Brider was visited by the Detective Police and so severely was she questioned, and so rudely was she treated, that she is now in a state of ill-health consequent upon this treatment.

I need hardly point out to you that it is a criminal offence to harbour an escaped convict, and at the first I advised my client to give information to the police in case she saw or heard anything. This she promised to do, but has, as I have said, received no information.

I desire to say, once and for all, that the police have no right to cross-examine my client, and I look forward to your good offices to prevent a recurrence of this most unconstitutional proceeding. If they call again, my client will shut the door in their faces. Furthermore, I shall communicate with the new Commissioner of Police with reference to the matter as soon as he is appointed.

Any further communications in the matter please address to Yours truly.
Signed Thomas O. Evans

That epistle arrived in Broadmoor on the 14th, and Dr Nicholson sent a copy to the Home Office on the same day, with a covering note:

No tidings have reached us of James Kelly since his escape.

My impression was and is that he may possibly have gone abroad. There was nothing whatever in his behaviour while at Broadmoor to indicate that he would be likely to prove dangerous to others. He was melancholic in his tendencies and more disposed to be suicidal at times. I have no reason, from anything I have seen about the condition of Kelly's mind for thinking that the murders in Whitechapel were committed by him. But, in this relation I enclose a copy of a letter which I thought it my duty to write to Mrs Brider the mother of Kelly's late wife and also a copy of the answer from her Solicitor.
Broadmoor
14.11.88

We shall probably never know for certain what caused the police to go in search of James Kelly on the day after Mary Kelly's body was found, but what seems curious at first sight is that they should have begun with his in-laws. He had, after all killed the Briders' daughter and one does not normally expect the parents of a murdered child to harbour the criminal.

In this particular case, however, matters were very different. James Kelly's inheritance had been worth over £26,000 in 1997 terms, although that sum had been greatly depleted by his solicitors' debits by the time he reached Broadmoor. In addition to the various duties payable, they had dipped into his account to the extent of, in present-day terms, £5,700 for administration expenses and £3,650 for his defence. Nevertheless, even after those deductions, and others in respect of cash advanced to Kelly or on his instructions, a not inconsiderable sum was to become his when he became twenty-five. That would be on April 20th, 1885, and there can be little doubt that Mrs Brider had been determined that all or part of it would come her way.

It will be recalled that she and her husband signed Kelly's Petition for Clemency, once again not something that one would normally do for the killer of one's child. In addition to that, however, Mrs Brider was a regular enquirer of the Broadmoor authorities about Kelly's health and well-being. He had made no will and therefore, had he died before his twenty-fifth birthday, no doubt the Briders could have made a good case to be his beneficiaries as it was generally accepted that he had no other relatives. If, on the other hand, he actually achieved twenty-five, and she had remained on good terms with him, Mrs Brider would have had high hopes of some of it coming her way – as, there is reason to believe, some already had.

Unfortunately, only one of Mrs Brider's letters remains in the Broadmoor file. Written to the Superintendent, and dated September 2nd, 1884, it reads (uncorrected) thus:

Dear Sir

Would you kindly let me know how James Kelley from City Roads health and mind his and if you think he will ever recover or get any better. Should feel it a great favour by your sending a reply.

Yours faithfully,

S. A. Brider.

The copy of the answer is unsigned, it reads:

Mrs S. A. Brider,
21, Cottage Lane,
City Road,
London

5th September, 1884

Dear Madam,

With regard to your letter of the second instant regarding James Kelly, his bodily health is not very good, and mentally there is little change.

Yours faithfully,

On January 24th, 1888, Dr Nicholson wrote to the Home Office about Kelly's escape the day before, and reported upon the steps which had been taken to try to apprehend him. The last two paragraphs of that communication read:

For a long time previously to his escape the *active* [my italics] indications of insanity had subsided and he conversed rationally. He showed no signs of being violent, or in any way dangerous.

Kelly is not unlikely to get in communication, personally or in writing, with his mother-in-law Mrs Sarah Brider, 21, Cottage Lane and who has always taken an interest in him since he came to Broadmoor.'

It is obvious, however, that Mrs Brider had kept her 'interest' of nearly five years a close secret. It would, after all, not have been regarded by her relatives and friends as 'the done thing' if they knew that she, apparently, bore her daughter's killer no ill-will. Even the Briders' solicitor was kept in the dark because, also on January 24th, 1888, the same Thomas Evans whom we have already met wrote the following letter to Broadmoor:

> Thos. Evans, Solicitors,
> 13, Bouverie Street,
> Fleet Street,
> London

The Superintendent,
Broadmoor Criminal Lunatic Asylum

> 24th January, 1888

Dear Dr Nicholson,

> *Re: James Kelly.*

I regret I have been out nearly all day and thus was unable to meet your messenger when he first called.

The announcement that the above has made his escape is quite unexpected, and I at once gave his relatives to understand that should he make his appearance in London he is to be detained and handed over to the police for the purpose of being taken back to Broadmoor.

He is not likely to get any help from the relatives, they are too bitter against him to assist, and as to the friend mentioned in the letter, I do not think his claim well-founded as Mr Sampson, the solicitor of Liverpool, has explained matters to me. He might make his way to Mr Sampson's offices as he has some fancied grievance against that gentleman, but I have no information and cannot believe that he would be able to obtain pecuniary assistance anywhere.

Pray treat this communication in strict confidence. Be assured I will make to assist you in any way I can, and that you have my deepest sympathy. I also wish Kelly a speedy return to Broad-moor.

I am, dear Sir,
Yours faithfully,
Thomas Evans

It is unfortunate that no copy of Dr Nicholson's letter has survived because it would be more than interesting to know what what prompted Mr Evans's reference to 'the friend' and Kelly's solicitor. As it is, we can only speculate, but the only friend of Kelly with whom the Superintendent of Broadmoor was likely to have spoken was George Stratton, who had eventually told everything he knew about the escape and Kelly's plans. From the little said in Evans's letter, it would seem that Kelly had hopes of obtaining money from Mrs Brider and/or his solicitor in Liverpool. What the 'fancied grievance' against Mr Sampson was can again only be a matter of conjecture. Two possibilities that spring to mind are that Kelly may have thought that the solicitor had taken too much in costs, and/or that the latter had refused to get money to Kelly via a third party.

Just in passing, what a change in tone Evans's letter of November displayed from the one above! That may well be because the police who arrived at Cottage Lane somehow gave the impression that they were there at the instigation of Dr Nicholson, and the delivery of his letter on the very next day would have tended to confirm the idea. Of course, for all we know, Nicholson may very well have spoken his mind to someone in the Home Office *before* he wrote his letter, because he knew full well of Mrs Brider's apparent – and very surprising – concern for Kelly's welfare.

It was because of the friendship which Mrs Brider had shown

towards Kelly that, on the night of his escape, Nicholson had despatched a Principal Attendant to Scotland Yard with specific instructions to ensure that No. 21, Cottage Lane would be watched by plain-clothes detectives. To be told by Evans on the following day that the family had no time for Kelly, planted suspicions about the Briders in Dr Nicholson's mind which were never to leave him and he communicated his feelings to the police. He always thought that Kelly made contact with the Briders after his escape, and had probably connived in it. As we have seen, he wrote to Mrs Brider almost ten months after the escape, despite the supposed bitterness, and even eight *years* later he would be telling the police that they should question *her* as to Kelly's whereabouts.

So, as I have said, it may very well be that Dr Nicholson was the person who prompted the actions which resulted in the police descending upon Cottage Lane the day after Mary Kelly's murder – perhaps, for instance, by jogging Monro's memory about Kelly.

We are not told whether the 'Detective Police' who interrogated Mrs Brider so roughly were Metropolitan or Section D men. Whoever they were, either they did not make the written report that one would expect – unless, as with many others in the file, it has been destroyed – and no word of their actions seems to have reached the ears of the men actually investigating the murders. The deed was done, and knowledge of it appears to have been restricted to but a few. Although the records now made public are packed with the names of suspects, there is not a single mention of James Kelly, or anything to do with him. Certainly Dr Anderson was kept in the dark, although he was casting around desperately for leads.

Anderson had been absent during the investigation into the murder of Annie Chapman, and had not returned to England until a week after the 'double event'. In consequence, he had little first-hand knowledge of the subsequent police actions and was reliant upon the evidence, reports and opinions of others. Some of those were so contradictory that he really did not know what to think, especially on the question of whether or not the killer possessed any surgical competence.

Logically, the doctors to whom he should have turned for guidance were M'Kellar, the Chief Surgeon of the Metropolitan Police, or Phillips, who had been called to three of the murder sites and had been present at four of the post-mortem examinations. It is therefore curious that Anderson, as we have seen, should, in fact, have consulted Bond, who had not been involved at all until the death of Mary Kelly. To be charitable, he probably chose Bond because he was better qualified, more experienced, nearer at hand and likely to submit a more objective opinion than anyone too closely involved with the murders. On the other hand, it could simply have been that he did not think very highly of the others!

Dr Bond's report makes interesting reading:

> 7 The Sanctuary
> Westminster Abbey
> November 10th '88

Dear Sir,
    Whitechapel Murders.
    I beg to report that I have read the notes of the four Whitechapel Murders
1. Buck's Row
2. Hanbury Street
3. Berners Street
4. Mitre Square

I have also made a Post Mortem Examination of the mutilated remains of a woman found yesterday in a small room in Dorset Street—:

1. All five murders were no doubt committed by the same hand. In the first four the throats appear to have been cut from left to right, in the last case owing to the extensive mutilation it is impossible to say in what direction the fatal cut was made, but arterial blood was found on the wall in splashes close to where the woman's head must have been lying.

2. All the circumstances surrounding the murders lead me to form the opinion that the women must have been lying down when murdered and in every case the throat was first cut.

3. In the four murders of which I have seen the notes only, I

cannot form a very definite opinion as to the time that had elapsed between the murder and the discovery of the body. In one case, that of Berners Street, the discovery appears to have been immediately after the deed. In Buck's Row, Hanbury St, and Mitre Square three or four hours only could have elapsed. In the Dorset Street case the body was lying on the bed at the time of my visit two o'clock quite naked and mutilated as in the annexed report. Rigor Mortis had set in but increased during the progress of the examination. From this it is difficult to say with any degree of certainty the exact time that had elapsed since death as the period varies from six to twelve hours before rigidity sets in. The body was comparatively cold at two o'clock and the remains of a recently taken meal were found in the stomach and scattered about over the intestines. It is therefore, pretty certain that the woman must have been dead about twelve hours and the partly digested food would indicate that death took place about three or four hours after food was taken, so one or two o'clock in the morning would be the probable time of the murder.

4. In all the cases there appears to be no evidence of struggling and the attacks were probably so sudden and made in such a position that the women could neither resist nor cry out. In the Dorset St case the corner of the sheet to the right of the woman's head was much cut and saturated with blood, indicating that the face may have been covered with the sheet at the time of the attack.

5. In the first four cases the murderer must have attacked from the right side of the victim. In the Dorset Street case, he must have attacked from in front or from the left, as there would be no room for him between the wall and the part of the bed on which the woman was lying. Again the blood had flowed down on the right side of the woman and spurted on to the wall.

6. The murderer would not necessarily be splashed or deluged with blood, but his hands and arms must have been covered and parts of his clothing must certainly have been smeared with blood.

7. The mutilations in each case excepting the Berners Street one were all of the same character and showed clearly that in all the murders the object was mutilation.

8. In each case the mutilation was inflicted by a person who had no scientific nor anatomical knowledge. In my opinion he does not even possess the technical knowledge of a butcher or horse slaughterer or any person accustomed to cut up dead animals.

9. The instrument must have been a strong knife at least six inches long, very sharp, pointed at the top and about an inch in width. It may have been a clasp knife, a butchers knife or a surgeons knife, I think it was no doubt a straight knife.

10. The murderer must have been a man of physical strength and of great coolness and daring. There is no evidence that he had an accomplice. He must in my opinion be a man subject to periodical attacks of Homicidal and erotic mania. The character of the mutilations indicate that the man may be in a condition sexually, that may be called Satyriasis. It is of course possible that the Homicidal impulse may have developed from a revengeful or brooding condition of the mind, or that religious mania may have been the original disease but I do not think either hypothesis is likely. The murderer in external appearance is quite likely to be a quiet inoffensive looking man probably middle-aged and neatly and respectably dressed. I think he must be in the habit of wearing a cloak or overcoat or he could hardly have escaped notice in the streets if the blood on his hands or clothes were visible.

11. Assuming the murderer to be such a person as I have just described, he would be solitary and eccentric in his habits, also he is most likely to be a man without regular occupation, but with some small income or pension. He is probably living among respectable persons who have some knowledge of his character and habits and who may have grounds for suspicion that he isn't quite right in his mind at times. Such persons would probably be unwilling to communicate suspicions to the Police for fear of trouble or notoriety, whereas if there were prospect of reward it might overcome their scruples.

It is remarkable how closely Dr Bond's conclusion resembles the profiling quoted at the start of this chapter, and how closely both match the disturbed personality of James Kelly.

One thing in particular worth noting about this murder is the description which Thomas Bowyer gave of the man whom, allegedly, he saw with Mary on the Wednesday prior to her death: 'Aged 27 or 28, with a dark moustache and very peculiar eyes.' Now look at the photograph of the twenty-eight-year-old James Kelly! According to John McCarthy, in an interview with the *Daily News*, she was with a similar man, in The Britannia, at eleven o'clock on the night of November 8th. Could those sightings have been of him preparing the ground?

Then came the murders of Alice McKenzie and Frances Coles. Very few seem to believe that Alice and Frances were Ripper victims, but I can see no reason why they should not have been. According to his statement, Kelly was in France when they were killed, but that does not preclude the possibility of his having been the perpetrator. For one thing it is difficult to know when to believe him, and for another it should be remembered that he stated that he hugged the northern coast for the whole of that period. He gave no reason for doing so, but it may well have been that it was in order to obtain work on the many cross-Channel boats. Were that the case, he would have had many opportunities for returning to London from time to time.

Be that as it may, I consider it significant that there were no more Ripper-type murders in London after that of Frances Coles, because it was about the time of her death that Kelly struck inland to Paris. After that he was in dire straits for a year, during which he was totally preoccupied with his struggle for survival.

Then, early in 1892, he went to America, and from that moment on there was not a single murder in London which could in any way have been likened to those of the Ripper. Of course we do not know what Kelly got up to in the USA, nor in the other countries which he visited.

He returned to England from New Orleans at the end of March, 1896. On October 14th of that year, a letter beginning 'Dear Boss' and signed 'Jack the Ripper' was received at the Commercial Street police station. It explained that the writer had *just come back from abroad* [my italics] but was now ready to resume his work.

Neither Chief Inspector Moore nor the now Superintendent Swanson attached any importance to that letter as the handwriting was not the same as in the two original communications, although Moore found many similarities. Nevertheless, it is a coincidence, is it not, that, after a minimum of five years since the last 'Ripper killing', a knowledgeable letter should be sent to the police in the very year that James Kelly came back to England?

To my mind, there are far *too* many coincidences between James Kelly and the activities of 'Jack the Ripper' for them to be merely that. In Kelly we have a man who:

1) Was the only convicted insane woman killer at large in the East End during the period of the killings.

2) Hated women generally, but prostitutes in particular.

3) Was the only man named by the Home Office as possibly being the 'Whitechapel Murderer'.

4) Was sought actively by the police immediately after the killing of Mary Kelly.

5) Fits virtually every profile of a serial lust killer.

6) Inflicted injuries to his wife's throat similar to those to Martha Tabram's.

7) Had an excellent knowledge of the geography of the East End.

8) Had sharp knives and ripping chisels as the tools of his trade.

9) Had handwriting similar to that in the two original Ripper communications, a connection to account for the Americanisms and every reason for giving 'Jack the Ripper' as his *trade* name.

In addition, as we have seen, there were many, many other correlations between Kelly and the Ripper, minor in themselves, but taken together and combined with the points set out above they form what I consider to be an overwhelming circumstantial case against him.

Without explanation, Kelly said that he had 'been on the Warpath' ever since escaping from Broadmoor, and I believe I know what he meant by that.

11

Cover-Up

PROBABLY THE GREATEST mystery surrounding James Kelly is why nobody had ever even heard of such a serious candidate for the title of 'Jack the Ripper' until John Morrison introduced him to a disbelieving world.

The Public Record Office at Kew says that the suffix 'HO 144', which appears on the Home Office files for both Kelly and 'The Whitechapel Murderer', denotes that the file concerned is part of the class of records HO 144 (Home Office Registered Papers, Supplementary) which consists of 'supplementary registered papers of the Home Office and includes files on criminal and certain other subjects, separated from the main file series in HO 45 *because of their sensitivity at the time of transfer* [my italics].

Obviously it is a very serious matter if a man kills his wife, or anyone else for that matter, but such murders were, and are, commonplace and so what was it about Kelly's case which considered to be so 'sensitive'? As I have remarked, all the 'Ripper' files bear the 'HO 144' suffix, but *they* are now open to public inspection whilst Kelly's remains securely under lock and key at the Home Office.

Why all the secrecy about him? Why is his file 'Closed until 2030', when those of far more recent, and apparently more infamous, killers are in the public domain? Why must his Home Office file 'never be destroyed', and why, that being the case, was it culled less than a fortnight before that instruction was written, and *which* documents were 'Destroyed'?

Curiously, and probably significantly, many documents have also disappeared from Kelly's Broadmoor file and, once again, we have no means of knowing to what they related.

Stories of official cover-ups are legion in the 'Jack the Ripper' saga, but what *are* we supposed to think about James Kelly's case?

Let us recapitulate the facts.

Here was an insane woman killer whose escape from Broadmoor was known not only to a department of Scotland Yard but also to James Monro, the then Assistant Commissioner of Police, CID. It is true that Monro did not have an official role in the 'Ripper' investigation, but there is no doubt that he was very active behind the scenes.

Now Monro is reputed to have been an excellent detective, and it is therefore unlikely that he had no thoughts at all of the throat-cutting Kelly when Martha Tabram, Polly Nichols and Annie Chapman were all murdered in similar fashion within a month. He had, after all, written the last of his several letters about James Kelly only just over five months before Martha was killed, and the escape of a murderer from Broadmoor, of all places, was not exactly an everyday occurrence. I think we may take it, therefore, that Monro at least had thoughts about the possibility of Kelly being the murderer and, as he was very close to the Home Secretary, Henry Matthews, it is likely that he mentioned them to him. That likelihood is increased when we remember that Matthews told his Private Secretary, Ruggles-Brise, that 'Monro might be willing to give a hint to the CID people if necessary.'

Whether Monro *would* have been willing to do so is debatable. He had, after all, resigned as Assistant Commissioner, CID, only three weeks before, and he may not have wished to help his successor, Robert Anderson, however amicable their personal relationship. It is also possible that he would have resented any suggestion coming from Ruggles-Brise, of whom he does not appear to have been particularly enamoured.

When one considers all the facts, it appears unlikely that Monro did mention Kelly to the CID, especially as there are no records of the hunt for him having been revived until after the murder of Mary Kelly some nine weeks later. The likelihood is that Monro sat on his hands, and all thoughts of Kelly were forgotten until Mary's death, when either one of two sets of circumstances arose:

1) The police discovered something in No.13 which pointed directly to Kelly and caused them to hasten to Cottage Lane. Their find, and the subsequent fruitless interview with Mrs Brider, was reported to the Home Office where Matthews recalled immediately any mention of Kelly which Monro may have made. He then decided that Broadmoor should be asked if, by any chance, they had any idea where Kelly might be, but ordered that the inquiry should be couched in casual terms in order to avoid suspicion that Kelly really might be the killer.

2) The murder of another 'Kelly' revived Home Office memories of the Broadmoor escapee, and their note to the Asylum of November 12th was coincidental with, and independent of, any police find.

Where at all possible, I tend to discount coincidences and therefore I plump for the first alternative. However, should I be correct in doing so, I must say that it was rather remiss of the Home Office not to have told Dr Nicholson that the police had already enquired at Cottage Lane. Had they done so he would not have incurred the wrath of Mrs Brider and her solicitor!

Of even more interest (and yet another coincidence?), on the evening of November 10th, i.e. of the same day that the police harassed Mrs Brider, the *Star* newspaper published an article in which it was stated that: 'It is believed by people who pass among their neighbours as sensible folk that the Government do not want the murderer to be convicted, that they are interested in concealing his identity, that, in fact, they know it, and will not divulge it.' Had someone spoken out of turn?

First thoughts must be that if both the Home Office and the police knew that Kelly was the murderer they would have lost no time in publicizing the fact. It is only when one considers all the possible consequences of such an act that the possibility of a cover-up arises.

Supposing they had revealed that they had been aware, all the time, that a named homicidal maniac was on the loose and yet not only had they done nothing to apprehend him but he *still* eluded capture? Even worse, what if it had transpired that even though the Home Office and James Monro had known of Kelly's escape nobody had had the wit to connect him with the killings? Heads would have rolled, and both the Home Office and Scotland Yard would have become laughing-stocks once the anger had subsided. Even the Government could have come under threat.

No, once the James Kelly/ 'Ripper' penny had dropped, far from the fact being made public the main concern would have been to keep it secret.

That could have been done only if most of the policemen actively involved in the investigation had not known that the killer had been identified, because it would have been impossible to silence them all. Who amongst them, therefore, would have known of any possible Kelly/'Ripper' link? Well it may well be that *none* of them did or, at the most, only a few, but that would depend upon the nature of whatever clue may have been found in Miller's Court.

Had it been something minor, the subsequent report about the Cottage Lane call could have been pooh-poohed by Monro and the Home Office, with whom alarm bells would have been ringing. On the other hand, a major find would have been followed up by only the most senior of the detectives, and they could easily have been sworn, or bullied, to silence because of the traditions of their department. That would explain why some of them never discussed the case thereafter, whilst others, constrained to silence about the killer's true identity, were nevertheless unable to resist the temptation of hinting that they knew more than they could say.

There were some, just as eager to boost their public image, who achieved their joint objectives of secrecy and bolstering their vanity by actually naming possible suspects. They merely added to the confusion caused by those who knew nothing but still put forward their wild inventions, thus creating red herrings which continue to deceive, and obscure the trail, to this very day.

It is also probable that Monro did his utmost to preserve secrecy by ensuring that any investigations involving Kelly or No. 21, Cottage Lane, were conducted by his own 'Section D' men.

Despite the foregoing, it may well be that there are some readers who still remain to be convinced that there was, and is, a cover up. Of those I would ask these questions:

1) Why is James Kelly's file still in the category of 'sensitive' subjects?

2) Why does no report of the call by detectives at Cottage Lane appear in any *known* file?

3) Why is it that the Home Office file does not contain the original of their enquiry to Broadmoor about the possibility of Kelly being 'the Whitechapel Murderer'? Broadmoor itself had no reason to be involved in any cover-up and so, yet again, we find a document in *their* file without which we should not know that the official finger of suspicion had been pointed at James Kelly.

4) Why, in 1906, did Scotland Yard state that they had no photograph of Kelly when we know that they were supplied with at least one when he escaped? Why did they not ask Broadmoor for one *if* the original/s had been mislaid?

5) As we have seen, there were many communications to and from Scotland Yard between 1888 and 1906; what, then, happened to *their* file on him which has, apparently, disappeared? The Metropolitan Police told me that all their papers, 'that have survived' (!), are held for permanent preservation at the Public Record Office at Kew, but that they are unable to trace anything about Kelly. Is that not peculiar? The Home Office and Broadmoor kept *their* files, albeit with documents destroyed or missing, but as far as Scotland Yard is concerned Kelly never existed. Why should that be?

6) From which 'main' file in the series HO 45 were Kelly's 'supplementary registered papers' separated, and where is it now?

7) Why do the Thames Valley Police have nothing on file about Kelly either? Why, despite the fact that it was in their name that the 'Wanted' notice about Kelly was published, did the Wokingham Police apparently make no connection between him and the 'Ripper'?

8) Why were there no replies from the Home Office when Kelly surrendered himself to the British Consuls at New Orleans and Vancouver?

9) Why, in their 1906 circular, did Scotland Yard give instructions that, should he be traced, Kelly was *not*, repeat *not*, to be arrested?

10) Why was it that the Metropolitan Police could not trace Kelly in 1906, and why were facts which would have aided his apprehension omitted from their defeatist circular?

11) Why, in view of the inquiry to them from the Home Office, was Kelly not questioned about the 'Ripper' murders by Broadmoor officials when he returned to the Asylum? Or is it possible that he *was*, but that his original statement is one of the documents that has been destroyed or gone missing? Certainly the extant statement shows no evidence of his having been interrogated in detail about *anything*, and some of the phraseology seems oddly vague. Is it possible that it was virtually dictated to him, just for the record? What adds emphasis to these questions is the fact that several details not contained in the existing statement have slipped into official documents.

12) Why did Monro declare that the 'Ripper' should have been caught, and why, after reading some papers which he left with his eldest son, did the latter tell his brother that their father's theory about the identity of the 'Ripper' was 'a very hot potato'?

A cover-up would explain:

a) Why Chief Inspector Walter Dew, a Detective Constable at the time of the murders, was told, and repeated in his memoirs, that inquiries were made at asylums 'all over the country, including the Criminal Lunatic Asylum at Broadmoor', but that 'No useful evidence was obtained'.

b) Why there is no police record of *anyone* in the Convict Office, or anywhere else in Scotland Yard, or in the Wokingham Police, having made any connection between the series of murders and the escaped lunatic killer whom they had all been seeking only months before.

c) Why the police presence in the East End was scaled down after Mary Kelly's murder.

d) Why the Home Office and Scotland Yard did not want Kelly back in England.

e) Why, when he did arrive in the country, he was able to elude capture, and instructions were given that he should not be arrested.

f) Why no record remains in the Broadmoor or Home Office files of the full results of the questioning to which Kelly was subjected upon his return to the Asylum, nor why the Home Office should have insisted he be kept in Broadmoor, despite the Medical Superintendent's opinion that he 'would not be certifiable as insane'.

g) Why he was given 'the chemical cosh' at Broadmoor 'in order to make him an idiot'.

h) What 'the whole matter' was which weighed on his conscience for all those years, and caused him to 'burst into tears' even as late as 1927.

i) Why no mention of James Kelly appeared anywhere, in connection with the 'Ripper' killings, for over a century until John Morrison put him forward as a suspect.

You will look in vain for Kelly's name in any of the memoirs, 'discovered' documents, books or public records, although they are littered with mentions of harmless Jewish lunatics, a drowned barrister, various poisoners, some society doctors, a royal duke, an assortment of Americans, a famous artist and Uncle Tom Cobley and all. Tenuous connections have been made between all of them and 'Jack the Ripper', but nowhere will you find serious mention of the *only* convicted, lunatic, throat-stabbing woman killer who was known by the Home Office and Scotland Yard to have been at large during 1888.

It is now extremely doubtful whether any conclusive and incontrovertible evidence about the identity of 'Jack the Ripper' will ever be discovered. Every candidate offered for consideration will therefore need to judged upon circumstantial evidence, and I submit that, if only in that respect, James Kelly's claim to infamy exceeds by far that of any other.

I am very conscious that his story is interspersed with blank periods, and that, on occasion, my reasoning has, of necessity, been tortuous. The only defence which I can offer is that readers ask themselves how many 'ifs' and 'buts' would have been included in any attempted twenty-first century exposés of the Watergate and Arms to Iraq conspiracies, had those intended cover-ups succeeded.

As far as we are allowed to know, James Kelly took his darkest secrets to the grave, and we do not even know where that is. At

Broadmoor, I was told that there is now no record of his particular burial place. The 'old' cemetery is a rather unkempt enclosure near the main gate, and the later one is merely a sizeable grassy area which sweeps down to the road. All the headstones have now been removed. A white marble statue of an angel, in the centre, is the only indication of what lies beneath that pleasant sward. James Kelly is there somewhere.

The actual whereabouts of his remains are now as unknown as those of most of his victims – those poor women who did nothing to justify the treatment meted out to them. Nevertheless their names live on, immortalized by their killer, and even today, despite the depredations of the ubiquitous 'developers' in Whitechapel and Spitalfields, it is sometimes possible to imagine their shadowy figures in the back-streets and alleys which remain.

They are gone, but not forgotten. May their souls rest in peace; they deserved better.

Bibliography

Books about 'Jack the Ripper'

There are scores of books on the subject and to list them all would be tedious. I have therefore contented myself with mentioning only those which I have consulted.

Adam, H. L., *Trial of George Chapman* (William Hodge & Co. Ltd, 1930)

Begg, P., *Jack the Ripper – The Uncensored Facts* (Robson Books Ltd, 1988)

Begg, P., Fido, M. & Skinner, K., *The Jack the Ripper A to Z* (Headline Book Publishing plc, 1991)

Farson, D., *Jack the Ripper* (Michael Joseph, 1972)

Fido, M., *The Crimes, Detection and Death of Jack the Ripper* (George Weidenfeld & Nicolson Ltd, 1987)

Harrison, M., *A Biography of HRH The Duke of Clarence. Was he Jack the Ripper?* (W. H. Allen & Co. Ltd, 1972)

Howells, M. and Skinner, K., *The Ripper Legacy* (Sidgwick & Jackson Ltd, 1987)

Knight, S., *Jack the Ripper: The Final Solution* (George G. Harrap & Co. Ltd, 1976)

McCormick, D., *The Identity of Jack the Ripper* (Jarrolds, 1959)

Matters, L., *The Mystery of Jack the Ripper* (Hutchinson, 1929)

Odell, R., *Jack the Ripper in Fact and Fiction* (George C. Harrap & Co. Ltd, 1965)

Rumbelow, D., *The Complete Jack the Ripper* (W. H. Allen & Co. Ltd, 1975)

Stewart, W., *Jack The Ripper: A New Theory* (Quality Press, 1939)

Sugden, P., *The Complete History of Jack the Ripper* (Robinson Publishing Ltd, 1994)

Underwood, P., *Jack The Ripper: One Hundred Years of Mystery* (Blandford Press, 1987)

Whittington-Egan, R., *A Casebook on Jack the Ripper* (Wildy & Sons Ltd, 1975)

Memoirs with references to 'Jack the Ripper'

Anderson, R., *The Lighter Side of My Official Life* (Hodder & Stoughton, 1910)

Dew, W., *I Caught Crippen* (Blackie, 1938)

Leeson, B., *Lost London – The Memoirs of an East End Detective* (Stanley Paul, 1934)

Macnaghten, M., *Days of My Years* (Edward Arnold, 1915)

Smith, H., *From Constable to Commissioner. The Story of Sixty Years, Most of Them Misspent* (Chatto & Windus, 1910)

Articles about 'Jack the Ripper'

Camps, F. E., *More About 'Jack The Ripper'* (The London Hospital Gazette, 1966)

Ogan, J., *Tabram Tabulated* (*Ripperana*, July 1994)

Pamphlet

Anon., *The Whitechapel Murders or the Mysteries of the East End*, Nos. 1 & 2 (Purkess, 280, Strand, London, WC)

Books about Broadmoor

Allen, J. E., *Inside Broadmoor* (W. H. Allen & Co. Ltd, 1952)

Partridge, R., *Broadmoor: A History of Criminal Lunacy and its Problems* (Chatto & Windus, 1953)

Thompson, P., *Bound for Broadmoor* (Hodder & Stoughton Ltd, 1972)

Books about Offender Profiling

Canter, D., *Criminal Shadows* (HarperCollins, 1994)

Holmes, R. M. and De Burger, J., *Serial Murder* (Sage, 1988)

Ressler, R. K. and Shachtman, T., *Whoever Fights Monsters* (Simon & Schuster, 1992)

Wilson, C. and Seaman, D., *the serial killers: A Study in the Psychology of Violence* (BCA, 1991)

Articles about Offender Profiling

Boon, J. and Davies, G., 'Criminal Profiling' (*Policing*, Autumn 1993)

Canter, D., 'Offender Profiles' (*The Psychologist*, Vol. 2, No. 1, 1989)

Eckert, W. G., 'The Ripper Project' (*The American Journal of Forensic Medicine and Pathology*, 1989)

Ogan, J., 'A Light In The Shadows' (*Ripperana*, Part 1, January, 1994; Part 2, April 1994)

Newspapers consulted

Bournemouth Visitor's Directory
The *City Press*
The *Daily Chronicle*
The *Daily News*
The *Daily Telegraph*
The *Eastern Argus & Borough of Hackney Times*
The *East London Advertiser*
The *East London Observer*
The *Eastern Post & City Chronicle*
The *Evening News*

Hackney Gazette
The *Islington Gazette*
Lloyd's Weekly London Newspaper
The *News of the World*
Pall Mall Gazette
Reynolds's Newspaper
The *Star*
The Times
The *Western Mail*
The *Western Morning News*

Books about social conditions

Besant, W., *East London* (Chatto & Windus, 1901)
Booth, C., *Life and Labour of the London Poor* (Macmillan, 1902)
Fishman, W. J., *East End 1888* (Duckworth, 1988)
London, J., *The People of the Abyss* (Thomas Nelson & Sons Ltd, 1902)
Mayhew, H., *London Labour and the London Poor* (Chatto & Windus, 1851)
Mearns, A., *The Bitter Cry of Outcast London* (Leicester University Press, 1970)
Morrison, A., *Tales of Mean Streets* (Methuen & Co., 1894)

Journals and magazines

The British Journal of Criminology
The Lancet
Illustrated Police News
The Police Gazette
Ripperana

Other publications

Post Office Directory of London
Alan Godfrey Maps

Archival Sources

All the following provided me with invaluable assistance but it would not, however, be practicable to list all the information which I received. I have therefore noted only the sources which hold primary documents without which no serious investigation into the 'Ripper' murders may be made.

Bank of England – Archive Section
Bethlem Royal Hospital and The Maudsley Hospital.
Bishopsgate Institute Library.
Bodleian Library.
British Library.
Broadmoor Hospital: File: 3510 – KELLY J.
District Probate Registry.
GMB National College.
Guildhall Reference Library.
Home Office: File H.O. 144/10064 – James Kelly.
Lancashire County Council, District Central Library, Preston.
City of Liverpool Record Office.

London:

1) Corporation of London Records Office: Coroner's inquest on Catherine Eddowes. (Ref: Coroner's Inquests (L) 1888, No. 135).

2) Greater London Record Office: MJ/SPC, NE 1888 Box 3 Case Paper 19. Mary Jane Kelly inquest, 1888.

3) Borough of Camden – Local Studies Library.
    Borough of Hackney – Archives Department.
    Borough of Islington – The Finsbury Library.
    Borough of Southwark – Local Studies Library.

Borough of Tower Hamlets – Bancroft Library.

National Postal Museum.
New Scotland Yard.
Office of Population, Censuses and Surveys.
Principal Probate Registry of the Family Division.

Public Records Office, Kew:
Metropolitan Police Files on the Whitechapel Murders,
References:

MEPO 1/48. Commissioner's letters.
1/54. Letters sent, 1890–1919.
1/55. Letters to Home Office, 1883–1904.
1/65. Letters from Receiver to Home Office, 1868–1891.
2/227. Police reinforcements for Whitechapel following the Pinchin Street murder.
3/140. Files on individual Whitechapel Murders.
3/141. Miscellaneous suspects and correspondence on the murders.
3/142. 'Jack the Ripper' letters.
3/3153. Miscellaneous documents concerning the murders.
3/3155. Photographs of the murder victims.

Home Office Files on the Whitechapel Murders.
References:

HO 144/220/A49301. Suspects.
,,   B. Rewards.
,,   C. Steps taken to catch the killer.
,,   D. Communications from abroad re suspects.
,,   E. Suggested use of dogs.
,,   F. Miller's Court murder.
,,   G. Police allowances.
,,   I. Castle Alley murder.
,,   K. Pinchin Street murder.

City of Salford – Local History Library.
Thames Valley Police.
University of Kansas, Wichita, United States of America.

Appendix A:
Maps

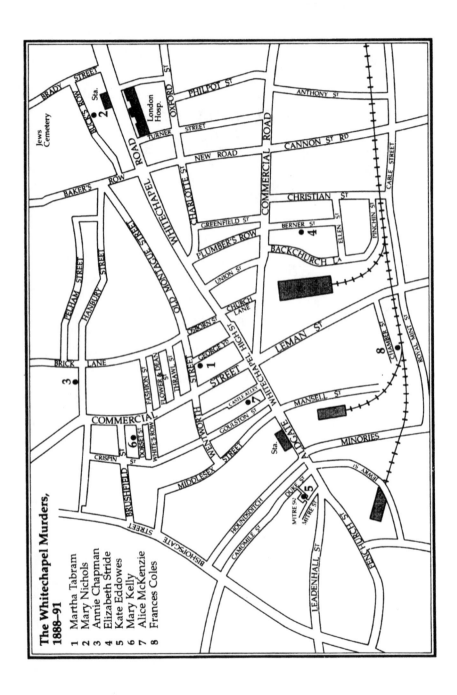

The Whitechapel Murders, 1888–91

1 Martha Tabram
2 Mary Nichols
3 Annie Chapman
4 Elizabeth Stride
5 Kate Eddowes
6 Mary Kelly
7 Alice McKenzie
8 Frances Coles

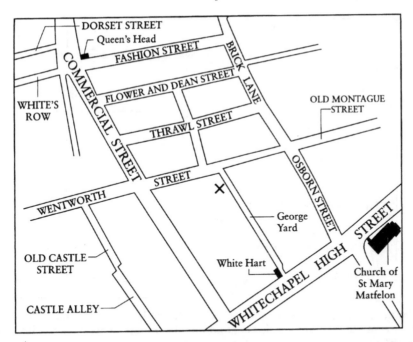

George Yard and its neighbourhood. George Yard Buildings, where Martha Tabram was found dead at 4.45 a.m. on 7 August 1888, is marked by an ✕.

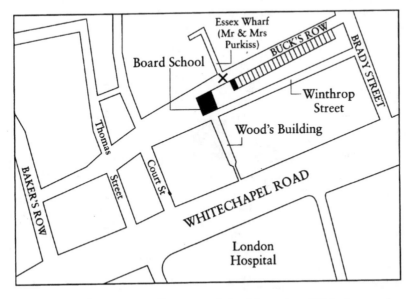

Buck's Row and environs. The spot where Mary Ann Nichols was found dead, at 3.40 a.m. on 31 August 1888, is marked by an ✕.

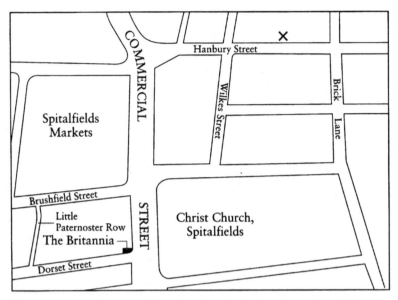

Hanbury Street and its neighbourhood. The body of Annie Chapman was discovered in 29 Hanbury Street at about 6.00 a.m. on 8 September 1888. ✕ marks the spot.

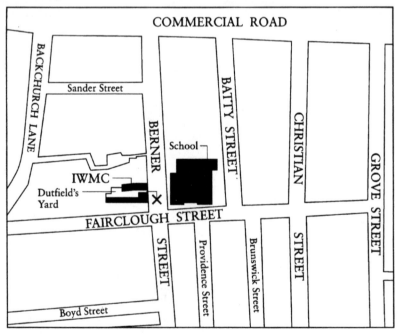

Berner Street and environs. The body of Elizabeth Stride was found beside the IWMC (International Working Men's Educational Club) in Dutfield's Yard at 1.00 a.m. on 30 September 1888.

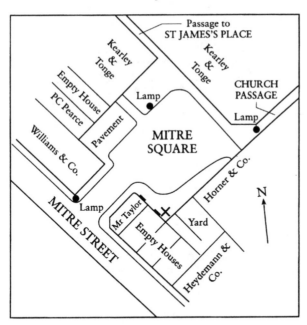

Mitre Square. Catherine Eddowes was found dead here, at 1.44 a.m. on Sunday, 30 September 1888. ✗ marks the spot.

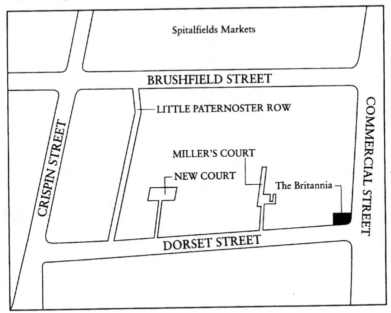

Dorset Street and environs, showing Miller's Court, where Mary Jane Kelly was found dead, and Little Paternoster Row, into which Annie Chapman was last seen disappearing.

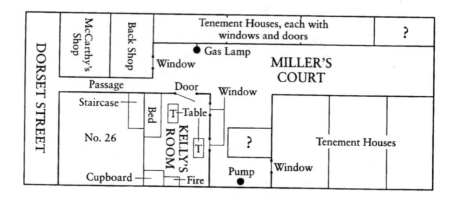

Miller's Court, showing Mary Jane Kelly's room. The use of the areas marked '?' is uncertain: see 'Points to Ponder', no. 14.

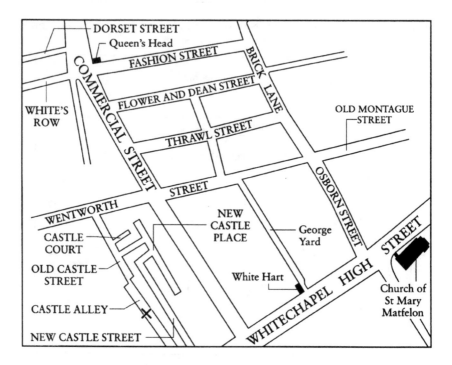

Castle Alley and neighbourhood. The body of Alice McKenzie was found here, at 12.50 a.m. on 17 July 1889. ✗ marks the spot.

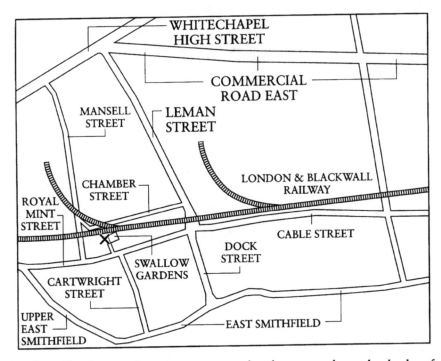

Swallow Gardens and environs. ✕ marks the spot where the body of Frances Coles was found at 2.20 a.m. on Friday, 13 February 1891.

Appendix B:
Points to Ponder

1. *Was William Turner living off Martha Tabram's immoral earnings?*

   He seems to have been much younger than Martha, and it does not appear likely that he was attracted by her physical charms. To all intents and purposes he was unemployed, so from where did his money come? At the inquest, he said that he gave Martha 1/6d on the Saturday before she died, for her to buy some stock. Now why should he do that when he knew very well that the money would go straight on drink? Far more likely, I think, that Martha gave *him* money, ostensibly for *him* to buy stock.

   His evidence presents him in a light altogether too good to be true. According to him, he was 'of sober habits', usually had Martha home by 11 p.m., never quarrelled with her, and even gave her money when she was on the bottle. He had no idea that she walked the streets, and every time she stayed out all night he took her word for it that it was because she had had a fit.

   What seems more probable is that he, knowing everything that Martha was up to, left her when she was on a drinking spree because she then had no money for him. Perhaps it is significant that, with Martha dead, he had been forced to resort to the Victoria Working Men's Home, for a roof over his head.

   It is probable too that Mrs Bousfield is not what she appeared. According to her, Martha was little short of a saint: she never drank, was a retiring person who 'scarcely knew two people in the street' and never brought anyone back to her room. It could well be that Turner and Mrs Bousfield got their heads together about what they were going to say at the inquest because both had something to hide.

Was Mrs Bousfield running what may be termed a house of accommodation, and providing a place where prostitutes could take customers if the weather was inclement, or if something more than a 'knee-trembler' up some dark and dirty alley was required? We know that Martha had a room there and two mattresses.

2. *Could 'Pearly Poll' have identified the soldiers with whom she and Martha had been had she so wished?*

The prostitutes who catered for the military often knew more about the various regiments than the soldiers themselves! It is therefore completely unbelievable that the two women had not known to which regiment their companions belonged, and equally incredible that 'Poll' had not noticed whether they were wearing side-arms.

To have picked out the men could, however, have had disastrous consequences for a woman in her situation. She would have risked retribution from the comrades of the men she had identified. She also knew very well how East Enders dealt with 'coppers' narks'. Self-preservation was therefore probably her main reason for not telling the police who the soldiers were.

3. *Where was the Old Montague Street Mortuary?*

In almost everything written about these murders, constant reference is made to 'the Whitechapel Mortuary in Old Montague Street', said variously to have been a shed in the grounds, or 'at the back', of 'the Old Montague Street Workhouse', or a shed at 'the Old Montague Street Infirmary'. Others have located the mortuary in Eagle Street or Eagle Place, and some have made definite mention of 'the green back gates' which were supposedly in 'Chapman's Court'.

Unfortunately, all those references are copied from previous books, or some contemporary newspaper reports which were completely fictional. Despite extensive research, I was unable to locate a mortuary, workhouse or infirmary in Old Montague Street, nor a 'Chapman's Court' – green gates notwithstanding!

The replies to my many letters of enquiry shed no light whatsoever on the subject until the Greater London Record Office wrote: 'Unfortunately we can find no reference to a mortuary in Old Montague Street from our maps or directories.

'The building shown on the first edition Ordnance Survey Map as the Whitechapel Union Workhouse, and on Stanford's map of London (1877) as the Whitechapel and Spitalfields Workhouse, is in fact the Whitechapel Workhouse Infirmary.

'Although it was used originally as the union workhouse (the workhouse in South Grove is a later institution), by 1879 it had become known as the "Baker's Row Infirmary". When Charles Street and Baker's Row had been renamed as Vallance Road, in 1896, the Infirmary likewise changed its name, to the White-chapel Union Infirmary.

'It was situated on the East Side of Charles Street/Baker's Row, just north of the Friends' Burial Ground. We can find no reference to a separate mortuary on any of our maps.'

So that was that. There was no mortuary, workhouse or workhouse infirmary in Old Montague Street. Baker's Row was, of course, at the eastern end of Old Montague Street. Was the information about the location of the mortuary mis-heard by the reporters of the day?

The answer came from two local newspapers.

The *East London Observer* of September 1st, 1888 states that the body of the next victim was taken to the mortuary 'which is situated in the Pavilion Yard close by'.

The following sentence appears later in the same article: 'The Whitechapel Mortuary is a little brick building situated to the right of the large yard used by the Board of Works for the storage of their material.'

Then, in an account of the inquest upon yet another victim, this appears in the September 15th edition of the *Eastern Post and City Chronicle*: 'The Coroner said Whitechapel had no mortuary. What was called the mortuary is simply a shed belonging to the workhouse official. It is not a proper mortuary at all.'

In the same report, Dr Phillips is said to have told the Coroner: 'Having received your instructions, sir, soon after two o'clock on Saturday afternoon I went to the labour-yard of Whitechapel Union for the purpose of further examining the body and making the usual examination.'

Reporting upon his post-mortem examination of Alice McKenzie, in 1889, Dr Phillips wrote that the body had been taken to 'the shed used as a Mortuary'. According to *The Times* of July 19th, 1889, at the inquest Dr Phillips elaborated that to 'the shed used as a mortuary in the Pavilion-yard, Whitechapel'. He then went on to describe the shed as 'a most inconvenient and ill-appointed place'.

So there, it seemed, we had it at last. What was used as a mortuary was a little brick shed located in Pavilion Yard; but was it?

Pavilion Yard adjoined the western side of the Pavilion Theatre, which was situated between Old Montague Street and Whitechapel Road, and had its entrance in Baker's Row. On its western side, the Yard was adjoined by a very much larger yard in which were situated several small buildings. It seems much more probable that it was this yard, shown on maps as 'Stone Yard', which was used as a labour yard and for the storage of materials, and that Dr Phillips was slightly inaccurate in his statement. There is confirmation of this probability from a report, also in the *East London Observer*, on the inquest of the next victim after Martha Tabram. Inspector Spratling had just finished his evidence when a juryman popped up with a complaint. He said that the body had been left outside in the mortuary yard for so long that it was in clear view of the children from St Mary's School when they arrived for morning lessons. St Mary's School adjoined the 'Stone Yard' and not Pavilion Yard!

We may now, therefore, and with some confidence, take it that 'the Whitechapel Mortuary in Old Montague Street' was, in fact, a small brick shed in the Stone Yard.

The three entrances to that yard were in St Mary Street, Eagle Place – which was an alley from Old Montague Street – and a covered entry from the Whitechapel Road. The last is almost certainly the 'Chapman's Court' referred to in so many accounts, although the name is not given on any map I have seen. In all probability the name was a colloquialism, as indeed the use of 'Pavilion Yard' may have been.

Identifying the 'Old Montague Street Mortuary' has, I am afraid, been something of a rigmarole; but if only a few of the more inquisitive students of these murders are spared the hours of searching I have endured I shall consider it justified. Future authors – be my guest!

4. *How did Polly Nichols's murderer escape detection?*

The murder must have occurred between 3.20 a.m. and 3.40 a.m. – let us say half past three. At that time PC Neil was at the part of his beat which was farthest from Buck's Row; PC Thain was also as far from the murder scene as his perambulations would take him; and Sergeant Kerby had already passed through Buck's Row on his nightly 'points' check. However, Sergeant Kerby was an unknown factor, insomuch as the whole concept of 'making points' relied upon the irregularity of such checks. The killer was therefore most fortunate that Kerby did not stumble across him.

In addition, there was a night gateman at the railway yard, a night watchman at Kearley and Tonge's warehouse, both in Buck's Row, and another night watchman in Winthrop Street. Perhaps, therefore, the killer had an intimate knowledge of that particular part of Whitechapel or a degree of forward planning was involved.

5. *How able was Detective Inspector Abberline?*

Thought of by many as having been in overall command of the 'Ripper' investigation, something of a legend has grown up around Abberline over the years, whereas the truth of the matter is that, although a cut above the average policeman of his day – a level which was not difficult to achieve – Abberline was no deductive genius. He was honest, methodical and competent, and had a great deal of success in the solving of routine crimes, but the sole reason for his secondment to the murder team was the length of time which he had spent in the area where the atrocities were happening. All in all, he was stationed in Whitechapel for fourteen years – five as an ordinary inspector and nine in charge of the local, 'H' Division, CID.

In 1887 he had been transferred to Scotland Yard but, with his virtually unrivalled knowledge of the district and its criminals, it is hardly surprising that he was called upon to lead the team of detectives on the ground when the killings began.

Superior to Abberline, although he had joined the Metropolitan Police five years later, was Detective Chief Inspector Donald Sutherland Swanson. It was he, in fact, who had overall direction of the day-to-day investigations, from the time of Polly's murder until the beginning of October, 1888. Then, as the number of killings mounted and another police force became involved, he became the desk-officer in complete charge of the case and acted in many ways as a rather superior modern-day police collator.

The Assistant Commissioner, CID, of the Metropolitan Police, Dr Robert Anderson, regarded Swanson as being 'the eyes and ears of the Commissioner in this particular case'. It was as a result of Anderson's recommendation that the Commissioner, Sir Charles Warren, made it known that Swanson had 'the whole responsibility' for the case, and ordered that every piece of paper should pass through Swanson's hands, and that he should be consulted on every aspect of the investigation.

Also superior to Abberline was Detective Chief Inspector Henry Moore, although he, also, had joined the Metropolitan Police far later than he – in this instance some six years later. When Swanson became desk-bound, it was he and not Abberline who took his place on the ground.

The legend of Abberline must therefore be looked at askance. He was a good, plodding copper, but he had nothing really special to offer except his local knowledge and, in the event, even that proved of little value. It says a great deal about how he was regarded by his superiors when one realizes that he served for twenty-seven years before he too was promoted to Chief Inspector, whereas Swanson and Moore, with less service, both achieved that heady rank after only nineteen years.

There is reason to believe that his delayed promotion rankled with Abberline, and caused him to have something of a chip on his shoulder. Perhaps that attitude became obvious to his superiors, because they, certainly, regarded him as being merely one member of a team, and there is evidence to suggest that any information passed to him was strictly on a 'need to know' basis. Any resentment on his part could also be the reason why he retired so young. Less than two years after gaining the rank he coveted, and having thereby become entitled to an increased pension, Abberline left the Force at the age of only forty-nine. There would appear to be no other reason for his leaving if he was, in fact, as dedicated to his job as some would have us believe, because he continued to work, as a *private* detective, for twelve more years.

6. *At what time did Annie Chapman die?*

According to Dr Phillips it was before 4.30 a.m., probably *well* before, but his opinion must be weighed against the evidence given by Elizabeth Long and Albert Cadosch. Mrs Long said that she saw Annie alive at 5.30 a.m., and Cadosch stated that he heard a woman's voice, followed by a fall against the fence, at around 5.20 a.m. So either the doctor was wrong or the evidence of the other parties must be suspect. When faced with such a conflict it is sensible to take the most likely possibility. Let us, therefore, see what that is.

Mrs Long had only a fleeting glimpse of the woman's face, and it was half-turned away from her at that. She could very well have been mistaken, especially when one considers how a face can change after death.

Then what about the barely-awake young Cadosch? People were all around him, both sleeping and awake, some with their windows open, and yet nobody but he heard any noise from the yard. He could have heard someone cry out in their sleep, or caught a snatch of conversation – he may have been misled by a couple of scuffling cats. All the evidence about the hole in the fence makes it quite clear that, whilst he would probably have needed to go right up to the fence, and look down, in order to see the body, from where he *actually* stood he was *bound* to have seen anyone moving about close to the recess.

Both of those witnesses could have been genuinely mistaken, but we should not ignore the possibility that one or both were mere publicity-seekers.

Annie Chapman and 'The Red Terror' were both creatures of the night. Somehow one just cannot imagine that they would stand haggling in broad daylight, and amidst all the hustle and bustle that always went on at that end of Hanbury Street on market days. Also, it is difficult to believe that Annie would have wandered around the streets for three and a half hours without either earning the extra pennies for her bed, or getting dossed down *somewhere*.

No, commonsense – and every instinct – dictates that the encounter with her killer took place within about an hour of her leaving Crossingham's, and that the murder took place under cover of darkness. That would accord with the doctor's opinion, but the big snag, of course, is that John Richardson said that the body was not there at 4.45 a.m. – so, was it?

Richardson went to that yard with only one objective, to ensure that the cellar door had not been tampered with. Cutting the piece of leather from his boot was an afterthought. All his attention would therefore have been directed to his right when he reached the back door, and the body, were it there, would have been in the recess *behind* him.

His next move was to attend to his boot, and he sat on the middle step to do so. The corpse would then have been to his left, and below him, and, as the legs were drawn up, it would not have projected as far forward as would otherwise have been the case. Richardson's statement that he could not have failed to see the body is therefore very open to question, and further doubts arise when the rest of his evidence is examined in the light of what is most likely to have happened.

The clue to the whole business is contained in his statement that, when he left, *the back door closed itself*. From that it is clear that, unless opened fully back against the wall, the door was so hung that its own weight would cause it to close and, having re-enacted his movements *in situ*, I can confirm that.

Picture the scene. Richardson goes along the passage, pushes open the quite substantial back door slightly and glances quickly to his right to see if the padlock is intact. *So* cursory, in fact, was his check that, it will be remembered, even Mr Baxter commented upon it at the inquest: 'You do not seem to have taken much trouble to see that it was all right.'

So, Richardson takes a quick look to his right, and then decides that he will do something about his troublesome boot. Still holding the door ajar, he sits down on the 'middle' step – which was actually nearer the top than the bottom – with the door now resting open against his body, and inclining him to his right and away from the recess. It was not completely light, and in that position, and with the door at that angle, it is quite conceivable that he would not have noticed the corpse.

On Richardson's own admission, he was not at the house 'more than two minutes at the most'. Later, when he viewed the body from No. 27 through the hole in the fence, he had all the time in the world, it was broad daylight, and the door was flung wide open. Under those circumstances, it would hardly be surprising if he had convinced himself that he *must* have seen the body had it been there on the Saturday morning.

If we take it that it *was* there then, is there any indication, however slight, of the actual time that the murder was committed? Only one comes to mind.

Both Amelia Richardson and John Davis were elderly and, it would seem, given to cat-napping. They both slept at the front of the house, and both were awakened at 3 a.m. Is it possible, therefore, that they were disturbed in some way by Annie and her killer before, or as they entered, the house, or by the front door slamming as, or more likely just after, the murderer left? If so, that would give a time of death rather similar to that of Polly Nichols's, and probably within Dr Phillips's rather elastic limit. Such a time would also provide a more credible interval for Annie's finding of a customer.

7. *When did Liz Stride die?*

Many deductions about this killing have been based upon the assertion of Louis Diemschütz that he had arrived at the Yard at 1 a.m. – a time based solely upon that shown by the clock he had seen, which was not necessarily accurate. Evidence given at the inquest casts doubt upon the one o'clock arrival.

PC Lamb testified that he was on duty in Commercial Road when 'shortly before one o'clock' Eagle and Isaacs told him of the murder.

Dr Blackwell stated that he arrived at the Yard at 1.16 a.m., and estimated that the woman had then been dead for between twenty and thirty minutes.

It is highly probable, therefore, that Diemschütz made his find between 12.45 and 12.50 a.m., and that the attack on 'Long Liz' took place much earlier than has been thought.

We shall never know all the facts about this case, but that should not discourage us from trying to bring some common-sense to bear in an effort to discover what is most likely to have happened. In so doing, it is just possible that we shall also shed some light upon what is, to my mind, one of the most puzzling questions about this killing, and one that I have never heard anyone else ask, namely why was Elizabeth Stride in Berner Street *at all* that night?

All the evidence was that Berner Street – or that section of it anyway – was not a regular beat for prostitutes. It consisted mainly of small terraced houses, from which watching eyes took in every movement, and there were very few, if any, dark corners where illicit coupling could take place without fear of interruption. Yet one irrefutable fact is that Liz *was* there, and so why? Let us try to unravel the threads, and probably the best way to start is to see if any of the alleged sightings may be discarded.

BEST & GARDNER. These two men stated that Liz left The Bricklayers Arms at just after 11 p.m., in company with a man sporting a thick black moustache. Presumably he had bought her at least one drink, and he was said to have been all over her – hugging and kissing her in a way that attracted attention.

Best and Gardner had ample time to observe the couple in a good light; there is no reason why they should have lied and their story sounds plausible – let us leave them 'in'.

PACKER. The trouble with his evidence is that he varied his times so much that one finds difficulty in giving credence to *any* of his statements. If he *did* sell some grapes to a couple on the Saturday night, all we can be sure of is that the man was not the one with whom Liz left The Bricklayers Arms, and that if the woman *was* Liz she did not eat any of the grapes.

What Packer had to say was of not the slightest use to the police nor, I fear, will it help us. I think we may put him to one side.

MARSHALL. This man said that he saw Liz talking to a man near his house at about 11.45 p.m., and that they then walked down Berner Street – away from the Club and towards Ellen Street. There is no reason to disbelieve him and, from the way the man and woman were behaving they may well have been those seen by Best and Gardner.

PC SMITH. Smith was a young man – only twenty-six years old. He appears to have been observant, and gave his evidence in a factual manner. His testimony was that he saw Liz talking to a man at 12.30 a.m., or just after. They were on the opposite side of the street from the Club and Packer's shop, and the man was carrying something wrapped in a newspaper.

I think we should retain Smith's evidence.

BROWN. He stated that he saw a man and a woman standing near the wall of the Board School at about 12.45 a.m. However he was not certain that the woman was Stride, and the rest of his evidence was equally vague.

We may forget about Brown' s evidence.

SCHWARTZ. It must have taken a great deal of courage for a foreigner, and a Jew to boot, who could not speak English, to have placed himself at the scene of the crime at about the time it was committed, thus running the risk of becoming a prime suspect. We should therefore take his statement very seriously indeed.

He said that he followed a drunken man down Berner Street at 12.45 a.m. He saw the man standing in the gateway of Dutfield's Yard trying to pull Liz into the street. She resisted and fell to the ground, and Schwartz did not see what happened after that.

Those, then, are the persons who thought that they saw Liz that night, and what are we left with from their evidence which is reasonably reliable?

(1) Stride leaving The Bricklayers Arms with man A, at just after 11 p.m.

(2) Stride talking to man B, towards the end of Berner Street, at around 11.45 p.m.

(3) Stride on the other side of the street from the Club, at 12.30 a.m. or just after, with man C who was carrying something wrapped in newspaper.

(4) Stride being attacked by man D, who tried to pull her out of Dutfield's Yard at 12.45 a.m.

The descriptions of men A and B are not that different. Could it be, therefore, that Liz was still with man A at 11.45 p.m.? It was only some 400 yards from the pub to where Marshall saw them just over half an hour later, but it could have taken them that long to walk there if they had sheltered somewhere else from the rain and/or if their stroll had been interrupted for more kissing and cuddling.

But why should they walk to Berner Street at all?

Could it have been, do you think, that Liz did not wish to run the risk of meeting Kidney, especially whilst with a customer, and therefore steered her companion in a direction away from Kidney's usual haunts? Could the reason for their stop near Marshall's house have been because the man objected to walking so far and Stride, with some tale, was trying to persuade him to go just a little further? Was that the reason for his 'You would say anything but your prayers'?

Let us imagine a scenario.

Liz takes man A to some dark spot at the bottom of Berner Street. Their business is concluded, and probably quicker than she had anticipated remembering his eagerness, and Liz, with at least the price of her bed in her pocket, begins to make her way to Flower and Dean Street. She walks back up Berner Street and is accosted there by the man with the newspaper parcel. Their conversation lasts only a short time, because Liz is anxious to return to Flower and Dean Street, and they part, with Liz continuing up Berner Street. Something then happens which causes her to retrace her footsteps and, a few moments later, she is seen by Schwartz as the drunken man tries to pull her out of Dutfield's Yard.

Were that what happened, all the reliable times of her sightings fit.

8. *Who wrote the slogan on the wall?*

Despite what the police thought at the time, it would seem fairly certain that 'Jack' left Mitre Square by way of Mitre Street because by doing so he would have avoided the busier and better lighted areas. After a quick dash across Aldgate, which PC Watkins must have missed seeing only narrowly as he turned into Leadenhall Street, the killer would have had access to a labyrinth of poorly lighted 'back doubles'.

According to the 'authorized version', and regardless of which exit he actually used, he then fled to his lair, pausing only to drop the piece of apron and write the message in Goulston Street. Now there can be no doubt that he *did* go that way – after all the scrap of cloth did get from Mitre Square to where it was found – but what is obviously wrong is the timing.

According to all the evidence, the murder must have happened at roughly 1.40 a.m. and, from what PC Long had to say, the piece of apron was dropped, and the message chalked, between 2.20 and 2.55 a.m. If, for the sake of argument, we take the latter time as being a conservative 2.40 a.m., it is immediately apparent that there was at least an hour between the events. Deduct a leisurely fifteen minutes to get from Mitre Square to Goulston Street and we are left with a minimum of three-quarters of an hour. For the whole of that time, we are asked to believe, the killer just waited around until, presumably, he saw the galloping Major Smith coming up the street. Then he sprang into action and nipped up Bell Lane to Dorset Street, where he stopped to wash his bloodstained hands before continuing his flight and leaving the Major to watch the water gurgling down the sink.

It just does not make any kind of sense and therefore, as Watkins's time is confirmed by the medical evidence, it must be concluded that the cloth and the writing were in place when Long passed that way at 2.20 a.m., if indeed he did, and that he did not see them. That would be quite understandable were it so. The writing was quite small, and Long only noticed it all because his attention was drawn to that part of the lobby by the relative whiteness of the piece of apron. As for the latter, either Long simply missed it on his previous patrol – and it is worth nothing that he was dismissed from the police in July 1889, for being drunk on duty – or it had been out of his sight at that time.

There was a particularly dark corner at right angles to the left side of the lobby as one walked in from the street. It would have been logical for 'Jack' to have stood there whilst he was cleaning himself or his knife, and if he had dropped the rag there Long would not have seen it on a casual examination. If, however, that hypothesis is correct, we must ask ourselves how it came to be moved the very few feet to where it was discovered.

Nearly an hour could have elapsed between the discarding of the cloth and the time it was found, and anything could have happened to it in that time. Indeed it need not necessarily have been dropped in the lobby at all. In that neighbourhood, and at that time in the morning, all manner of furtive creatures were shuffling around to whom, in the darkness, a piece of material would have had a potential value. Only when it had been examined under some form of light would its true disgusting nature have been revealed, and then it would have been rejected immediately. Similarly, it could have been picked up from the corner by a tenant of the Dwellings and, after scrutiny, dropped just as hastily. It is even possible that the smell from the rag attracted the interest of an animal who moved it in the process of investigation.

Somehow I have never taken to the notion of the killer pausing in mid-flight to write a cryptic message in the blackness of that lobby, and with a piece of chalk that he just happened to have in his pocket. I agree with Superintendent Arnold. It seems far more likely that it was just one of the many anti-Semitic daubings in the area, and nobody would have dreamed of associating it with the 'Ripper' had the portion of Kate's apron not been found beneath it.

There appears to be a general assumption that it was chalked in large, bold letters high upon the wall. However, Halse made it quite clear that it was in a schoolboy's 'round hand', and that the largest of the letters were only three-quarters of an inch high. It is highly unlikely that such small and careful writing could have been made in the dark, and by a killer who was, quite literally, on the run from the police – and who just happened to have a piece of chalk in his pocket!

I strongly suspect that Halse's words hold the solution, and that there was a youth in the neighbourhood – even perhaps living in Wentworth Dwellings – who could have shed a great deal of light on the mystery.

9. *Where were Kate's tattoos?*

Although there were no official records of any tattoos on Kate's body, there were newspaper reports of her having the initials 'TC' tattooed either on her left or on her right arm. There may be a simple explanation for the confusion: a close examination of the mortuary photograph reveals a distinct 'T' on her right forearm, and what could be a 'C' in a similar position on her left.

10. *What are we to make of the Lusk kidney?*

All my instincts tell me that the kidney was a hoax, but I am impressed by a point made by my friend Dr Hocking. He suggested that the reason why only half the kidney was sent may have been that the murderer damaged it during removal. To have despatched the whole kidney in such a condition would have exploded the useful myths about surgeons and doctors; the sender therefore cut off the damaged portion to disguise his incompetence.

11. *Who was John McCarthy?*

Not a lot is known about Mary Kelly's landlord, and the census return for 1891 hinders rather than helps. Listed as living at No. 27, Dorset Street, is a John McCarthy, aged forty-two, 'General Shop Keeper', born in Spitalfields. His wife is shown as being Mary McCarthy, aged thirty-eight, also born in Spitalfields, and there is a dependent son, George, aged sixteen. *At the same address*, however, *another* John McCarthy appears. He also is aged forty-two, and is described as a 'Grocer', born in Dieppe, France! This John McCarthy's wife is aged thirty-eight also, but *her* name is given as Elizabeth, born in Shoreditch, and there are four dependent daughters.

It is a mystery that I do not pretend to understand.

12. *Who locked the door at No. 13?*

The riddle of the supposedly locked door has exercised innumerable minds over the years, but too few have asked what kind of key was involved. I visited the houses of what was then called Duval Street. Originally, their doors had been fitted with large, heavy, mortise 'box' locks, with large heavy keys to match, which must have been cumbersome to carry around. Some of the original locks were still in place when I saw them, although used only on a secondary basis; Yale locks had been added, and had apparently been in use for many years.

It is pure surmise but, as the Yale lock was patented in 1844, it would seem likely that the lock in use at No. 13 in 1888 was of that type. (There are newspaper reports that Bowyer looked through the keyhole but that would still have been possible were the old lock unused.) This would fit in with what Barnett is alleged to have told Abberline: that, in order to unlock the door, he and Mary 'put their hand through the broken window, and moved back the catch' – actions that indicate a Yale-type lock.

Why then did the door have to be forced? Dr Phillips and the police could see into the room, and surely they would have realized the ease with which the catch could be released? Failing that, why did neither Barnett nor McCarthy put them right?

All that comes to mind is that something – the overcoat,

perhaps – was hanging in such a way as to obscure any view of the lock inside and that the police assumed that the older mortise lock had been used. Barnett, having been detained by the police, was not in Miller's Court and so unable to demonstrate the opening procedure, while McCarthy would have assumed that the police had already exhausted all other possibilities.

13. *What did happen at the Lord Mayor's show?*

This point is hardly something upon which to ponder, but it deserves to be mentioned, as we are most fortunate that not only was some of the atmosphere of the Lord Mayor's Show of 1888 captured on canvas but that it is still on public display.

The artist was a Lincoln man, William Logsdail, who won gold medals for his works, and exhibited in the Royal Academy from 1877. In 1888 he had recently returned from Italy and was so impressed by the Lord Mayor's Show that he decided to paint a large depiction of the event.

It took two and a half years to complete, but the result, to my mind, was well worth the effort and expense. I cannot count the number of times, going back to my childhood in pre-war London, that I have stood, enthralled, before the magnificent *The Ninth of November* in the Old Library at Guildhall.

This splendid painting is oil on canvas, and is 73¾ inches by 107¼. Most of the individual figures were painted from friends or professional models, but Logsdail went to great lengths to capture the event accurately. The coachmen and footmen went to his studio in their liveries; the Corporation mace was put at his disposal; and he was able to visit the stables in Fore Street and have the horses harnessed to the coach. Logsdail was disappointed that the painting did not sell for the price he wanted. After its exhibition at the Royal Academy in 1890 it went to America and was awarded a medal. Upon its return it was bought by the then *Sir* James Whitehead for the low price of £500, but on the understanding that it would be presented to the Guildhall Art Library. However, once he had acquired the painting, Sir James decided to keep it! Logsdail was bitterly disappointed, but his work was eventually bought from Sir James's son, in 1933, for £250.

If you are ever in the vicinity of Guildhall, go and see it. I shall be most surprised if you are not impressed, but whilst gazing at it spare a thought for the poor young woman who, was at that very moment, on that very day, lying cut to pieces in a small back room in Spitalfields.

14. *Where was the 'shed' in Miller's Court?*

Miller's Court is usually described as containing six two-roomed houses, and indeed it did. What does not appear to be known generally, however, and even where it is no comment is forthcoming, is that there were two additional buildings. One was on the left, at the far end of the Court and adjoining the last crib. The other jutted into the yard at right angles from the first dwelling on the right and towards the windows of No. 13.

Of these two additional buildings, only the one in the yard appears ever to have been mentioned, and then merely in passing. Those references do not appear in the Coroner's Notes, nor in any statements to the police. It is in the *Daily Telegraph* of November 13th that a Mrs Prater is reported as having said, in her evidence at the inquest: 'I live at 20 Room, in Miller's Court, *above the shed*'. [My italics], and the *Western Mail*, of November 10th, states, rather ambiguously: 'The ground floor of the house to the right of the court is used as a store, with a gate entrance and the upper floors are let off in tenements.'

The *Daily Telegraph* of November 12th has a plan of Miller's Court upon which the structure jutting into the yard is marked 'Dustbin', but unless it was a sizeable and permanent building, I doubt whether it is the one shown on some contemporary maps. The same plan has the front room of No. 26 marked 'Shed', and, in its edition of only two days earlier, the same newspaper – again referring to No. 26 – stated that: 'It has seven rooms, the first floor front, facing Dorset-street, being over a shed or warehouse used for the storage of costers' barrows.'

Well I may be wrong, but I doubt very much whether that

ground-floor front room was ever used for such a purpose. Its size and the width of the front door would seem to be against the idea – unless they were very small barrows! As far as I can ascertain, only the *Daily Telegraph* ever attributed such use to that room and, unusually, it appears to have been in error. That view tends to be confirmed by the fact that, in the same article on the 10th, and referring to the passage leading to Miller's Court, it stated: 'On the right-hand side of the passage there are two doors.' It goes on to say that the first 'leads to the upper floors of the house' and, a little later, that the second was to No. 13. Now that is patent nonsense. There were no doors *at all* leading from the passage, and even if it were considered that the door to No. 13 did so – which it did not – then that was the *only* one. So if the newspaper made such a basic mistake perhaps it was also wrong about the use of the downstairs room.

It is interesting to note that, in the same edition of the 10th, the *Daily Telegraph* reported an interview with the above-mentioned Mrs Prater, whom it described, incorrectly, as the occupant of the first-floor front room. Is it possible therefore, do you think, that she was speaking loosely when she, apparently, told the reporter that she lived 'above' the shed, and really meant to say that she *overlooked* the building in the yard? (Which she did.) Were that the case, then it would be understandable how the newspaper came to think that the ground-floor room was a 'shed'. I just do not know, but what *is* certain is that Mrs Prater, could not have lived above No. 13 *and* the front room of No. 26 – 'shed' or no 'shed'.

So what were 'the shed' and the other building? A privy and a wash-house, or a store for McCarthy's shop, are the answers which spring most readily to mind, but whatever they were it is strange that they have never been mentioned before. What did they contain? Were they locked? Were they searched? Every nook and cranny of Dutfield's Yard was investigated and reported upon, and even the privies were mentioned, but a mysterious silence about the two buildings in Miller's Court has reigned down the years.

15. *Why was MacDonald in such a hurry to close the inquest on Mary Kelly?*

Some possibilities are worth pondering:

(a) The police knew who the murderer was, but did not think they would ever be able to bring him to justice even if he was caught, and therefore any further evidence was deemed superfluous.

(b) They knew the identity of the killer, and already had sufficient evidence to convict him, could he but be apprehended.

(c) Some incriminating evidence had come to light which they did not wish to be made public for fear of altering the murderer.

(d) MacDonald had been told by the police that they were confident of an imminent arrest, and therefore the 'minutiae of evidence' *would* be brought out at a police-court.

(e) There *was* a conspiracy of some sort, and MacDonald had been instructed, or persuaded, to bring the inquiry to an untimely halt.

(f) Phillips and the police just wanted an inquest free of criticism, and the sooner it was finished the better.

(g) MacDonald wanted to demonstrate that an inquest could be held, and a verdict reached, without the several adjournments that other coroners, especially Wynne Baxter, felt necessary.

(h) A combination of some of the above.

Did James Kelly leave some clue, possibly in No. 13, which led the police to him? Is that why they arrived in Cottage Lane the following day? If so, they would have known that there was little point in bringing a man already judged insane before a court. He would merely have been returned to Broadmoor.

(It is sometimes alleged that MacDonald deliberately failed to sign the verdict form. I checked. There were in fact two forms. One had his signature and those of the jurors; the other contained the verdict. Presumably he clipped them together. This error, due perhaps to inexperience, does not justify any conspiracy theory.)

16. *Should we trust Detective Inspector Reid?*

Detective Inspector Reid told the inquest that he discovered a broken pipe and a farthing when Alice Mackenzie's body was lifted on to the ambulance.

Dr Phillips reported that, some twelve hours later, an old clay pipe was found on the body, was broken by the attendant and then disappeared.

We have therefore to consider two possibilities:

(a) *That there were two pipes.*

This possibility has one great drawback. If there *were* two pipes, and the first was discovered under the body, why was Reid the only person in Castle Alley to see it?

Dr Phillips makes no mention of it, nor a farthing for that matter, despite his known proclivity for recording such details.

Sergeant Badham, who was present when the body was lifted, and actually took it to the mortuary, makes no mention in his report of any such finds.

There is not a word from anyone but Reid about the alleged discoveries.

(b) *That there was but one pipe, and it was the one found by the mortuary attendant.*

Were that the case, Reid must have invented the tale of the pipe under the body – but why should he do that?

All I can think of is that it was a fabrication to cover up his shortcoming in failing to discover the pipe when he searched the body. Imagine his discomfiture if he heard of the attendant's find and realized that he, a Detective Inspector no less, had overlooked the pipe in his search. Somehow his blunder would have to be concealed before he became the laughing stock of his men.

It would have been a simple matter for him to have retrieved the pieces of pipe from the mortuary on the evening of the 17th, and then – voilà – produce them at the inquest the following day. Not only would he have saved his reputation, he would have enhanced it!

Dr Phillips, as one might expect, made no mention at the inquest of the finding and breaking of the pipe in the mortuary, and Reid was therefore spared any embarrassing questions from

Wynne Baxter. He must have thought himself home and dry, and the only reason that we know anything about it is because of the mention tucked away in Phillips' long report of four days later.

It may be thought unlikely that a policeman of Reid's rank would have lied on oath about such a trivial matter. I must confess that at one point I felt the same, but then I remembered people I had known who would have lied about *anything* rather than admit to an error – and Reid was not known for his accuracy.

Two things resolved the doubts which I had.

Badham's report was written on the day of the murder and is signed by both him and his inspector, Thomas Hawkes. Underneath their signatures, however, there is an addition in Reid's handwriting, made at a later stage. It reads: 'An old clay pipe and a farthing were found under the body.' On no other police report in the whole of the 'Ripper' files have I come across a similar *unsigned* addition to a colleague's report, and I can only suppose that Reid made it in order to give some support to his tale.

My hypothesis also offers an explanation for why Phillips never 'recovered' the pieces of pipe.

When Reid produced them at the inquest, Phillips would have realised what had happened to them but, being a police surgeon, he was not going to rock the boat. I think that the only reason why he made mention of the pipe in his report was because others had witnessed the discovery and breakage.

Some may consider that this whole business of the pipe/s is much ado about nothing. I would, however, make the point that if a policeman would lie on oath about such a small matter we can take his word for nothing else.

There is an interesting link between Alice Mackenzie's farthing and an odd story about Annie Chapman's death. At Alice's inquest, according to *The Times* of July 19th, 1889, Reid stated: 'In another instance of this kind – the Hanbury Street Murder – two similar farthings were found.'

Certainly, in almost every book written about these murders, one will find mention of some rings and coins being found at

Annie's feet. Yet there is nothing about them in the extensive official reports. No police officer, apart from Reid, ever mentioned any coins, and Reid was not involved in the investigation. If coins were discovered, it was kept secret by the police and Reid was the only officer to break ranks. On the other hand he might merely have been repeating earlier rumours.

The evidence confirms that Annie was indeed wearing three rings on the night she was killed, and that when Dr Phillips examined the body they were gone. The coins pose a far more difficult problem, but Annie's own words provide a very strong clue that she had cash on her when she disappeared into the dark and dangerous streets of Spitalfields on that fateful morning. Consider her remarks to Donovan and Evans. She did not say that she had no money for her bed, but that she did not have *enough*. The implication is obvious, and would explain why she was so confident that she would not 'be long' in getting whatever she needed to make up the required sum.

Yet neither rings nor coins were found on her after her death. Where did they go? I feel that we need look no further than the killer for the thief. He almost certainly took Polly's wedding ring, and Annie's rings would have been another bonus. As for the coins, I think it is probable that the murderer heard them jingle in Annie's pocket as he threw up the clothes. 'The Red Terror' killed and mutilated because of a rage generated by many emotions, but he was probably not above profiting from his crimes if opportunities arose.

That leaves, however, the puzzle of who was responsible for the story that the rings and coins were laid out at her feet. The earliest mention of the rings appears to have been in a special edition of the *Pall Mall Gazette*, in an article written by their reporter Oswald Allen. The edition was published on the day of the murder. There is no copy extant, but William Stewart quotes from it in his book. He also says that Allen told him that he had only a fleeting glimpse of the body and implied that his piece was largely based on a 'number of statements' which he took down. It is quite possible that someone told Allen of Annie's rings, and that when he heard that 'all her belongings were laid out at her feet', he assumed that they included the rings and so put that in his piece.

As for who originated the story of the coins, the short answer is that we do not know. *The Jack the Ripper A–Z* claims that the story was 'in press reports the following day', but I have been unable to confirm that statement, and, if it is true, one has to wonder from whom the reporter(s) received the story, and why Allen and all the others missed it. All we do know for certain is that Detective Inspector Reid used it for his own purposes.

17. *Whom were the police looking for?*

I find it intriguing that, apparently, all the Metropolitan police stations had been provided with a description of the supposed killer of Mary Kelly so soon after her death.

You will recall that in the early hours of November 14th, Mr Galloway had pointed out a suspicious 'carroty moustache' man to a PC. However the constable had refused to act because he was looking 'for a man of a very different appearance'.

Now that was a mere three and a half days after something had sent the police rushing to Mrs Brider's, and only just over thirty hours after Hutchinson's statement that the description of the man whom he had seen had been 'Circulated to A.S.', but there is no record of a similar circulation of Kelly's description, although we know that the police were searching for him. In fact, as we have seen, no records whatsoever survive of the search for Kelly, and we should know nothing of it but for the letter from Mrs Brider's solicitor. It hardly seems logical, however, that the police would circulate the suspect description given by Hutchinson and fail to do the same in respect of James Kelly. Whose description, therefore, did the constable have in mind, that of the stranger seen by Hutchinson or Kelly's?

The *Eastern Post*, of November 17th, stated that: 'The theory originally stated by Dr Forbes Winslow that the murderer is a homicidal lunatic is gaining ground daily. It is therefore satisfactory to learn that inquiries are still being made at lunatic asylums, and that the police will soon be in possession of a fairly complete list of homicidal patients recently discharged as cured. *It is stated that several houses at which the murderer is believed to call occasionally under the closest police surveillance.'* [My italics.]

That last sentence conveys a sense of positive police information. It does not, for instance, mention 'a suspect' but, quite definitely, 'the murderer', and there appears to be fairly certain knowledge of his likely contacts. Those able to read between the lines will also suspect that the conjunction of mention of homicidal lunatics is not coincidental. Everything points to the fact that the police not only had sure information that the killer was a homicidal lunatic, but that they were also armed with the names and addresses of those likely to help him – as they were with James Kelly.

Unlike so many other newspaper articles, this one has a ring of truth and certainty about it, and one wonders from whom the information came. It is hardly likely that senior police officers would have risked alerting the murderer, whereas one of lower rank who knew of the swoop on No. 21, Cottage Lane, may have had no such scruples had the price been right.

There can be no doubt that it was good information, and it seems to have been exclusive to the *Eastern Post* because I can find nothing similar in any other newspaper. Indeed a veil of secrecy appears to have been drawn over the whole operation. Had Mrs Brider not complained about the treatment meted out to her we should have known nothing of it, and that leads me to wonder how many calls were made on others less vociferous. The police had a list of James Kelly's friends, one of whom lived in the heart of the murder area, and of those who had visited him in Broadmoor. There is also a strong probability that George Stratton and other inmates at the Asylum gave vital information, yet there are no newspaper reports about Mrs Brider's interrogation, let alone any other police visitations. The police files are also strangely silent on the subject. There is no mention of the circumstances which led them to Cottage Lane, or of the conversation there; nor are any other interviews or surveillances recorded. Unless the newspaper article was entirely fictional, we are therefore driven to conclude either that the police made no notes of their activities or that any such records are now lost to us.

Be all that as it may, it would not have lessened any impact which the report may have had on the killer. By confining his murderous activities to the small area which he knew best, he had ensured that the odds against him would be increased after each atrocity. So far he had been very fortunate, but now it must have seemed that his luck was fast running out, and that it was time to make himself scarce. It was hardly surprising therefore that there was no further attack that year.

18. *Who or what was Matfelon?*

As we have spent a great deal of time in Whitechapel, let us end there with our final Point to Ponder.

The Parish Church of Whitechapel was that of St Mary Matfelon, the original structure having been built in the fourteenth century, as a chapel of ease to Stepney. Several explanations have been given for its strange name.

(a) That Matfelon was a Hebrew word for a woman carrying, or recently delivered of, an infant son, which was brought back to this country by the Crusaders.

(b) That Matfelon was a benefactor to the church.

(c) That, around 1428, a Frenchman murdered a widow with whom he was lodging. He was apprehended, and as he was taken past the church, the locals threw things at him and he was killed. The murderer was a felon, and a frightened person was said to be 'mated'.

(d) That a bell was tolled when *any* criminal passed the church, and then he was 'mated' (frightened).

(e) That the church was built in a field full of a variety of knapweed known as 'matfelon'.

For what it is worth, I incline towards the last.

Index

Note: JK in the index refers to James Kelly. AC, FC, CE, MK, AMc, MN, ES, refer to the enquiries into the murders of, respectively, Annie Chapman, Frances Coles, Catharine Eddowes, Mary Kelly, Alice McKenzie, Mary Nichols, and Elizabeth Stride.